EMPTY HOUSES

EMPTY HOUSES

Theatrical Failure and the Novel

David Kurnick

PRINCETON UNIVERSITY PRESS

Princeton & Oxford

Copyright © 2012 by Princeton University Press

Published by Princeton University Press, 41 William Street,
Princeton, New Jersey 08540
In the United Kingdom: Princeton University Press, 6 Oxford Street,
Woodstock, Oxfordshire OX20 1TW
press.princeton.edu

LIBRARY OF CONGRESS CATALOGING-IN-PUBLICATION DATA
Kurnick, David, 1972–
Empty houses : theatrical failure and the novel / David Kurnick.
p. cm.
Includes bibliographical references and index.
ISBN 978-0-691-15151-9 (hardcover : acid-free paper)—
ISBN 978-0-691-15316-2 (pbk. : acid-free paper) 1. English fiction—
History and criticism. 2. American fiction—History and criticism.
3. Fiction—Technique—History.
4. Drama—Technique—History. I. Title.
PR826.K87 2011
823.009–dc22   2011014630

British Library Cataloging-in-Publication Data is available

This book has been composed in Garamond Pro
Printed on acid-free paper. ∞
Printed in the United States of America
1 3 5 7 9 10 8 6 4 2

For Jo Thomsen and Helen Greenberg

IN MEMORIAM

It seems so safe at home, it seems so frightening on the streets, but this is a delusion. It is not safe at home; it is only safe on the streets. Don't go home.

—DECLAN DONNELLAN, *The Actor and The Target*

CONTENTS

Thanks to Jessica Brent, Amanpal Garcha, Ayelet Ben-Yishai, Crisi Benford, Gage McWeeny, and Kent Puckett, friends and colleagues who sustained me through the early and late stages of this writing. It's been my good fortune to have Steve Biel, Jeff Melnick, Werner Sollors, Martin Puchner, Margaret Cohen, Franco Moretti, Elaine Scarry, and the late Eve Kosofsky Sedgwick as inspiring teachers, and Sharon Marcus as an expert adviser and interlocutor. Bruce Robbins and Nicholas Dames were unfailingly generous with their time, and have never quite allowed me to thank them for how much they continue to teach me. Colleagues at Rutgers University have provided encouragement and stimulation over the last four years; special thanks are owed to Lynn Festa, Jonah Siegel, Carolyn Williams, Billy Galperin, John Kucich, Dianne Sadoff, Kate Flint, Carter Mathes, Meredith McGill, Elin Diamond, Michael McKeon, George Levine, Rebecca Walkowitz, and Henry Turner. Kate Marshall and Sianne Ngai's responses to a portion of the manuscript proved invaluable in drafting the introduction. Rae Greiner, Andrew Miller, Ivan Kreilkamp, Ben Katchor, Nancy Henry, Gerhard Joseph, Anne Humpherys, and Jonathan Grossman were excellent hosts at institutions where I presented portions of the book; my gratitude also to those engaged audiences and colloquia. Rita Bernhard and Manuel Betancourt gave invaluable assistance in preparing the manuscript, and Hanne Winarsky and Christopher Chung shepherded the book through the publication process with enthusiasm. Detailed and exciting readings of the manuscript by Kevin Ohi, Leo Bersani, Alex Woloch, and anonymous readers for Princeton University Press were crucial in helping me see what this book wanted to do.

For their long friendship, I thank Jalaa' Abdelwahab, Mark Bates, Jared Hohlt, Chad Kia, Michael Miller, Molly Murray, Laura Pinsky, Iohann Pita, Janeen Potts, Esther Rhee, Francisco Rodriguez, Becca Rugg, Rachel Saltz, Mimi Schultz, Jake Short, Jonathan Taylor, Colm Tóibín, Mike Vazquez, and Vineeta Vijayaraghavan. Luann, John, Katie, Dutch, and Sally Kurnick, and Nia, Jou, and Ever Quiñonez, continue to give pleasure and support in equal measure.

I owe deepest thanks to D. A. Miller, who believed in this project before a word of it was written, and whose example as a teacher, reader, and friend has been a great gift; to

Joe Rezek, whose sharp eye and big heart are present for me on every page; and to Heather Love, companion in conversation. This book would not have been started or finished without them.

* * *

Parts of this book were written with the support of the Huntington Library, the Columbia University Society of Fellows, and the Center for Cultural Analysis at Rutgers.

An early version of a section of chapter 1 appeared as "Empty Houses: Thackeray's Theater of Interiority," in *Victorian Studies,* 48.2 (winter 2006): 257-267; reprinted with permission of Indiana University Press.

Early versions of two sections of chapter 3 appeared in *The Henry James Review* as "'Horrible Impossible': Henry James's Awkward Stage," *The Henry James Review* 26.2 (2005): 109-129 (copyright © 2005 Johns Hopkins University Press) and "What Does Jamesian Style Want?" *The Henry James Review* 28.3 (2007): 213–222 (copyright © 2007 Johns Hopkins University Press). The author thanks the Johns Hopkins University Press for permission to reprint both articles, and Susan Griffin at *The Henry James Review* for her editorial expertise.

EMPTY HOUSES

Introduction

INTERIORITY AND ITS DISCONTENTS

Theater Demetaphorized

In at least one version of the story, the modern novel is born from theatrical failure. Henry James is famously supposed to have learned his lesson in the theater, and the lesson was to stay out of the theater. Fortunately for literary history, this account goes, he alchemized his personal embarrassment into narrative innovation. In the years immediately following the *Guy Domville* disaster of 1895, James conducted a series of formal experiments in his fiction, arriving at a set of rules that made the novel into an object of undeniable artistic merit. Chief among these were the strict limitation of point of view to one or two focalizing characters and the avoidance of narrative summary in favor of tightly recounted scenes. The name James gave to these dicta, which were to have major implications for his explorations of interiority in the novels of the new century, was the "scenic method." This was a canny rhetorical recuperation of his theatrical failure, at once praising the theater and sidelining it: if on the one hand the novel thus conceived appears to aspire to the condition of theater, on the other it is understood adequately to displace and replace the drama as an embodied social event. In the scenic method the theater is remade as metaphor. James's theatrical debacle has become one of the better-known critical allegories for the birth of the modern novel for a number of reasons, perhaps the most obvious being the pleasure of seeing humiliation reworked as aesthetic triumph. But this account also confirms our sense that the privileged subject of modern literature is the psychic interior, and, more darkly, buttresses a story of the modern novel as the exemplary genre of social forgetting, a sublimation of collective life into a self-enclosed technicism and aestheticism.

Empty Houses troubles this story by noting, first, that the Jamesian transmutation of dramatic frustration into narrative accomplishment has resonances in other important novelistic careers. In addition to analyzing James's post-theatrical work, this book explores the afterlife of frustrated dramatic projects in the careers of William Makepeace Thackeray, George Eliot, and James Joyce. My most immediate claim is that what might seem a series of perplexing or amusing biographical anomalies merits recognition and analysis as a literary historical fact. That all these writers had serious ambition to write for the stage, and that all of them reworked their theatrical concerns into innovative and influential fiction, indicates that the novelistic turn to and away from the living theater was not a punctual event but has been an ongoing aspect of novelistic development. The list of important novelists who have written for the theater is long, stretching at least from Aphra Behn to Samuel Beckett. But the presence of the theatrical imagination is particularly striking in the four writers who are the subject of this book precisely because it seems so incongruous in them. The example of James makes clear two features of that incongruity: first, while theatrical writing is by definition committed to the absence of a narrative voice, these writers' signal contribution to literature consists of the perfection of a series of sophisticated narrative techniques; second, while the theater demands and depends on the literal fact of collective assembly, each of these writers routed their representations of social forces through various forms of inwardness. To examine the novelistic refunctioning of these writers' theatrical ambitions is thus to examine the collision of the most collectively oriented of forms with one that seems axiomatically individualistic. Thackeray's novels turn obsessively around the micropolitics of family and the affective exclusiveness of domesticity; Eliot is the great poet of sympathy, the advocate of a rigorous internal training in right feeling; James's fictions explore the tortuous workings of consciousness and intimate relations; Joyce made the sexual "core" of the self available for narrative exploration. The term by which I designate this tradition, the novel of interiority, is meant to capture this mapping of ever narrower interior geographies.[1]

The novel of interiority seems to offer irrefutable support for Ian Watt's canonical description of the novel as "less concerned with the public and more with the private side of life than any previous" literary form, as well as for Sylvie Thorel-Cailleteau's recent claim that "the history of the genre is related to that of contracting space."[2] In a series of influential critiques, each of the writers treated here has been faulted for a betrayal of the collective imagination. Georg Lukács devotes several pages of *The Historical Novel* to denigrating Thackeray's psychologization of history, while Raymond Williams's *Culture and Society* attacks Eliot's dubious portrayals of democratic assembly.[3] Fredric Jameson memorably describes Jamesian perspectivalism as one of literary culture's "more desperate myths of self," "a powerful ideological instrument in the perpetuation of an increasingly subjectivized and psychologized world."[4] And Franco Moretti credits Joyce's aggressive multiplication of perceptual data with providing the individual with an alibi of "innocent passivity" in the face of capitalist exploitation.[5] Although these novelists have received the harshest assessments from Marxist analysts, the terms of those critiques chime with descriptions of the novel of interiority articulated from a host of perspectives—from post-structuralist feminist Nancy Armstrong's claim that the novel's "phobic representations of the human aggregate" indicate that "the novel of course was not made to think beyond the individual" to sociologist Pierre Bourdieu's assertion that "the psychological novel . . . maximize[s] denial of the social world."[6]

Provoked by such unanimity, this book develops a counternarrative about what novels are and what ideological work they do. *Empty Houses* asks what contribution these writers' theatrical ambitions made to their invention of what by many accounts are among the most "novelistic," and thus reputedly individualizing, of novels. It argues that when we recognize the role of the theater in the creation of the novel of interiority, that novel emerges as a record of the discontents historically sedimented in interiority—less propaganda for the inwardly focused, socially atomized individual than a rigorous account book of interiority's exclusions. Historians and social theorists have long recognized the nineteenth century as the moment when the increasing abstraction and massification of public culture produced a hypercaloric interiority as its imaginary compensation—a situation virtually guaranteed to keep subjects shuttling between hunger for what they have lost and nausea at what has been offered in its place.[7] The novelists this book treats are often taken as apologists for this bargain—as if the very act of making interiority narratively interesting argued for interiority's adequacy as a substitute for a robust public culture. But *Empty Houses* demonstrates that the novel's interior spaces are lined with longing references to the public worlds they would seem to have left behind. In its contradictory character, at once inwardly oriented and outwardly desirous, the tradition explored here confirms the fundamental ambiguity embedded in the logic of the public/private distinction. Demonstrations of its ideological character have not made the public/private divide any less indispensable as an analytic tool, precisely because its ideological character means it is not susceptible to being "disproven." As Susan Gal has recently argued, the indexical sign of "privacy" powerfully marks realms of human experience by recursively nesting private zones inside one another.[8] Thus, while a suburb seems private in comparison with a business district, once inside that suburb the front lawns seem more private than the quiet streets—and, once inside the house, the front hall is marked as public over against the living room. This logic is of course headed for the bedroom, but it does not stop there: sexuality, the body, and the desires that drive them are themselves susceptible to further such subdivision. As Michael McKeon puts it in *The Secret History of Domesticity* (a book tracking the early modern emergence of the dynamic Gal is describing), "the 'privacy' of the individual can be conceived to consist not only of interrelations with other private individuals and institutions . . . but also of the intrarelations that exist within any single individual."⁹

In tracing a line from Thackeray's obsession with the domestically enclosed family to Eliot's preoccupation with the sympathetic exchange between two characters to James's attention to subtleties of consciousness and finally to Joyce's plumbing of the sexual depths, this book might seem to verify the novel's inexorable drive inward. But I take these writers' desire to enter the theater as the symptom of a powerful ambivalence at the heart of their novelistic projects. In each career the experiment with theater occupied a pivotal moment, often directly preceding and always deeply imbricated with the novelistic innovations for which they are now better known. The turn to the theater indexes in each case a desire for a palpable relation to an embodied public and an impatience with the inward gaze of narrative fiction, in the process opening a self-critical perspective on these writers' apparent project of making domestic and psychological interiors seem narratively important. The empty houses for which the book is named refer both to the theatrical spaces their plays were unable to fill and to the domestic and psychological containers their novels appear to encourage readers to desert. Indeed, the novel of interiority bears out not only Gal's account of nested privacies but also the sense, implicit in her analysis, that intensified interiority can have surprisingly publicizing consequences. As in a process of atomic fission, the subdivision of ever more particularized realms of privacy builds a correspondingly explosive pressure toward exteriority, so that even as these texts push inward they fantasize about collective responses to the isolations of privacy.¹⁰ The interior spaces traced in these novels bear the visible impress of a frustrated will to performative exteriority and collectivity, recalling what Hannah Arendt calls "the original privative sense" of the concept of privacy, its root meaning of being deprived access to an ample social world.¹¹ The novel of interiority is a record not only of relentless intensifications of interiority but of the desire to escape from it.

Far from confirming what Armstrong terms "the novel's irreversible contraction of the imagined community,"¹² *Empty Houses* demonstrates the novel's abiding interest in various scales of collectivity. The theatrical energies encoded—genetically, as it were—in the novel of interiority continually point beyond the enclosures represented by the family, the home, individual psychology, and sexual identity. Thus in Thackeray's theatrical work, as in the fiction he made from it, the family is haunted by the possibility of bohemian sociability; the intensity with which Thackeray maps the domestic enclosure prompts his readers to imagine more various arrangements of social space than those provided by the idealized family of mid-Victorian England. Eliot's half-finished play *The Spanish Gypsy* imagines a fragile but radical democracy among characters, and this expansive sense of the boundaries of human community lingers into her later fiction, where the suspicion that her characters

are participating in a universal theater threatens to undo the psychological clarity of the scenes of sympathetic exchange for which she is famous.
Henry James's fascination with the scandal of sexual betrayal seems oddly
beside the point in the novels he wrote immediately after his theatrical failure. His experimental novels do not depict the "typically Jamesian" situation
of individuals isolated by perspectival and moral difference; instead, those
novels present coteries of erotic dissidents united by an interest in evading
late-century codes of sexual meaning. Similarly, Joyce's interest in the theater constitutes an auto-critique of his tendency to fix characterological truth
through the exposure of sexual secrets. While his most recognizable narrative techniques are governed by an apparent desire to put the sexual core of
human personality "on stage," Joyce's theatrical experiments also allowed him
to imagine collective spaces where perverse sexual desire has no identificatory
implications.

In every case the theatrical energy formally encoded in the novelistic representation of interiority turns that interiority inside out, prying open the
closures of home and psyche and rethinking human identity and human
pleasure in radically collective terms, while simultaneously tracing the obstacles to such collective conceptualization. The antimoralistic, antipsycholo-
gistic tradition I trace here might seem to constitute an underground line in
literary history, so little does it fit our received sense of what novels do; but it
is my argument that this allergy to interiority is weirdly central to the main
tradition of the novel of interiority. Concurring with Jameson's claim that
"all literature must be read as a symbolic meditation on the destiny of community," this book argues that the novel of interiority offers more compelling evidence of the persistence of the collective imagination than has been
acknowledged.[13] The theatrical endeavors of these prominent novelists constitute a literary historical testament to the malaise inherent in inwardness
and individuation as such. To be sure, these writers' theatrical ambition was
in each case failed or frustrated—their plays were either never completed,
never accepted for performance, or (if performed) often dismal flops—but
these frustrations did not close down the theatrical imagination. The dramatic texts these writers created instead asserted themselves over a period
of years. In several cases these dramatic efforts were recast in narrative form,
and in each instance they came to inform stylistically and formally what are
still routinely described as un- and even antitheatrical novels. In tracking this
theatrical persistence, I have resisted the temptation to read these careers tel-
eologically, as if the dramatic efforts were regrettable detours on the road to
aesthetic integration. Instead, the chapters that follow register the depth of
these writers' attachment to their theatrical failures, an attachment indexed
most vividly by their habit of writing novels that ruefully refer to the plays
they might have been.

One way to describe the method of this book is as a reverse engineering of the metaphorization at work in Henry James's conversion of his theatrical failure into an aesthetic program. The depth of these writers' interest in the theater has been difficult to see in part because their signal aesthetic and ethical concerns employ a figurative use of terms that might also be taken to refer to scenes of literal performance. Thackeray's popularization of Bunyan's image of "vanity fair" is of course an attack on hypocrisy and petty snobberies —but it also makes reference to the urban fairgrounds that were a concrete (if obsolescent) reality in mid-Victorian England; Eliot's sympathetic aesthetics so routinely work by disciplining characters into a heightened awareness of what she calls the "inward drama" of consciousness that we may forget that drama is also the name for a collective social event; and Joycean epiphany originated not only from a secularization of Aquinian aesthetics but from Joyce's deep engagement with the naturalist (especially Ibsenian) drama's strategies for putting psychological truth on stage.

The concepts of "vanity fair," the "inward drama," the "scenic principle," and "epiphany" thus open an imagistic and conceptual traffic with the idea of concrete theatrical space, and so with the energies of publicity and collectivity. The tradition of novelistic longing for the theater is legible as the history of the yearning to reliteralize these figures; *Empty Houses* takes these authors' real-life theatrical endeavors as license for such a reliteralization. I ask what fairs mean in Thackeray's novels and if we can imagine live audiences to James's meticulously constructed scenes; how our sense of the plots of Eliot's novels might change if we imagine her characters preparing for their searching conversations by consorting in the wings of a real theater; and why Joyce's moments of epiphanic exposure so frequently invoke concrete performative spaces. The goal in each case is to revive a sense of the lost social referent of such figures.

This literalism is what most sharply differentiates this book from existing studies of the crucial figurative role theater plays in the novel. Although this scholarship sometimes notes the actual theatrical efforts of major novelists, the substance of those efforts has almost wholly escaped analysis.[14] This focus has hypostatized the novel and the theater as independent traditions, and my emphasis on the erratic trajectory of individual careers is meant as a reminder that these forms are not produced in isolation from each other. It also aims to complicate the antagonistic model of generic evolution that has shaped critical accounts of theater and the novel. Perhaps inspired by Bakhtin's claim that the novel "gets on poorly with other genres," critics have tended to assume the novel's expansionist ambition, its desire to absorb or otherwise neutralize the generic antagonist represented by the theater.[15] A guiding hypothesis of much of this criticism has been that when the novel engages theater, it does so homeopathically—to expel it, punish it, or marginalize it.

This assumption of generic competition has in turn buttressed the notion of the novel's essentially interiorizing function. The story of the novel as an agent of privatization has frequently been told as a tale of two genres, in which the novel's achievement of cultural hegemony over the course of the nineteenth and early twentieth centuries entails the eclipse of theater in the same period. The claim in these accounts is not that the theater disappeared in these years (it can easily be shown that the Victorian theater in particular was a growth industry)[16] but rather that the novel increasingly set the terms in which both forms imagined subjectivity. Historians of theater have traced the changes in theater architecture, playwriting, acting styles, and urban space that effected what has been called the gradual "novelization" of the theater over the course of the nineteenth century.[17] An overview of these changes makes evident their general thrust toward interiorization. The disappearance of urban fairgrounds; the shortening of theatrical bills of fare to fit the schedules of suburban trains; the evaporation of the stage apron and thus the curtailing of interaction between actor and audience; the new emphasis on realism in stage design and characterization and on decorum in the audience; a focus on interior settings, domestic entanglements, and the complexities of psychological motivation that reaches its apotheosis in the "wallpaper horizon"[18] of Ibsen's and Shaw's naturalism; finally, an acting style (known first as the System and then as the Method) that achieves dominance in the twentieth century by ontologizing these developments via a quasi-religious emphasis on authenticity and interiority: together these changes transformed theatrical culture to reflect the new prominence of the domestically oriented and psychologically absorbed subject presumably called into being and sustained by the realist novel.[19] The supposed generic competition between theater and novel also allegorizes the creation of the modern subject as the socially deactivated subject par excellence. It is precisely the publicity, exteriority, and collectivity of the theater (we might just say the "theatricality" of the theater) that need to be disciplined in a culture of the novel, and by most accounts this is just what happened.[20]

But assuming such a disciplining occurred, what were its affective features? While theater historians have disputed the notion that the theater was somehow in retreat in the nineteenth century, the "decline thesis" was such a commonplace of the era that everyone from intellectuals like G. H. Lewes (who complained of "dramatic degradation") to Dickens's fictional Mrs. Curdle (who sniffs that "the drama is gone, perfectly gone") could agree on it.[21] The rhetorical conflation here—in which a supposed falling off in dramatic quality is rewritten as the disappearance of the theater itself—anticipates the ways that literary history has tended to ignore the dramatic efflorescence of the nineteenth century. It is, for example, notoriously difficult to reconstruct from the page the sensory and intellectual pleasures of the 1871 melodrama *The Bells*: although the play achieves effects of considerable psychic complexity, these are not primarily verbal in nature, depending instead on the subtle management of stage effect via shifting tableaux and musical accompaniment.

Moreover, the power of *The Bells* had much to do with the notoriously psy-chologized, hyper-realistic acting of Henry Irving in the role of its guilt-ridden anti-hero, and Irving's name was associated much more closely with the play than was that of its author, Leopold Lewis.[22] Music, stagecraft, and Irving himself are all of course absent from the play's text, which thus presents itself to readers as a notably thin artifact of a more vivid event. In response to the lack of specifically literary interest presented by most plays in the nine-teenth century, literary history has until recently proceeded as if there simply were no drama in the years between Sheridan and Shaw.

While it is worth correcting this misperception, it is just as important to recognize that the idea of the theater's disappearance expresses a crucial truth about the period's economies of literary value. Sharon Marcus has argued that the features of nineteenth-century theater we have just reviewed—the weakness of its author function, its lack of literary prestige—make it fertile ground for critics seeking to "deconstruct the institution of literature."[23] We might add that it offers an equally promising viewpoint from which to canvas the constitution of the literary as an autonomous field, with all the attendant ambivalences of that process. The estrangement of literature from theatrical culture was a feature of Victorian contemporaneity: at once omnipresent and symbolically sidelined, the nineteenth-century theater was already an em-blem of the felt abstraction of literature from social life, and thus a symbolic magnet for the culture's recessive energies. Given this complexly contoured symbolic terrain (in which the theater is both losing ground and expand-ing, both gone and omnipresent), *Empty Houses* questions the notion that the models of "contest" and "competition" provide the best rubric through which to comprehend relations between literary forms.[24]

The careers examined here make clear that writers do not always know what is good for "their" genre, or even which genre is theirs. Even if the novel were definitively established to be in competition with the theater, we should recall that competitors view one another with longing as well as with enmity, and that victors often ambivalently memorialize the values of their defeated rivals. Far from triumphing in the eclipse of the theater, some of the peri-od's most important novelists registered their symbolic ascendancy ruefully. Where a loose Darwinism informs most existing accounts of the novel's rela-tion to the theater, the economy structuring the generic negotiations tracked in this book corresponds better to Freud's classic analysis of melancholia. Freud distinguishes mourning from melancholia in part on the grounds of the latter's potentially interminable nature: melancholia, he claimed, is a way not to mourn—which is to say not to get over and not to forget. Because the melancholic incorporation of the lost object is also a way to sustain a relation to the energies and possibilities represented by that object, Freudian melancholia is a technology of retention.[25] In stubbornly refusing to abandon their theatrical projects—by reworking theatrical failures in narrative form,

creating novels that convey a sense of the plays they might have been, or re-
minding readers of the embodied public their works have failed to convene
—these writers make visible the regrets that accompany a genre's process of
becoming unmistakably itself. They offer evidence of what we could call the
melancholy of generic distinction.

Tracing this melancholy requires attending at once to the ways the novel
seeks to resemble theater and to the ways it understands itself as irremediably
distinct from theater. This involves some necessary terminological blurriness.
The pages that follow sometimes contrast "novelistic" with "theatrical" logic,
and I want to stress two points about this usage. The first is that this is a
heuristic and not an essential distinction. My claim that some of the most
formally innovative novels introject the "theatrical" deeply into their texture
is meant to upset our certainties about the ideological orientation of either
form. Still, such binarizing terminology has been unavoidable in discussing
a span of time increasingly invested in the binary. The critical elevation of
the novel in the nineteenth century proceeded by marking the novel's formal distinctiveness from the theater. Victorian critics followed classic Aris-
totelian poetics in paying particular attention to the different compositional
possibilities of narrative and dramatic modes, and the theater remained a
more salient generic comparand for the novel than, say, poetry or epic.[26] This
leads to a second point: despite the fact that the novel described in *Empty
Houses* looks more determinedly "theatrical" than has been acknowledged,
it is inescapably true (and essential to understanding the novel of interiority)
that the novel and drama operate according to distinct protocols of storytelling and consumption. Because there are unavoidable distinctions between
plays and novels, I have omitted scare quotes from the words "theatrical" and
"novelistic" in the pages that follow; but this usage should not be taken to
suggest that these modal distinctions can be invested with firm ideological
significance.[27]

This terminological difficulty proceeds from the instability and inescapability of generic difference, and it suggests a further irony in the careers examined in *Empty Houses*: these would-be playwrights have all been noted for
their antitheatricality. From Thackeray's hatred of pretense and Eliot's suspicion of vain women to James's early diagnoses of the culture of publicity and
Joyce's contempt for Buck Mulligan's performative flourishes, these writers are
capable of rhetorically employing "theater" as a synonym for everything they
most despise. But the mobility of the idea of theater in their work suggests an
affective compound that the label "antitheatrical" handles too crudely.[28] The
psychic alchemy whereby we abuse an object that has disappointed us is, of
course, familiar enough. But Freud's conception of melancholia, sensitive as
it is to the radical fungibility of bad feeling about self and other, instructively
complicates this apparently clear psychic logic. Specifically, his essay suggests
that these writers' antitheatricality might express not just personal anger at

a theatrical frustration but also a more sociohistorically resonant resentment at the theater's increasing resemblance to the novel. Freud claims that the lost object in melancholia cannot be submitted to the work of mourning because its loss is unconscious—and in the essay's most arresting moment, he clarifies that such unconsciousness can result even when the subject is "aware of the loss giving rise to the melancholia, that is, when he knows whom he has lost but not *what* it is he has lost in them" (166). One reason for an inability to mourn a lost object, in other words, is an inability to specify the qualities in it that might be worth mourning.

The antitheatricality of these writers should be understood as a second- or third-order affect such as Freud sketches here—an expression all at once of distress at a personal theatrical failure, at the increasing remoteness of theatrical values from the inward-looking fictional worlds they were constructing, and at the existing theater's assimilation of precisely the "novelistic" values they had turned to the theater to escape. The conditions for such knotted emotions only increased as the two forms came more and more to resemble each other toward the end of the nineteenth century. As the novel becomes ever more focused on interior spaces and as the theater that once promised to provide an alternative follows suit, the vitriol directed at the theater also becomes the carrier of a frustration with the increasing virtuality of the publicity and externality that theater emblematizes: anger at the object can represent the object's failure to represent a viable alternative. While the novelists I treat have been interpreted as establishing the generic superiority of the novel at the expense of theater, I read the intense desire and bitterness they attach to the theater as a complaint against the polarization itself. This book argues that the cohabitation in these writers of antitheatrical rhetoric with deep theatrical desire expresses not an acquiescence in the fortified boundary between novel and theater but a protest against their felt convergence on the terrain of the interior.

Theater Dethematized: Spatializations of the Novel

The novel of interiority registers that protest in a variety of ways. The strategy that features most consistently in the chapters that follow is these novels' habit of referring their readers to performative spaces. This is true first of all in a thematic sense. These texts consistently incorporate their creators' theatrical preoccupations through the depiction of public spaces; often these spaces are so heavily invested that they function as fantasy images of the novel itself. Bakhtin's word for this phenomenon was "chronotope," the term he invented to denote the spatio-temporal figure providing a work's texture and the generative matrix for its plot. The essay in which he introduced the term specifically invokes Thackeray's *Vanity Fair* as an example of the theater as chronotope.[29] As chapter 1 shows, Thackeray's obsession with theatrical space in that novel extends from the fairgrounds that give the book its title to the children's puppet theater that provides its closing image. The relay the novel sets up between these chronotopes means that even the domesticated toy theater becomes a monument to fairground sociability. A similarly insistent depiction of theatricalized space informs George Eliot's career, notably in the city square where the heroine dances in *The Spanish Gypsy* and the casino that provides the setting for the opening of *Daniel Deronda*. As spaces where the boundaries of ethnic groups and human personality are strangely irrelevant, they are peculiar "containers" for what seem to be intensely psychologized narratives. Similarly, James's *Awkward Age* is centered on a salon whose principal activity is the fostering of sexually loose and psychologically confounding "talk," while the "Circe" chapter of Joyce's *Ulysses* is a closet drama set in a street in Dublin's red-light district and inside an improbably capacious brothel.[30]

These public spaces are overtly thematized in the fiction. But there is a further dimension of these texts' spatial imagination, one that, though more difficult to describe, is also more radically unsettling—precisely because it derives not from thematically represented spaces but from the text's formal presentation. If the chronotopic effects I have just discussed suggest that the novelistic world can be analogized to a theater, this second type of spatialization intimates, more troublingly, that the events of the novel might actually be transpiring inside one. With surprising consistency the novels examined in *Empty Houses* undergo a warping in their phenomenological texture, so that the narrated action appears suddenly to be taking place in a theatrical frame, and the characters to be self-consciously performing parts before an imaginary body of spectators. Perhaps the strangest feature of these theatrical spatializations, as we will see, is that they derive from a series of formal devices familiar to students of novelistic innovation, among them interior monologue, free indirect discourse, and the careful restriction of point of view. These devices are frequently read as handmaidens of interiorization, deeply individuating and psychologizing narrative technologies. But I argue that these novelists' inflection of such devices has a genetic relation to their failed theatrical experiments, and that these techniques thus smuggle the memory (or more properly the fantasy) of the crowded theatrical space into the psychic interior. The collectivization and spatialization attendant on these narrative devices only becomes visible when we perceive their intimate relation to theatrical form. If one result of studying theatricality in the novel without considering the theatrical projects of novelists themselves is to reify the sense of generic independence, another is to overlook the specifically formal traces the theater leaves in the novel. Critics, especially of the nineteenth-century novel, have tended to thematize theatricality as another name for duplicity, pretending, and self-difference: the ambivalent Victorian romance with theatrical artifice has long been perceived as central to the period.[31] But too fixed a focus on this particular and heavily moralized understanding of theatricality ignores the other meanings it had even for the morally obsessed nineteenth century; in particular, it misses the consistent association of theater with the more properly formal project of gesturing toward collective space. This consciousness of theater as a publicizing and collectivizing technology is powerfully legible in the narrative devices I have mentioned; bearing the traces of these novelists' will to collectivization, these devices function as monuments to interiority's discontents. Among the most notable effects of these formal innovations is to sideline characterological distinction, and in the process to turn psychological questions into social ones.

We have seen, for example, that Thackeray's *Vanity Fair* conveys a palimpsestic vision of the home as an enclosure that keeps referring to the public spaces it excludes. But this torsion toward theatrical spaces is conveyed with equal power by the very texture of the narration. Chapter 1 examines the tonal shifts of the narrative voice in *Vanity Fair* as encoding a yearning for public scenes of performance. Moving between public speechifying and chastened intimate address, the Thackerayan narrator offers readers an acoustic map of different imaginary scenes of reception. The pitch of Thackeray's voice—both its tone and its reach, its sound and the spaces it organizes—indexes various fantasmatic scenes of readerly witness, conveying in the process a vivid sense of the erosion of public space in the face of the exaltation of the domestic sphere. The sociohistorical imagination evident in *Vanity Fair* was given a new intensity of focus in his unperformed play *The Wolves and the Lamb* (1854) and the novel into which he later adapted it, the formally innovative *Lovel the Widower* (1860). In retreating from the stage, Thackeray both amplified his critique of mid-Victorian domesticity and pioneered the practice of interior monologue. The novel's theatrical genesis crucially inflects Thackeray's version of this hallmark technique of narrative interiorization: *Lovel the Widower* is one of Thackeray's most psychologized works, with a narrator who constantly gives away his insecurity and bitterness in the face of the domestic comedy he relates. But his habit of speaking as if from a vanishing stage transforms this slight marriage comedy into a dark meditation on the restrictions of point of view; and it transforms this psychological portrait into a social diagnosis of the disappearance of a pre-Victorian culture of performance.

George Eliot's tangled engagement with the drama is the subject of chapter 2, which begins with an analysis of the mutual constitution of theatricalized space and characterological interiority in *Romola* (1863) and *Felix Holt* (1866)—transitional novels in which Eliot's emphasis on psychological inwardness works at the expense of demonized crowds. But during this period she also undertook a dramatic work that challenged her most fundamental formal and ethical commitments. Conceived as a play but published as an epic poem mixing dramatic and narrative forms, *The Spanish Gypsy* shows Eliot refusing both the novel as a form and the inward cultivation it seems designed to encourage. *The Spanish Gypsy* includes narrative passages that take the grammatical form of free indirect discourse, in which a character's habits of mind are mimicked by the narrator's prose. But the exteriorized perspective demanded by the dramatic origin of *The Spanish Gypsy* assures that these eminently psychologizing sentences emanate from and attach to no character in particular, instead appearing to echo in an auditorium populated with spectators. Eliot carried this experiment in externalized forms of psychological narration into the novels she wrote next, *Middlemarch* (1871–72) and especially *Daniel Deronda* (1876)—in the case of the latter imparting to the characters a suspicion that the plots in which they are entangled are playing out in a giant performance space. Indeed, Eliot originally considered writing her last major novel as a play, and we will accordingly track the ways in which the thematically represented theaters of *Daniel Deronda* infect the narrative fabric of the text, so that the novel seems constantly on the verge of turning itself into that unwritten performance piece.[32] *Deronda* is famous for the harshness with which its two central plots ("English" and "Jewish") are kept ethnically and ethically separate; but the text's theatrical hangover continually intimates to its characters and to its readers that those plots share greenroom space backstage.

Such spatializations become more emphatic in the texts analyzed in chapter 3. Henry James conceived of *The Other House* as a play but published it as a novel in 1896. Almost exclusively reliant on dialogue and dense with the notation of movements that frustrate readerly visualization, the novel constantly alludes to the theatrical status it appears to have abandoned; James reworked the novel back into a play in 1909. Both versions suggest that the domestic tragedy constituting the plot is contained in the space of a theatrical auditorium: in perhaps the oddest moment in the 1909 version, an indisputably pathological character actually looks out challengingly at "the spectators."[33] Similar invocations of theatrical space haunt 1899's *The Awkward Age*, a novel whose characters begin to play to an imaginary theatrical audience that James posits just beyond the "footlights" of the diegetic universe. *The Other House* and *The Awkward Age* bookend James's experimental period of 1895–99, years often understood as a preamble to his perfection of the psychological novel in the new century. But in abandoning James's fabled "center of consciousness" in favor of elaborating a group subject, these drama-novels document James's ambivalence regarding the interiorizing narrative approach of which he would become the acknowledged master. We will see that the sense of collective endeavor is kept alive in James's late career by his work's most unmistakable feature, its style. In *The Wings of the Dove*, Jamesian style—precisely because it is a shared resource in his fictional world—emerges as the bearer of what I call performative universalism, conveying a sense that his characters are participants in a shared effort to evade psychic distinction.

Chapter 4 traces this trajectory into the twentieth century, examining the collective spaces invoked in Joyce's career-long obsession with dramatic form—from the epiphanies he wrote as a teenager through his 1918 play *Exiles* to the closet drama of the Nighttown (or "Circe") episode of *Ulysses*. Joyce's experiments with theatrical form constitute a running commentary on his interest in the "depths" of the psyche. The different conceptions of theatrical space embedded in the idea of epiphany lend a dual valence to this keystone of Joycean aesthetics. If, on the one hand, epiphany imagines a humiliating theater of psychic exposure, on the other it gestures toward a perverse collective space where such exposures would lose their policing force. These isolating and collectivist impulses are both visible in Joyce's play *Exiles*, which follows Ibsenesque naturalism in its representation of psychic motivation but allows its characters to mount a notable collective resistance to the diagnostic imperative structuring their stage existence. And when he came to fold a play text into *Ulysses* itself in the Nighttown episode, Joyce rejected the psychologizing logic that grounds personality in sexuality. Nighttown is commonly read as a theater of exposure, a making-manifest of the sexual depths, but its status as a play script drains its revelations of psychic significance. Like an actor who knows that the "aesthetic frame he occupies . . . protects him from the abyss"[34] of his socially ratified identity, the characters in the brothel-cum-playhouse that is Nighttown take a performative step back from their emphatic sexual individuation by pointing us to the space they collectively occupy; the episode becomes a meditation on the possibility of an eroticized public culture released from the reign of psychosexual meaning.

As this overview indicates, the theatrical spatializations discussed in each chapter typically occur when someone inside the novel "breaks character" to gesture beyond his immediate diegetic context. Because this repeatedly occurs at these texts' most psychologized moments, this warping partially neutralizes what would otherwise appear their most interiorizing effects. We might describe these spatializations as formal paroxysms: moments at which the conventions of the genre become visible, even—strikingly—to the characters themselves. In these moments the text's awareness of its status as a novel reaches a fever pitch, and the novel pushes against its own novelness by pointing to the possibility that it might instead have been a play. Because this twinned sense of generic identity and generic contingency is imparted to characters themselves, those characters are thereby briefly lifted from their position "inside" the fiction—abstracted or formalized by means of a double consciousness akin to that of actors participating in a theatrical performance. These are moments in which the novel imparts to its characters what Bert States, in his phenomenological account of the performative event, terms "the permission of the mimesis," the ability to lay claim to one's dual status as performer and as character.[35] In other words, these are moments in which the novel imbues its characters with the double aspect every character enjoys as a matter of course in theater.

The technical term for the making-explicit of this duality is parabasis, which designates the moment in classical Old Comedy when the chorus "came forward without their masks to face the audience and delivered . . . views on topics such as politics or religion about which the dramatist felt strongly."[36] The term is best known to contemporary literary criticism from the work of Paul de Man, who made use of it in his reading of the concept of irony in German romanticism. For de Man, parabasis vitiates a text's referential seriousness; as the trope "by means of which the illusion of the fiction is broken," parabasis is the deconstructive device par excellence.[37] This conclusion, however, may have more to do with de Man's lack of interest in the embodied theater than with the trope's inherent function. De Man notes the theatrical origins of the term but quickly translates it into a purely literary operation, where it becomes a figure for the expression of textual self-consciousness. But the term's derivation from the classical theater—and its etymological meaning of "a coming forward"—suggest that theatrical parabasis does not so much (pace de Man) detract from the substantiality of a fictional universe as it heightens the spectators' awareness of the fiction's spatial and social grounding. If theatrical parabasis reveals a certain brittleness in the diegesis, it also and at the same moment socially substantializes the performance: the robustness subtracted from the drama as story is rendered to the theater as space and as event.

Of course, this transfer only literally occurs in the case of the embodied theatrical event: in the moments of novelistic parabasis sketched above, the theatrical surround toward which the characters gesture remains imaginary. This designating of a ghostly theatrical frame is a crucial aspect of these novelistic self-spatializations, one just as significant as their supposed deconstructive function, and these writers' theatrical ambition should alert us to the proximity of the embodied theater as a referential destination of their writing. Rather than blanketing the diegetic universe in a self-conscious textuality, such spatializations should be recognized as, more oddly, adding a further imaginary spatial dimension to that universe. In each of the cases I have just discussed, the referential texture of the fiction is warped not by an awareness of its textuality but by the sudden interpolation—"between" the reader and the diegetic action, as it were—of a hypothetical theatrical context for that action. If under normal narrative protocols the reader is "alone" with the diegetic universe, in these moments the intimacy of novel reading is aerated with an idea of public space: we suddenly sense not only the crowd of spectators of which we are an imagined part but also the architectural fact of the space we imaginarily share with them. In this sense, novelistic parabasis is more accurately characterized as constructive than as deconstructive.

It is important to recognize that this fantasmatic spatialization is also a fantasmatic collectivization: to refer to the theatrical frame in which the action takes place is both to designate one's status as one player among many and to gesture out toward the collectivity of witnesses that fill that space.[38] As I have suggested, the theater's role as an agent of collectivization needs to be stressed in a contemporary critical context that tends to understand theater primarily as a figure for duplicity. Our current tendency to take theater as a metaphor may simply be a result of the relative marginality of theatrical performance in modernity. But it was not always thus; in the nineteenth century it is notable how frequently discussions of theatrical artifice modulate into meditations on the collective space of the performative project. In an essay titled "Stage Illusion" first published in 1825, for example, Charles Lamb deflected the question of the actor's professional duplicity onto a consideration of the theater's collective address. "Why are misers so hateful in the world," Lamb asks, "and so endurable on the stage?" His answer is that our awareness of the feigned nature of stage occurrences inevitably inflects their meaning. If the conclusion is unsurprising in its substance, it is strikingly phrased: theatrical events "please by being done under the life, or beside it; not *to the life.*" Lamb elaborates on the claim in a discussion of cowardly characters: the stage coward makes

> a perpetual subinsinuation to us, the spectators, even in the extremity of the shaking fit, that he was not half such a coward as we took him for ... We saw all the common symptoms of the malady upon him; the quivering lip, the cowering knees, the teeth chattering; and could have sworn "that man was frightened." But we forgot all the while—or kept it almost a secret to ourselves—that he never once lost his self-possession; that he let out by a thousand droll looks and gestures—meant at *us*, and not at all supposed to be visible to his fellows in the scene, that his confidence in his own resources had not deserted him.[39]

"Meant at *us*": Lamb's emphasis nicely indicates that every instance of theatrical pretending is by the same token an instance of public address; an acted gesture implicitly convenes a collective body of witness. This exteriorizing tendency is, of course, one source of antitheatrical pronouncements against the essentially meretricious nature of performance.[40] But if we join Lamb in forestalling such moralized thematizations (theater equals duplicity, theater equals meretriciousness) we can register the underlying formal promise of collective awareness heralded by theatrical performance. Note how the remarkable locutions and neologisms of Lamb's essay—"under the life," "subinsinuation," "meant at *us*"—take their distance from the particular characterological qualities of miserliness and cowardice that occasion them. These examples are, importantly, *only* examples, interesting less in themselves than for the way they highlight an extradiegetic assertiveness that is a general feature of theatrical performance.[41] Indeed, it is easy to see how one could make a different version of the point with a wholly distinct set of attributes. Cruelty, gullibility, delusion, loyalty, warmth: all, if performed adequately, will convey that surplus of intention that Lamb describes as a subinsinuation. I refer to theatricality as a dethematizing energy in order to register this formalizing tropism of performance, its tendency to encase these qualitative differences among attributes within a shared structure of address. Theatrical pretending may "mean" duplicity; but it also always subinsinuates the bare fact of our collective presence.

While the collectivity indicated by the actor's performance is first and foremost that of the audience, it is also true that theatrical performance normally occurs through a collective body of performers. Important as it is in accounting for the distinctive phenomenology of the theatrical event, this fact may seem so obvious as to appear unremarkable. Note how casually, for example, the novelist Olive Schreiner invokes the collective nature of the theater in the preface to her 1883 novel *The Story of an African Farm*. Defending the book's downbeat plot, Schreiner contends that "human life may be painted according to two methods." She continues:

> There is the stage method. According to that each character is duly marshalled at first, and ticketed; we know with an immutable certainty that at the right crises each one will reappear and act his part, and, when the curtain falls, all will stand before it bowing. There is a sense of satisfaction in this, and completeness. But there is another method—the method of the life we all lead.[42]

Schreiner goes on to celebrate her novelistic practice at the theater's expense. But in the process she emphasizes that the theater is a mode in which the unfolding of story is premised on a collaborative effort. This fact, Schreiner suggests, underwrites even the most violently divergent narrated fates with an image of collective survival: "When the curtain falls, *all will stand before it bowing.*" The words signal that the necessarily collective ground of theatrical presentation inflects at every point the meaning of whatever story is getting told: the curtain call serves to make this collective grounding explicit, but it is perceptible to spectators whether or not the entire cast assembles at the play's end. The phenomenology of performance thus effects a fundamental alteration both in the ontology of character and the meaning of plot. In the theater, even the bitterest characterological oppositions are premised on a foundational cooperation; even when, in the closing gesture of *A Doll's House*, Nora slams the front door of Helmer's house, we are aware that this definitive rupture is sponsored by necessarily collaborative preparation.

This is an ineradicable feature of theatrical performance. But literary critics, who tend almost by definition to approach plays via the medium of print, are perhaps especially prone to underestimate its implications for the texture of performative events. One of these implications is that performance tugs against individuation with a collective impulse that assimilates the most discrepant characters into a common category.[43] The collaborative nature of the theater—like theatrical impersonation—can to that extent be described as powerfully dethematizing: no matter the plot, what happens on stage communicates first and always the fact of collective endeavor. If "collective endeavor" sounds like an idealization of theater, it might more properly be understood as its definition. To recognize, with Darko Suvin, that "politics—the organization of people's living together—is always implicit in theatre performance," or, with Fredric Jameson, that theater is "the very figure for the collective," is not to claim the political virtue of collectivity per se.[44] My argument is not that theater is always politically beneficent (theater of course can enforce or disguise pernicious ideologies) but that the formal trace the theater leaves in the novel indexes the collective horizon that is the necessary ground of any meaningful political engagement.

This conception of theater animates one of the most provocative projects in recent critical theory, the work of Jacques Rancière. Accepting the terms of the Platonic invective against "theatrocracy" while inverting its value sign, Rancière makes the case that pretending and collectivity, far from contingently linked features of dramatic enactment, are always mutually entailed in theatrical performance. The theater in Rancière's conception is the privileged site of political subjectivization because it is at once a space of assembly and a space of licensed self-difference: if democracy is "the collective embodiment of the capacity of anybody, the power of those who have no 'entitlement' to exert power by the privilege of possessing a quality—whether birth, wealth, science or other," the theater's externality makes it impossible to stably ascertain who possesses those prerequisites of participation.[45] In Rancière's conception, in other words, the theater's *modal* difficulty in ratifying interior distinctions among subjects is key to its democratic orientation. In the space-for-seeing that is the theater, the predicates of political belonging are appropriable: anyone might claim to possess them by mimicking them. Indeed, in licensing such mimicry, the technology of theater invites such disruptive appropriations.

Rancière's linkage of theatrical mimesis and the collective has its roots in his archival work on nineteenth-century French theatrical culture.[46] In his account, the urban *théâtres du coeur* were spaces of "a disorder that expresses itself in various ways: the agitation of the queue and the overcrowding in the gallery; the din raised by a group of hired clappers frequently composed of tailors who were particularly able to disguise themselves as fashionable dandies; disorders of the imagination produced by the drama or the prestige of the actors."[47] In the wake of the 1848 Revolution, French authorities issued a series of edicts regulating the use of music, costume, dance, and crowd scenes; the new rules were designed to

> make the performance space merely the space of execution of a text or music, a place where nothing happened, where the singer or the actor would function only as an executor and the public as consumer. The multitude of prohibitions . . . aimed . . . above all to suppress all theatricality . . . anything that could become the basis of an illusion or of a wink, any incitement of the public to active participation.[48]

If the state was clearly troubled by theater's ability to convene tumultuous crowds and by its provisional suspension of codes of class and sexual propriety, Rancière insists that these facts were connected to the work of theatrical mimesis as such, the "illusion" or "wink" that in his account addresses the crowd and licenses its disruptive self-constitution as a collective body.

Although the situation was distinct in the less explosive political context in England, Rancière's analysis accords in its outlines with accounts of early-nineteenth-century British theater by Elaine Hadley and Marc Baer depicting the Regency and early Victorian theater as channels of popular resistance to the logics of privatization and the market economy.[49] But while Hadley, Baer, and Rancière all tell a story of the progressive taming of the radical disruptiveness of the existing theater, Rancière's point is that this democratizing potential can never be totally expunged and in fact inheres in the technology of dramatic representation and assembly. The nineteenth-century commentary we have already examined indicates that an awareness of the collectivizing possibilities Rancière locates in the theatrical situation survived into and throughout the Victorian period, even after changes in theatrical culture had stratified the public along class lines and enforced stricter rules of decorum both on- and offstage. Rancière's interest in the theatrical "wink," for example, derives less from that gesture's ironizing effects than from its capacity to address an assembled crowd—precisely the function, as we have seen, of the actor's "subinsinuation" in Lamb's account. When Rancière notes (à propos the melodramatic audience's lack of interest in plot) that "it is assuredly difficult to make people profit from a moral if they do not make the analytic link between the crime and the punishment," his description accords well with Schreiner's complaint about the failure of theatrically presented fates to "stick."[50] Similarly, Rancière's emphasis on the collectivizing possibilities of disguise would have been familiar to Victorian audiences, who typically witnessed a troupe of actors appear in changing constellations of roles in several different pieces over the course of a single night at the theater. Deborah Vlock describes the resulting theatrical culture as entailing a "loosening of plot and character" and an emphasis on the troupe's self-constitution rather than the stories it presented—a dethematizing point Rancière puts more abstractly when he claims that it "is not the value of the message conveyed by the mimetic *dispositif* that is at stake [in aesthetic forms], but the *dispositif* itself."[51]

Such comments suggest that the intimations of collaborative existence embedded in the theatrical apparatus are subtly but importantly anti-closural, even anti-narrative. As Schreiner's preface indicates, performance disconcertingly suggests that the narrated fates of individual characters are accompanied and in some sense negated by the fact of performative cooperation: the "share" doled out to one character is haunted by the sharing inherent in the collective performative project as such; the presence of the "cast" underwrites the casting of individual lots the plot narrates.[52] This fact in turn suggests that identification is an inadequate rubric with which to approach the phenomenology of theatrical forms. The theatrical event asks its spectators not only to identify with one of the parties to a conflict but, at a more basic level, to cathect the staging of the conflict itself; it asks them not only to feel along with one character to his or her end but to be present at the collective enactment of that ending. The concept of identification neglects the fact that what draws an audience to a scene is often less the ambition to be or to possess a particular character than the more fundamental desire that this project be maintained, that these characters coexist and play out what conversations or conflicts they will—in short, that this collectively maintained world exist and be given sufficient spatial ground.[53]

If this collectivist imagination is particularly relevant to the theater, *Empty Houses* seeks the traces of such de-individualization in the novel of interiority by attending to the spatializations through which it summons a virtual theater. The anti-narrative torsion of these novels' invocation of theatrical space serves as a reminder that the narratological category of closure derives from a spatial metaphor: closure in this sense refers not to what happens to individual characters but to the more elementary fact of their co-presence, their shared containment in the space of the work.[54] An awareness of the work as a kind of social container can be central even to the experience of a temporally articulated form like the novel. Indeed, this is an experience to which we pay colloquial homage when we say (for example) that *Daniel Deronda* has a famous actress and a consumptive Jewish mystic "in" it—even if we cannot recall these characters' relations to each other or what happens to either of them. In accounting for the spatialized and denarrativized senses in which we can apprehend a novel, it is useful to speak less about the book's plot than about its characteristic climate or pervasive atmosphere—features that derive more from elements of tone, style, and narrative presentation than from what actually "happens" in the book. Accordingly, *Empty Houses* sometimes takes what will seem a perverse distance from the plots of the novels in order to attend to the phenomenological texture conditioning the fictional world. I am less interested in the story of victimization that structures James's *The Awkward Age* than in the visually hazy atmosphere blanketing the action, less intrigued by the marriage comedy Thackeray rehearses in *Lovel the Wid-ower* than the sourness with which he maps the domestic space that comedy supposedly sanctifies, less preoccupied with *Daniel Deronda*'s Zionism than with its characters' intimations of their shared theatrical condition, less in-trigued by the characters' fantasies in "Circe" than by the fact that Joyce's exteriorizing presentation refuses to say whether these are *their* fantasies, or fantasies at all.

If the themes of victimhood, marriage, Zionism, sexual fantasy, and so on, remain undeniably important to the meaning of these novels—and es-pecially to the divergent character fates they narrate—their formal presenta-tion insinuates a dethematizing element into the narrative fabric by ignoring or sitting athwart the movements of plot. The spatial imaginary indexed by this dethematizing theatricality suggests that novels can be read not only as records of fictional events but also as shelters for imagined forms of collective being. While their narrated events may support the notion that these novels are devoted to the mystique of the interiorized individual, their persistent encodings of theatrical space demand that we read them with an eye for their institutional erotics: these novels express at the most basic level a demand that these collective spaces exist, even if only in the provisional medium of the fictive world. And quite contrary to the received idea of the novel as de-voted to the all-importance of interiority, the theatrical spaces conjured in these novels facilitate a distance from the notion of identitarian consistency. These are collective spaces conditioned by a suspension of hermeneutic atten-tion. We might define a theater as a space marked by the ambition to make the permission of the mimesis publicly available—a space devoted to the non-traumatic collective consumption of slippage between human essence and human signification. In invoking the theater—in attempting, against the grain of narrative, to *become* theater—the novel of interiority that emerges in *Empty Houses* similarly shelters an agnosticism about what constitutes the truth of human personality.

To put this in terms of a contemporary critical lexicon that has been important to this book: these novels conjure a series of paradigmatically queer spaces. The formalizing gesture that inaugurates queer critique has strong resonances with the dethematizing projects operative in the novel of interiority; as many commentators have noted, the term "queer" takes its distance from the fixity of gay and lesbian identities in order to under-take the more properly formal project of articulating a critical relation to sexual norms. Moreover, this book's emphasis on issues of sexual difference and sexual shaming—an emphasis that grows more pronounced in the final chapters—has a historical rationale. A focus on sexuality is inescapable when treating a period (the mid-nineteenth to early twentieth centuries) in which, as Foucault most powerfully articulated, the question of human interiority has a privileged relation to the question of sex.[55] The intensification of the linkage between sexual and identitarian truth is borne out by the trajectory mapped in the following chapters, in which the domain of the interior moves from the domestic enclosure in Thackeray to the depths of sexual secrecy in Joyce. And as the question of interiority migrates to the subject's supposed sexual core, the communitarian energy I locate in the novel of interiority comes to center on the representation of sexual minorities: in the cases of Joyce and of James Baldwin, the subject of my epilogue, the male homosexual is the privileged site for the examination of interiority and its discontents.

The focus on homosexuality in these writers is notable but not exclusive: it is a feature of the theaters conjured by the novels analyzed here that they do not demand identification at the door. Michael Warner notes that queer theory is characterized by an "aggressive impulse of generalization"—a dethematizing refusal to specify where queer insights stop or to whom they might apply.[56] In keeping with that impulse, I have chosen not to read the collectivities these novels imagine, address, and desire as circumscribed by any particular sexual identity. The novel of interiority suggests that if sexual minorities have felt most intensely the isolating ravages of a culture obsessed with self-scrutiny, that particular experience has a broader relevance. As Eve Kosofsky Sedgwick has shown, a radical oscillation between particularizing and generalizing paradigms—what she calls minoritizing and universalizing ways of understanding sexual difference—is hardwired into modernity's thinking about sexual subjectivity. Her *Epistemology of the Closet* is a study of the emergence of male homosexual identity in the later nineteenth and early twentieth centuries, but her sense of that particular group's proximity to broad questions of identity justifies her claim to be speaking not just about gay men but about what she frankly labels "Western culture as a whole."[57] For Sedgwick, the "radical and irreducible incoherence" (85) of minoritizing and universalizing paradigms means that it is always unclear in this period whether sexual deviance is a problem for a localized group or an aspect of human populations more generally. *Empty Houses* covers nearly the same chronological spread as Sedgwick's book, and in demonstrating how frequently the question of deviance abuts the issue of collective forms of life, it supports her claims about sexuality's adjacency to questions of the public broadly conceived. In conjuring a series of emphatically non-normative spaces with emphatically undefined outer boundaries, the novels examined here suggest that collective aspiration in modernity is lodged in the minor places of sexual and private life.

That sexual subjectivity is not in itself an adequate field for the achievement of such aspiration perhaps goes without saying; at any rate, this has been one insight of politically oriented criticism of the novel, which has consistently emphasized the containment of political desire in romantic and psychological structures. *Empty Houses* grants this point while insisting on the multivalence of the novel's increasing sexualization. The novel's intensified attention to the representation of sexuality—and particularly of sexual minorities—in fact spotlights the traumatic closures of individualism, and this spotlighting of interiority is not equivalent to an ideological assertion of its political adequacy. In the wake of what has been called "homonormativity" —the emphasis in gay and lesbian politics on a consumerist version of identity, and on such issues as adoption, military service, and marriage equality— it has become tempting to read the history of queerness as always having tended toward our current moment of neoliberal accommodation, and to read any emphasis on sexual difference as reinforcing the privatized imaginary.[58] But in the years on which *Empty Houses* focuses, this particular future (that is, our present) was far from clear. Eli Zaretsky's recent history of the social meanings of psychoanalysis, for example, offers a complex account of how the late-nineteenth-century intensification of meaning around the question of sexuality made "personal life . . . the site of deep wishes and utopian imaginings."[59] Zaretsky's point is the ambivalent one that such localization could be both mystifying, encouraging an inattention to the "political, economic, and cultural preconditions" of interiority, and liberatory, "deepening the meaning of modernity" by encouraging the emancipation of women and sexual minorities (7–8).

For a certain stripe of left criticism, of course, the fact that the utopian imagination finds expression in the representation of specifically sexual community will seem to mark its insufficiency. In his essay "Pleasure: A Political Issue," for example, Jameson endorses a politics of sexuality only with the caveat that "the proper political use of pleasure must always be *allegorical* . . . The thematizing of a particular pleasure as a political issue . . . must always involve a dual focus, in which the local issue is meaningful and desirable in and of itself, but is also *at one and the same time* taken as the *figure* for Utopia in general, and for the systematic revolutionary transformation of society as a whole."[60] *Empty Houses* takes the force of this claim seriously but tarries at greater length with the sexually minoritized figure and his pleasures than does Jameson (in "Pleasure: A Political Issue," that length is limited to the sentence I have just quoted). To trace the history of interiority's investment with utopian longing is not merely to tell a story of mystification; far from occluding the non-fit between interiority and large-scale social transformation, the novel of interiority makes that inadequation painfully visible. This book's epilogue argues that the novel of interiority reaches an impasse and a breakthrough in the work of James Baldwin precisely when the contradictions inherent in the attempt to think collective problems through sexual interiority becomes unavoidably insistent—and does so through Baldwin's negotiation with the generic difference of the theater. Baldwin's career makes clear that if the novel relentlessly personalizes collective issues, its theatrical preoccupation constitutes a record of the political costs of that reduction, one that demands to be read at the level of form.

The Vocation of Failure

Put another way, *Empty Houses* constitutes an argument about the ideological valences of the aesthetic. I have claimed that novels "summon" theaters, that they "invoke" spaces, and that they "imagine" the creation or maintenance of forms of community. If in one sense these are traditional descriptions for what art does, only a slight change in the angle of vision is required to make them look like notably modest claims. In contrast to much recent criticism that argues for fiction's role in solidifying or even creating some central feature of modern life, *Empty Houses* claims that these novels are intensely aware of their relative marginality and powerlessness. "Universalizing the individual subject . . . is what novels do," Nancy Armstrong flatly claims.[61] But the writers examined in *Empty Houses* are not so sure about the performative efficacy of their own work, let alone about the sanctity of the "individual subject" that work might be said to model. Many critics have noted that the historical transition from high Victorianism to high modernism intensified the aesthetic's status as supplementary to "real" life; the fracturing of the Victorian reading public had, by the turn of the century, created a high art whose cultural status was in inverse proportion to its actual readership. This fact is clearly of central relevance to the authors discussed in the second half of this book: James's New York Edition of his complete works (1907–9), a prestige collection that sold dismally, can be taken as the epitome of this process, and the notion that *Ulysses* was essentially destined for the professoriat was clear even to its creator.[62] But a sense of artistic irrelevance may have been evident even before sales fell toward the end of the nineteenth century. Isobel Armstrong has noted that the post-Kantian "purity" of the aesthetic realm could double as a sense of inconsequentiality: "the Victorian poets," she writes, "were the first group of writers to feel that what they were doing was simply unnecessary and redundant."[63] I argue that similar doubts about artistic efficacy obtained for the period's novelists; my claim that Thackeray and Eliot intimated the peripheral nature of art even from within their popularity is thus also a claim for their prescience and their modernity.

Just as important is the fact that these writers' failed theatrical projects became charged sites for their thinking about the efficacy of the artistic in general. In an essay on the little-known theater of Baudelaire, Roland Barthes writes, "What is interesting about Baudelaire's plays is not their dramatic content but their embryonic state: the critic's role is therefore not to dissect these sketches for the image of an achieved theater but, on the contrary, to determine in them the vocation of their failure."[64] One need not agree that failure is quite as purposeful as Barthes implies to see the suggestiveness of his phrasing. The types of theatrical frustration discussed in the following chapters range from the failure to complete plays to the inability to get them performed to (more or less definitive) negative popular reaction to staged productions—and it is not my purpose to claim that these are all equivalent forms of failure, or to explain whether or why these plays were fated to fail.[65] Rather, I argue that—whatever the reasons for it—theatrical frustration offered a visceral experience to these writers of the failure to establish successful contact with an audience. Thus these biographical failures became potent emblems of larger concerns: whether these plays needed to or were designed to fail, their authors "vocationalized" that failure, retroactively repurposing it as significant and productive of fictional experimentation. The novelistic texts most influenced by these theatrical failures are marked by a sense of incompletion that becomes a meditation on the marginality of the aesthetic in modernity. In place of making the (perhaps more galvanizing) claim that the novels I treat are forceful political statements, my point is that the limited extent of their force is one of the things they most powerfully consider.[66]

Thus where literary critics frequently speak of texts themselves as "performances" or "enactments" of an authorial project or ideological script, I have resisted such terminology and its silent metaphorization of the idea of theatrical performance. By insisting on the stubbornly literal fact that novels are not performances, I aim to make visible the sense of non-achievement and virtuality embedded in these texts. Such virtual or "failed" enactment holds especially for the effects of fantasmatic spatialization this introduction has been describing: the theater these devices sustain in the heart of the novel of interiority is an imaginary one. The performed theater is, of course, necessarily an affair of real bodies in real space; it is peculiarly strong in what Hans Ulrich Gumbrecht calls "presence effects."[67] As theater historians often have occasion to lament, writing about theater transforms the event into an artifact, bleaching it of the color, heat, noise, and social contingency that properly constitutes it.[68] The novel has often been understood as eliding this fact by co-opting the living theater into the two-dimensional form of metaphor. I suggest, to the contrary, that these novels are supremely aware, and work to make their readers aware, of their failure to be theater. This failure effect radiates most notably from the aspiration these texts often evince to approximate the appearance of play texts. Each of these authors makes recourse—sometimes sudden, sometimes sustained—to the look of the theatrical script in their narrative texts. Sometimes this effect proceeds from the simple fact of having dialogue massively preponderate over narration, as in the novels of James; at others, the effect is more blunt, as when Thackeray and Joyce suddenly adopt the typographic conventions of play texts, with speech marked by character tags and narration ceding to the notation of stage directions enclosed in parentheses. In still others, as in Eliot's typographic invocations of the theater in *Daniel Deronda*, the effect of ambient theatricalization is fleeting but productive of powerfully uncanny effects.

It is tempting to see such code switching as a sign of the novel's incorporative drive, its much bruited habit of ingesting other forms into its texture. Novel studies has often understood the novel as the assimilative form par excellence, and self-confidence—of its centrality, its inevitable "rise," and its ability to absorb whatever material while still remaining itself—as its defining affect.[69] But the phenomenological oddity attending these writers' inclusion of theatrical cues suggests that this gesture should be read not as an emblem of assurance but as a self-conscious marking of the limits of the novelistic project. Far from signaling the triumph of the novel's expansionist ambition, such invocations of theater involve the narrated world in a deep sense of wrongness, clouding the text's referential clarity, frustrating readers' attempts to visualize the action, or pointing us toward a theatrical enactment that by definition we cannot attend.

The theater semiotician Keir Elam has noted that the sensory vehemence of theatrical performance frees the dramatic text from the responsibility of making the diegetic world linguistically available. The grammar of theatrical texts, as a result, is notably heavy with shifters and deictic expressions that simply *refer* to the world given to the spectators via the undeniable facts of stage, set, and bodies. The theatrical text counts on performance as its sense-making complement: as Elam puts it, "A mode of discourse, like the dramatic, which is dense in such indexical expressions, is disambiguated—acquires clear sense—only when it is appropriately contextualized . . . It is, in other words, *incomplete* until the appropriate contextual elements (speaker, addressee, time, location) are duly provided."[70] When novelistic discourse mimics what Elam calls the "deictic density of dramatic language" (131), the result is to court a sense of incompletion that will never be appeased by the text's animation.[71] These novels' encryption of theatrical codes thus adds another, phenomenological, variety of "failure" to the biographical one: the theatrical spatialization of the novel is a frustrated or failed deixis. It does not absorb or discipline an imaginary theater but points to it as an absent referent. In the process, it underscores the novel's necessary alienation from the embodiment and collectivity of the theatrical event.[72] But the pathos of incompletion inherent in the theatrical text is at the same time a provocation to imagine the theatrical event that would give the text referential density. Elam's emphasis on the insufficiency of the theatrical text intimates as much. "The language of the drama *calls for* the intervention of the actor's body in the completion of its meanings," Elam writes (130; my emphasis); his language suggests that the dramatic text indexes a desire, or a demand, that the enactment take place. In reading a play text (and, I argue, in reading the novels that invoke them), we are being asked to imagine a performance, and this is also implicitly a demand to imaginarily convene a public and to hypothesize the space in which it might congregate.

To recognize this demand—even if only to register the impossibility of fulfilling it—is to respond to the petition that the text has made of us. It is to recognize what J. L. Austin terms the perlocutionary dimension of a speech act. "Saying something will often, or even normally," Austin writes in introducing the concept, "produce certain consequential effects upon the feelings, thoughts, or actions of the audience, or of the speaker, or of other persons: and it may be done with the design, intention, or purpose of producing them."[73] Perlocution here encompasses a wide range of response, from having an emotion in reaction to a speech event to being moved to do something about it. One form of perlocutionary response Austin does not name is that whereby we are made to feel with particular severity the difficulty in traveling along this spectrum, the restraints on our moving from response to action.[74] This sense of being enjoined to do something one is in no position to do is precisely the dimension of response in which we find ourselves in reading a play text, with its string of directives to actors who remain phantoms and set designers who are only conjectural—and its implicit invocation of an audience whose absence is a constitutive feature of our reading in the first place. Because the reader of a play text is asked to imagine both a collective space and the collective project that would populate it, the play text must in the first instance be understood as a solicitation to a collective project—at an even more basic level, as a solicitation to collective thinking. The thinness of the play text is a form of ghostly prompting; when we read a play, what is paradoxically invoked is an event in which our solitary status *as* reader will be canceled. If "all dramatic texts are hypotheses, yearnings," perceiving the formal trace the theater leaves in the novel should make us newly aware of the sense of petition embedded in the novelistic text.[75] The novels explored here perversely aspire to the world-hunger, the sense of incompletion and the corresponding ontological neediness, characteristic of the theatrical text. The novel of interiority thrusts its reader into a situation of solicited and blocked response when it points her toward a space of theatrical enactment from which her identity as a reader alienates her.

It is not clear to me that the desired or expected readerly response to this situation is one of resignation or of accommodation. Many forms of progressive criticism assume that what a text wants is for its reader to resemble it; this assumption of a basically mimetic desire frequently takes the form of a suspiciously neat compound verbal form, as in the claim that the bourgeois subject is both "described and reproduced" by the text.[76] This formulation underestimates the disequilibrium that can obtain between a text's narrated concerns and the effects it may have on its consumers. To put it simply, while interiority and privacy may find representation in the novel, it does not follow that interiority and privacy are recommended by the novel. The political consequences of reading are notoriously difficult to specify. But the assumption that the novel of interiority makes interiorized subjects, and that this ideological work occurs without remainder, imputes an efficaciousness to the literary artifact that is hard to square with these texts' awareness of their potential irrelevance. Indeed, it is difficult not to suspect that by crediting the text with the power to remake life in its image, we permit ourselves to smuggle an officially discredited language of appreciation into our work under cover of a hardboiled political skepticism. The marginality of the aesthetic in modernity suggests that the literary artifact does not merit this particular form of ambivalent praise.

If *Empty Houses* subtracts something from our sense of the novel's political potency, it aims to augment our sense of the novel's political insight and its political desire. The story of the novel's rerouting of properly public energies into private scenes of contemplation is one we have perhaps become too fond of telling. The very repetitiveness with which novels are said to close down the social imagination they arouse would appear to betray the inadequacy of this model: a collective imagination so continually in need of re-containment must, despite appearances, be startlingly persistent. It is more responsive to its formal and tonal textures—more responsive to its intense desire for *response*—to say that in its continued invocation of an absent theater the novel of interiority works to make the reader dissatisfied with his status as a reader by rendering palpable to him the fact of his social apartness. "Performance" derives etymologically from the Middle French for "to furnish forth," "to carry forward," "to bring into being."[77] The perlocutionary demand issued by these texts is to furnish something they have revealed as missing in the world as it exists. We might take the recurrent theatrical longing of these major novelists as striving to make readers aware of the availability of the social, even its inevitability, as an ethical and political horizon for what seem the most inwardly oriented literary forms. Today especially, when the prestige of the private and the privatized could scarcely be greater, we should hesitate before ratifying that prestige analytically. Criticism has suggested that our failure to recognize the pressure of the collective is the result of our seamless reception of the novel of interiority. *Empty Houses* argues that that novel's injunction has yet to be absorbed.

ONE

Acoustics in the Thackeray Theater

If there was nothing new on the boards, Thackeray turned to novel
reading. —Gordon Ray, *Thackeray: The Uses of Adversity*

"The Play"

Passing through London on his way to Cambridge, an eighteen-year-old
Thackeray paid a visit to family friends, bought some new clothes, and, in
the words of his biographer Gordon Ray, attended "the play."[1] The definite
article is not Ray's affectation; in fact, the formulation was at the root of an
exchange on the theater recorded by an earlier Thackeray biographer, Her-
man Merivale, who reports that

> like all good and unspoiled souls, [Thackeray] loved "the play." Asking
> a listless friend one day if he liked it, he got the usual answer, "Ye-es—I
> like a good play." "Oh! get out," said Thackeray, "I said *the* play; you
> don't even understand what I mean."[2]

Thackeray's enthusiasm is for the theatrical apparatus as such: every individual play—no matter how bad—partakes of the expansiveness of "the play";
Ray cites Thackeray's contempt for his cautious friend as evidence of a "lifelong passion" for theater (151). But Thackeray's theatrical passion was riven
by ambivalence: a perennial theatergoer, Thackeray was also volubly disappointed by "the" play, which figures frequently in his work and letters as a
transcendental signifier of disillusion, disgust, and ennui. A few paragraphs
after his catalogue of the teenage Thackeray's London weekend, Ray shifts
into a quotation from the autobiographical novel *Pendennis* (1848–50) in
which the narrator casts a backward glance over his youth. "The young man's
life is just beginning . . . He has no idea of cares yet, or of bad health, or of
roguery, or poverty, or tomorrow's disappointment. The play has not been
acted so often as to make him tired."[3] We seem to have stepped into a world of

precisely inverted values: every local instance of "the play"—no matter how good—is, in the end, just another play.

The note struck here is so characteristic of Thackeray's stance toward the theater that it is tempting to take this as his final word on the matter. Enthusiasm so reliably translates into disappointment that we may remember the terminus as the whole story. Indeed, Thackeray's frequently expressed contempt for "sham" would seem easily to qualify him as the most antitheatrical of nineteenth-century novelists. Other writers devote more energy to explicit disavowals of theater—think of the heavy weather attending *Mansfield Park*'s theatricals or *Villette*'s school play—but the relative dearth of theatrical set pieces in Thackeray's work only points up the way a hatred of pretense saturates his narrative universe. Less an issue of plot than of tone, Thackeray's distaste for "theater" seems too omnipresent to require narrative elaboration.[4] To be sure—as generations of critics have shown, and as my opening anecdote suggests—it is possible to demonstrate that Thackeray's hatred of theatricality coexists with a powerful attraction to it. But focusing on Thackeray's moral ambivalence about an abstraction called "theatricality" may obscure the most interesting aspects of his overinvestment in the question of the theater.

His hatred of "sham" notwithstanding, Thackeray's work is everywhere animated by an attachment to an existing theatrical culture—including the fairground that was not only an image he drew from Bunyan but also a concrete if visibly dwindling aspect of the mid-century urban environment in which he wrote. Just as important, Thackeray's work is shot through with an attachment to the publicity and social promiscuity for which the theater stands. This is an attachment whose coordinates are more ethical than moral—more concerned, that is, with the social spaces the theater creates and the forms of life it fosters than with the necessity of judging performance according to a rubric of right or wrong. "Theater" in Thackeray is very rarely merely the sign of moral disapproval. In *Vanity Fair*'s preface, for example, Thackeray concedes theatricality's blameworthiness precisely in order to subordinate this binary moralism to something more supple: "Some people consider Fairs immoral altogether, and eschew such, with their servants and families," he writes. "Very likely they are right. But persons who think otherwise, and are of a lazy, or a benevolent, or a sarcastic mood, may perhaps like to step in for half an hour, and look at the performances."[5] Thackeray's casual allowance of the moral point ("very likely they are right") ushers in a modular, potentially expandable grammar of *or . . . or . . . or . . .* One of the affordances of this grammar is its loose correlation of emotional tonalities: laziness, sarcasm, and benevolence are in no clear sense "opposites" of morality, nor do they stand in any necessary relation to one another. Thackeray's association of theater with the sheer variety of affective and relational possibility becomes invisible when the question of theater is subsumed in the issue of moral decision.[6]

Thus if Thackeray's "typically Victorian" obsession with artifice—his ambivalence about disguise, duplicity, and deceit—is still an unavoidable feature of his career, it is worth noticing the other topics to which theatricality attaches itself in his work: the shape of the home and the rhythms of the city, the changing intimacies of the family and the contours of interiority, the sociability of playgoing and the solitude of the study. The theater in Thackeray is a densely impacted emblem of social change, one that contains a capsule history of its moment and envisions possible futures. In particular, Thackeray's work about and for the theater imagines forms of domestic life open to penetration by the street and less rigidly focused on the nuclear family. Although Thackeray's theatrical ambition offers the most palpable evidence of these fantasies, his most famous novel canvassed the sociohistorical meanings of theater long before his attempt to write a play canalized them in the formal narrative innovations of his late career. We will see that the much remarked theatricality of *Vanity Fair* is a melancholy gauge of the reorganization of affective space at the Victorian mid-century to privilege the domestic hearth, and that Thackeray's affection for "the play" should be understood as a form of depressive dissent from this restructuring of social and intimate space.[7] Moreover, the figure and the reality of theater in Thackeray's career provide a social genealogy for two key features of his narrative technique. The first is the markedly melancholy attitude of the Thackerayan narrator, the second his interest in the representation of interior experience. Seen in proper relation to Thackeray's theatrical preoccupation, both features emerge as records of a traumatized reaction to the felt contraction of the public sphere.

Celebrated by his contemporaries for its satiric energy, castigated by modernists as intrusive and moralistic, Thackeray's voice is perhaps the most distinctive feature of his work. I have called that voice melancholic; other critics have volunteered "depressive," "disenchanted," "deflated," and "dissociated."[8] Saturated with disappointment, regret, resentment, bitterness, insecurity, sarcasm, sentimentality and rancorous antisentimentality, accusation and self-accusation, Thackeray's voice is the bearer of an insistent affective surplus. We will see that these varied tonalities, and the panicked movement among them, provide a record of a perceived diminishment of public space. In particular, the modulations in the *Vanity Fair* narrator's tone call attention to the domestic as a forcefield of enclosure and miniaturization, a space in which the public world of fairground theatricality is drawn indoors and shrunk to child-sized scale. While these miniaturizing energies shape *Vanity Fair*'s plot as well as Thackeray's illustrations for the book, the central figure for these processes of enclosure and diminishment in the novel is the puppet theater. A symbol of the impoverished relational possibilities of the mid-Victorian present in which Thackeray writes, the toy theater encapsulates the transition from the fairground to the nursery. In doing so it becomes an emblem of a public domesticated and a visible corollary to the Thackerayan narrator's chastened voice.

Thackeray's obsession with the theater became literalized in the ambition to write for the stage that resulted in the 1854 domestic comedy *The Wolves and the Lamb*. His inability to see the play staged rankled to the end of Thackeray's life.[9] The play's composition—and, just as important, its failure—will be central to our exploration of the second feature of Thackeray's narration mentioned above, its interest in exploring interiority. *The Wolves and the Lamb* represents a "failure" in at least two senses: both because it never convened the public of which Thackeray dreamt and because it acquiesced in a celebration of the domestic sphere that had been the object of Thackeray's ambivalence. But its failure, ironically, allowed him to explore a lush narrative space of interiority when he adapted it into the short 1860 novel *Lovel the Widower*—a text that has been credited with pioneering the modernist techniques of the interior monologue and stream-of-consciousness narration. Tracing the mutations the story undergoes in its retreat from the theater, we will see that the energy invested in this late novel's most distinctive formal feature derives from a melancholic relation to the lost possibility of performance. In *Lovel the Widower*, novelistic interiority emerges as a container for an unaccommodated theatricality.

I refer to these distinctive narrative features as aspects of Thackerayan "acoustics" in order to foreground the spatializing effects of these techniques; the term allows us to think the reciprocal way spatial contours determine tonal qualities even as voice and tone provide guides to the shape and social uses of space. If sound is "equivalent to the articulation of space," if "it indicates the limits of a territory and the way to make oneself heard within it, how to survive by drawing one's sustenance from it,"[10] speaking of Thackerayan acoustics permits us to ask what social spaces are mapped by this narrative voice and what forms of life might be sustained there: Does the Thackerayan narrator speak to the attendees at a fair or to children in the home? If the former, is the fairground crowded? If the latter, can we read the pitch of his voice to determine whether the children are well-mannered or raucous, and how he feels about the difference? What is the shape of the stage from which he projects his voice? Is he alone on that stage? Is the "house" he addresses empty or bustling—or does he modulate his voice for an intimate fireside gathering? What social meaning do we attach to the fact that so many of his best-known utterances appear to assume that no one is listening? Why do Thackeray's asides seem to echo with the tones of his interlocutor's anticipated rebuttal? And if he speaks to the reader in his room—as, of course, Thackeray also always does—what effect does the promiscuous invocation of these other spaces have on that reading experience?

In provoking these questions, Thackeray's voice becomes both a sensitive index to the distribution of social space and a powerful means of insinuating a theatrical spatialization into the heart of the narrative universe.[11] The effect is to reveal the social undergirding of the psychological and moralistic energies of Thackeray's narration. *Vanity Fair*'s famously melancholy jester, we will see, conveys not only indignation at duplicity but the discomfiture of a busker whose fairground bravado is inappropriate to the domestic enclosure in which he suddenly finds himself: the speaker's abruptly lowered tone provides an acoustic map of both spaces and a record of the movement between them. Similarly, the interior monologue developed in *Lovel the Widower* registers less as a psychic confession than as a soliloquy spoken into the echo chamber of an empty theater. Where the common understanding of interior monologue presumes a mimetic model of the relations between reader and text, in which one private self reflects and models another, attending to the acoustics of Thackeray's voice refers us instead to the pathos of a deserted collective space. Seen this way, interior monologue does not encourage inwardness in its readers so much as it makes them perceive with discomfort—perhaps with discontent—the quiet of their reading chamber.

While these effects are particularly central in Thackeray's work, we might take his extraordinary sensitivity to the contours of domestic, psychological, and theatrical space as an index of the public desire of realism more broadly. The features of Thackerayan narration on which we will be focusing—its disenchanted tone and its interest in individual psychology—are central pillars of the realist tradition. Thackeray's special interest in demystification and individual experience supports George Levine's claim that Thackeray "develops the model for . . . certain basic conventions of Victorian realism"; in Levine's account, Thackeray emerges as the writer most representative of realist representational habits.[12] An inquiry into the genealogy of those representational habits thus promises to offer insight into the social discontents at the heart of the realist project. Thackeray's work makes movingly explicit the extent to which some of the most salient features of that project derive from a curdled appetite for publicity. Linking the archetypal elements of Thackerayan narration to a frustrated theatrical desire makes perceptible the novel's constitutive element of social longing.

Trivializing History, or, Domesticity

> Miniaturization is . . . the cipher of history.
> —Giorgio Agamben, *Infancy and History*

Vanity Fair is set in "the past"—but is it a historical novel? Published in 1847–48, the novel centers on the Napoleonic Wars. Its pivotal chapters take place during the June 1815 Battle of Waterloo, a battle the novel names "the greatest event of history" (339). But Thackeray's unorthodox attitude toward this benchmark of the Real strikingly undermines the novel's claim to historical status: his well-known reticence about depicting the battle itself has led one critic to maintain that the novel is "built around a thunderous void."[13] Moreover, the book's welter of period detail can seem suspiciously fussy, a kind of window dressing that, far from signaling a deep historical sense, instead marks its failure. In a representative comment, H. M. Daleski claims that "it seems reasonable to believe that the society portrayed in it is, in essentials, that of Thackeray's own day"; he opines flatly that *Vanity Fair* is "not a historical novel," and complains that "historic battles, no matter how momentous, are implicitly reduced—amid a barrage of drawing-room war imagery—to an analogous scale."[14]

It is important that this complaint attacks both Thackeray's superficiality and his sense of proportion. In Daleski's remark about the battlefield being scaled down to fit the drawing room, the reproach to Thackeray's historical sense takes the form of unease with the literally reductive use he makes of the materials of the past.[15] But accusations of superficiality and trivialization miss the fact that Thackeray's interest in period detail is by no means a constant feature of his novel: there is a movement over the course of *Vanity Fair*, a gradual alteration in the way Thackeray handles the pastness of his material. The novel opens with a compulsive insistence on the temporal distance separating the moment of narration from the events themselves: in the novel's first sentence we learn that our story takes place "while the present century was in its teens" (3), and Thackeray quickly tells us that Napoleon is among the living (14) and that Dr. Johnson was recently so (5). In early chapters the temporal markers are everywhere: it is difficult to read long without some reminder of "those days" (24), "the period of which we write" (27), "forty years ago" (41), "those times" (58), "those famous days" (59).

While these signposts build toward *Vanity Fair*'s marker of the historical real, Waterloo, the obsessive temporal indices virtually vanish after the battle's occurrence at the novel's midpoint. The markers of pastness in the book's latter half are increasingly sporadic and half-hearted; when they do occur, they rely on vague reminders that, for example, a fashionable gown would today be pronounced "the most foolish and preposterous attire ever worn" (602) or a passing allusion to historical events: we hear about the death of Napoleon (729), Catholic Relief (782), and the Reform Act (872), but these events click so desultorily by—they have so little effect on the characters, their actions or their fates—that, like the "rudely audible . . . tick-tock" of the clock on the Osbournes' mantelpiece (271), they seem merely to mark the fact that time keeps going. Though Thackeray provides dateable events allowing readers to deduce that the novel ends sometime in the 1830s, the attenuation of historical meaning in the novel makes the second half read more and more like the mid-century present in which Thackeray writes—a fact that justifies in part the critical sense of Thackeray's historical carelessness. Rather than ratifying this judgment, though, we might recognize that Thackeray pursues a specific historiographic technique in starting his novel so definitively "in" history before moving so abruptly "out" of it. Abandoning a fictional universe of historical meaning for one characterized by a blurry, empty temporality, Thackeray imagines the mid-Victorian present as a de-historicized temporal zone. *Vanity Fair* narrates the absorption of History into the Everyday, the defeat of events by trivia. It offers a genealogy of the mid-century that understands the present as, precisely, the end of history.[16]

Or, to put it somewhat differently, the shrinking of history. Another name for the presentism pervading the second half of the novel might be miniatur-ism: in many ways the second half is a smaller version of the first—a place (like the Regency court as described by Thackeray in *The Four Georges*) of "prodigious littlenesses."[17] This is clearest in the novel's generational struc-ture. The novel's two heroines, Becky Sharp and Amelia Sedley, conceive their sons in the weeks around Waterloo, and the effect is to suggest that the battle provokes a narrative mitosis: at the moment it leaves History behind, the novel's character population undergoes a multiplication in number and a demotion in size, as the center of interest shifts from the amorous intrigues of four young adults to the domestic travails of two young families. Equally striking is the way the novel recycles in miniature its own climactic moment. Compare, for example, the treatment of Waterloo with that of the English "invasion" of the fictional German principality of Pumpernickel late in the novel. The dimensions of the German vacation destination (which the char-acters visit for no discernable reason) echo in a spatial register the tininess of the motivation that has brought us here. A "duchy which stretches for nearly ten miles," Pumpernickel is a "little comfortable ducal town," "a cheery social little German place," "the pleasantest little place" (800, 793, 797). But the figurative links between this cozy locale and the killing fields of Belgium are everywhere. The town is filled with "stout trim old veterans . . . such as have invaded Europe any time since the conclusion of the war" (783). In stark con-trast to the precision of Waterloo, the "any time" here highlights the ahistori-cism of the novel's second half, the increasing sense that the postwar period might as well be contiguous with the "now." A parodic sense of repetition pervades the episode: in Pumpernickel, war is replayed as society squabbling (as prominent ladies rally their followers to the English or French party at teatime [805]) or as kitsch entertainment (in the form of Beethoven's *Die Schlacht bei Vittoria*, a symphonic piece commemorating Waterloo with the orchestrated sounds of artillery fire and the groans of dying men [794]). The episode rehearses the historical maelstrom of war as queasy-making tourist whimsy.

It is not just in Pumpernickel that History suffers corrupting reduction; such diminutizing repetition is endemic to the world of *Vanity Fair*. Al-though the book diegetically presents this reduction as a *change* hinging on the climax of Waterloo, on an imagistic and tonal level the text is pervaded by a sense of miniaturization, so that the world the novel portrays seems both to be always getting smaller and to have always been small. The novel in fact describes itself in diminishing terms even in its opening pages. When its heroines take leave of the Pinkerton Academy for Girls in the first chapter of the novel, Thackeray writes that "it is probable that we shall not hear of [Miss Pinkerton] again from this moment to the end of time, and that when the great filigree iron gates are once closed on her, she and her awful sister will never issue therefrom into this little world of history" (7). Who is being confined, and what is the space of confinement, in this ambivalent narratorial farewell? If the "great filigree iron gates" are entombing the Pinkerton sisters in an extra-narrative limbo, why is it the world of the novel that is described as "little"? And if the world of the novel (which in an earlier draft Thackeray referred to as "this little three-volumed world of history"[18]) is to be defined in opposition to the space in which the Pinkertons are shut up, why is it something one comes "into"?

The sense that *Vanity Fair* not only narrates the movement into a miniature world but in fact starts there is rendered most literally visible in Thackeray's illustrations for the initial capital letters of each chapter.[19] The effect of miniaturization is built into the form of these initial-letter decorations, since the field of the drawing usually requires that a figure be encompassed by a single letter of type—as, for example, with the ogre curled up inside the "O" which opens chapter 39 (fig.1). But beyond these constraints of the form, Thackeray is concerned to set up internal size differentials in the illustrations, so that even in the space defined by a single capital letter, vast differences of scale become visible. Thus the piper who introduces chapter 6 aims his instrument sharply downward at the tiny cat at his feet, and the gargoyle/jester holding the letter "A" to start off chapter 10 looms gigantically over the tiny human figures gathered around his pedestal (figs. 2–3). The corpulent Joseph Sedley looks pint-sized astride the elephant decorating the initial letter for chapter 17, and the slender Becky looks huge holding the puppet in the decoration for the initial "L" in chapter 21 (figs. 4–5).

A related miniaturizing effect radiates from the many images in the book of children doing "adult" things. A boy in oversized livery pushes a letter twice as big as his head through a door in the little drawing that concludes chapter 13; an infant couple huddles under a downpour at the beginning of chapter 38 (titled "A Family in a Very Small Way"); two toddlers in oversized military hats cross swords at the beginning of chapter 5; little George, decked out in the baggy garments of his royal namesake, lounges at the head of chapter 56; and so on (figs. 6–9). The most striking of these images may not seem at first to belong in their company. The little self-portrait of the bespectacled Thackeray, jester's rod and mask in hand, that punctuates chapter 9 has been much remarked as a pictogram of the bitterly melancholic tone suffusing the novel's narrative voice (fig. 10). But we should note that this jester's head is fully as big as the rest of his body, and that the hand that grasps the mask has the pudgy under-articulation of a baby's fist. The texture of the image's famous melancholy is intimately related to the conjunction of its evidently adult head and its chubby baby's body: Thackeray's jester is not only disillusioned—he is also strangely infantilized.

We have seen that the pervasiveness of the miniaturizing linguistic and visual rhetoric in *Vanity Fair* collides strangely with the novel's attempt to narrate a *process* of miniaturization. On the one hand, miniaturization is something that happens; on the other, miniaturization is something that has always already happened. One reason the historical force of *Vanity Fair* has been hard to perceive is that its diachronic aspects are overwritten with images of this movement's finished achievement: the process of diminution is at once a story the novel tells (in its movement from the eventfulness of history to the emptiness of the present) and a matter, more amorphously, of atmosphere (in the constant images of precocity and usurpation, and in the condescending tone that serves, precisely, to belittle the novel's subject matter). If this temporal conjunction, in which the end of the story is interleaved with the story's unfolding, is entirely appropriate to the genealogical project Thackeray undertakes in *Vanity Fair*, we still need to ask why miniaturization should be the mode in which Thackeray presents the historicity of the Victorian present. What is the sociohistorical referent of this rhetoric of diminution, these relentless images of shrunken scale? Susan Stewart has argued that the miniature has a specific relationship to the contours of the home, and to the forms of individual experience it shelters. "We cannot speak of the small, or miniature, work," she writes, "independent of the social values expressed toward private space—particularly, of the ways the domestic and the interior imply the social formation of an interior subject."[20] If, as Stewart argues, the very form of the miniature invokes privacy and the home, another name for the end of history in *Vanity Fair* is domesticity.

It is thus fitting that while the war, suitably trivialized, becomes the blueprint at Pumpernickel for society battles and evening entertainment, the most jarring use of the novel's bloody past is as material for domestic pedagogy. Amelia's long-suffering admirer William Dobbin no sooner earns fame as a hero of the British war effort than he begins repackaging his feats for consumption in the home. On his first visit to Amelia and her baby son, he brings with him "a wooden horse, a drum, a trumpet, and other warlike toys, for little Georgy, who was scarcely six months old, and for whom the articles in question were entirely premature" (448). His next gift is a chess set whose "pawns were little green and white men, with real swords and shields" (495). Later, in Pumperknickel, Dobbin's "good military knowledge of the German language" makes him useful as a tour guide for Amelia's traveling domestic entourage, "and he and the delighted George fought the campaigns of the Rhine and the Palatinate" (787). These efforts serve to trivialize not only the Napoleonic Wars but Dobbin himself, whose new nickname "Major

Prodigious
Littlenesses

Figure 1

Figure 2

Figure 3

Figure 4

Figure 5

Figure 6

Figure 7

Figure 8

Figure 9

Figure 10

Sugarplums" fits his military identity snugly into the domestic frame of the novel's second half. But as the reference to Georgy's prematurity hints, this reduction of war to child's play never feels entirely as *gemütlich* as Dobbin's cute nickname suggests. For all his avuncular consideration, Dobbin's haste to fill Georgy's nursery with toys redolent of the conflict that has just killed his father flirts with crassness. The shrinking of history for domestic consumption—borrowing as it does the contemptuous rhetoric of diminution that informs the book as a whole—is so unsettling that it becomes difficult to distinguish the domestic from a kind of grotesque shrinking.

This making-grotesque is crucial to Thackeray's project of defamiliarizing what might otherwise appear, "naturally," as mere child's play. This becomes clearer when we notice how consistently Thackeray—despite his incessant production of the miniature—violates its formal conventions. Stewart maintains that the miniature world is typically self-contained: "It is absolutely necessary that Lilliput be an island. The miniature world remains perfect and uncontaminated by the grotesque so long as its absolute boundaries are maintained" (68). But it is precisely the violation of that boundary that Thackeray continually enacts—visually (in the fantastic size differentials internal to his illustrations), tonally (in the condescension with which he regards the pettiness of his novelistic world), and narratively (in his repetition of his own novel's material in a miniature mode). The grotesqueness that results from Thackeray's contamination of the miniature world serves as a reminder of the unnaturalness of the domestic, the sociohistorical contortions that have been necessary to produce it. And if the always miniaturizing, always miniaturized world of *Vanity Fair* traces the production of the home as the privileged space of intimate relations at the English mid-century, it is clear that Thackeray regards that privileging with something close to rancor. "I'm sick of that miniature," Amelia's mother complains somewhere in the timeless stretch of the novel's second half (496). She is referring to her daughter's devotion to the tiny image of her dead husband. But her words might equally be Thackeray's, his comment both on the miniature and on the domestic enclosure it references.

In his classic description of the consolidation of domestic space in the nineteenth century, Eli Zaretsky proposes a now familiar thesis that the gradual removal of productive labor from the middle-class home resulted in the glorification of the family as the natural container for "the newly discovered worlds of childhood, emotional sensibility, and compassion."[21] The family begins, in the nineteenth century, to be lauded as the essential unit of social organization, "a little church," "a little state," "a little commonwealth" (42, 57): Zaretsky's Thackerayan epithet points to the affinity between the process of miniaturization and the shape of the emergent domestic hearth.[22] His work also suggests why child's play should function as such a charged synecdoche for the home in this period. The images of tiny people discussed above can, of course, be apprehended as images of the pettiness (the "vanity") of human striving, but they can also all be understood in more frankly denotative fashion as pictures of children—the littleness of whose forms renders grotesque their adult activity. Understood not as metaphors of some changeless human condition but as a commentary on a historically specific social form called childhood, one of the pillars of domestic ideology emerges as an image of historical degradation—a replaying of history's tragedy as domestic farce.[23]

But if childhood is the emblem of the supposed pettiness, privacy, and exclusivity of the Victorian domestic enclosure, it also functions paradoxically as a monument to the energies of publicity and to a quite distinct organization of affective space. According to the well-known thesis of historian Philippe Ariès (whose research focused on France), childhood as the nineteenth century knew it was a melancholic repository of a diminishing public culture. Ariès depicts a premodern social world, traces of which survive into the eighteenth century, in which a cross-class, cross-generational public existed for such now stereotypically "childish" pastimes as oral storytelling. Similarly, the books of the Bibliothèque Bleue were originally aimed at a general audience; only with the solidification of childhood did "children [become] their last public."[24] Ariès's research on the puppet theater finds the same pattern: "the Guignol of early nineteenth-century Lyons was a character of lower-class but adult theatre, while today Guignol has become the name of a puppet show reserved for children" (70). In Ariès's account, childhood emerges as a living archeological exhibit of the transformations necessary for the consolidation of the modern family and the domestic sphere.

Nineteenth-century childhood thus confronts us as a historical palimpsest. On the one hand, the child's game, as a miniature activity taking place in a domestic world itself understood as a miniature kingdom, is the very image of fortified privacy, the prototype of what Stewart calls the "within within within" of the domestic miniature (61). Home, family, child, toy theater: a set of shrinking boxes figuring with increasing intensity both the pathos of diminishment and the alienation from a public culture. On the other hand, that spectacle's resemblance to the public world points, as if through the looking glass, back into a world of fairground sociability. Childhood is thus at once the centerpiece of domestic felicity and the note of discord at its heart—a conjunction that explains why children are the site of such ambivalent overinvestment in Vanity Fair. With a miniature size that functions as an objective correlative of the pettiness of the present, and a raucous playtime activity that recalls an alternative arrangement of social space, the child gives both form and content, so to speak, to Vanity Fair's historical melancholy. A machine for importing the theatrical past into the domestic present, the miniature is a Janus-faced sign of social change, functioning ambivalently both to contain that theatrical energy and to keep it intact for possible future regeneration.

Diminishing Returns: *Vanity Fair*'s Theatricality

The prominence of the theatrical chronotope in Thackeray's work has most often been read as a commentary on the transhistorical duplicity of human-kind ("all the world's a stage"). But the connection of the theater to the mel-ancholic repetitions of child's play indicates that theatricality in *Vanity Fair* also functions as a mechanism to resist the seemingly natural chronologies of the domestic novel. This use is most clearly indicated in Thackeray's re-marks in chapter 26, shortly after Amelia's marriage. "As his hero and heroine pass the matrimonial barrier, the novelist generally drops the curtain, as if the drama were over," we read; and with more than half of the novel yet to come, it is clear that this novel will not follow this pattern (319). The theatrical chronotope here staggers the temporality of domestic ideology, drawing us into the wings of the performance of happy union to reveal affective residues not absorbed by what Karen Chase and Michael Levenson have termed the Victorian "spectacle of intimacy."[25] In the scene the narrator goes on immedi-ately to relate, a just married Amelia returns to her family home to gaze wist-fully on her childhood bed, while her husband spends the evening in town watching Kean perform as Shylock. Here again theater symptomatizes the survival of historically excessive energies into the domestic present.

This pattern, whereby theater blurs the outlines of the marriage plot and the home that is that plot's destination, is incessant: when Sir Pitt Crawley scandalizes his family by openly pursuing a liaison with his housekeeper, he exults that it is "as good as a play to see her in the character of a fine dame, and he made her put on one of the first Lady Crawley's court-dresses" (504); these illicit sexual pleasures almost inevitably work by theatrically refunctioning the trappings of respectable domesticity. Becky, declining to go upstairs to comfort her sobbing son, "[falls] to talking about the Opera" with the reprobate Lord Steyne (476), as if her theatergoing more than her adultery constituted the essence of her failed motherhood. The theater's violation of the home is clearest in the charades scene at Lord Steyne's: when Thackeray specifies that the thunderous applause greeting Becky's performance sounds through "the whole house," it is hard to know whether we are to take the phrase in the theatrical or domestic sense (646). In all these instances the theater becomes an emblem for what stubbornly resists accommodation in the domestic sphere—what threatens its spatial integrity by luring its inhab-itants out into the streets or inviting the public inside, or what menaces its temporal sanctity by symbolizing, and occasioning, the persistence of pre-or extramarital attachments. While these obsessive rehearsals of the home's violations could be taken as tributes to the fantasy of its sanctity,[26] Thack-eray's work represents less a slavish celebration of the domestic interior than a protest against a world in which it has come to seem the sole location of happiness. Because the home and the theater work as imagistic complements in the novel, becoming attuned to the tones of this disappointment makes more clearly audible the social longing encrypted in Thackeray's love of "the play." More specifically, we will see that the Thackerayan narrator's melancholy insistently points us to a story of enclosure, in which the noise and multiplicity represented by the theatrical apparatus have been reduced and contained in the space of the home.

Perhaps the most fruitful place to look for the characteristics of this theatrical desire is, paradoxically, the manifestly antitheatrical "Before the Curtain" preface to *Vanity Fair*. In addition to introducing the novel's governing theatrical chronotope, the preface functions as a spatializing promontory from which to survey the sociohistorical terrain canvassed in the text that lies beyond it. With his opening words Thackeray strikes the depressive keynote to *Vanity Fair*: "As the Manager of the Performance sits before the curtain on the boards and looks into the Fair, a feeling of profound melancholy comes over him in his survey of the bustling place" (1). From his vantage point the speaker notes the "great quantity of eating and drinking, making love and jilting, laughing and the contrary, smoking, cheating, fighting, dancing, and fiddling" in the crowd. Soon the activity pulls the speaker off the stage and down into the fair; by the second paragraph our "man with a reflective turn of mind" has surrendered his visual prospect for a phenomenologically detailed immersion. He is now down among the stalls, and "not . . . oppressed" by the hilarity he sees there:

> An episode of humour or kindness touches and amuses him here and there;—a pretty child looking at a gingerbread stall; a pretty girl blushing whilst her lover talks to her and chooses her fairing;—poor Tom fool, yonder beyond the wagon, mumbling his bone with the honest family which lives by his tumbling;—but the general impression is one more melancholy than mirthful. When you come home, you sit down, in a sober, contemplative, not uncharitable frame of mind, and apply yourself to your books or your business. (1)

In accounting for the evident overdetermination of this speaker's melancholy, we should start by noting his words' richly equivocal relation to social space. At first glance, the ambiguity of the speaker's positioning seems to defeat any attempt to map its spatial contours: he appears to circulate rootlessly, now on the stage, now down among the stalls, now off sharing a meal with Tom Fool's family, now anticipating a lonely afterward of retreat. The speaker's ubiquity almost becomes a kind of placelessness, so that he seems to be in none of these sites precisely, less a location than a kind of moving seam—a curtain, or fourth wall—separating these variously configured spaces. (In an important sense he is just that, and we will see that in his later fiction Thackeray "works" that seam as a position affording insight into the constitution of domestic and public space.) And yet a trajectory is clearly perceptible in these lines, a definable movement between two social spaces, and between two relational regimes: the sentences carry us from a space of social multiplicity to an anticipated domestic enclosure. This social reduction is also an affective one, as we move from a space of public hilarity, kindness, embarrassment, and eroticism to a private one defined by melancholy sobriety. The speaker insists that this substitution is not so much the result of a movement as an unmasking, a revelation of the secret truth that has been lurking behind this multiplicity; and it is of course a willingness to take him at his word that has led to the critical sense that these are "antitheatrical" sentences. But once we register the care with which Thackeray has undergirded this abstract point with a specific spatial trajectory, we might suspect that the Manager's sadness as he sits "before" the curtain refers not to the calamitous spectacle on view in the crowd he beholds but to his imminent withdrawal from this scene of promiscuous publicity. If, as one critic claims, "Before the Curtain" functions as "a kind of epitome of the whole novel,"[27] this owes less to its insistent melancholy than to the social genealogy it provides for that melancholy. The domestic end point of this story comes to seem not the undisputed site of truth but a contingent sociohistorical location.

Indeed, the story encapsulated in these sentences is the story of the novel itself: the genealogical project animating Thackeray's prose at the level of sentence and paragraph also organizes its macrostructural elements. I have already suggested that the novel recounts the enclosure of historical, social, and affective variety in the space of the home. We can perceive this trajectory even more vividly if we compare the prologue to that part of the book that lies most distant from it in narrative terms, the final pages. These are the bookends, so to speak, of the novelistic arc, and the movement they trace emerges with particular clarity in comparing Thackeray's illustration for the monthly wrappings to the one he made for the novel's finale. This comparison reveals that, although the idea of "theatricality" remains central over the course of the narrative, we end up indoors, and in a world of children. In the initial image, which serves as a kind of pictorial version of "Before the Curtain," the speaker addresses an assembled crowd composed of loose aggregates of people of all ages; by the closing image, that narrator has evaporated into pure voice, while the children he addresses have taken on the singularity of icons (figs. 11–12). "Ah! *Vanitas Vanitatum!*" the narration concludes. "Which of us is happy in this world? Which of us has his desire? or, having it, is satisfied?—Come, children, let us shut up the box and the puppets, for our play is played out" (878). The image that confronts us is of two children closing a box containing miniature figures representing the novel's characters. The serene pose of the paired boy and girl echoes that of the Dobbin and

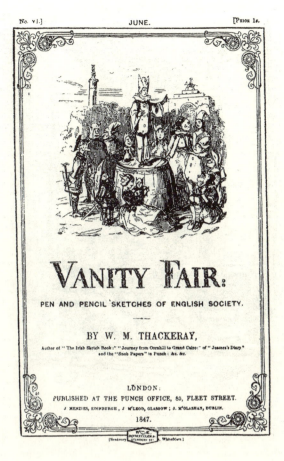

Figure 11

Figure 12

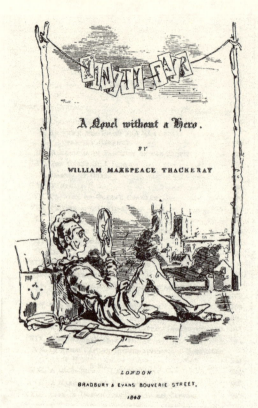

Figure 13

Amelia "puppets" who peer out of the toy box, and the uncanny juxtaposition of gigantic children with miniature adults makes it dizzyingly unclear who precisely is putting whom to sleep: gazed at long enough, the children's eerily adult equanimity provokes in the viewer, via a kind of fantasmatic compensation, the suspicion that the barely discernible features of the tiny family are signaling an infantile desire to stay up, to get out.

The force and originality of this image become more apparent when we recall puppetry's connections to the outdoor fair and the popular theater. For example, in Punch and Judy—whose repertoire of behavior essentially consists of a public display of what we now term domestic violence—we see the tendency of the puppet tradition to turn the private out toward the world. But the trajectory of the puppet show in *Vanity Fair* moves in precisely the opposite direction. Thackeray's preface refers to the novel as an itinerant puppet show, but the book ends up indoors; it has become a play theater under the control of two children whose bedtime shutting up of their toy box repeats the puppet show's own historical movement from fairground performance into the domestic enclosure. Thackeray's critics have remarked the *memento mori* tonality of this image, but we should note that, in superimposing an image of the claustration of death on that of domesticity, Thackeray suggests an understanding of the domestic *as* death.

The puppet theater offered itself to Thackeray as a particularly dense symbolic container of sociohistorical change. In his history of Victorian toy theaters, George Speaight attests to such toys' emblematic position in the nineteenth century's discursive fortification of the domestic as a parallel and sanitized universe.[28] Speaight's history confirms for the English context the trajectory traced by Ariès in France, whereby public adult entertainment gradually becomes lodged in the enclosure of the nursery. Originally conceived of as souvenirs of theatrical productions, toy theaters came into their own as a lucrative business in the nineteenth century when their producers began to market them not as mementos of performances but as miniature, domestic versions of them. A commodity that began life as an emblem of crossing between public and private entertainments thus became over the course of the nineteenth century an index of their distinction.[29] The movement indoors "naturally" also meant a reorientation of the toy theater toward the child. As Speaight exults, "Here, then, was a complete drama in miniature . . . What an idea for boys!" (21). Because the movement to the domestic was accompanied by a diminutization in audience, the toy theater alludes to a clamorous world of publicity—but, crucially, one rendered smaller. If, as Ariès suggests, the miniature world of childhood games reflects the detritus the "official" culture has left behind, then in the toy theater the Thackerayan narrator sees the palimpsestic superimposition of two epochs, and a vision of the hardening of that domestic enclosure.

This removal from the public—more than the supposed mendacity of that public—thus merits attention as the story the novel tells. Once we perceive the lineaments of this narrative of withdrawal, it becomes apparent how fully it underwrites the funereal tonality so distinctive to Thackeray's narrative voice and to his rhetorical and visual repertoire. Roger Wilkenfeld notes that the monthly wrappers Thackeray designed for the novel show a fool on his barrel haranguing the crowd, but that in the engraving he made for the frontispiece of the book version, "the audience has disappeared and the fool has moved from his barrel stage to one more prominently detached from the bustle of the fair"; a puppet box supports the jester's depressive slump (fig.13).[30] Similarly, when Thackeray picks up the fairground motif in the middle of the novel, it would be easy to see him as castigating "theatricality": "This, dear friends and companions, is my amiable object—to walk with you through the Fair, to examine the shops and the shows there: and that we should all come home after the flare, and the noise, and the gaiety, and be perfectly miserable in private" (228). As in "Before the Curtain," the harshly downbeat conclusion of the sentence may make us forget the affective variety (curiosity, excitement, fear, and tenderness) in what has gone before. But, again, we may look to the sentence's spatial dynamics to explain the reductive trajectory whereby emotional multiplicity becomes emotional deprivation: is it the nature of the spectacle that makes miserable—or the fact that public "gaiety" has been exchanged for private isolation? Like "Before the Curtain," this passage ruefully anticipates the movement indoors that the novel as a whole narrates, the miniaturizing process by which the public sphere becomes a tinny and tiny replica of itself. At the root of Thackeray's ambivalent attraction to "the play" is less an appetite for the self-dissolving energies of artifice than a nostalgia for the social spaces that allow that self-dissolution to function as a lived possibility.[31]

It might seem counterintuitive to read Thackeray as mourning a culture of public theatricality when historians demonstrate that the theater, far from declining in the period, was in fact dramatically expanding.[32] But the terms of that expansion, and the shape of it, offer remarkable echoes of the historical movement traced in the trajectory from fairground to indoor puppet theater over the course of *Vanity Fair*. The years immediately preceding the publication of the novel saw the so-called battle for the free stage, in which "illegitimate" theaters wrested the monopoly on "straight" (i.e., nonmusical) drama from the two patent theaters, Drury Lane and Covent Garden. Before the passage of the Theatres Act of 1843, all other theaters were forced to include music in their theatrical offerings—a restriction abetting melodrama's spectacular rise in the early part of the century. The Theatres Act multiplied the locales in which plays were acted but also expanded the reach of the Lord Chancellor's censors to include all the spaces newly defined as playhouses; the increased purview of the censor's office gave a more consistent moral tone to the London theater, and etched a sharper demarcation between approved middle-class fare and music-hall carousing. Even in farce—where elements of the rowdier "illegitimate" drama survived in the new dispensation—the subject matter had been given over to such an overwhelming hominess that theater historian Michael Booth describes the genre as "Dionysus domesticated."[33]

These shifts in theatrical fare were mirrored by those in acting style, perhaps best represented by the ascendancy of William Charles Macready, who, in managing both Covent Garden and Drury Lane during the 1830s and 1840s, had eschewed grand gestures for a mannerly style—even when playing Shakespearean tragedy. Critical opinion on Macready's acting was divided, but everyone agreed on its domestic orientation: one enthusiastic observer still deplored the fact that, as Macbeth, Macready appeared with "a fashionable flowered chintz dressing-gown, perhaps the one he usually wears, loosely thrown over his armour," while Leigh Hunt, a vocal detractor, managed to praise Macready's representations of "domestic tenderness."[34] Meanwhile, equally profound changes were under way regarding the shape of the stage itself and the contours and rhythms of urban neighborhoods.

In 1840, according to Jim Davis and Victor Emeljanow's history, the West End "resembled a rather haphazard fairground, with each booth displaying its wares for a passing trade." But in the 1840s the West End, under pressure from theatrical impresarios and with the assistance of journalists, began to remake itself as a "Crystal Palace, which would lure an increasingly assertive middle class to a theatrical theme park." In pursuit of this goal, the 1840s saw the launching of a public relations project to "legitimize" the theatrical spaces of the West End, to create a kind of facsimile public sphere unmarked by the impropriety, class mixing, crime, and sheer social contingency by which public space is often recognized.[35]

While journalists sang the praises of the sleek new crimeless theater district, inside the theaters a parallel civilizing process continued: showtimes were moved back and programs compressed to allow suburbanites to catch the last train home; children's matinees, with suitably tame material, were instituted to accommodate weekend family outings; the last spectators had been exiled from the stage at the end of the eighteenth century, and by the middle of the nineteenth, the stage apron—the "point of acknowledged contact between actors and audiences"[36]—was also being phased out. With it went the epilogues and prologues through which the actors had broken character and addressed the audience (and on which, not incidentally, "Before the Curtain" is modeled). Instead, actors were increasingly confined to the space of the new box set, in which painted flats—outfitted with workable doors and windows—ensured that a realistic interior setting gradually replaced the stylizations of the proscenium stage: this last innovation was particularly associated with Mme Vestris's Olympic Theatre, which, starting in the 1830s, became, according to contemporary tributes, "a life-boat to the respectability of the stage" by having "drawing-rooms . . . fitted up like drawing-rooms, and furnished with care and taste."[37] Middle-class spectators now gazed through a "fourth wall" into a stage world increasingly resembling the home they were temporarily escaping. Half-price seats were abolished, keeping out poorer audiences or ensuring that their attendance would be less casual. A Select Committee headed by Edward Bulwer-Lytton in the early 1830s had stressed before Parliament the importance of sponsoring smaller theater spaces whose acoustics would assure that "serious drama of an intimate modern kind could . . . properly be heard."[38] In short, as one historian writes, "the conditions of theatre-going needed to reflect the sense of comfort and well-being that visitors associated with their own private spheres of activity."[39]

Thus, during precisely the period in which the urban fairgrounds were shut down (the last, Smithfield's Bartholomew Fair, closing in 1855), a theater district was being created in which the difference between indoors and outdoors would be more difficult to ascertain; in the theaters, the spaces on either side of the footlights increasingly confronted one another as mirror images of mutually regarding privacies, the faultlessly realistic interiors on the stage offering a spatial model for the interiority of the audience members in their darkened seats. All these changes could be described as efforts to halt the promiscuous movement of the speaker of "Before the Curtain": to dismantle the stage apron on which he stands to address the public; to drench in darkness the audience at which he gazes; to prevent him from wandering among the booths of the fair; to shut down the fair itself and send its attendees, precisely, home. "Come, children, let us shut up the box and the puppets, for our play is played out": it is easy to hear the moralist speaking here, the stern advocate of the mid-Victorian reality principle. But the words also echo with the tones of elegy.

We do not begin to appreciate Thackeray's distinctiveness by deciding that in allegorizing the triumph of domesticity his novel works to accommodate us to it. It is tempting to read Thackeray's depressive narrative voice as insisting that the isolation of everyone in a domestic unit is an indisputable good—or at any rate a nonnegotiable fact of existence. But this would be to reduce the extraordinary complexity of this voice to a series of propositions, and to assume that telling a story is the same thing as endorsing it. The sheer mournfulness with which Thackerayan narration infuses that story, the intensity with which it stages and restages the contraction of public space, and the ingenuity with which it invents tonalities to make us hear that contraction —all this demands that Thackeray be read not as renouncing a relation to the public but as stubbornly retaining it in the face of the most severe (domestic or psychological) isolation. Giorgio Agamben writes that the miniature is the source of "a counter-echo in which the rigidified world . . . entrusts its hope of historical awakening."[40] Thackeray's glum directive elicits precisely such a counter-echo, a protest against a world where "the play" and the social energies it represents have migrated indoors.

The Box-Opener: A Note on Becky Sharp

If the murmur of that counter-echo is audible even in the dour final moments of *Vanity Fair*, it is because the novel's trajectory toward enclosure never itself quite reaches closure. Thackeray's narrator instructs us to shut up the box, but a glance at the accompanying image shows that the puppets representing Becky and Lord Steyne are lingering outside, in an image of exile (or escape?) from the domestic space of the toy box. The facing page carries an image of Becky at a booth in Vanity Fair as she confronts Amelia and Dobbin's family group. Thackeray's identification with Becky—the Victorian gentleman's covert attraction to the "vitalism" and "gusto" of the reprobate—has long been a staple of Thackeray criticism.[41] This account is both irrefutable and incomplete: while she is certainly identified with the qualities of ingenuity, fluidity, energy, and "theater," Becky is more particularly the sign of a longing for the social spaces in which those qualities are cultivated. She represents a historical inaptitude, a discomfort with the protocols of the Victorian present and an attachment to the theatrical past whose supersession is already under way.

Perceiving the historical wish secreted in Becky's person requires, to be sure, some inattention to the luridness with which she is denigrated in the final chapters of the book. As the novel reaches its close, the contest between Becky and the home achieves ever starker focus. Dobbin, as if taking his cue from the images juxtaposed on the novel's final pages, declares to Amelia his horror that the sanctity of "the *house*" (his emphasis) should be violated by Becky's presence (845). Meanwhile Becky happily resides at a hotel alive with all the "*fumum* and *strepitus* of a German inn at fair time" (842). But the strenuousness of Dobbin's repudiation might almost be compensating for the curious lack of horror evinced by the narrator on this point. "She was happy enough at the period of her boarding-house life," Thackeray writes (820), and he seems happy enough to leave her to it. Moreover, in the climactic confrontation between Becky and Amelia, Thackeray remains notably uninterested in delivering the blame that the resolution of his domestic comedy demands. The scene might be described as a battle of the miniatures: Amelia, "in the company of her miniatures," is visited by Becky, who, in turn, has just been looking at the "miniature" image of Joseph Sedley on his elephant (865, 859).[42] In preparation for the encounter, Thackeray tells us, "Becky took down her elephant, and put it into the little box which she had had from Amelia ever so many years ago" (864); the absurdity of putting an elephant in a "little box," coupled with the fact that "Elephant" is also the name of the disreputable inn in which Becky is lodging (838), suggest that Becky's is the miniature that is not one, a tiny container that threatens to smuggle a burgeoning publicity into Amelia's airless domestic surround.

Crucially, the episode also marks Becky's closest approach to usurping the plotting function of her narrator. The exasperated tones in which she serves Amelia with the letter proving her dead husband's adulterous intentions ("Look there, you fool") resonates with the ambivalence of the narrator's celebration of Amelia, a few pages later, as a "tender little parasite" (866, 871). This convergence between Becky and her narrator betrays the investments of a narrative system that has been straining to maintain their distinction throughout the novel's second half, as Becky absorbs the identitarian slipperiness that is the lifeblood of *Vanity Fair*'s narrator. In the early sections of the novel our narrator's coordinates are discomfitingly hard to pin down—now an omniscient speaker with "the privilege of knowing everything" (31), now a bachelor at Vauxhall (65), now the scraping husband of "Julia" longing for a handout from a wealthy aunt (104). But among the most striking containments enacted in the second half of the novel is that of its multiplicitous narrator in the person of a gossipmonger at Pumpernickel. "It was on this

very tour that I, the present writer of a history of which every word is true . . .
first saw Colonel Dobbin and his party," our narrator—now reduced to the
status of a mere character—startlingly relates (793). Only a vaguely choral
"we"—to indicate the other chatty bachelors who discuss the principle characters around the gaming tables—provides a chastened echo of our narrator's identitarian promiscuity. Meanwhile, as Becky's wanderings escalate, she
floats ever freer of the novel's diegetic purview. "We must pass over a part
of Mrs. Rebecca Crawley's biography with that lightness and delicacy which
the world demands," our narrator sniffs. "Her taste for disrespectability grew
more and more remarkable" (812, 822). This taste coincides with a multiplication of her *noms-de-voyage*, and Becky appears in rapid succession as Madame de Raudon, Madame Rebeque, Mrs. de Rawdon, Circe, Doll Tearsheet.

As the protean mobility of the narration is transferred more and more to
Becky, as her identity dissolves in a blur of artifice, it is worth inquiring into
what we do in fact know about her. Where does she come from? What, to
put the question differently, are the social and historical coordinates of her
vitality? "How much gayer it would be to wear spangles and trousers, and
dance before a booth at a fair," Becky muses toward the end of the novel. She
might seem merely to be fantasizing, from deep within the domestic drift of
the novel's second half, about a possible future. But she is also remembering:

> "I recollect," Becky continued, pensively, "my father took me to see a
> show at Brookgreen Fair when I was a child; and when we came home
> I made myself a pair of stilts, and danced in the studio to the wonder of
> all the pupils . . . I should like to do it now." (638)

Becky is the only character for whom the book's overarching figure is more
than a metaphor: she has been to Vanity Fair, and would like to go back.
The convergence of vehicle and tenor in her life history marks her as the site
of the novel's most intense affective investment. That she experiences this
convergence in the mode of alternating regret and anticipation signals that
for Thackeray, too, the idea of Vanity Fair is an account of social change as
much as a tool to castigate hypocrisy. Becky's exile to the outskirts of polite
society indicates less the fallen woman's inevitable slide to the gutter than a
shifting social landscape in which the transformative energies of the fair are
being consigned to the symbolic margins. Late in the novel we learn that in
her travels Becky "discovered a relation of her own, no less a person than her
maternal grandmother, who was not by any means a Montmorenci, but a
hideous old box-opener at a theatre on the Boulevards" (824). If this genealogy reveals, as genealogies are supposed to do, Rebecca's truth, this is not that
she harbors unseemly relations (whom would this surprise?). It is that she
contains the historical memory necessary to pry open the box of the home
that is otherwise poised to shut for good.

Empty House Theatricals: *The Wolves and the Lamb*

> Public discourse says not only "Let a public exist" but "Let it have this
> character, speak this way, see the world in this way." It then goes in search of
> confirmation that such a public exists, with greater or lesser success—success
> being further attempts to cite, circulate, and realize the world understanding
> it articulates. Run it up a flagpole and see who salutes. Put on a show and see
> who shows up.—Michael Warner, *Publics and Counterpublics*

No one showed up for Thackeray's 1854 play *The Wolves and the Lamb*, for
the good reason that it was never publicly performed. Gordon Ray reports
that Thackeray composed the "melancholy comedy" during a difficult winter
in which he struggled with health problems, depression, and fitful progress on
The Newcomes.[43] He intended the play for the West End's Olympic Theatre—
the venue that the recently retired Mme Vestris had made a center for theatrical reform with her box sets, realistic domestic interiors, and showtimes specifically designed "to enable families to reach their homes before midnight."[44]
But the new manager rejected it after a hasty reading, as did the manager of
the Haymarket to whom Thackeray next submitted it. In fact, its only performance occurred at an 1862 party Thackeray threw when he moved with his
daughters into the large house in Kensington where he would spend the rest
of his life. The playbills Thackeray printed for the party punned badly on his
initials in calling this a performance of the "W.M.T. House Theatricals." The
reference to an "empty house" both alluded to the fact that the furnishings
had yet to arrive and reminded spectators of the play's inability to command
the attention of a real theatrical "house." As important, by metaphorically
hollowing out the space of domestic felicity, Thackeray imparted a strangely
melancholic note to his housewarming.[45] The effect is to overlay this com-
memoration of private happiness with an image of public refusal—even to
suggest the former as a paltry compensation for the latter.

The sour pun is the more striking when considered alongside the blandly
orthodox domesticity celebrated in the play itself. *The Wolves and the Lamb*
is a desultory domestic comedy of the type finding increasing favor in mid-
century London (particularly at the Olympic): perhaps one reason for its
failure to gain a place on the stage is the unconvincing, indeed almost parodic, eagerness with which it mimics the dominant coziness of the West End
theater. The play's headnote indicates that the stage represents "MILLIKEN'S
villa at Richmond; two drawing-rooms opening into one another."[46] Thackeray
thus offers his hypothetical viewers an image of the domestic receding into
itself, as if to remind us of the derivation of the term "drawing room" from

the word "withdraw"; the resulting stage picture is that of an exponentiated domesticity. The stage directions continue with an impeccably realistic vision of upper-middle-class comfort:

> *The late MRS. MILLIKEN's portrait over the mantelpiece; book-cases, writing-tables, piano, newspapers, a handsomely furnished saloon. The back-room opens, with very large windows, on the lawn and pleasure-ground; gate, and wall—over which the heads of a cab and a carriage are seen, as persons arrive. Fruit, and a ladder on the walls. A door to the dining room, another to the sleeping apartments, &c.* (373)

As the trailing "*&c.*" indicates, Thackeray seems uninterested in the details of this space beyond what is necessary to signify its placid respectability. So unremarkable is this interior vision that it is difficult at first to notice what it most unsettlingly suggests—namely, that a writer who made his name sneering at domestic comedy is attempting in all earnestness to do one. This disconcerting shift is best exemplified by the totemic use of children in composing the stage picture. Where in *Vanity Fair* the teeming images of mischievous infants suggested the undoing of the domestic scene they might otherwise signify, here the children who shuffle dutifully across the stage at the play's first and last moments are quite literally at home.[47] Under the pressure of the domestic stage's literalization, *Vanity Fair's* allegorically charged gaggle of human miniatures has become a bunch of characters: no longer the bearers of an ambivalent sociohistorical bitterness, they are, simply, Milliken's kids.

This visual frame offers an apt introduction to the plot of the play, which pays insistent homage to the space of the home. The lamb of its title is the widower Milliken, a *"wealthy City Merchant"* (372) who falls in love with his children's governess Julia Prior, to the dismay of his imperious mother-in-law and his sanctimonious mother. When these older women discover that Miss Prior has been employed on the stage—dancing for ten shillings a week in an "Oriental ballet"—they react to the news with predictable horror (one of them sputters, "When do you intend to leave, madam, the house which you have po—poll—luted?" [412, 434]). But Julia's theatrical past proves surprisingly anodyne. In notable contrast to Becky Sharp and to Thackeray's other theatrically marked heroines (*Pendennis's* Blanche, *Henry Esmond's* Beatrix), Julia Prior is fully assimilable in the Milliken family. The marriage comes off in the end, and Julia is more than willing to repress her theatrical past in exchange for a position in the home. In a series of reshufflings that dutifully expresses the play's irreproachably middle-class ethos, Milliken's aristocratic in-laws are ejected and the stage-Cockney butler John departs his service in order to start up his own family and a small business as a pub owner. John takes leave of the Millikens with a vision of multiplying spaces of bourgeois privacy that could serve as the play's motto: "I wish to sit in my own little

home, with my own little wife by my side" (443). *The Wolves and the Lamb*
ends shortly after (in a phrase that recalls the concluding lines of *Vanity Fair*
without conjuring their tragic resonance) with the children being summoned
to "come in" to their tea (445). In this closing tableau, as in the play as a
whole, there is virtually no breathing space for the Thackerayan melancholy
that functions in *Vanity Fair* as an expression of social and historical discontent. It is as if, in the context of a theatrical culture made over in the image
of the home, Thackeray can barely work up his customary interest in the
theatrical; or as if, denied access to the space "before the curtain"—denied,
that is, the embellishments of his acid narration—he can only rehearse, quasi-
mechanically, the domestic ideology the form demands of him. Finally "in"
the theater, he treats it like a toy box.

If there remains any place on this stage for the Thackerayan narratorial
sensibility, it lies in the curious person of Captain Touchit—a character who
(not unlike the "I" who suddenly pops up on the margins of *Vanity Fair*'s
domestic comedy) has no place in a summary of its plot. An old friend of
the hero who is visiting the house as the action transpires, Touchit remains
entirely peripheral to the unfolding of the action. His externality is signaled
most clearly by the fact that he is the only character who seems aware of the
theatrical medium in which the play necessarily unfolds. Stumbling on to
the climactic scene, for example, he exclaims, "What is this comedy going
on, ladies and gentlemen? The ladies on their elderly knees—Miss Prior
with her hair down her back. Is it tragedy or comedy?—is it a rehearsal for
a charade, or are we acting for Horace's birthday?" (437). The declamatory
mode in which the line is offered is one pointer to Touchit's contiguity with
Thackerayan narration. Even more remarkable is its content, which gestures
at the multifarious theatrical culture otherwise ignored in *The Wolves and
the Lamb*. If the play as a whole slavishly participates in the domestication
of the theater, it is only Captain Touchit who registers that that process is
under way.

Aside from his narrative marginality, a connection to theatrical space
turns out to be what most characterizes Touchit. A former tenant in a boardinghouse kept by Julia Prior's family, Touchit is the sole character with a living experience of the governess's theatrical past. He is also much more eager
than she to discuss it, to bring those theatrical spaces to verbal life on this
stage. When, in his only tête-a-tête with Julia he reminisces about one of
their fellow lodgers ("What a heap of play-tickets, diorama-tickets, concert-
tickets he used to give you!" [401–402]), Julia cuts short this drift into the
past, and into theatrical spaces distinct from the drawing room in which they
find themselves. Gendered reasons clearly underlie Julia and Touchit's differing responses to the unseemly memories they share: Touchit never stands
in danger of exclusion from the Milliken home on account of his past. (As
Lenore Davidoff and Catherine Hall have argued, the ideology of separate

spheres obscures a central facet of male privilege—namely, that the pleasures of both home and street were much less problematically available to men than to women.)[48] And in keeping with a certain misogynist logic, Thackeray makes clear that even as Julia abjures the public culture of the theater, she has in no way renounced its artifice, her experience with which serves her well in performing her way into bourgeois entitlement.

But if Touchit is unlikely to suffer ejection from the home on grounds of propriety, there are indications at the play's end that he may be discarded for his sheer irrelevance. "And you will come down and see us often, Touchit, won't you?" Milliken asks vaguely in the play's penultimate line, but the question goes unanswered by Touchit, who a moment earlier has indicated his intention not to "interrupt this felicity" and to dine instead at his club (445). This non-exchange makes evident the increased demarcation between inside and outside, home and world—and between the spectacle of domesticity and the pleasures of the theater—that is characteristic both of the refortified Milliken home and of the paradoxically withdrawn theatrical space it occupies. Touchit is the lone repository of the memory of those external spaces the play ignores. In this, he (and not the governess Julia) is the heir to Becky Sharp, whose distinctiveness lies not only in her personal experience of the world of publicity and performance but in her insistence on remembering that world. Touchit's silence at the finale mirrors the play's confusion about what to do with this extra-domestic character. His exile from the conclusion of *The Wolves and the Lamb* suggests that a stage committed to mirroring the enclosure of the home can afford no space for that theatrical memory.

Paradoxically, it is only in the novel that this repository of the theatrical past will find his voice. *The Wolves and the Lamb* forces us to imagine Touchit's interior response to the play's final question; but the 1860 novel *Lovel the Widower* that Thackeray adapted from his play opens with and is sustained by a torrent of Touchit's language. Retreating from the scene of his theatrical frustration, Thackeray discovers a subtly contoured and expansive space of interiority.

In the Recess of Consciousness: *Lovel the Widower*

> But these are mute personages in our drama; and having nothing to do or say,
> need occupy a very little space here.—Thackeray, *Vanity Fair*

The emotional focus and innovative force of *Lovel the Widower* derive from the way it gives formal expression to the experience of dramatic failure. But that late novel's acoustic experimentation has a precedent in Thackeray's career: the Christmas book *Mrs. Perkins's Ball* was published in 1848, as *Vanity Fair* was appearing in biweekly numbers. Like many of Thackeray's casual productions, it is generically ambiguous: so heavily illustrated that it is unclear whether image or word is meant to hold our attention; chopped into miniature "chapters" sometimes less than a page long; constantly shifting between narrative and dramatic modes. It is a text full of weird and startling effects, one of which can be taken as a precursor to the experiments of *Lovel the Widower*. The narrator of *Mrs. Perkins's Ball* is Thackeray's alter-ego Michelangelo Titmarsh. He is hanging back from the whirling couples on the dance floor, indulging in the mental quips that are the wallflower's consolation:

> Poor Hely, if he were advancing to a dentist, his face would not be more cheerful. All the eyes of the room are upon him, he thinks; and he thinks he looks like a fool.
>
> Upon my word, if you press the point with me, dear Miss Jones, I think he is not very far from right. I think that while Frenchmen and Germans may dance, as it is their nature to do, there is a natural dignity about us Britons, which debars us from that enjoyment. I am rather of the Turkish opinion, that this should be done for us. I think ***
>
> "Good-by, you envious old fox-and-the-grapes," says Miss Jones, and the next moment I see her whirling by in a polka with Tom Tozer, at a pace which makes me shrink back with terror into the little boudoir.[49]

We might take this moment as offering a capsule genealogy of Thackeray's narrative voice, one that hints at the origins of that voice's extraordinary sensitivity to the contours of public and interior space. What is most disconcerting at the passage's conclusion is the revelation that we are not alone with Titmarsh's narration. No quotation marks frame his discourse, and the "dear Miss Jones" who is apostrophized in the second paragraph appears to function only as the kind of apparitional interlocutor Thackeray rapidly summons and dismisses throughout his fiction; she seems, that is, to be no more than a figure (momentarily graced with a suitably anonymous proper name) for the reader. Titmarsh appears to speak to us merely in the metaphorical sense that we employ in discussing narrative "voice." But in speaking up, "Miss Jones" disconcertingly interposes a flesh-and-blood character between Titmarsh's words and our reception of them. She *places* those words, and their speaker, in the social landscape of the narrated world: Titmarsh's observations at first seem to enjoy the screen of silence, but Miss Jones's out-loud interruption of his acrimonious reflections call him out of his private rumination to hold him accountable for the social derivation of his discontent. Soliloquy turns into colloquy.

More exactly, soliloquy is revealed to have always been colloquy, narration to have always been interlocution, the hanger-back to have always been on display.[50] In the space between the two paragraphs marked by Thackeray's row of asterisks, the social coordinates of the apparently placeless voice become abruptly, embarrassingly, visible. As important: no sooner is this voice exposed as "dramatic"—as a partner in dialogue—than a very public rebuffing makes it recoil into a redoubled privacy, a "little boudoir" of consciousness now definitively impenetrable by the social surround. We can be sure as the passage ends that we are alone with Titmarsh's hushed confession. If we are now decidedly "in" Thackerayan narration, what is most distinctive in that narration is its origin in a bitterness about the niceties of bourgeois behavior—here, the courtship rituals whose violation presumably causes Miss Jones's irritation. If Titmarsh's brief internal comments make halting steps toward the development of interior monologue, this episode suggests that this innovative technique for the exploration of the psyche derives from a marginality to the demands of domestic comportment.

The movement from soliloquy to colloquy to silent interior speech occupies only a brief moment of *Mrs. Perkins's Ball.* But such acoustic warping is the narrative principle at the heart of *Lovel the Widower.* The later novel indicates that Thackeray's narrative experimentation awaited his theatrical effort, and his theatrical failure, in order to come to fruition. In adapting his failed play Thackeray found himself confronted with a fortuitous collision of sociohistorical content (the transformations in Victorian theatrical culture we have examined) and a formal transformation that serves as a resonant allegory of that content; the coincidence appears to have sparked the prolonged experiment of *Lovel the Widower.* The story remains essentially the same as in the play, but Thackeray transforms its meaning by giving power of narration to the most peripheral character. The 1860 novel creates its flamboyant interior monologue out of that liminal space between theatrical past and domestic present inhabited by Captain Touchit. "Who shall be the hero of this tale?" the novel opens. "Not I who write it."[51] The words signal a minor-key dissent from the Dickensian opening that is its most immediate point of reference: unlike David Copperfield coyly wondering whether he will turn out to be the hero of the life story that bears his name, this narrator flatly refuses to move center stage. "I am but the Chorus of the Play," he clarifies—and takes off on a fifteen-page rant in which we tour an echo chamber reverberating with past and present arguments, blandishments, resentments. No one else speaks, but we are nonetheless awash in voices:

> I am but the Chorus of the Play. I make remarks on the conduct of the characters: I narrate their simple story. There is love and marriage in it: there is grief and disappointment: the scene is in the parlour, and the region beneath the parlour. No: it may be the parlour and the kitchen, in this instance, are on the same level . . . I don't think there's a villain in the whole performance. There is . . . an old haunter of Bath and Cheltenham boarding-houses (about which how can I know anything,

never having been in a boarding-house at Bath or Cheltenham in my life?) ...

The principal personage you may very likely think to be no better than a muff. But is many a respectable man of our acquaintance much better? ... Yes; perhaps even this one is read and written by—Well? *Quid rides?* Do you mean that I am painting a portrait which hangs before me every morning in the looking-glass when I am shaving? *Après?* Do you suppose that I suppose that I have not infirmities like my neighbors? ...

I wish with all my heart I was about to narrate a story with a good mother-in-law for a character; but then you know, my dear madam, all good women in novels are insipid. This woman certainly was not. ... Aha! my good Lady Baker! I was a *mauvais sujet*, was I?—I was leading Fred [Lovel] into smoking, drinking, and low bachelor habits, was I? I, his old friend, who have borrowed money from him any time these twenty years, was not fit company for you and your precious daughter? Indeed! ...

Before entering upon the present narrative, may I take leave to inform a candid public that, though it is all true, there is not a word of truth in it; that though Lovel is alive and prosperous, and you very likely have met him, yet I defy you to point him out; that his wife (for he is Lovel the Widower no more) is not the lady you imagine her to be. (197–202)

Are you talking to me? we may well ask. Where are we? *When* are we? Is this voice telling a story, conducting a quarrel, rehearsing a grudge, announcing a performance—speaking to a public, to Lady Baker, to itself? How many of us are there in here? Some of these sentences take up the tone of the stentorian moralist derided by Thackeray's modernist critics, and some could be characterized as the "confiding garrulities" beloved by his nineteenth-century readers.[52] But there is a new mobility and restlessness that have led Geoffrey Tillotson to describe *Lovel* as anticipating the development of stream-of-consciousness narration.[53] This metaphor may be too placid, however, to account for a speech act so fitful, devious, and panicked. In the opening pages of *Lovel*, we enter a narrative space where the referential trajectory of language is prone to odd inflections, where the scope of the audience and the status of the utterance undergo incessant warpings: curse shades into entreaty, narration into quarrelsome conversation, reminiscence into hallucination. The effect is as if Titmarsh has retreated so far into the recesses of his mind that it scarcely matters whether he speaks or only imagines his words, or whether there is any Miss Jones there to register the difference.

Is it possible to trace the contours of the shadow theater mapped by this surge of language? We are both upstairs and downstairs (in the "parlour" and the "kitchen"); we are at once in the home (in the seat of "love and marriage") and out of it (our speaker unconvincingly disavows familiarity with "boarding-houses"); we are at once at the temporal threshold of Lovel's story ("before entering upon the present narrative") and beyond that story's close ("he is Lovel the Widower no more"); we are on the stage but peripheral to its action.[54] So apparently ubiquitous is this narrative voice that it might seem to partake of a casual Balzacian omniscience—if it weren't for the fact that it is also so drenched in tones of spleen, loss, resentment, and sheer embodied breathlessness. This speaker appears to suffer in his person the exhausting effects of every narrative swerve, every spatial and temporal translation.

We have seen that the characterological location of this ubiquity that has no place to rest is *The Wolves and the Lamb*'s Captain Touchit. But he appears here under a name that offers an oddly bald explanation for his placelessness and for his overcompensating, quasi-paranoid narrative style: "I shall call myself Mr. Batchelor, if you please" (216). Meanwhile, his friend Milliken has been rechristened with a name, "Lovel," that rounds out the domestic sphere's logic of affective exclusivity. If, as our narrator assures us, "there is love and marriage in it," Frederick Lovel is clearly where it's at—and Mr. Batchelor is just as clearly out of it. The love/Lovel semi-pun offered in the first lines of the story constitutes an almost crass joke against those who find themselves unaccommodated by the domestic present: it's not merely that the bachelor is excluded from the domestic hearth in a culture where "only marriage could yield the full privileges of masculinity."[55] More damaging, this hearth has now explicitly become the space of "love." The obviousness of this effect is clearly part of Thackeray's intent and a large component of the story's pathos. It may be possible to understand Titmarsh's shrinking from courtship ritual as an offhand joke, but it is much harder to ignore the social abjection and sheer tactile need embodied in a Batchelor whose "real" name is Touchit.[56]

Batchelor's sourness in these opening pages suggests that the wellsprings of Thackerayan narration lie in a resentment about the equation between the domestic and affective plenitude.[57] But it is crucial to notice that Batchelor's eminently novelistic voice is given its affective contours by his obsession with the memory of theater. His social need, that is, is a symptom of the disappearance of a "stage" that could accommodate him, and is therefore as much a historical as a psychological phenomenon. If Tillotson is correct that Batchelor's voice anticipates the modernist stream of consciousness, *Lovel*'s theatrical background indicates that this technique for the exploration of interiority derives not from a push toward psychological realism but from the vacuum created by the loss of a commonly accessible public culture. The interior monologue would thus owe less to the representational demands of a generic subject than to the specific social melancholia of the "*mauvais sujet*" who is exiled from the domestic enclosure and who stubbornly holds onto a social space fading into oblivion. Batchelor's narration is a panicked report from an evaporating culture of public theatricality, and his interior monologue signals not an accommodation of the new novelistic order but alienation from it.

J. Jeffrey Franklin has argued compellingly that nineteenth-century realism disciplines theatrical characters to supplant the "subject of performance" with the "subject of reading."[58] The subject of performance—the exteriorized, action-oriented subject Franklin contrasts with the "inwardly directed and self-reflexive, socially isolated and deactivated" reading subject (32)—is indeed rendered obsolete in *Lovel the Widower*. But this supersession is not only mourned by the novel but is mourned as one of its most important formal innovations. Far from constituting a triumphant alternative to the theatrical, novelistic interiority emerges as a container for an unaccommodated theatricality. The sociohistorical melancholy saturating this formal innovation is underscored by the fact that, in morphing from Touchit into Batchelor—in departing the stage for the "boudoir" of interiority—Thackeray's non-hero has also gained a *past* that would have been literally unrepresentable on the domestic set of *The Wolves and the Lamb*. Where in the play Touchit's relation to Julia Prior is passed over in a few lines, here the details of their shabby shared history dilate to occupy a third of the text. This past is a space of a decidedly undomesticated theatricality, a risqué world represented by the "places of public amusement" where Julia (here renamed Elizabeth) Prior dances to help support her family (222). More surprising, it is also a space of children—not the allegorical apparitions of *Vanity Fair* but a collection of hungry, grubby "little folks" for whom Batchelor displays notable affection. "I went to Prior's: I took the rooms," Batchelor recalls.

> I was attracted by some children: Amelia Jane (that little dirty maid before mentioned) dragging a go-cart, containing a little dirty pair; another marching by them, carrying a fourth well nigh as big as himself. These little folks, having threaded the mighty flood of Regent Street, debouched into the quiet creek of Beak Street, just as I happened to follow them. . . . The aspect of these little people, which would have deterred many, happened to attract me. I am a lonely man. (215–216)

Where elsewhere in Thackeray's work children are unfailingly associated with the scene of domestic interiority, these children are emblems of the home's permeability, its openness to incursion from the city. We notice also that what Geoffrey Tillotson identifies as Thackeray's favorite derogatory adjective—"little"—has here been transformed into a wholly positive quality, almost a fetish: Mr. Batchelor does not only like little children, he likes to *say* that they are little.[59] His language betrays a fixation on the cuteness and tininess of their persons and accoutrements. In the space of a single paragraph lamenting the fact that Elizabeth's delinquent father confiscates her "little slender pocket-money," Batchelor claims that Eliza uses the money to perform "kindnesses to the little brothers and sisters," as well as to purchase her own "little toilette ornaments" or "little knicknacks" and toys for her brother "little Bill" (206). It is as if the littleness that is irksome to Thackeray is the littleness that is enclosed, that is inaccessible. Released onto the scene of public consumption, littleness becomes a mark of tenderness.

Even Batchelor's irritability exudes pleasure in asserting his importance to the extended boardinghouse family. Scandalized by Mr. Prior's abuse of his children and by his habit of pilfering his lodgers' foodstuffs, Batchelor threatens to revoke his gifts:

> I vowed a tremendous vow . . . I would quit the lodgings, and never give those children lollipop, nor pegtop, nor sixpence; nor the pungent marmalade, nor the biting gingerbread-nut, nor the theatre-characters, nor the paint-box to illuminate the same; nor the discarded clothes, which became smaller clothes upon the persons of little Tommy and little Bill, for whom Mrs. Prior, and Bessy, and the little maid, cut, clipped, altered, ironed, darned, mangled, with the greatest ingenuity. I say, considering what had passed between me and the Priors—considering those money transactions, and those clothes, and my kindness to the children—it was rather hard that my jam-pots were poached, and my brandy bottles leaked. (206–207)

The passage in one sense reproduces the logic of diminishing scale familiar from *Vanity Fair*: big narrator gives discarded clothes to little Bessy, who cuts them down for even littler baby brothers. (And the inclusion of "theatre-characters" in the catalogue of gifts recalls the earlier novel's emblem of domesticated publicity). Just as familiar, the passage's humor depends on the boomeranging energies of diminution at work in Thackeray's language: invoking his adult beneficence, Batchelor sounds like nothing so much as a big baby. Yet despite the absurdity of his grandiose rhetoric, Batchelor is a useful person to the Prior household, and he does not leave. Where in *Vanity Fair* the circulation of goods results in a zero-sum game of universal alienation and frustration, here Batchelor describes what is in fact a mutually beneficial emotional economy.[60] What today would be called Batchelor's parenting style (unorthodox and self-aggrandizing though it may be) has real dividends—in clothes, food, and attention—for the children of the Prior household. "Little Dick Bedford used to sit many hours asleep on my landing-place," Batchelor recalls. "I used to like to help the little man from my breakfast, and see him enjoy the meal." The "touching little picture" of the printer's boy dozing in the stairwell is a spectacle enjoyed by "the whole house" (221); the palpable nostalgia in Batchelor's tone is intimately tied to the interpenetration in this vision of outside and inside, privacy and publicity. In its unanxious mingling of adults, children, and classes, as in its mixture of scenes of work and leisure, the Priors' boardinghouse creates a loosely assembled domestic economy that shelters what we could call the bohemian bachelor's family values.

To put it this way, of course, is immediately to identify the sentimentality of this novel. But it would be overhasty to dismiss *Lovel* on these grounds without first registering the depth of sentimentality's expressiveness—the way it gives voice to the social dissatisfactions of those subjects Lauren Berlant has called "the intimately disappointed."[61] Batchelor's vision of boardinghouse utopia is also the vessel of an insistent sociohistorical longing. In its facilitation of interfamilial, interclass mingling, the Prior boardinghouse is typical of the rooming houses that Sharon Marcus has described as sites of "social and spatial blending."[62] Although Marcus emphasizes that boardinghouses were an established middle-class phenomenon in nineteenth-century London, she also demonstrates that the social mixing they occasioned was increasingly identified with the working class, and held up in contrast to an idealized bourgeois privacy (88). Marcus's period of focus, the middle decades of the century, corresponds to the era of theatrical reform detailed above—a fact suggesting that Batchelor's stubborn attachment to the early Victorian stage and his fondness for the Prior household are images of each other. The Prior house, in other words, is not a home, and this seems precisely what makes it such an appealing memory for the bachelor who finds himself stranded at Lovel's in the domestic comedy of the present.[63]

It is only in this present—only after the dissolution of the boardinghouse's ad-hoc extended family—that Batchelor pushes his quasi-parental fondness for little Eliza into a romantic register, as if in a fictional world structured by the dictates of the marriage plot, the only way to claim a relation to Elizabeth and the family she represents is to court her. But Batchelor's conspicuous consumption of romantic chagrin seems beside the point in *Lovel*—not least because the "elderly Tiresias" (244) who narrates the story goes by a name that clearly signals his externality to the marriage plot. Released from suspense over who gets the girl (Elizabeth marries Lovel, we recall from the first pages [202–203]), the reader is at liberty to notice other affective relations proliferating in the margins of that domestic comedy. Indeed, when Batchelor hits the most "romantic" notes of his narration, he sounds as if he hankers not for Elizabeth herself but for the Prior—the prior—household with which he associates her:

> Why didn't I say to her, "My dear brave Elizabeth! as I look in your face, I see you have had an awful deal of suffering. Your eyes are inscrutably sad. We who are initiated, know the members of our Community

of Sorrow. We have both been wrecked in different ships, and been cast
on this shore. Let us go hand-in-hand, and find a cave and a shelter
somewhere together?" I say, why didn't I say this to her? She would
have come, I feel sure she would. We would have been semi-attached
as it were. (251)

The sense of shared anachronism is as strong here as that of desire, and it is not
clear whether Batchelor is proposing marriage or a sort of aerated intimacy.
Batchelor's last words pun lightly on the "semi-detached" suburban villa, an
architectural style designed to impart an air of privacy to houses built in clus-
ters. Thackeray's adjective (perhaps coined here)[64] inverts the contemporary
architectural term to make it resonate with tones of communication rather
than isolation. The semi-attached future he posits so hesitantly sounds more
like the boardinghouse past they share than the till-death-do-us-part proximity Eliza is actually heading for with Lovel. Although it is expressed in the
language of courtship, this would-be proposal in fact gestures toward a quite
different domestic arrangement. If in *Vanity Fair* the identification between
the narrator and Becky on the ground of historical longing could only give
rise to an anxious denial, here a shared past facilitates a rapprochement between the "bad" woman and the melancholy bachelor.

To be sure, attending to the possible worlds outside the purview of domesticity requires some distance on the marriage plot that anchors the narrative. It is the dilated spaciousness of Batchelor's narration that affords that
distance in *Lovel the Widower*. Emerging from the voluble margins of *Lovel's*
love plot is the suggestion that Batchelor is occupied less in a competition
for Elizabeth's hand than in a rivalry with the whole affective vortex represented by Lovel, his deceased wife, his adorable children, his in-laws—with a
domesticity, in short, for which the bachelor is now revealed as a constitutive
limit, a just-barely-inside outsider. And this plot is accentuated by the formal
improbabilities attendant on Thackeray's addition of an observer to his text's
necessarily narrator-less precursor: part of *Lovel's* peculiar force derives from
its creation of a narrator out of thin air. "Out of this room, which I occupied
for some few days, now and subsequently, I looked forth as from a little am-
bush upon the proceedings of the house, and got a queer little insight into
the history and characters of the personages round about me" (256–257).
Lodged in the middle of the house, in a sound-permeable room that affords
him a front-row view of the domestic dramas unfolding there, Batchelor sees
everything, but at the social cost of approaching near invisibility.

Indeed, Batchelor never seems more characterized than when his narration verges on an I-am-a-camera objectivity. In *Lovel's* third chapter ("In
Which I Play the Spy"), the novel's plot hews closely to that of the play, and in
places Thackeray resorts to play-dialogue typography to represent the characters' conversations. But unlike the play, where Touchit's supernumerary status

is only nonplussing, here the disappearance of narrative elaboration signaled by dialogic form registers *as* a disappearance, if only because Batchelor keeps interjecting reminders that he is the conduit of the story, our window onto this home: "I had been some thirty hours in the house, and what a queer little drama was unfolding itself before me!" he exclaims (271). It is difficult to know whether he is bragging about his insight or lamenting his nonparticipation. In any case, Batchelor's boasts about his "profound knowledge of human nature" (277) and his access to "the secrets of the house" (278) become entangled with a sense that these are paltry compensations for the loss of an ampler and more various organization of social space. If he was a vital participant in the teeming Prior household, Batchelor's only role in the "queer little" dramas of the Lovel household is as a kind of fourth wall—a principle of narrative omniscience that exults in its superior insight as a way to compensate for its liminality. The effect is to locate the genealogy of this omniscience in social placelessness. In Batchelor's opening harangue, he badgers the shade of the prim Lady Baker, who has accused him of "low bachelor habits": "No, madam, it was your turn to bully me once—now it is mine and I use it" (201). "It" here is the very position of narration—a position that now stands revealed as fueled by resentment, loss, and fantasmatic revenge. The fourth wall talks back, and in the process demonstrates the constitutive social exclusions that have pushed it out to the edge of the performance—to the outskirts of the domestic comedy that is the only play that remains to be staged.

Throughout *Lovel*, Batchelor's obsessive use of dramatic metaphors acts both as a rhetorical hangover of the novel's theatrical genesis and as a reminder that the theater he desires no longer exists: Batchelor's theatrical imagery insistently finds him backstage, in the wings, too late for the performance. Ashamed at having hung back as the novel's romance plot reaches its climax (he eavesdrops through a window as another man makes a pass at Elizabeth), Batchelor pretends to have been out for a walk: "As the battle was over, I—I just went round that shrubbery into the other path, and so entered the house, arriving like Fortinbras in 'Hamlet,' when everybody is dead and sprawling, you know, and the whole business is done" (319). If in this case the figure of the theater indicates belatedness, elsewhere it suggests that Batchelor's displacement is a kind of ghostliness. Late in the novel, he describes his aimlessness in the domestic world by comparing himself to one of the stage's most famous walking dead: "Suppose Hamlet (Père, and Royal Dane) comes back and finds Claudius and Gertrude very comfortable over a piece of cold meat, or what not?" Faced with the prospect of this spectral irrelevance, Batchelor resolves to stay away: "Open, Trap-door! *Allons*: it's best to pop underground again" (347). The facetious tone of these lines should not occlude the genuine sense of loss they register. If the shape of the psyche is determined by the history of its abandoned attachments, then Batchelor's richly contoured interiority here is structured by the lost public culture that the theater signifies for him. Batchelor's interior monologue may make him the herald of a narratological principle of privacy, but his is an inwardness given essential form by the disappearance of what we might term his theater of action. His interiority is a narrative memorial to his social obsolescence, a space echoing with the intimate publicity of the prologue spoken from the now evaporated apron of the old stage.

Among the ghosts of the Prior household that Batchelor calls up in the opening sections of the novel is that of Mr. Slumley, the newspaper editor who secured Elizabeth her job on the stage, and in whose muckraking paper *The Swell* "you would find theater and opera people most curiously praised and assaulted," Batchelor recalls. He continues:

> I recollect meeting him, several years after, in the lobby of the opera, in a very noisy frame of mind, when he heard a certain lady's carriage called, and cried out with the exceeding strong language, which need not be accurately reported, "Look at that woman! Confound her! I made her, sir! . . . Did you see her, sir? She wouldn't even look at me!" (210)

Slumley—associated by name with the boardinghouse and by occupation with the stage—makes luridly obvious the investments that equally propel Batchelor's narrative. The invective Slumley hurls at the bourgeoisified actress expresses the fury of the displaced; his peroration here is an angrier manifestation of the social and historical melancholy that infuses Batchelor's voice. In entreating this placidly respectable operagoer to remember her time on the boards, Slumley gives voice to a plea for the boardinghouse in the face of the home's ascendancy, a call to remember the sociability that persists in the privatized self, an insistence on the retention of the past in the present. Batchelor's supple narrative voice is similarly insistent, without making Slumley's equation between resentment of the new order and hatred for the woman who has become ambiguously ensconced in it. Batchelor's ineffectual attachment to Elizabeth Prior may be no less real for being only halfheartedly romantic. For all its manifest absurdity, his desire for her approaches tragic status when we recognize in it the desire for a sociability now inaccessible to the domestic present: "Elizabeth means a history to me" (229).

TWO

George Eliot's Lot

The book I am writing is *not* a novel.
—George Eliot to George Smith, July 1867

Theater and Abstraction

In her essay "Notes on Form in Art" George Eliot argues for the insepara-bility of artistic form and content by reviving a metaphor so close to death that we may not at first recognize it as a metaphor. "Poetic Form," she writes, "was not begotten by thinking it out or framing it as a shell which should hold emotional expression, any more than the shell of an animal arises before the living creature . . . The beautiful expanding curves of a bivalve shell are not first made for the reception of the unstable inhabitant, but grow & are limited by the simple rhythmic conditions of its growing life."[1] Eliot's image of the shell condenses a complex set of meditations on the use and misuse of figurative language. Considered as a physical object that both houses and is shaped by a living organism, a shell is a tangible reminder of the intimacy of life and form. In its metaphoric usage, however, it evokes something close to the opposite phenomenon, the tendency of artistic form to harden and erase its reference to life: Eliot's first use of "shell" in the above passage evokes not the "beautiful, expanding" organic membrane she goes on to describe but the empty casing that the word more routinely connotes. Most striking, as a figure no longer commonly perceived as one, "shell" itself embodies this os-sifying movement from the first, "live" sense to the second, "dead" one. Eliot's words remind us that to use the word "shell" as if it were simply a synonym for empty form is to bypass the organic object which itself gives rise to the figure. A dead metaphor for the phenomenon of dying metaphor, the shell is both a powerful reminder of form's reference to life and a figure for the im-minent ossification of all figurative language. At once a record of the organic and the sign of its erasure, the shell Eliot invokes here is a monument to, and a betrayal of, life itself.[2]

In the essay's immediately following lines Eliot links her discussion of life and form to the origins of literary genres:

> It is a stale observation that the earliest poetic forms arose in the same spontaneous unreflecting way—that the rhythmic shouts with clash of metal accompanying the huntsman's or conqueror's course were probably the nucleus of the ballad epic; that the funeral or marriage sing-song, wailing or glad, with more or less violent muscular movement & resonance of wood or metal made the rude beginnings of lyric poetry. But it is still worth emphasis that this spontaneous origin is the most completely demonstrated in relation to a form of art which ultimately came to be treated more reflectively than any other—the tragic & comic drama. (*E*, 435–436)

Eliot's abstract discussion of form has become a story about the social origins of the generic system. In this account, the epic, lyric, and drama emerged out of an intimate relation to a living social world. They might all, Eliot implies, be likened to the shell as organic entity, formed by and along with the pulsing life inside it. But some genres, it seems, are more shell-like than others: the drama's social genesis is "the most completely" evident. Where Eliot supports her claims about epic and lyric by specifying the practices (hunting shout, marriage song, funeral lament) from which these forms arise, in the case of the drama she foregoes such detail. The reason, it seems, is that for a form that by definition relies on embodiment and congregation, no reminder of archaic collective origins is necessary: as if in anticipation of Rancière's observations about the theatrical *dispositif*, Eliot insists that the social is still the inalienable precondition of the drama. But Eliot also suggests that the drama is peculiarly prone to a formalization that can estrange it from its necessary relation to collective life. The drama's susceptibility to "reflective" artistic treatment makes it resemble not the shell as the container of life but the shell as hollow casing. This short passage suggests that while all art is a memorial to the rhythms of collective life, the drama is the form where this fact should be most apparent but is most in danger of being stylized away.[3]

The question of drama's proximity to—or alienation from—the social fact of performance was very real to Eliot as she composed "Notes on Form in Art." She wrote the essay in 1868, the same year she published her generically ambiguous book-length poem *The Spanish Gypsy*. It had had a particularly tangled creative history. Its final form, which mixed dramatic and narrative techniques—awkwardly, in the opinion of Eliot's contemporaries—represents a kind of archeological image of the work's evolution. In its journey from conception to publication, *The Spanish Gypsy* traversed the distance between drama as embodied event and drama as abstracted, "reflective" literary form that is the subject of "Notes on Form in Art." Eliot began *The Spanish*

Gypsy in 1864 (the year after *Romola* had appeared in book form) at a moment in which she was preoccupied with the possibility of writing for the theater: she was rereading Euripides in December 1863, and her companion G. H. Lewes's journal entry for 8 February 1864 indicates that Eliot was considering writing a play for the actress Helen Faucit.[4] Eliot's letter in April to a friend relating that Faucit's performance in three Shakespeare plays had been "a flash of real acting in the evening twilight of the stage" suggests she was still toying with the idea two months later (*L*, 143).[5] This project was abandoned, but by early September 1864 Eliot recorded that she was "*reading about Spain and trying a drama on a subject that has fascinated me—have written the prologue, and am beginning the First Act. But I have little hope of making anything satisfactory*" (*J*, 120). The journal's early allusions to this new work refer to it always as "my drama," and its constituent sections are designated "Acts." But persistent illness and depression exacerbated Eliot's doubts about the play, which she was arduously composing in prose and then translating into blank verse. It is with a sense of relief that Eliot reports her abandonment of the project in February 1865: "Ill with bilious headache, and very miserable about my soul as well as body. *George has taken my drama away from me*" (*J*, 123). The next month she recorded with excitement the beginnings of work on a new novel. *Felix Holt* was published by Blackwood in June 1866.

But by October Eliot noted that she had "recommenced 'The Spanish Gipsy,' intending to give it a new form." The centrality of the formal issue for Eliot is underlined by the fact that in this entry she begins referring to the project not as a drama but as "my poem" (*J*, 129). Eliot retained the term as a constant in all her subsequent discussions of *The Spanish Gypsy*—insisting on it when her interlocutors seemed hazy or indifferent about the work's form. In March 1867, recently returned from a trip to Spain during which she had conducted research for the poem, Eliot wrote to John Blackwood that "the work connected with Spain is not a Romance. It is—prepare your fortitude—it is—a poem"; she went on to explain its original dramatic conception and her new idea for its form (*L*, 354). Blackwood's response indicated doubt about how to discuss this announcement: "I shall be very curious indeed," he wrote, "to see the Spanish Poem or Drama" (*L*, 357). By November Blackwood had forgotten Eliot's insistence on the work's nontheatrical status, as he wrote inquiring whether she wanted to see "some of the drama in type to see how it looked" (*L*, 394). Eliot silently corrected Blackwood's designation: "The length of the poem is at present uncertain" (*L*, 396). Ten days later Lewes, acting as Eliot's intermediary, again stressed the work's new formal identity in a letter to Blackwood: "By this post I send you part I of the poem" (*L*, 399). Blackwood finally took the point; his next letter exults in having received "the precious M.S. of Part one of the Poem" and the letter after that reverently refers to "the great Poem" (*L*, 400, 402). But the Leweses would have to reassert *The Spanish Gypsy*'s nontheatrical status a few months after publication: Blackwood wrote in June 1868 that a friend of the actress Mary Frances Scott Siddons had inquired "whether the author would be willing to adapt or have it adapted to the stage" (*L*, 452). Lewes, writing again on Eliot's behalf, responded that *The Spanish Gypsy* was "eminently unsuited for an *acting* play. To put it on stage would be to spoil the poem—and it could not be shaped into an effective drama" (*L*, 453).[6]

This confusion over the generic name for *The Spanish Gypsy* suggests that the book's composition gave Eliot a heightened awareness of the importance of such formal distinctions. As we have seen, this is exactly the topic that preoccupies her in the contemporaneous "Notes on Form in Art." That essay's interest in the always disappearing social roots of aesthetic forms suggests that it is the special tendency to abstraction of the concept of "drama" that is at issue in her correspondence with Blackwood. He is happy to keep "drama" as a loose designation for her work—and that looseness authorizes a willingness to consider *The Spanish Gypsy* as potentially (perhaps lucratively) destined for the stage. But Eliot's insistence that her work *was and is no longer a drama* resists this definitional flexibility; her resistance to metaphorization is also a resistance to the tendency to transport the notion of "drama" from the stage to the page, and from the social to the abstractly formal. Rhetorically marking her text's distance from performance, Eliot both emphasizes the specificity of collective embodiment and insists on her text's distance from that original goal.

If Eliot is keen to specify the nontheatrical status of her writing, modern critics have argued that she does so to insulate it from the vulgarity of the theater. The tendency of critics who treat Eliot and theater is to place her firmly on the side of abstraction, disembodiment, and sublimation. Joseph Litvak, for example, has argued that *Daniel Deronda* enforces a "hierarchy of genres . . . whose aim is to appropriate and neutralize the theatricality that threatens to infect the novel," while J. Jeffrey Franklin, in a discussion of *Felix Holt*, contends that the novel endorses Felix's antipathy to performance: "Everyone in *Felix Holt* is theatricalized in one or more ways except Felix himself . . . Felix is depth and authentic concern, the representative of the novel's own prose."[7] In both accounts Eliot's demonization of theater coincides with a troubling political agenda: for Litvak, the "text-genre system" that privileges poetry over theater is tied to the "sex-gender system" that punishes wayward female characters like Gwendolen Harleth (158), and, for Franklin, Felix's antitheatricalism curtails "the threat of working-class suffrage" that is the novel's central concern (97). The liberal values with which Eliot's work is associated—sincerity, privacy, reformism—seem scarcely imaginable without the denigration of a theater that stands for falsity, publicity, and revolutionary agitation. Despite the centrality of theatricality in these accounts, neither mentions Eliot's struggles with the form of *The Spanish Gypsy*, a fact suggesting that for these critics "drama" and "theater" have already undergone a process of metaphorization. Because the novel remains the ultimate generic ground of analysis, the theater that figures in these accounts has already been absorbed into the narrated world of fiction: Eliot's flatly literal invocation of "*my drama*" does not factor here.

In aligning Eliot with abstraction and with the interiorizing work of the novel, these accounts chime with a critique frequently leveled at her aesthetics. For Daniel Cottom, Eliot's "narrative supervision" results in "the sublimation of politics in the rules of sentimental psychology"; Franco Moretti argues that Eliot's narrator exalts "meditation at the expense of active and practical concerns"; John Kucich claims that Eliot's narration involves a "displacement of the site of identity away from social relations"; and Catherine Gallagher presents Eliot as an advocate for a "cultural" realm aloof from traffic with the realm of political or social "fact."[8] Despite their varying emphases, these accounts agree that Eliot's narrative practice abstracts the political, the social, and the collective in favor of an ethics of consciousness. What unites these critiques to the theatrically centered discussions of Litvak and Franklin is an alignment of Eliot's ideological position with the very form of the novel: for all these critics, it is Eliot's narrative voice that contains the social world, redirecting appetites that pertain to the collective into the psychological interior. In punishing, expelling, or disciplining a series of performative characters, Eliot's narrator becomes the deliteralizer par excellence, sublimating a potentially collective theater into an individualized and individualizing drama of consciousness.

But in *The Spanish Gypsy* Eliot undertook a major project that by virtue of its conception as a play resisted the inhabitation of characters' consciousness so important to the interiorizing abstractions of her narrative fiction. Indeed, if Eliot had fulfilled her original intention for *The Spanish Gypsy*, she would have had to abandon not only the privilege of narratively penetrating characters' thoughts but the use of narration *tout court*. This is a far from insignificant privation: *The Spanish Gypsy* appears to express the desire of Eliot's narrator *not to be*—and Eliot's desire to imagine a form of life unregulated by a supervisory narrative gaze. Given the centrality of narration to the ideological work supposedly performed by Eliot's texts, this suicidal ideation on the part of the Eliot narrator should be taken seriously as an index of her doubts about the limitations of the novel as a form. Indeed, throughout the generic evolution of *The Spanish Gypsy*, one thing that remained clear to Eliot was that (as she put it to a correspondent in April 1867) "the book I am writing is *not* a novel" (*L*, 377). We might register this emphasis by refusing to take for granted the inevitability of the novel in Eliot's oeuvre. The following pages undertake the unlikely project of reading Eliot's later career from the vantage point of the formal and ideological provocation represented by *The Spanish Gypsy*. Centering an analysis of Eliot's late work on this odd text seems less improbable when the following facts are considered: because Eliot turned to this dramatic poem when she had started to venture beyond the provincial English settings of her early fiction but had not yet arrived at the full complexity of her final work, it is a major work situated at the juncture between the "early" and "late" periods; because she worked on it intermittently for four years, *The Spanish Gypsy* was a living project in Eliot's mind for longer than any of her novels; and because it shares a Renaissance setting with *Romola*, an interest in the politics of collective assembly with *Felix Holt*, a plot of a woman's frustrated reformist destiny with *Middlemarch*, and a concern with ethnic outcasts with *Daniel Deronda*, *The Spanish Gypsy* thematically abuts each of her last four novels.

These facts, combined with its resolute strangeness, suggest that *The Spanish Gypsy* maps the outer boundary of what Eliot's realism could make ideologically and formally meaningful—and that attending to it might change our understanding of the interlocking logics of form and ideology in her work. We have examined the critical consensus according to which Eliot sides with inwardness against exteriority, privacy against collectivity, consciousness against action, "culture" against society. These are powerful and unavoidable oppositions in Eliot's work. But all of them are unsettled by *The Spanish Gypsy*, a work that departs from Eliot's customary ideological positions along with the formal devices that convey them.[9] This chapter begins by looking at the two novels whose composition bracketed Eliot's first attempt at *The Spanish Gypsy*. On the surface, no two Eliot novels look more dissimilar than 1863's *Romola* and 1866's *Felix Holt*—the first a laboriously researched exploration of intrigue in Renaissance Florence, the second a return to the pre-Victorian English midland setting that earned her fame. But they are united by a preoccupation with the problem of political assembly and, more particularly, with interiority's relation to democratic politics. Each book posits a different solution to the relation between novelistic interiority and collective assembly—the first depicting duplicitous interiority as a mirror of the politicized crowd, the second positing interiority as an antidote to that same crowd. In their different ways these novels confirm the sense of Eliot's exaltation of inward-looking self-consistency. We will see that Eliot turned to *Felix Holt*, and to the novel as a form, in 1865 to rescue her from the formal difficulties (and emotional distress) she had encountered in her initial efforts to write *The Spanish Gypsy* as a play.

But Eliot followed the publication of that novel by returning to the dramatic poem that had so troubled her. Thus while *Felix Holt* resolved a local creative stalemate, Eliot's return to *The Spanish Gypsy* indicates that her embrace of the novel appeared less final to her than it has to many critics. *The Spanish Gypsy* reopens the formal and ideological questions that Eliot might seem to have definitively closed with *Felix Holt*. Indeed, where Eliot's immediately preceding fiction implies that dignity inheres in the moral education

of the individualized self, *The Spanish Gypsy* proposes an ethics of exteriority. Moreover, while the notion that feminine love of performance requires
a painful moral correction is a veritable law of Eliot's fictional universe, it
is one she violates in *The Spanish Gypsy*: alone among her major works, it
features a heroine whose association with theatrical display goes unpunished
and is in fact seen as vital to her ethical trajectory.[10] These thematic issues
are closely tied to the formal traces of its performative origin retained in the
final text of *The Spanish Gypsy*: even in its narrative sections the poem hews
to the externalized perspective of the theater and confusingly incorporates
the typographic conventions of play scripts, with major effects on the poem's
texture and meaning. We will see how the poem's exteriorized perspective
remakes Eliot's famously deft use of free indirect discourse, introducing a
psychic unlocatability in the heart of this supremely psychologizing literary
device and allowing thought to peel free from discrete psychological containers. Just as strangely, *The Spanish Gypsy* imagines a human community radically enlarged—not by the piecemeal work of sympathy but by means of the
collectivist technology of the theatrical imagination.

That the poem does not coherently sustain these experiments is one reason for its near invisibility in most accounts of Eliot's career. As a number of
recent analyses have shown, on some fundamental level *The Spanish Gypsy*
doesn't "work."[11] While it is therefore tempting to see the dramatic poem as
expressing—and disposing of—a series of doubts about the interiorized fiction Eliot went on to perfect, we might conversely want to remain attuned to
the ways a collectivist theatrical imagination continues to inform her major
fictional achievements. A brief discussion of *Middlemarch* will show how
that novel registers the pressure of sheer social magnitude at the level of its
imagery; I suggest that even this most supremely psychologized fiction—
for many critics, the realist novel that most effectively displaces the social
through emphasis on the privatized interior—is haunted by a theatrical collectivization that functions as an after-image of the crowds of *The Spanish
Gypsy*. Even more striking is the way that *The Spanish Gypsy*'s status as play
script threatens to carry over into *Daniel Deronda*, undermining both that
text's ethnic determinism and the stability of its psychological portraits by
envisioning the novelistic cast of characters as a promiscuously intermingling
collective body. Lewes's diary indicates that Eliot's last major novel may have
been conceived as a play—and in its strangest moments *Deronda* still seems
to aspire to become one.[12] In its possible theatrical origins and its evident
connection to *The Spanish Gypsy*, Eliot's final novel challenges us to read it
as offering an alternative to the protocols of readerly identification. We will
see that the theatrical imagination of the novel upstages the divergent fates
narrated by its plot, in the process offering an alternative way to understand
the ethical provocation of realist fiction. At its most powerful Eliot's realism
solicits her reader not to align himself fantasmatically with the fates of one

or two privileged characters but to imagine the conditions of participation in collective life.

Romola, Felix Holt, and the Uses of Inwardness

One way to describe the plot of *Romola* is by saying that it traces the submission of a secretive and opaque character to narrative surveillance. Another is to say that it details the punishment of a demagogue by the crowd he has attempted to manipulate. While these summaries seem to fit, respectively, the stories of the invented bigamist Tito Melema and that of the historically real church reformer Girolamo Savonarola, the oddest thing about the novel is that each description applies equally well to either character. The confusion of these two apparently distinct crimes makes clear that for Eliot the problem of mass assembly is inextricable from the problem of interiority. Both, we will see, are crucially related to the issue of the theater.

Romola's eighth chapter offers an allegory for the narrator's relation to Tito's irritating inexpressiveness. Titled "A Face in the Crowd," the chapter hinges on the young scholar's perception that he is being watched one day in the Piazza del Duomo: "he saw a man's face upturned towards him, and fixing on him a gaze that seemed to have more meaning in it than the ordinary passing observation of a stranger."[13] This exchange of glances turns out to have momentous consequences for Tito's plot, but it also gives legible form to the narration's suspicious perusal of its central character. Thus far in the novel, the narrator has suggested that the "bland liveliness" (85) of Tito's face might indicate nothing beyond its own much remarked beauty. "Tito had an innate love of reticence—let us say a talent for it . . . and, like all people to whom concealment is easy, he would now and then conceal something which had as little the nature of a secret as the fact that he had seen a flight of crows" (94). Much like that hypothetical flock of birds, though, Tito's beauty is ripe for augury. A few pages later Tito stands staring at a handful of florins, and the narrator describes him "looking down, in that transfixed state which accompanies the concentration of consciousness on some inward image" (97). Such impenetrability, one suspects, will not be tolerated for long, and on the next page Tito loses his staring contest with the narrative eye: having survived close to a hundred pages as a provoking emblem of meaninglessness, Tito's reticence yields its inner depths.[14] We now hear of Tito's "first real colloquy with himself" (98)—a colloquy that reveals the criminal origin of that fistful of coins and Tito's essentially corrupt nature.

Granted access to its protagonist's interiority, the narrator revels in it. Backtracking from the earlier assertion of the possible meaninglessness of Tito's serene exterior, the narrator now assures us that Tito harbors a "guilty secret," "guilty wishes," "inward shame" (the last phrase is repeated twice)— and recommends "the purifying influence of public confession" as a curative

(100–101). The almost salacious emphasis here suggests that the guilty content of Tito's interiority has been produced as punishment for the presumption of having shielded that interiority from the narrator's epistemological access. The arc traced in these few pages—from Tito's sensing that he is the object of perusal to his abject surrender to psychic penetration—establishes in miniature *Romola*'s conception of subjectivity as a series of repeated dramas of occlusion and disclosure. The narrative now offers the reader insight into every "strange complication in [Tito's] mental state" (134), even as it continues to produce figures of observation within the diegesis who stand as surrogates for that narrative proximity. "Tito had become aware," we later read, "that there was some one not far off him by whom he very much desired not to be recognised" (193). And again: "he had an uncomfortable undercurrent of consciousness which told him that Tessa had seen him and would certainly follow him . . . the sense that Tessa was behind him, though he had no physical evidence of the fact, grew stronger and stronger" (194).

The frequency with which Tito feels himself watched exceeds even the demands of a verisimilar depiction of spy-ridden Renaissance Florence: the elevated sense of cloak-and-daggery, though in each case explicable by the presence of some actual onlooker, appears finally to refer to Tito's status as a novelistic protagonist—as someone, that is, who is always watched by a multitude of readers. "There would be *no witness by*," Tito later tells himself as he anticipates contracting a false marriage with the peasant girl Tessa (305). He is correct, in a strict sense: none of the novel's important characters observes his betrayal of this simple-minded young woman. But he is also deluded: the narrative—and readerly—proximity to his interiority means that even when he is alone Tito is attended by what the narrator elsewhere calls (citing Hebrews) a whole "cloud of witnesses" (436). The paranoid world of Florentine politics in this sense functions as an objective correlative to the heightened specularity of novelistic existence, in which involuntary self-disclosure is normal and compulsory. "Tito winced under his new liability to disesteem" (477), we read later when Tito deserts the Medicean party and has to deal with his former friends' awareness of his political opportunism. But there is nothing new about this state—and not just because this is Tito's umpteenth betrayal of someone or other. Novelistic character as Eliot understands it is virtually defined by this liability to disesteem. What distinguishes Tito in Eliot's work is less his thoroughgoing evil than the fact that he suffers so visibly from a condition afflicting all his fictional peers.

If only by virtue of his status as a real historical figure, Savonarola would seem to offer more resistance to narratorial oversight. And, in fact, the issue with which Eliot initially links Savonarola is not duplicity but demagoguery: long before granting her reader access to Savonarola's interior struggles, Eliot repeatedly frames him at the head of a threatening crowd. As the novel opens, we learn that Lorenzo de Medici's death has provoked republican fantasies, and the city is rife with "the murmured desire for government on a broader basis" (84). Eliot consistently yokes Savonarola narratively and imagistically with the Florentine populace's bid for political clout. In her first extended description of Savonarola's oratorical powers, Eliot remarks on the size—and the socially mixed nature—of his audience with the same compulsive repetitiveness she brought to bear on Tito's guilty conscience. The Frate, Eliot writes, speaks to a "vast multitude of warm, living faces," and a few lines later she repeats that the "multitude was of all ranks" (225). When Savonarola dissolves into stagey sobs, the "multitude . . . vibrate[s]" in responsive excitement (230), and, as if in explanation of this overwrought emotionalism, Eliot again specifies that on this occasion "the Frate's audience, always multifarious, had represented even more completely than usual the various classes and political parties of Florence" (232). Eliot's association of Savonarola with expanded political representation clearly resonates with the Victorian agitation for the extended franchise that was contemporary with the book's writing: "There was a force outside the palace which was gradually tending to give the vague desires of that majority the character of a determinate will," Eliot later writes. "That force was the preaching of Savonarola" (313).

This linkage of Savonarola to majority rule makes it all the more surprising that the crime for which the novel ultimately condemns him is not political agitation but hypocrisy. Chapter 64 finds Savonarola "kneeling in audible prayer" in search of divine guidance about his upcoming trial by fire. But "he had ceased to hear the words on his lips. They were drowned by argumentative voices within him that shaped their reasons more and more for an outward audience" (524). As a number of critics have noted, Eliot thus psychologizes Savonarola's orientation toward the assembled multitude.[15] More precisely, she makes that orientation the basis of his psychological plausibility as a realistic—which is to say internally conflicted—character. "The doubleness which is the pressing temptation in every public career, whether of priest, orator, or statesman, was more strongly defined in Savonarola's consciousness as the acting of a part, than at any other period in his life" (532), Eliot writes in the next chapter as the Frate prepares to submit to the flames. Savonarola is spared the melodramatic trial by fire by a downpour, but not before having surrendered, like Tito before him, to psychic oversight by the narrator. What Savonarola loses in remote greatness, he gains in novelistic depth. Now that we finally have access to "that dissidence between inward reality and outward seeming" (525), Savonarola begins to enjoy that eminently novelistic privilege: he becomes convincing. Tito, of course, has been so all along, in accordance with a dictum Eliot's narrator offers elsewhere in the novel: "It is easy to believe in the damnable state of a man who stands stripped and degraded" (578).[16]

The convergence between the fates of Eliot's two central characters is made startlingly clear in the narrative chiasmus that structures their deaths.

Although the novel begins by prescribing for Tito a purgative confession, he is never permitted this outlet. His death is caused by a raging mob with no interest in whatever Tito may want to get off his chest: Eliot describes a "crowd pouring from the bridge" that identifies Tito, contradictorily, as belonging to each of the city's rival factions ("Piagnone! Medicean! Piagnone!") before resolving to "throw him over the bridge!" (545). And while Tito thus seems to be murdered by the crowd that Savonarola has riled up, the confession prescribed for Tito is weirdly extracted from Savonarola: "Not long after [Tito's death]," Eliot writes, "Savonarola was being tortured, and crying out in his agony, 'I will confess!'" (548). This confession signals Savonarola's final submission to the interpretive regime of the psychological novel. Through it he ends up where Tito begins, an object of readerly scrutiny: toward the end of the novel we read of Romola's "long meditations over that printed document" (571) as she tries to distinguish what is coerced in the confession from what is sincere. But in the regime of moralized visibility the novel has elaborated, this is a distinction without a difference. Eliot concludes her narration of Savonarola's death by asserting that "justice is like the Kingdom of God—it is not without us as a fact, it is within us as a great yearning" (549). This is, to say the least, a counterintuitive conclusion to draw from *Romola*, given that Eliot's two central characters have just succumbed to "justice" of the most violently external kind.[17] The statement comes alarmingly close to aligning Eliot's providential narrative with a lynch mob, on the one hand, and with state torture on the other. Even more brazen, it locates the blame for this violence in the "within" of her characters. The conclusion is hard to avoid that Tito and Savonarola have been killed for their resistance to novelistic intelligibility.[18]

Despite the wide difference in their temperaments, each makes that resistance under the sign of the theater. Tito has been associated with performance from his first appearance in the novel, when a Florentine woman responds to his good looks and what the narrator describes as his "glance provokingly free from alarm" by proclaiming him "a minstrel or a mountebank" (26). Savonarola, meanwhile, does not only work the crowd with histrionic precision but is also a consummate engineer of stage effect: with the Bonfire of the Vanities he creates "a scene of so new and striking a sort" that it marks "an epoch in carnival keeping," a "new Carnival, which was a sort of sacred parody of the old" (417–419). Thus even before they exchange fates at their deaths Eliot's two protagonists are linked, and their crimes rendered equivalent, through the figure of theater. In conflating the hypocrite and the politician, theatricality thus allows Eliot to posit a connection between two activities that might seem to have nothing to do with each other: pretending and assembling. This yoking is particularly striking in the peasant fair during which Tito contracts his false marriage to Tessa. Eliot explicitly depicts this as a scene of theater, a "mimic ceremony" officiated by a "conjurer" whose "sham Episcopal costume" and "altar-like table" produce a "sufficiently near parody of sacred things to rouse poor little Tessa's veneration" (149, 148). But perhaps the strangest thing about the scene is that it seems motivated less by Tito's duplicity than by the popular assemblage that almost upstages it in Eliot's narration. The chapter opens with an image of "the moving crowd" in the piazza and a description of Tito's "pleasure in the hooting and elbowing" that engulfs him (137). He leaves the "hellish hubbub" of the square to enter the church of the Nunziata, only to be confronted inside by a second crowd, a "multitude" composed, like Savonarola's public, of both "coarse bronzed" peasants and "the softer-lined faces" of the better-off (144). And, as if in response to the unsettling vision of social mingling, this crowd is surreally doubled by yet "another multitude . . . spreading high and far over the walls and ceiling" (144). The fantastic image has a rational explanation: "It was a crowd of votive waxen images, the effigies of great personages, clothed in their habit as they lived" (144). In this phantom crowd of mannequins, the human gathering appears spontaneously to secrete a material emblem of its socially multifarious nature.

The imagistic alchemy of this scene rewrites social mixture quite literally as doubleness; the assembled social body emerges as inherently duplicitous. When Tito shortly after performs his most cynical action—partaking in the rudimentary marriage ceremony that makes him a bigamist—he is only conforming to the logic of doubling just modeled by the crowd he has been watching. In suggesting that the crowd does not merely embody duplicity but also compels it, the scene prefigures the narrative's assimilation of Tito and Savonarola: the Frate, too, is led into doubleness by the pressure of the assembled crowd. Democratic excess thus characterizes Eliot's two male leads in the most intimate sense. Indeed, democracy and hypocrisy become mutually implicated in a dizzying relay that makes distinctions of form and content difficult to maintain: mass assembly appears as the structuring formal precondition for the hypocritical content of these men's being, even as the "argumentative voices" of the public seem the natural content of that interiority.

That theatricality in *Romola* provides the figural frame whereby assembly becomes a problem of duplicity makes it all the more noteworthy that Eliot's next project involved not the vilification of the idea of theater but a serious approach to the reality of it: she tried to write a play. In embarking on *The Spanish Gypsy* she undertook a major work whose form would resist the moralized narratorial access to interior space on which *Romola*'s depiction of democratic excess depends. If Eliot's initial effort at writing in this unfamiliar form was attended by intense mental anguish, her correspondence reveals a strange resonance between the formal problem she has tackled and the figures she employs to discuss her distress. A letter written on 19 February 1865 to Maria Congreve complained of a tiresome party: "I turn my inward shudders into outward smiles, and talk fast with a sense of lead on my tongue" (*L*, 178). Two days later Lewes insisted that she abandon work on *The Spanish Gypsy*, but on the 27th Eliot reported to Mrs. Congreve that she is still struggling not to "diffuse my inward trouble" (*L*, 179). Shortly afterward Eliot wrote to apologize for her foul mood during a recent visit: "When one is bilious, other people's complexions look yellow, and one of their eyes higher than the other—all the fault of one's own evil interior" (*L*, 182). These descriptions of Eliot's "deep depression" (*L*, 184) are also reports on her creative frustration; we have seen that her journals from this period ascribe her anxiety to an inability to make progress on *The Spanish Gypsy*. The consistent references to Eliot's own moralized interior space suggest a kind of rebound between her mood and the form in which she works—as if, denied access to the interior of a demonized character, she herself begins to inhabit what she had labeled in *Romola* the "dissidence between inward reality and outward seeming." Even after she has abandoned work on her drama, she suffers from an exacerbated sense of her own interiority—a variety of psychic pain it is not too fanciful to call Tito's revenge.

Perhaps unsurprisingly, it is a return to the novel that assuages this pain. Lewes's journals indicate that shortly after Eliot began work on *Felix Holt* she felt well enough to go into their garden, where she avidly discussed "psychological problems" and her new novel (*L,* 194).[19] If Eliot's descriptions of the first effort at *The Spanish Gypsy* suggest that the lack of narrative access to characters' interiority informed her descriptions of her mental suffering, the opening chapters of *Felix Holt* indicate that the cure for this condition was an emphasis on "evil interiors" even more strident than that structuring *Romola*. *Felix Holt* opens with a veritable orgy of inwardness. The novel no sooner introduces the proud provincial widow Mrs. Transome than it informs the reader of her "sharp inward struggle" and makes us privy to the visions she is "inwardly seeing."[20] Where *Romola*'s secretive characters submit gradually to psychic display, Mrs. Transome's surrender is total and speedy. Unpleasant information that in the earlier novel would have merited a drama of revelation is here perfunctorily unveiled: for example, we learn almost casually that Mrs. Transome was seized years ago by the "desire that her first, rickety, ugly, imbecile child should die, and leave room for her darling" (23). And although the narrator withholds the details of her secret sin for a few chapters, the early announcement that "sensibility and dread . . . lay screened behind all her petty habits and narrow notions, as some quivering thing with eyes and throbbing heart may lie crouching behind withered rubbish" (31) makes Mrs. Transome's adultery, when it is specified, feel oddly inadequate to the hyperbolic imagery. As E. S. Dallas put it in his review of the novel, Mrs. Transome's secret fairly "oozes out" of her.[21] Her legibility as a character with something to hide overshadows whatever it may be that she's keeping under wraps.

Mrs. Transome may be the novel's most abjectly readable character, but she is far from unrepresentative. Jermyn is "inwardly irritated" (41); Harold is at first "inwardly amused" (43), but as he finds himself increasingly subject to "inward argument" (219) and "inward debate" (338) he becomes "inwardly vexed" (365); Christian "inwardly" determines to cut short a conversation (342); Mr. Lyon is "inwardly torn by doubt and anxiety" over whether to reveal Esther's parentage (169); and Esther herself, most protractedly, suffers from "an inward strain" (260) and "inward flutter" (222), painful intrusions on "her inward vision" (447) and "inward incommunicable debate" (428). The word is a favorite of Eliot's throughout her work. But its abrasive repetition in *Felix Holt* makes the novel a startlingly thorough—even gloating—assertion of penetrative power on the part of Eliot's narrator. So insistent is this declaration that it is hard not to suspect that it represents Eliot's relief at her escape from the resistant medium of the drama. The only character partially to elude this pandemic of exposed secrecy is the strangely inert Felix Holt himself. But his lack of psychic depth makes him uniquely suited to serve as a spokesperson for inwardness. It is an inward revolution he recommends as an alternative to electoral reform when he addresses an assembled crowd at the novel's midpoint: "all the schemes about voting, and districts, and annual Parliaments, and the rest, are engines," he speechifies, "and the water or steam—the force that is to work them—must come out of human nature—out of men's passions, feelings, desires" (293). By connecting Felix's strange brand of "radicalism" to the narrator's obsessive inward gaze, the speech makes clear the political implications of the novel's narrative mode. In making his case that an inward transformation take the place of outward agitation, Felix speaks to a character population well prepared to accept his teaching. Tenderized to within an inch of their psychic lives by the constant analysis of their interior states, the denizens of *Felix Holt* model precisely the attention to the inward for which Felix proselytizes. *Felix Holt* thus inverts the relation between democracy and interiority proposed by *Romola*: where the earlier novel posited the two as inevitably corrupt versions of each other, here interiority has become an alternative to democracy. Interiority in *Romola* functions as a reflection of the crowd's nightmarish duplicity; in *Felix Holt* inwardness functions as crowd control.

The ideological nature of the novel's linkage of interiority and mass agitation becomes most visible in the climactic trial scene. This is the second major public gathering in the novel—the first being the election riot that has resulted in the death of an innocent man of which Felix now stands accused. If the earlier scene demonstrates the danger of the mob undisciplined by inward restraint, the trial scene rectifies that danger by convening a public for a display of interiority. "His nature is very noble," Esther testifies on Felix's behalf. "He is tender-hearted; he could never have had any intention that was not brave and good" (449). The narrator's comment that Esther sounds as if she is "making a confession of faith" (448) confirms that it is *her* inwardness that is put to use here; Esther vouches for Felix's relatively opaque interiority by advertising her own. The novel indulges a strangely naïve faith in the effectiveness of this display, as Esther's self-revelation releases enough energy to move the legal apparatus marshaled against Felix, and to override the substantial evidence for his guilt. *Felix Holt* thus concludes with a startling profession of belief in the power of interiority to have external force in the world.

But the novel also thereby involves itself in a clear contradiction: Esther's "inward revolution" (464) must become outwardly legible in order to take narrative effect. The disavowed theatricality of the trial scene has been well described by J. Jeffrey Franklin, who notes the irony in Eliot's turn to the "inherently theatrical" trial to validate her novel's insistence on inwardness.[22] "What is on trial in Felix's trial," Franklin writes, "is the efficacy of interiority, the form of the novel itself" (101). Esther's testimonial to Felix's goodness makes her into a characterological embodiment of that character-witnessing constantly performed by Eliot's narration. But is the scene as efficacious as Franklin goes on to suggest? "Felix and Esther live happily ever after in the model nuclear family," he writes, "and the reader, if successfully constructed, loves it" (103). The sarcasm of this summary implies that Franklin at least has escaped interpellation by the novel's showy recommendation of inwardness and its corresponding denigration of democratic politics. And in fact, this is the most reviled conclusion in Eliot's fiction: critics have labeled it "romantic," "perfunctory," "politically crude," "petty," "cynical," and "absurd."[23] If the trial scene gives voice to the Arnoldian fantasy of culture's performative force, these responses suggest that it also inadvertently reveals the pathos of that fantasy along with the politically repressive ideology motivating it.

Eliot's immediate return to *The Spanish Gypsy* suggests that the solution of *Felix Holt* was not satisfactory to her either. This alone should make us take note of what usually remains an invisible moment in critical accounts of Eliot's career. If *Romola* and *Felix Holt* represent Eliot's experimentation with the ethical consequences of a narrative focus on inwardness, this experiment resulted in the suggestion that the crowd is a dangerous social body that will invade the space of interiority unless it is controlled *by* the space of interiority. The novels make this case by setting individual consciousness—the novel of interiority's proper object of attention—against demonized scenes of theatrical assembly. But in going back to *The Spanish Gypsy* Eliot was returning not to a narrated theater but to an attempted one. The distinction has major consequences for the ideological possibilities explored in the text. Although *The Spanish Gypsy* made its way into the world as a printed poem, not a performed play, Eliot left the traces of her book's theatrical intention troublingly evident in the final text. In doing so, she created a theater that cannot be disciplined or expunged—precisely because it haunts the text as its referent and intention. In *The Spanish Gypsy* Eliot disciplines not the theater but the obsession with interiority entailed in the theatrical thematics of *Romola* and *Felix Holt*. And where *Felix Holt* created an equality among its characters in submitting them to a universal narrative surveillance, *The Spanish Gypsy*'s formal peculiarity points toward a democracy ordered on very different principles.

The Spanish Gypsy's Universal Theater

The Spanish Gypsy introduces its heroine in a scene of public assembly. Book 1 opens in 1492 in Bedmár, a fortress town in southern Spain a few miles from the Moorish border and a crucial outpost of the Catholic reconquest effort. As a group of minstrels plays to the crowd in the central square, Eliot lays on the southern trappings: peasant maidens, gamboling infants, the "breath of flowers and aromatic leaves," "recumbent dogs," and youths with "large lazy eyes."[24] Meanwhile, the music "knits the crowd / Into one family" (I.1147–1148); the "wingéd sounds exalt the thick-pressed crowd / With a new pulse in common, blending all / The gazing life into one larger soul / With dimly widened consciousness" (I.1221–1224); "vibrations sympathetic stir all limbs" (I.1282). Shared pulsations, sympathetic vibrations, widened consciousness: Eliot's trademark concerns are perceptible even through the aromatic breezes of the Plaça Santiago. If this scene of assembly escapes the demonization of crowds otherwise constant in Eliot's imagination, it appears that the southern setting allows for the exemption; this idealized image of Eliotian community is authorized by exoticist kitsch. The arrival of the lady Fedalma confirms this impression. "Lithe" and "saffron-robed" (I.1305) on the eve of her wedding to the handsome Count Silva, Fedalma erupts from this gathering as its spontaneous embodiment. "Swayed by impulse passionate" (I.1315), she begins to move to the music. The crowd is enchanted, and one can imagine that Eliot anticipated the same reaction among London theatergoers when she conceived this set-piece for her Spanish play.

This vision—every detail of which signifies The South—could easily be aligned with the nineteenth-century tradition of exoticist spectacle that Edward Ziter describes as a co-partner with anthropology and ethnology in constituting "the modern British colonial imaginary."[25] In Ziter's account (which focuses on representations of the Orient), the exoticist drama depends on the legibility of the performance space. For all its sensual grandeur, exotic spectacle was overwhelmingly *meaningful*; the detailed, intensely researched mise-en-scène of orientalist productions, Ziter claims, trained "Europeans to interpret the surface of objects and people as manifestations of internal laws and organic processes" of alien societies (3). Eliot may have hoped to capitalize on the vogue for exotic spectacle when she invented her tale of Moors, Jews, Catholics, and gypsies dueling, dancing, and serenading under southern skies. But conventional as the scenographic imagination informing this opening dance may be, it is also atypical in Eliot's work: the primitivist setting licenses not only a collective gathering but a frank pleasure in a performance where auto- and alloeroticism are hopelessly entangled. While feminine self-display in Eliot's work is almost always the precursor to self-correction, Fedalma's dance comes with no such self-canceling moral tag.

> Swifter now she moves,
> Filling the measure with a double beat
> And widening circle; now she seems to glow
> With more declaréd presence, glorified.
> Circling, she lightly bends and lifts on high
> The multitudinous-sounding tambourine,
> And makes it ring and boom, then lifts it higher
> Stretching her left arm beauteous; now the crowd
> Exultant shouts, forgetting poverty
> In the rich moment of possessing her. (I.1414–1423)

This is a startlingly eroticized image of public self-display without the alibi of interiority, and it is the only such moment in Eliot's work that goes narratively unpunished.[26] Where Tito's pleasure in being traversed by the crowd signaled his psychic duplicity, for example, Eliot's agnosticism about the contours of Fedalma's interiority permits the passage to float free of the narrator's intrusive moralizing. Despite the passage's "epic," or narrative, form, then, Eliot abides here by the exteriorized gaze inherent in her original theatrical conception. In crucial respects Eliot's depiction of Fedalma's dance recalls Lewes's discussion of Spanish theatrical characters in his 1846 book *The Spanish Drama: Lope de Vega and Calderon*.[27] Lewes sketches a familiar opposition between the sensual southerner and the intellectual northerner as a contrast between performative and novelistic conceptions of subjectivity: "Nowhere throughout the Spanish drama can you find a character," he writes. "If you remember any person in these dramas, it is by what he *did*, and not what he *felt*; because the difference is only in the actions, not in individualities."[28] For Lewes, the "Spanish" emphasis on action drains interest from interiority; similarly, Eliot's poem scrambles any coherent psychological account of Fedalma's dance. The scene is notable for its consistent recourse to images of depersonalization. The "dimly widened consciousness" (I.1224), for example, is attributed not to Fedalma but to the crowd surrounding her, while other images seem designed to blur our sense of their psychological referent: when we are told that "the spirit in [Fedalma's] gravely glowing face / With sweet community informs her limbs" (I.1330-1331), the play on "community" suggests at once that Fedalma's limbs move in graceful coordination and that those limbs are instinct with the collectivity for which she dances.

A little later Eliot accounts for Fedalma's passion in a passage whose main effect is a dispersal of agency:

> The exquisite hour, the ardour of the crowd,
> The strains more plenteous, and the gathering might
> Of action passionate where no effort is,
> But self's poor gates open to rushing power
> That blends the inward ebb and outward vast—
> All gathering influences culminate
> And urge Fedalma. (I.1406–1412)

The grammatical structure of the sentence strung across these lines indicates Fedalma as the passive object of a list of "gathering influences"—and yet those influences also figure the crowd's loss of psychic boundaries and volitional control: the abstract "self" whose "gates" stand conquered by an equally abstract "power" might belong to the spectators as much as to Fedalma; the decentered "action passionate where no effort is" could accommodate either Fedalma's spontaneous dance or the crowd's instinctive appreciation of it; and the "blend" of "inward ebb and outward vast"—itself a figure for the nondifferentiation of person and context—dizzyingly refuses to clarify whose inwardness is under discussion. Although it would be possible to assign these affects either to Fedalma or to the crowd, the passage keeps both possibilities in ambient play. If it is easy to perceive the exoticism that denies interiority to hot-blooded southerners, it is crucial also to acknowledge the psychic and ethical possibilities allowed by that exoticism. Eliot's sentimental vision of peasant *Gemeinschaft* permits her to envision a working-class collectivity outside the purview of novelistic interiority—a collectivity convened around the ecstatic image of a solitary woman in a city square.

Moreover, this exteriorized perspective has disruptive consequences for the moment of "racial" recognition that this scene goes on to recount. Fedalma's dance is interrupted by the arrival of a procession of gypsy prisoners being led away in chains by their Spanish captors. At their head is Zarca, the man she will soon learn is her father and at whose behest she will abandon her Spanish fiancé to join the gypsy fight against Catholic oppression. If the most striking feature of Fedalma's dance is its refusal of the moralizing and individualizing energies such scenes customarily catalyze in Eliot's fiction, something similar occurs with the logic of racial recognition: the performative orientation of the text disperses the location of racial identity that we typically think of as inhering in individual persons. Eliot hangs back from specifying the racial fellow-feeling that presumably draws Fedalma, instead employing a figure that displaces the psychological recognition onto the scene in general. As Fedalma stares at the gypsies in the stillness heralded by the chiming church bell, Eliot imputes a "thought" to the bell itself: "the great bell's hidden thought / Now first unveiled—the sorrows unredeemed / Of races outcast, scorned, and wandering. / Why does he look at her? why she at him?" (I.1466–1470).

Who, we might ask, wants to know? Eliot relates the scene in a narrative mode; indeed, the questions take the grammatical form of the free indirect discourse Eliot practiced so expertly and which in most circumstances augments the effect of characterological coherence.[29] But Eliot here makes free indirect discourse the vehicle of an uncanny psychic mobility, refraining from the interior penetration that mode makes possible in favor of an externalized perspective that refers the question out to an undefined body of spectators. If free indirect discourse typically limns the contours of the psychic interior, these sentences achieve a quite distinct spatialization—a projection outward onto an implicitly performative frame. The result is that the "racial" consciousness at issue here veers away from either of the scene's two central characters: far from specifying the content of the charged connection between Fedalma and the man she will shortly know as her father, the externalized perspective achieves a proto-Brechtian abstraction that puts the nature of that connection in question.[30] Indeed, although this is identifiable as a scene of recognition, it is not at all clear that it is Fedalma who is doing the recognizing, or that what is being recognized is her "racial" connection to the chained gypsy chief. The consciousness in play here is better described as pertaining to the scene itself than to its players: the "thought" belongs to the bell that punctuates the tableau rather than to the psychologically opaque beings who inhabit it. While the poem's narrative momentum encourages the sense that Fedalma undergoes some revelation here, the externalizing thrust of the poem's rhetoric suggests that this is less Fedalma's revelation that she *is* a gypsy than that she *must identify* with their collectivity. To put it this way is to highlight what the poem's critics, early and late, have noted: *The Spanish Gypsy* is psychologically incoherent. William Dean Howells observed that Fedalma's "sudden sympathies" with gypsydom suffer from an "insufficiency of motive," and the complaint remains the same more than a century later when Sylvia Kasey Marks faults the poem's "lack of psychological character development."[31] At the root of both comments may be a more radical confusion: the poem is not merely psychologically unconvincing but actively frustrates the sense that it is populated by coherent and discrete psychological beings.

To ascribe Fedalma's impulse to join the gypsies to the "thought" of a church bell, after all, is potentially to universalize that impulse: there is no reason why the others in the square might not feel themselves addressed by the bell's appeal. And although at the level of plot this does not happen (*The Spanish Gypsy* narrates the apparent inevitability of racial distinction), a decidedly cosmopolitan group of characters does in fact play a central role in the text's introduction, as if to keep before the reader the possibilities that the plot will not encompass. The group of minstrels led by the singer Juan performs the musical accompaniment to Fedalma's dance scene. Although it provides the music cementing this scene of ethnic definition, the group itself is notably hybrid—clearly an anomaly in a fifteenth-century Spain undergoing ethnic cleansing at the hands of the Inquisition. Just as striking, Eliot indicates a close relation between the dramatic orientation of the text and its ability to do justice to that hybridity. She introduces these characters in the poem's first, "epic," stanzas of Book I. In addition to "JUAN there, the spare man with the lute" (I.288), we also meet "MINE HOST" (I.235), a Jew named Lorenzo who has strategically converted to Christianity in order to ply his trade as an innkeeper. The next introduced is "BLASCO . . . a prosperous silversmith from Aragon" who is said to be "as solemn as [Lorenzo's] dog" (I.279–281). Beside him is "the silent ROLDAN," a glum jester whose lined face Eliot compares to that of a servile butler prematurely aged by his "hard industry in apishness" (I.339, 355). His lame son "little PABLO has his spangles too, / And large rosettes to hide his poor left foot / Rounded like any hoof" (I.376–378). Eliot has introduced this catalogue with the strange remark that "the souls are five, the talkers only three" (I.232). Not unlike Gertrude Stein's four saints uncomfortably parceled out among only three acts, Eliot's words suggest a foundational inadequation of textual structure to human unit: quite literally, not everyone will get his "say" in a world so ordered.

In fact, the relation between text and subjectivity is even stranger than this line suggests. Eliot seems to have reached the end of her list when she suddenly prevaricates: "I said the souls were five—besides the dog. / But there was still a sixth" (I.380–381). The qualification here about the dog's possible claim to a soul may seem only an offhand joke. But the sixth "soul" Eliot goes on to describe puts this in doubt:

> But there was still a sixth, with wrinkled face,
> Grave and disgusted with all merriment
> Not less than Roldan. It is ANNIBAL,
> The experienced monkey who performs the tricks,
> Jumps through the hoops, and carries round the hat. (I.381–385)

Eliot goes on to give the "experienced monkey" nearly thirty lines of characterization—far more than most of his comrades in the minstrel troupe. On several occasions later in the text Eliot will go on to impute mental deliberation to Annibal, describing him as "cautiously neutral" (I.772) during a heated conversation between his human acquaintances or as "morose / In private character" (II.443–444). And in a scene in which Annibal finds himself present at a conversation between Don Silva and the Jewish astrologer Sephardo, we read in a stage direction that the monkey, "*having waked up in alarm, shuts his eyes quickly again and pretends to sleep*" (s.d., 145). The perplexing quality of the attention lavished on this animal is heightened by Eliot's assurance that Annibal is "a serious ape whom none take seriously" (I.404). What, aside from the labored drollery it affords, accounts for Eliot's attribution of higher linguistic comprehension and deliberative rationality to a monkey?

Unusual as it seems, the vehemence of Annibal's humanization recalls many other moments in Eliot's work, which consistently uses animals to mark the equivocal boundaries of the human. In *Adam Bede*, the text in which the figure of the animal is perhaps most sustained, we are repeatedly asked to wonder, only half-facetiously, about the opinions that Adam's dog is forming on the ongoing action (*AB*, 129) and about whether the schoolmaster Bartle Massey understands he is using a figure of speech when he refers to his dog as a "woman" (*AB*, 258). With equal and opposite insistence, Eliot signals Hetty Sorrel's shallowness by analogizing her to a "kitten" or a "bright-eyed spaniel" (*AB*, 390, 149). And as if to round out the overlapping logics of animality and humanity, Hetty's dubious claim to full human status is underlined most emphatically by her incuriosity about the lives of animals: when Adam tries to interest her in the mechanics of an ant colony, she replies "indifferently, not caring to know the difficulties of ant-life" (*AB*, 241). Eliot's condemnation of a character for her inability to care about insect sociability may seem absurdly harsh; and of course there are cognitive distinctions among ants, dogs, and apes. But the more important point to take from this thread of images is its implicit argument that the subject with the best claim to inclusion in the category of the human may be she who is least confident about the outer boundaries of that category; the animal is the primary figure by means of which Eliot worries the frame of human community.[32]

Because *The Spanish Gypsy* is mostly concerned not with animals but with a despised ethnic group, Eliot's insistence on the definitional drama around the "person" of Annibal is also a meditation on the ways in which humans are excluded from human collectivity. (It may be helpful to recall here that Adam Bede's dog is named Gyp, a choice suggesting that even in her first novel Eliot's imagination aligned excluded human groups with the claims of the animal). This experiment treads close to the oppressive rhetoric it interrogates, and *The Spanish Gypsy* does not hesitate to take up brutal images of racist dehumanization: the poem's characters compare gypsies to "rats / Or swarming flies, or reptiles of the sea" (I.2751–2752), label them a "tribe / Of human panthers, flame-eyed, lithe-limbed, fierce" (IV.85–86), and claim that Fedalma's "blood / Is as unchristian as the leopard's" (I.1715–1716). But these instances do not so much reiterate these comparisons as interrogate their power to police the boundaries of the human. Annibal's introduction has been prefaced by a prevarication about the conditions of inclusion: Does one "count" simply by virtue of having a soul, or is an articulate account of oneself necessary for participation in the human community? By what criteria do we number those present? What specifically takes us from three to five to six—and why should we stop there? James Buzard has argued that Eliot's fiction "flirts with the idea of a novel in which *every* character might become 'major.'"[33] *The Spanish Gypsy* experiments with the more radical idea of an art form in which those excluded from the human might accede to the status of a character. More precisely, Eliot's inclusion of Annibal not only questions why and whether the "animal" should constitute the limit of the human, but also challenges us to imagine a collectivity that could do justice to the "inhuman" in the human. At the edge of the human community but pressing his claim for inclusion with a weird effectiveness, Annibal represents the ethical pressure exerted by the sheer particularity of those beings who have only their particularity to recommend them. Like the poem of which he is such an odd feature, he implicitly calls for a community modeled on its literally most disconcerting element.[34]

The Spanish Gypsy's hybrid form is crucial in registering this ethical pressure: the idea of the theater, however virtual that theater remains, is central to the effect Eliot cultivates here. In Eliot's fiction the extension of human sympathy paradigmatically takes the form of one interiority recognizing another—one character's painstakingly narrated apprenticeship to the lifelong project of broadening the ambit of her sympathetic attention. But *The Spanish Gypsy* indicates that the drama, precisely because its modal exteriority predisposes it to remain agnostic about interiority, promises to *start* from the possibility of a broadened view of human inclusiveness. What the novel narrates as a gradual process of extension, the drama achieves as if by fiat. The clearest marker of how Eliot's experiment here is related to theatrical form is her typographic decision to represent characters' names using the play-script convention of small-capital letters, a decision that carries an implicitly universalizing tendency. Even when her characters are introduced in narrative passages, the fact that their first appearance is made in small capitals indicates that their "destination" is performance. And any subject so designated, human or otherwise, unequivocally attains the rank of character: he or she will be a member of the company that collectively activates that coming performance. We do not need to wait for Eliot's amused descriptions of ANNIBAL's personality to understand that he is in some essential way not different in kind from ROLDAN, JUAN, DON SILVA, SEPHARDO, ZARCA, FEDALMA, PABLO, BLASCO and his other colleagues on the virtual stage of *The Spanish Gypsy*. The typographic mark of a theatrical desire, these capitals also insist on depicting these characters as a cast, a collectivity or troupe collaboratively involved in the presentation of the text. A potentially infinite additive logic governs the very look of the text, as if this series might keep accruing members indefinitely.[35] There is moreover a visible ontological flatness to the characters thus introduced—a sameness that cuts across ethnic and even species divisions.

Such a democratizing typographic intention is normally foreign to the novel—where, for example, a minor character can be "disappeared" in a subordinate clause or a passive verb form.[36] Bruce Robbins has shown how servants in literature—often from within such semantic confinement—nonetheless exert a democratizing ethical pressure on the narratives that contain them. Robbins connects servants' frequent function as agents of narrative resolution to the Greek concept of *moira*—a word designating both the concept of fate and that of a share or allotment of resources. For Robbins, the dual nature of *moira* means that the serving classes in realist fiction demand a more equitable distribution of goods even as they work to conclude the novel's plot: the "servant as agent of an archaic fate" also "asserts the ultimate power of the community and presses obscurely toward social inclusiveness."[37] Something similar is at work in the "cast" implicit in Eliot's typographic presentation of characters in *The Spanish Gypsy*. In a theatrical context "cast" is, of course, both a verb denoting the allotment of parts in a play and a noun indicating the collective body of performers created by that allotment. Similar to Robbins's *moira*, "cast" enacts a conceptual pun between the idea of the individual's portion or lot and the ethical pressure toward distribution exerted by the claims of the social whole: just as the share doled out to one character is haunted by the sharing inherent in the collective project as such, the presence of the cast underwrites the casting of lots that determine social hierarchy.

The secret sharing of these two kinds of "cast" illuminates a democratic tendency or demand implicit in theater as a form. Here, too, *The Spanish Gypsy*'s failure to achieve performance is crucial to its ethical dimensions. In an actual staging, the democratic tropism implicit in the collectivity of the theatrical "cast" would be affected by the semiotics of stage management: certain characters are designated to stay in the spotlight, just as others will remain subordinated by the mise-en-scène.[38] But in the textual realm, this democracy reigns as a typographic fact, and as an injunction: the theater *The Spanish Gypsy* convenes is one that posits an ineradicable ontological sameness to "DON SILVA," "ANNIBAL" and "PABLO." The disorienting flatness of the resulting character world was noted by the poem's earliest readers. A *Macmillan's* reviewer objected to what he described as an unsettling similarity among characters one would expect to be differentiated by race, ethnicity and background: "One feels it churlish and ungracious to complain," he complained, "that a Jew astrologer, a gypsy chieftain, a Spanish duke, and a gypsy maiden bred in a Spanish palace, should all habitually manifest moral tempers or mental modes so nearly identical."[39] These characters, the writer implies, seem more like members of a theatrical company who have been trained in a uniform house style than the bearers of distinct personalities and fates. Despite this writer's disdain for *The Spanish Gypsy*, the review provides a subtle account of the ethical possibilities licensed by the text's formal oddity. His words suggest that Eliot's failed play-poem constitutes what Jacques Rancière calls a "theatrocracy," a regime of the perceptible premised on the principle of "the equality of anyone with anyone."[40]

Of course *The Spanish Gypsy*'s nonperformance also means that such equality remains only gestural. This frustrated ambition—the sense of longing, strain, and futility—is perhaps the ultimate meaning of *The Spanish Gypsy*'s formal hybridity. We have seen how Eliot's anxiety over the generic designation of her text—first drama, then poem, always "*not* a novel"—highlighted its distance from an original project of embodiment. In its determination to underline the failure of its performative ambition, the book buttresses Isobel Armstrong's claim that nineteenth-century poets emphasized textuality in order to underline the "overwhelmingly secondary" status of the aesthetic in modernity.[41] But *The Spanish Gypsy* is not reconciled to this situation: having abandoned its performative ambition, the poem insists on retaining a record of it. The pathos of *The Spanish Gypsy* has less to do with its hackneyed star-crossed-lovers plot or its familiar narrative of a sacrifice to duty than with the traces of its will-to-performance—those stage directions that lend it such an insistent, and insistently frustrated, performative texture. In publishing this record of disappointment, Eliot powerfully interrogated the fantasy of culture's efficacy on which cultural producers depend.

During the years of *The Spanish Gypsy*'s composition, Matthew Arnold was elaborating an appeal to culture's potency in the essays collected as *Culture and Anarchy* in 1869; it is clear that Eliot's work of the 1860s is in dialogue with Arnold's program.[42] Arnold's stress in those essays is so consistently on culture's "*inward spiritual activity*" that the question of what concrete "outward" effects culture may have on society appears deferred indefinitely. Yet despite his lack of interest in precisely how culture's power would manifest itself, Arnold insists on this outcome. After defining culture as "a knowledge of the universal order," Arnold urges that "culture [be] considered not merely as the endeavour to *see* and *learn* [this order], but as the endeavour, also, to make it *prevail*." The passage speaks to what we may term Arnold's performative ambition—the desire that culture involve two phases, the first of perception, the other of action.[43] Eliot's poem, in gesturing toward a performance that will not take place, offers a more distressed account of culture's distance from enactment, and a more frank acknowledgment of culture's restricted power. Toward the end of her life, in an essay published posthumously as "Leaves from a Notebook," Eliot referred to *The Spanish Gypsy* to underline precisely this sense of cultural frustration, describing her heroine Fedalma's devotion to the lost cause of her people as embodying a "magnificent futility" and a disdain for "a prudent calculation of results" (*E*, 451). Behind the praise for Fedalma's heroism is audible an agonized suspicion that the script of culture may never be performed—that the proposals offered by the aesthetic realm may "work" no better than *The Spanish Gypsy* itself.

Arnold prescribed a course of study as a remedy to social ills: "knowing and spreading the best which has been reached in the world," he wrote, is "an object not to be gained without books and reading" (109). Eliot's most radical thought experiment in *The Spanish Gypsy*, by stark contrast, is to hypothesize a culture existing beyond the authorizing aegis of the literary. If the poem's bookishness is central to the achievement of its most striking effects, this is a bookishness that aspires to self-cancellation. A distance from the book is in fact a recurrent trope in Eliot's account of *The Spanish Gypsy*'s conception and of the text's image repertoire. The gypsy chieftain Zarca maintains that his people's specificity consists in their vulnerable distance from a legitimating discourse of culture. A people "whom no God took knowledge of / To give them laws," with "no dimmest lore of glorious ancestors" to validate their coming together, the gypsies in his description—unlike the Christians, Jews, and Muslims they live among—are not people of the Book (I.2742, 2746).[44]

Eliot reported that she was inspired to write *The Spanish Gypsy* when she saw a Titian *Annunciation* in Venice. She claimed to find in the angel Gabriel's arrival the inspiration for the story of a woman learning that she has been "chosen to fulfill a great destiny."[45] Eliot's preference for this particular rendering may have to do with an iconographic detail that characterizes Titian's annunciation: Mary is leaning over a book, so that the angel in the picture resembles someone quietly entering a library. In the image of a woman being called away from her reading, Eliot appears to have glimpsed a summons to imagine a collectivity that cannot be brought to book.

Middlemarch, Daniel Deronda, and the Cast of Mind

What happens in Eliot's later career to the collective vision of the dramatic "cast" visible in *The Spanish Gypsy*? One answer is that this interest in theater migrates into metaphor—that Eliot sublimates the theater of collective life into an abstracted drama of consciousness. One of the most famous statements from the novel she began to write while completing *The Spanish Gypsy* suggests the central role such a deliteralization of the theater plays in Eliot's novelistic imagination. Chapter 11 marks the *Middlemarch* narrator's first reflection on the multiple plots she is about to begin interweaving. Tertius Lydgate and Dorothea Brooke have just met, but neither has an inkling of the role they will come to play for each other:

Certainly nothing at present could seem much less important to Lydgate than the turn of Miss Brooke's mind, or to Miss Brooke than the qualities of the woman who had attracted this young surgeon. But any one watching keenly the stealthy convergence of human lots, sees a slow preparation of effects from one life on another, which tells like a calculated irony on the indifference or the frozen stare with which we look at our unintroduced neighbour. Destiny stands by sarcastic with our *dramatis personae* folded in her hand.[46]

Implicitly contrasting "indifference or the frozen stare" with the fullness of responsive attention, the passage offers a virtual definition of Eliot's gospel of sympathy—one that marks that gospel's psychologism and gradualism. The work of the novel is to make visible the "slow preparation of effects" through which lives inhabiting different "lots" from our own become legible to us. Because the passage's emphasis on consciousness, slowness, and small-scale social interaction offers such a clear vision of the novelistic aesthetic, the "*dramatis personae*" invoked here seems less a reference to collective endeavor than a sign of an intensely interiorizing aesthetic agenda. Certainly it has been read this way by Eliot's most insightful critics: George Levine glosses these sentences with the claim that "it is rather easy to see that such a way of understanding relationships must almost inevitably lead *both* to the multiplot novel . . . and the complications of point-of-view narration."[47] For Levine, Eliot's invocation of the drama is so thoroughly metaphorized that it signals the necessity not just of narration but of its most interiorized variety. Nothing could seem further from the collective and depsychologized vision of *The Spanish Gypsy*.

But is the theatrical imagination nevertheless visible in the "stealthy convergence of human lots"? There are a lot of "lots" in *Middlemarch*—by which I mean in the first place that there are a lot of narrative outcomes in *Middlemarch*, many characters' plots to be tied up. But there is also a strangely pronounced emphasis on the word "lot": fifty-two occurrences if we count the plural—more than ten times the frequency of its near synonyms "fate" or "destiny."[48] The large majority of these cases employ the word in the sense we have just seen, as a way to describe the finality of our separation from others: "Scenes which make vital changes in our neighbours' lot are but the background of our own" (326); "no lot could be so cruelly hard as hers" (756), and so on. But a few of these occurrences use the word in the sense of a plurality, as when Alfred Garth laments his sister Mary's plan to work as a governess because it will mean "being among a lot of nincompoop girls" (400) or when the auctioneer Borthrop Trumbull describes a tray of jewels as a "recherchy lot" (606).[49] The sheer frequency of the word's occurrence in the novel sets up a kind of traffic between these meanings similar to those embedded in the dual meanings of the words "share" and "cast" explored above. The lot of lots in *Middlemarch* convey not only the ethical demand to acknowledge our difference from others but a more properly social awareness of the contingency of those differences and of the collective ground of existence.

While for many critics Eliot's work effects the sublimation of the social into the psychological, a notable feature of *Middlemarch*'s most psychologized moments is how populated the psychic interior feels. When Bulstrode's mental anguish reaches a peak late in the novel, we read that his mind was "crowded with images and conjectures" (697), and when Dorothea passes Will in her carriage, Eliot's narrator reports that she feels as if a "crowd of indifferent objects had thrust them asunder" (635). And at the moment Dorothea first allows herself to imagine that she and Will Ladislaw might love each other, she arrives at this suspicion not through an unmediated communion with her private sentiments but via the "revelation that another [i.e., Rosamond] had thought of him in that light"—a revelation Eliot describes as filling Dorothea with a "hurrying, crowding vision" (490). The "crowds" that imagistically press on these characters in their most interiorized crises indicate that an apprehension of sheer social density structures their most intimate psychic experience. It is presumably such passages that Fredric Jameson has in mind in his claim that nineteenth-century realism—and *Middlemarch* in particular—is, contrary to popular report, not introspective: "What was wrongly identified as a self-consciousness or reflexivity of the individual self," he writes, "can on closer inspection be seen to be a minute and microscopic negotiation with the shock and scandal of the Other."[50] The imagistic content of these scenes may indicate an even more radical openness than Jameson specifies here—less an encounter with "the Other" than simply with *others*. Preoccupation with one's lot results in the sense that one is simply one among a lot of others—perhaps an interchangeable one among a lot of others, as Dorothea intuits in the final example above.

That Eliot connects this pluralizing possibility with the theater is clearest in the novel's flashback to Lydgate's romance with the actress Mme Laure. The episode is notorious for its presentation of theatrical performance as a black box of agency. Acting a murder scene, Laure does the deed for real, stabbing her husband and co-star in the presence of the assembled spectators; her confession to Lydgate is incoherent, claiming both that her "foot really slipped" and that she *"meant to do it"* (153). But Lygdate's reaction focuses less on the epistemological conundrum these words attribute to the theatrical apparatus than on the sense that his relation to her has been deprivatized and rendered common: "He saw this woman—the first to whom he had given his young adoration—amid the throng of stupid criminals" (153). In conjoining the theatrical mise-en-scène to a vision of leveling collectivization, the moment makes thematically explicit the pattern we have already identified at a semantic level: the crowds, lots, and throngs pressing on these characters suggest that even in the psychologized world of

Middlemarch the metaphor of the "dramatis personae" is always poised to reliteralize itself—that a sense of collective plenitude is always ready to reassert itself as the phenomenological ground of the fictive world. We might think of *Middlemarch*'s strange insistence on these collectives as a trace of the throngs on the Plaça Santiago, a sign that Eliot's most supremely psychologized fiction retains an afterimage of *The Spanish Gypsy*'s vision of collective assembly.[51]

If in *Middlemarch* the collective is mostly detectable at the level of such verbal or imagistic echoes, in Eliot's final novel the theatrical haunting of psychic space moves into stark thematic focus. Of the novels that followed *The Spanish Gypsy*, *Daniel Deronda* most explicitly takes up the concerns of Eliot's failed foray into the drama. The plots of the two texts are clearly related: each recounts a protagonist's awakening to an affiliation with oppressed outsiders; each explores the rights of racial "others" in a world where ethnos and nation are supposed to be aligned; each concludes with a call to found an ethnic nation for the marginalized group at its center.[52] But perhaps the most striking resonance between them is the way *The Spanish Gypsy*'s gesturing toward a universal theater persists in the later book. It has been widely noted that *Daniel Deronda* is awash in theatrical imagery and themes, but at first glance it appears that the novel engages theatricality in order to denigrate it in favor of the inward gaze.[53] The novel opens with a minatory epigraph whose stress on interiority could not be more emphatic. The hyperbolic insistence of these words is the first indication that the novel's inner space is under peculiar stress:

> Let thy chief terror be of thine own soul;
> There, 'mid the throng of hurrying desires
> That trample on the dead to seize their spoil,
> Lurks vengeance. [54]

Gwendolen Harleth is the clearest referent for the epigraph, the last in Eliot's series of performative protagonists whose fate is to be redeemed into novelistic depth. The instrument of Gwendolen's redemption is Daniel himself; his protracted tutelage of Gwendolen is easy to read as an allegory of the theater being disciplined into contrition by the novel. The first paragraph of the novel sets the terms of this allegory.[55] Gwendolen is seated at a gambling table in the fictional German city of Leubronn, and the text immediately presents her as an interpretive problem: "Was she beautiful or not beautiful? and what was the secret of form or expression which gave the dynamic quality to her glance? Was the good or the evil genius dominant in those beams?" (7). Read literally, the opening question in fact offers little to ponder: we quickly learn that there is no doubt about Gwendolen's physical attractiveness. But of course the question is better read as pertaining not to Gwendolen's observable body but to her invisible soul; the straightforward query demands to be translated into its moral equivalent: Was she beautiful *inside*? Here, though, the interiorizing agenda encounters static. In addressing a series of questions to an enigmatic spectacle, Eliot's words recall those narrating Fedalma's encounter with the gypsy chieftain in *The Spanish Gypsy*: "Why does he look at her? why she at him?" (I.1469). The resonance between the two moments is instructive; as we saw, the earlier lines depersonalized Eliot's free indirect discourse, so that the psychic origin of the question became impossible to locate. Similarly, the opening sentences of *Daniel Deronda* only arrive at their characterological source after a perceptible delay: by the first sentence of the next paragraph we learn that these inquires are transpiring "in Daniel Deronda's mind" (7), but in briefly withholding that information, the lines introduce a stutter into the machinery of the interiorizing imagination.[56]

If these opening paragraphs achieve a psychological coherence— interested man watches interesting woman—it is a decidedly tenuous one. Moreover, that coherence looks ever less secure as Eliot colors in the surroundings to this scene of psychic attention. "About this table fifty or sixty persons were assembled, many in the outer rows, where there was occasionally a deposit of new comers, being mere spectators, only that one of them, usually a woman, might now and then be observed putting down a five-franc piece with a simpering air, just to see what the passion of gambling really was" (8). The sentence's syntax obeys the same accretive dynamic as the collective under description: one clause is stacked improbably onto another just as the crowd of "fifty" becomes "sixty," and the sentence goes on to absorb "a deposit of new comers" before swelling one final time to accommodate the hypothetical person, "usually a woman," whom we might witness on the edges of the action. If this expansive grammar conveys the sense of a narration constantly extending its ambit of attention, the sentence immediately following redescribes this logic of promiscuity in terms of social categories. "Those who were taking their pleasure in a higher strength, and were absorbed in play," Eliot writes, "showed very distant varieties of European type: Livonian and Spanish, Graeco-Italian and miscellaneous German, English aristocratic and English plebeian" (8). Like *The Spanish Gypsy*'s minstrel troupe, this catalogue seems as if it could go on forever. And as in that catalogue, the qualitative differences among the items are subordinated to the quantitative logic that assembles them: nationalities are mixed with ethnicities, language groups interspersed with subnational descriptors, one nation (but not the others) subdivided by class.

The tonal ambiguity of the dry comment that punctuates this catalogue —"Here certainly was a striking admission of human equality" (8)—is augmented by the uncertainty around focalization we have noted: Is this a narrator's flat description, Daniel's sardonic observation, or some ironizing compromise between them? The scene's blurred psychic boundaries find an analogue in its corporeal confusions. As the paragraph continues, body parts become verbally dissociated from discrete persons: "The white bejeweled fingers of an English countess were very near touching a bony, yellow, crab-like hand stretching a bared wrist to clutch a heap of coin" (8). The nightmarish vision culminates in a statement that makes the scene's theatrical underpinnings explicit: "But while every single player differed markedly from every other, there was a certain uniform negativeness of expression which had the effect of a mask" (9). The burgeoning crowdedness of this scene, its sense of bodily and psychic nondifferentiation, and its additive visual grammar are only halted by Daniel's decision to isolate the spectacle of Gwendolen from what surrounds it; to put it somewhat differently, Daniel's fixated attention to this one woman, and his decision to turn her into a psychological puzzle, transform this theater into a drama: "But suddenly he felt the moment become dramatic. His attention was arrested by a young lady" (9). Three pages into the novel's first chapter, then, we arrive via a narrative loop back at the moment of psychic attention that opens the text; the effect is that those inaugural interiorizing questions stand revealed as a control on the encounter with sheer social plenitude that the scene depicts.

It is possible to see the novel that follows as a long narrative recovery from the originary trauma of this scene. At the level of story, *Daniel Deronda* works to sort its heterogeneous character population into distinct ethnic plots, and this narrative of implacable ethnic difference proceeds via precisely the antitheatrical logic exemplified in this opening scene. Daniel eventually will adopt frankly punitive tones in his conversations with Gwendolen. "Take your fear as a safeguard," he advises her during one of their later interviews (452). His words paraphrase the epigraph's opening line, and they signal his affiliation with the novel's administration of salutary psychologizing terror. Gwendolen's moral education into the novel depends on her learning actively to desire Daniel's supervisory gaze: "I wish he could know everything about me without my telling him," she thinks to herself at one point (430)—rather precisely defining the novelistic narrator's privilege. The words indicate Gwendolen's acquiescence to the interpretive regime of the novel as a genre, and her abandonment of performative impenetrability. Gwendolen's humiliating failure to succeed as an actress and singer is a central concern of the novel, which brutally tracks her transformation from a "Vandyke duchess" (558) into a penitent widow who literally learns to appreciate "kindness, even from a dog, as a gift above expectation" (795). But this trajectory is only a narrative elaboration of a defeat Gwendolen suffers by virtue of her existence as a novelistic heroine. Her awakening to Daniel's moral teaching might simply be described as the aspiring actress's realization that she has wandered into the world of the novel.

Gwendolen's submission to the regime of novelistic depth is *Daniel Deronda*'s most protracted antitheatrical allegory, but it is hardly the most spectacular. In many ways Gwendolen's capitulation is a dress rehearsal for that of the text's most accomplished actress, Daniel's mother. Unlike Gwendolen, Leonora Alcharisi (now known as the Princess Halm-Eberstein) has had a decade-long career as one of Europe's foremost performers, and her climactic account of her decision to conceal Daniel's Jewish ancestry and pursue her profession is delivered in speeches as "perfect as the most accomplished actress could have made them" (629). But Eliot's novel appears to concede this poise the better to break it. The Princess summons Daniel to their meeting in Genoa to admit that she can no longer keep up her pose of self-sufficient opacity. "I can maintain nothing now. No faith is strong within me," she confesses. "My father's threats eat into me with pain. If I tell everything—if I deliver up everything—what else can be demanded of me?" (638). As these words indicate, Leonora's acknowledgment of the confessional imperative has implications for the ethnic separatism to which *Daniel Deronda* is narratively committed. The Princess presents her pursuit of a theatrical career as a rejection of her upbringing, and because this decision coincided with her occlusion of her son's Jewishness, her dedication to the theater has quite literally started Daniel on the search for roots that constitutes *Daniel Deronda*. The novel's coherence, then, depends on breaking the Princess's will to theatrical self-transformation. She is tolerated in *Daniel Deronda* only long enough to make obeisance to its mutually reinforcing logics of narrative supervision, ethnic truth, and psychological legibility. Like Gwendolen before her, Leonora appears to testify to the triumph of the narrative form whose logic she has dared to resist.

That Daniel's meeting with Leonora is the crux of the novel is a central claim of one of the most powerful recent readings of *Daniel Deronda*. Amanda Anderson's analysis of the novel turns on this scene, and her discussion merits detailed attention both because of its sophisticated sense of the ways that novels might be said to offer ethical propositions and because it exemplifies some of the costs of retaining a characterological orientation in extracting an ethical vision from the novel. In Anderson's account, *Deronda* "articulates a complicated cosmopolitan ideal that promotes critical detachment . . . as the basis for an ever-expanding horizon of ethical and political engagement."[57] Although Deronda becomes committed to the foundation of a state for his people, Anderson argues that his Zionism is founded on a notion of dialogic openness to the claims of the other; Daniel "consistently attempts to enfold civic principles into a fundamentally ethnic nationalism" (131). Still, Anderson recognizes that Leonora stands for a self-fashioning at odds with Daniel's narrative of ethnic self-discovery. Her identity as a professional artist and sexually autonomous woman is premised on what Eliot portrays as a ruthless commitment to the claims of the self. She poses a challenge that even Daniel's reconstructed ethnic nationalism cannot accommodate: as Anderson puts it, "Eliot's model of reflective dialogism, as represented by

Daniel, cannot remain open to the transgressive possibilities" Leonora represents (141). Anderson regrets the painful conventionality of Daniel's response to his mother, as well as *Daniel Deronda*'s painful inability to tolerate
her presence for more than a few excruciating pages. Narratively scapegoated
for daring to defy the nationalist project the novel sketches, Leonora represents all those who suffer from the text's "violent blindnesses and exclusions"
(145–146).

Anderson's solution to this situation is not to abandon her faith in Daniel's dialogism but to redouble her investment in it. Her hope is that a more
thoroughgoing commitment to detachment (it is a strength of Anderson's
book that this is not an oxymoron) would do justice to the claims articulated
by Leonora. "If raised to a *higher level of consistency* . . . Eliot's project should
be better able to accommodate Leonora's enactment of postconventionality"
(143; my emphasis). In effect, Anderson seeks to out-Deronda Deronda, to
remain truer than Eliot's hero to his professed ideals of flexibility and openness. In the pages in which she makes this argument, Anderson performs a
striking critical mimesis of the openness she recommends, oscillating between
the claims of the parties she wants to reconcile. At first, Anderson defends
the principle informing Daniel's liberal cosmopolitanism, commending him
for "evad[ing] a too-great disengagement from cultural norms" (138). A few
pages later, however, Anderson concedes a large part of Leonora's case when
she describes Daniel as "engag[ing] in mystification" and "rigid traditional-
ism" (142). But Anderson grants Leonora's point only to reassert her agree-
ment with Daniel: "Daniel's practices of detachment and reaffiliation are
never marked by fixity and complacency," she writes (143)—a peculiar claim
given her immediately preceding exposure of Daniel's hypocritical rigidity.
Perhaps sensing that her ideal of dialogism is verging on self-contradiction,
Anderson's next sentence insists that "a recuperation of Daniel's character
should not be made at the expense of Leonora, who represents a viable and
deeply felt response to her own cultural context and personal past" (143).
While the remainder of Anderson's chapter returns to a defense of Daniel's
cosmopolitanism, she spares one more backward glance for Leonora: "And
of course we must also do justice to the fact that the plight of Leonora bears
witness to the limits of Deronda's own dialogism" (145).

This oscillation does not discount Anderson's argument, which is after
all committed to the notion of gradual self-correction. But it does point to
a discomfort in her position, and to certain limits in its rhetorical capaci-
ties (Leonora's partisans will no doubt feel slighted by the casual sound of
the sentence I have quoted from Anderson's concession: "And of course we
must also do justice" . . . to those whom we seem to have just forgotten.) The
reason for this argumentative wavering seems clear: it results from the fact
that Anderson is forced to posit a counterfactual (more precisely, counterfic-
tional) outcome to the novel. The policy of vigilant inclusiveness Anderson

commends does not coincide with that pursued by the "real" Daniel, and she thus asks us to imagine a Deronda who would not disavow his mother. But her sense of responsibility to the plot of Eliot's novel requires that she continually correct this vision with an acknowledgment of what he does do. Anderson's defense of Daniel's liberalism has been critiqued for its own blindnesses.[58] But the more intransigent issue here is less the content of Anderson's cosmopolitan ideal than the characterology that underwrites it—not her effort to imagine a more inclusive cosmopolitanism than that modeled by Daniel but her modeling of such a cosmopolitanism *on* Daniel, however modified a version of Daniel she implicitly asks us to imagine. Anderson's argument is constricted by her reliance on the novel as a form or, more precisely, on the protocols of readerly identification which the novel is commonly understood to foster. That argument takes for granted that to extract a political or ethical vision from Eliot's text is to extract a political or ethical vision from one of its characters: we are compelled to identify with that character and take up fantasmatic residence with him in the novel's plot. Being committed to a character means being committed to what happens to him: in the allegory mapped by Anderson, we can choose Daniel or we can choose Leonora. To pose the alternative in this way inevitably stacks the deck in favor of the narrative "winner," as Anderson's chapter suggests: we may value the ethical force of Leonora's protest, but in a novel whose closure depends on her expulsion, we can only look sympathetically back as the narrative marches with Daniel into the promised land.

And yet, as Eliot's narrator might put it, "the driest argument has its hallucinations" (514). The Princess's testimony to Daniel—and her submission to *Daniel Deronda* itself—is not quite as uniform in its meaning as her confession implies, and her resistance to the novel's plot is more successful than the narrative of her expulsion suggests. That resistance is closely tied to her articulation of a theatrical ideal, and perhaps its most striking effect is to loosen the characterological closure Anderson assumes in favor of the collective and depersonalized phenomenological texture Eliot associates with the theater. Leonora's appearance, in other words, reveals the extent to which *Daniel Deronda* seems to want to be a play.

One of the most curious features of Leonora's appearance is that it happens twice. Leonora confirms Daniel's ethnic provenance in their first interview. Narratively, her second appearance is redundant, simply rehearsing issues covered in the prior conversation—but with the crucial difference that Leonora has recovered her theatrical self-assurance. Where the first interview shone a harsh light on her ambition to self-making, we now meet her in a room "much darkened with blinds and curtains," in which she "seemed even more impressive in the sombre light, the eyes larger, the lines more vigorous" (659). Where she earlier admitted to crushing guilt, she now remains analytically detached as she appraises the novel's punitive workings: "You

rebuke me," she tells Daniel. "Well—I am the loser. And you are angry because I banish you . . . You shall be happy. You shall let me think of you as
happy. I shall have done you no harm" (663–664). In their strange temporal
orientation, the sentences refuse the past tense of confession. Veering into
the future perfect, Leonora's words take up residence slightly to the side of
the narrative of ethnic truth whose key she is in the process of providing.
In staggering the Princess's appearances across these two scenes, and in allowing her to take back the self-sufficiency she earlier ceded to the novelistic
imperative, Eliot reverses the logic otherwise structuring her career, according to which a character's initial opacity yields to narrative penetration. The
Princess's ability to survive her submission to the novel—even to comment
skeptically on its progress—makes her an unprecedented instance in Eliot's
work of the theater being permitted to look back dubiously at the novel that
would contain it.

More important, there are indications that the resistance Leonora registers to the logic of the novel is simply the most lurid example of a more
evenly distributed phenomenon. Returning to his hotel from the first interview with his mother, Daniel finds a long letter from his friend Hans Meyrick that occupies much of the novel's fifty-second chapter. Leonora has just
finished testifying to the immutability of ethnic identity, but Hans's letter
reports on a series of unsettling performative substitutions: "I am consoling
myself for your absence," Hans writes, "by finding my advantage in it" (641).
He has begun to study Hebrew with Mirah's brother Mordecai, and boasts
of a proficiency we are not sure the now certifiably Jewish Daniel has himself
achieved. Hans claims to be boning up on Jewish history and to have acceler-
ated his friendship with Mirah—a "Jewess I should not mind being slave to"
(644). Hans's efforts to Judaize himself may appear facetious, but his letter,
in suggesting that Jewish roots might be acquired along with the "tri-literal
roots" of Hebrew grammar (646), lends support to Leonora's claims to self-
fashioning. When Hans goes on to tease Daniel about his supposedly intellectual relationship with Gwendolen, it becomes clear that his ironic vision
is connected to theatrical form. Picking up on his old joking comparison of
Grandcourt to the Duke in Donizetti's opera *Lucrezia Borgia*, Hans threatens to turn *Daniel Deronda* into a theatrical script:

> Shall you by chance have an opportunity of continuing your theologi-
> cal discussion with the fair Supralapsarian—I think you said her tenets
> were of that complexion? Is Duke Alphonso also theological?—per-
> haps an Arian who objects to triplicity. (Stage direction. While D. is
> reading, a profound scorn gathers in his face till at the last word he
> flings down the letter, grasps his coat-collar in a statuesque attitude
> and so remains with a look generally tremendous, throughout the fol-
> lowing soliloquy, "O night, O blackness, &c. &c.") (645–646)

Hans's letter indicates that Leonora's theatrical desire is formally infectious, as the text threatens to jump a generic barrier and become the play as which Eliot had once considered writing it. In Hans's "stage direction," the theater becomes not simply a theme or image in the narrative but the very condition of the text; Leonora's most intriguing function in *Daniel Deronda* may thus be to force the novel's theatrical desire into formal expression. Equally striking is that this stage direction appears to take performative effect in the narrative: Hans's words provide an entirely adequate physical description of the melodramatic pose one imagines Daniel striking a few pages later at the conclusion of his second interview with his mother. Eliot writes at the conclusion to chapter 53 that Daniel "had gone through a tragic experience which must for ever solemnize his life and deepen the significance of the acts by which he bound himself to others" (667). If we keep in mind Hans's description of Deronda's attitudinizing, our hero might seem to be an actor taking instruction from his friend's letter—an effect confirmed when, in his final interview with Gwendolen, Daniel "grasp[s] his ... coat-collar" (850) in precise obedience to his friend's stage direction.[59]

Eliot interpolates one additional scene into the gap between Leonora's appearances—a scene that functions like Hans's letter to suggest the instability of *Daniel Deronda*'s novelistic medium, and its characterological boundaries. After Daniel has absorbed his friend's letter, the narrative shifts to London, where Mirah is discussing Deronda with the Meyrick sisters and their friend Anna Gascoigne. The Meyrick girls have just discovered that Anna knows Deronda, too, and the company is absorbed with this coincidence: "Oh, this finding out relationships is delightful!" Mab Meyrick exclaims. "I feel sure something wonderful may be made of it, but I can't tell what" (654). Mirah, however, is obscurely alarmed by the news: "A confused discontent took possession of her at the mingling of names and images to which she had been listening" (655). Eliot provides a psychological rationale for this discontent: Mirah is in love with Daniel, and the news of his existence in this larger world—in particular his friendship with Gwendolen—poses a threat to the exclusivity of their relation to each other. But Mirah's comment a few lines later suggests that her disquiet stems less from jealousy than from her intimation of *Daniel Deronda*'s desire to turn itself into a theater. Asked her opinion of Gwendolen, Mirah answers, "I think she is like the *Princess of Eboli* in *Don Carlos*." Eliot clarifies that Mirah "was pursuing an association in her own mind not intelligible to her hearers—an association with a certain actress as well as the part she represented" (656).

Like *The Spanish Gypsy*, these sentences achieve several disconcerting effects because of a typographic decision: Eliot's italicization of both the title of Schiller's 1787 play and of the name of a character in that play suggests, in the first place, an unsettling traffic between the ontological levels of person and work, as if Eliot means to momentarily make us wonder about our habit of equating a text's viewpoint with that of its eponymous hero (prompting us to question, for example, how *this* novel's rejection of Daniel's mother would look if we began referring to her as "*The Alcharisi* in *Daniel Deronda*"). Relatedly, Eliot's promotion of the Princess to the same typographic status as Don Carlos suggests the spectacle of this minor character in Schiller's play rivaling the priority of its titular hero. Finally, in typographically setting off the name of this character, the sentence recalls the small capitals of *The Spanish Gypsy*, and thus bizarrely suggests that Mirah is reading from a play script or theatrical program.

These effects are a preamble to the more properly psychological discomfort Eliot goes on to specify: Mirah's uneasiness in the scene conflates a sense of unwanted social promiscuity with that of an uncanny doubling between character and actress. Mirah knows whereof she speaks: she is herself an experienced professional actress, and if she knows a woman who played the Princess of Eboli in Schiller's *Don Carlos*, it is most likely because she too was a member of the cast.[60] The allusion to Schiller's play is less interesting as an intertextual citation than as a reference to a social space in which Mirah and Gwendolen might be collaborators. Mirah verges here on the suspicion that the conditions of her fictional existence are set not by the separatist logic of the ethnic *Bildungsroman* but by the collectively oriented form of the theater. The threat embedded in these scenes is that the world of *Daniel Deronda* may not be one where everyone retires to his assigned ethnic corner, but instead a kind of "show" whose collective nature renders such stabilizing rubrics beside the point. We have seen that the form of the theatrical text intimates a democracy among its characters—even when they occupy roles of greater and lesser importance or suffer divergent fates. The democracy posited by the theatrical text—a "state" in which difference is subordinated to formal sameness—is precisely what alarms Mirah at this juncture. It is this alternative phenomenology that is powerfully legible in *The Spanish Gypsy*'s typographic invocation of a world that ignores ethnic (and even species) difference in the name of the social whole. A similar desire to cancel the plots of national and characterological difference informs these crucial scenes in *Daniel Deronda*.

Fredric Jameson has defined theater as "an experimental space and collective laboratory" which "is lacking, except figuratively, in the novel."[61] But the scenes we have examined conjure a theater that exceeds a figurative or thematic localization in the text by becoming the condition of the text. In permitting Hans to invent a functioning "stage direction" for her hero, or in giving Mirah a suspicion that the figures of her life are mingling in the wings of some great stage, Eliot gives voice to a desire to exceed the constraints of her form. Most provocatively, she challenges readers to understand *Daniel Deronda* without recourse to the identificatory practices supposedly native to the novel as a form. Jameson's description of theater as "the very figure for the collective" (11) suggests that, rather than asking us to imaginarily align

ourselves with one character or other, the theater solicits a more basic ca-
thexis of the scene itself, and the ongoing vitality of the collective situation
it represents. Jameson claims that such a provocation is unavailable to narrative fiction—but just such a collectivist imagination invades *Daniel Deronda*
in the narrative hiatus opened by Leonora's double appearance. Hans's letter and Mirah's unsettled theatrical imagination prompt the following questions: What if *Daniel Deronda* were indeed the play Eliot considered making
it? Can we read it as if it were anyway? What happens if one conceives of the
world of her final novel on the model of performance? To imagine *Daniel
Deronda* as if it were onstage is to imagine a world where Daniel's set-piece
with his mother is repeated nightly; a world where the painfully separate participants in the "Jewish" and "English" halves of the plot consort backstage,
and where the English widow Lydia Glasher and the Jewish actress Alcharisi
could be played by the same woman; a world where HANS MEYRICK and
MORDECAI COHEN and ANNA GASCOIGNE and JULIUS KLESMER might
appear hand in hand when the curtain falls, in that theatrical afterglow where
the bodies of the actors retain the mystique of character but have become
openly indicative of their contiguity with the real. In other words, a world
that had universalized the theatrical condition that in the novel's plot is quar-
antined and expunged with Leonora.

In the face of the wrenching divisions effected by the plot of *Daniel
Deronda* (between Daniel and his mother, between Daniel and Gwendolen, between England and "Israel") such speculations are bound to sound
utopian. But the Victorian theater was a space where such depersonalization and collectivization were functioning realities. The use of stock melodramatic types meant that even characters from quite different diegetic
environments—a Bohemian peasant and a Midlands gentleman are the examples Deborah Vlock offers in her study of the Victorian theater—could
seem like versions of the same character.[62] The palimpsestic effect whereby
past performances inform the current offering, or where novelistic characters would be imagined on the basis of recently viewed stage productions,
resulted in an enhanced consciousness of the group whose collaboration is
literally necessary in making characterological distinction visible. It is this
theatrical condition to which *Daniel Deronda* aspires. We might then be less
preoccupied by its narrative attempt to segregate its ethnic plots than by its
desire to maintain a world where such plots coexist in the same fictive space.
To perceive *Daniel Deronda*'s performative desire is to perceive the novel's
overriding interest in "putting on" the collective world it depicts. Almost all
the characters in *Daniel Deronda* believe that ethnicity is destiny.[63] But insofar as those characters resemble a cast, as Mirah intimates, they are haunted
by a sense of their potential interchangeability—their status as members of a
collective body we could call George Eliot's lot. The novel's most startlingly
egalitarian vision derives from its suggestion that the mutual participation of

its "players" in constructing their world undermines their interest in erecting characterological boundaries.

"I meant everything in the book to be related to everything else," Eliot wrote to her friend Barbara Bodichon in 1876, complaining about the tendency of critics to separate Gwendolen's plot from the Jewish sections of the novel (*L*, 6:290). It is precisely such a possibility of universal relatedness that so disturbs Mirah in the scene examined above, and it is this possibility that is the most radical aspect of Eliot's book as well as its most concrete inheritance from *The Spanish Gypsy*. In speaking for that connectedness, Eliot might be imitating the Princess, the performer who insists impenitently on the possibility of "another life" (666). She claims to speak only for herself, but the effects that radiate outward from her appearance touch all the characters who find shelter in Eliot's novel. As Olive Schreiner might put it, there is indeed a sense of satisfaction in *Daniel Deronda*, and of completeness—a completeness that has less to do with novelistic perfection (something *Deronda* clearly and happily does not achieve) than with its persistent invocation of the collective possibility named by the theater.

THREE

Henry James's Awkward Stage

As I heard you were going to try to turn the club into a Theatre And as I was asked w'ether I wanted to belong here is my answer. I would like very much to belong. —Henry James, aged thirteen, to Edgar Beach Van Winkle

Other Almost Anyhow

Two things quickly become clear to the reader of *A Small Boy and Others*, a book frequently described as the first volume of Henry James's auto-biography. The first is that the book is not about Henry James. The balance promised by the title tips continually in the direction of those "others," as omnipresent as they are indistinguishable. "Discrimination among the parts of my subject . . . [was] difficult—so inseparably and beautifully they seemed to hang together," James writes on his first page.[1] The memories that follow emanate as if from a composite consciousness anchored in but never coextensive with the James family: James speaks of "our shame" (16), "our effort" (19), "our circle" (29, 60), "the cousinship" (29), "*our* admonition," "our muddled initiations" (59), "our intelligence" (62), "our small inquiring steps" (63), "our party," "our sensibility" (85). This group consciousness, "with the generations and sexes melting together and moving in a loose harmonious band" (90), functions at once as the text's source and as a badge of pride. We are accustomed to seeing James as a purveyor of exclusivity, but it is notable that this "our" is given its peculiar libidinal charge by its definitional porousness, the sense that it encompasses an in-group of shifting scale. Perhaps uniquely in a genre usually intent on establishing its author's singularity, *A Small Boy and Others* is an autobiography given over to the glamour of the plural.[2]

The second thing to become clear is that, if the book is not in any straightforward way about Henry James, it *is* about the theater. James recounts his breathless attendance at adaptations of Dickens and Stowe, recalls his regret at missing plays judged too risqué for "our infant participation" (60), expresses delight at the Christmas pantomime, and lovingly describes the lettering on the theatrical placards along lower Fifth Avenue. Waiting for the curtain to rise for his first play imparts a "sense of sacred thrill" to the young James, and attending the stage version of *Uncle Tom's Cabin* is a "great initiation" (55, 85). So repetitively does James insist on the wonder of performance that the theater becomes a kind of ghostly referent for any number of the text's high points. Recording his memory of looking on as his cousin Marie is told by her mother not to "make a scene," James describes the event as "epoch-making" for his eleven-year-old self, and the moment's importance is clearly related to the theatrical atmosphere conjured by the common phrase (96–97). The insistence on the uniquely pivotal nature of these events does curiously little to distinguish them from numerous other scenes in the book. Toward the end of *A Small Boy*, for example, we find an account of the "initiation" at the Louvre in which the vision of French paintings allows James to "happily cross that bridge over to Style"; recalling a day spent ill next to a window opening onto a London street, James reports that he then "first tasted the very greatest pleasure perhaps I was ever to know—that of almost holding my breath in presence of certain aspects to the end of so taking in" (180, 145). In this peculiarly besotted text, we are never more than a few pages away from witnessing James being floored by "wonder" (129), by "a certain perversity of romance" (105), by "glamour" (203), by the "apprehension [of] something vague and sweet" (215), by "prodigies and mysteries of fifty sorts" (183).

It seems fruitful to locate the generative grammar for these moments not in any particular content (since that shifts so frequently) but in the topography they share—one modeled on the spatial and affective relations of the theater.[3] In every case, James occupies a spectatorial position vis-à-vis some situation described as mysterious, romantic, and, importantly, unapproachable —as if kept off-limits by the same convention that keeps spectators in their seats at a play. After one such moment (a visit to the prison at Sing-Sing during which James is struck by an inmate coolly cleaning his nails), James analyzes the emotion underwriting these scenes:

> Though in that early time I seem to have been constantly eager to exchange my lot for that of somebody else, on the assumed certainty of gaining by the bargain, I fail to remember feeling jealous of such happier persons—in the measure open to children of spirit. I had rather a positive lack of the passion, and thereby, I suppose, a lack of spirit; since if jealousy bears, as I think, on what one sees one's companions able to do—as against one's own falling short—envy, as I knew it, at least, was simply of what they *were*, or in other words of a certain sort of richer consciousness supposed, doubtless often too freely supposed, in them. They were so *other*—that was what I felt; and to *be* other, other almost anyhow, seemed as good as the probable taste of the bright compound wistfully watched in the confectioner's window; unattainable, impossible, of course, but as to which just this impossibility

and just that privation kept those active proceedings in which jealousy seeks relief quite out of the question. A platitude of acceptance of the poor actual, the absence of all vision of how in any degree to change it, combined with a complacency, an acuity of perception of alternatives, though a view of them as only through the confectioner's hard glass— that is what I recover as the nearest approach to an apology, in the soil of my nature, for the springing seed of emulation. (91–92).

The specular and spatial logics here epitomize what the theater historian David Wiles terms the "Cartesian theatrical dichotomy."[4] As in the theater, we see in James's account the primacy of vision at the expense of other sensory coordinates, the uni-directionality of the gaze from spectator to actor, the passivity of the observer contrasted with the spotlit activity of the observed, and a political quietism—a "platitude of acceptance of the poor actual"—that seems the result of all of these. Although James is not always in the theater when struck by "envy," the theater represents in purest form the topography implied by that emotion as he defines it. "Before the porticoes of the theatres," he writes later, "all questions melted for me into the single depth of envy" (200).

But we should be wary of limiting the meanings of Jamesian envy to those represented by the Cartesian mise-en-scène. Jamesian theatricality quite often fails to stay in its place, and so refuses to respect the contours and the politics —including the body politics—of Cartesian theatrical space. In the above passage, for example, it is striking how "lack" becomes curiously "positive," and how closely the avowed "lack of passion" abuts "an acuity of perception of alternatives." One of the strangest effects of James's late style, one much in evidence here, is the way its feats of grammatical subordination achieve the effect of a purely lateral, or additive, syntax. Rhetoricians note that an excess of hypotaxis has the effect of parataxis, so that on our way through a rigorously subordinated sentence, we end up perceiving less the intricately graded relation among clauses than the mere fact of their co-presence, in a defeat of the sentence's temporal axis by a spatial one: in this case, the phenomenology of the Jamesian sentence replicates precisely the situation of the young James whose overwhelmed perception it describes. Is it certain that such a perceptual surfeit must lead to the "platitude of acceptance of the poor actual" that James avows? Or, more forcefully: Does it even matter that James here says it does? Rather than take at face value the anti-sensuality of James's claim that the vision through the "confectioner's hard glass" is "as good as" the delicacy itself, we could note how that transparent sheet takes on the properties of the "bright compound" onto which it provides a window. Transfigured by James's distended syntax, that hard glass becomes a sugar-sweet compound in its own right, one that does not so much prohibit us from participating in the social as eroticize the conditions under which we might do so.

The impossibility invoked here seems a familiar version of a Jamesian ethos of renunciation, but it is also a rhetorical gesture that makes space for that eroticization. If we are attuned to the excess of social desire evident here, the passage reads as an incitement to transgress the protocols of spectatorship as much as an endorsement of them, so that in making sense of these ostensibly well-behaved sentences we may find ourselves imagining James pressing his tongue lovingly to the glass at the confectioner's shop. Such effects become explicit later in the memoir when, in a description of a cousin's room in Paris, vision slides into other senses, and spatial separation becomes a spur to spatial convergence:

> The closed windows, which but scantly distinguished between our own sounds and those of the sociable, and yet the terrible, street of records and memories, seemed to maintain an air and a light thick with the mixture of every sort of queer old Parisian amenity and reference: as if to look or to listen or to touch were somehow at the same time to probe, to recover and communicate, to behold, to taste and even to smell—to one's greater assault by suggestion, no doubt, but also to the effect of some sweet and strange repletion. (198)

That the windows —the marker of the physical boundary—are precisely what "maintain" the sense of "sweet and strange repletion" indicates that specularity here is a preamble to sensory overload rather than the means of sensory deprivation, a goad to sociability rather than a confirmation of isolation. Read otherwise than for their "plots," such passages can be seen (whatever their explicit investment in the hard glass of the impossible) to eroticize the clamorous world beyond the self and its domestic containers. Jamesian style achieves perlocutionary leverage over Jamesian content.[5]

The homology between the topography of these scenes and James's experience of the theater suggests that Jamesian theatricality disrupts both the identitarian boundaries of the spectator and his social isolation. But if the eroticization of the spectacle of the social rhetorically overbalances James's explicit renunciation of social participation, it is also capable of rebounding into the audience, of being absorbed into the relations between spectators, so that an energy sparked by an exciting spectacle lends a libidinal charge to that audience's sense of its collective being. Watch in the following passage as James starts to feel, in several senses, his companions in the audience at his first attendance at a stage adaptation of *Uncle Tom's Cabin*: James introduces the episode ensconced in an ambiguous first-person plural—"We lived and moved at that time, with great intensity, in Mrs. Stowe's novel"—and soon finds himself wondering whether his companions share his perspective: "To have become thus aware of our collective attitude constituted for one small spectator at least a great initiation . . . I am not sure I wasn't thus more interested in the pulse of our party, under my tiny recording thumb, than in the beat of the drama and the shock of its opposed forces" (83, 85). The moment on the one hand confirms the potential quietism of this particular collective imagination, as James finds himself more intrigued by his friends' reactions than by the "opposed forces" in the national struggle over slavery being represented. On the other, it indicates that the theatrical apparatus renders such closures politically ambiguous, as the first-person pronoun in the passage hovers between James's small party, the totality of the assembled spectatorship, and the national public.

Even from within its evident closures, then, Jamesian theatricality names the possibility of ever amplifying scales of sociality: the theatrical provides the space for a boy to identify himself with a female cousin or for the middle-class tourist to imagine himself a hardened convict; it merges his consciousness with that of the family and then dissolves that family into "the cousinship" and then allows that enlarged group to spill onto the sociable street.[6] The theater here is only in the first instance a way for the individual to imagine himself otherwise; it is more precisely a technology of collectivization, a mechanism for the production of the plural. It is also the name for a social space—an architectural and institutional context—that fosters such self-difference and collective awareness. James's earliest extant letter, which serves as this chapter's epigraph, suggests that James's appetite for the theater is also an institutional erotics. The letter does more than show that James's designs on the theater predated any pecuniary reward he eventually glimpsed there.[7] It also reveals that one of his earliest acts of extra-familial affiliation coincided with a project of spatial and social transformation ("I heard you were going to try to turn the club into a Theatre . . . I would like very much to belong"). *A Small Boy and Others* records not only a desire to be "other almost anyhow" but a desire for the social contexts that would house and foster such self-transformations. Jamesian theatricality is a world-making as much as a self-enhancing energy, promising an experience of sociality and an apprehension of a world in which it would be durably on offer. It fosters a fantasy of worlds otherwise arranged, of social "possibilities that were none the less vivid for being quite indefinite" (64). This is an erotics of alterity in the largest sense, a general will toward the counterfactual and toward the structures that encourage it.[8]

In this chapter, what I will frankly be calling the utopian strain in James mostly pertains to his interest in collective forms of sexual dissidence.[9] I also claim that two essential features of James's reputation need to be reevaluated: his association with the triumph of the novel and with the project of glamorizing interiority. "No genre has ever been more invested in the creation of private subjects or in the accumulation of inner capital than the nineteenth-century novel of psychological depth," Paul Morrison writes—and, we might add, no nineteenth-century writer has been more identified with the novel of psychological depth than Henry James.[10] Two of the most unusual works from James's experimental period—novels defying the equation of the name Henry James with the novel and of both with "inner capital" and "psychological depth"—receive the bulk of my attention here. The last years of the nineteenth century have long been understood as transitional in James's career, bridging the naturalist novels of the middle years and the works of the "major phase." This period also has an important relation to the questions of the theater and the psychologically knowable subject: it immediately followed five years in which James attempted to write for the contemporary stage. The debacle of 1895's *Guy Domville* marked a return to what James was later at pains to represent as his true calling of fiction. James's formal experiments in these years led him to two of the principles that he would expound in the prefaces to the New York Edition, and which his expositors from Percy Lubbock on have adopted as the dogma of the novelist's art: the scenic principle and the doctrine of a central consciousness. In the account offered by Lubbock and his followers, the Jamesian novel reaches its apotheosis in renouncing theater; "the master" is born from the death of the playwright.[11]

Leon Edel's biographical reading of the period makes clear the bearing such generic questions have on issues of sexual identity. If that reading now seems unconvincing in its pop-Freudian reductions, it usefully demonstrates the lengths to which critics will go to read resolutely depsychologized texts through a psychological hermeneutic. Edel considers the works of the experimental years an autobiography in drag, with James appearing in succession as the toddler Effie in *The Other House* (1896), as the precocious protagonist of 1897's *What Maisie Knew* (who is six when the story opens), as the slightly older Flora in *The Turn of the Screw* (1898), as the unnamed telegraph-girl in "In the Cage" (1898), and as the sixteen-year-old Nanda in 1899's *The Awkward Age*. According to Edel, this series answered in James "some compulsion to revisit, step by step, the hidden stages of his own development, within his safety-disguise of a little girl."[12] The snug fit between aesthetic and sexual meanings here makes for a potent story of artistic and psychic development: only when James abandons his theatrical misadventure is he able to incorporate the theater's lessons into the novel, now grasped as his true form. In the process he both produces a series of novels that trace the truth of his psychic life (defined here by a cross-gender identification that implicitly means homosexuality) and perfects the narrative technology that gives this kind of reading cultural purchase.

Given the neatness of these equivalences, it is striking that the pillars of this arc, *The Other House* and *The Awkward Age*, fail completely to support it. Far from returning triumphantly to his chosen form, James embraced the novel after *Guy Domville* in a mood of ambivalence manifest in these deeply un-*novelistic* novels. In these works the scenic principle takes the form not merely of avoiding narrative summary but of a near total suppression of the narrative voice. The books are so devoted (as James indicated in his preface to *The Awkward Age*) to "dialogue organic and dramatic, speaking for itself, representing and embodying substance and form," that they could be used as play scripts with little alteration to the texts.[13] The singularity of these novels in the Jamesian canon and in the tradition of the novel has not yet been fully gauged, and we will see that their formal provocation is intimately connected to the ethical and social challenges they pose. In their dramatic form these novels allowed James to anatomize and reject the psychologizing thrust his career is often taken to epitomize, and to resist the closure of sexual definitions at the historical moment in which Foucault located the "incorporation of perversions" in discrete individuals.[14] It is when James is least the master of the psychological novel that he offers the most sustained challenge to the demand to be oneself on which sexual identity is based; it is when James is least obedient to his prescriptions for the novel that he comes closest to envisioning the social formations that could protect a collective impenetrability to psychological knowingness.[15]

The following analysis does not deny that these texts can be maddening in their difficulty and generic uncertainty, nor does it claim that they are "successful." Rather, I argue that James designed them to feel wrong—as if they were written in some impossible genre, and with the purpose of creating for the reader a sense of cognitive discomfort and sensory blockage. The value of these novels for James was clearly closely tied to his sense of their failure. He called *The Other House* his "blest . . . precedent, a support, a divine little light to walk by"—and "a little thrifty pot-boiling turning-to-acc[oun]t of the scheme of a chucked-away 3 act play."[16] In the preface to *The Awkward Age* he called the novel "triumphantly scientific"—and conceded that his executing it almost wholly in dialogue had rendered it a "comparative monster" and almost a "disaster" (*AN*, 117, 98, 115). For a writer who claimed that "an acted play is a novel intensified; it realizes what the novel suggests," the decision to compose novels that invoke the acted plays they might have been indicates a deliberate highlighting of a lack of intensity perhaps endemic to the novel as a form—a purposeful courting of the unrealized, the incomplete, the merely suggestive.[17] Accepting these books' challenge means noting their failure to be "good" novels—attending to the otherness and awkwardness they smuggle into the genre.

This theatrical resistance to the logic of the novel is far from simple. Although theater remains a valorized concept in this stretch of James's career, it is important to register James's ambivalence about a naturalist theatrical culture that was, under the influence of Ibsen, adopting a notion of psychological truth in turn borrowed from realist fiction. The theater, paradoxically, was becoming more and more novelistic at precisely the moment James turned to it in order to achieve distance on the interiorizing thrust of the psychological novel.[18] The results of this situation on James's practice were complex but far from paralyzing. In their necessary distance from performance these pivotal works gesture toward the public event of the theater while remaining unbound by the orthodoxies of the naturalist drama. In a theatrical culture in which, in Elin Diamond's words, "realism's eternal room" was becoming the scene of psychological legibility, James's inability to make those heavily significant interiors materialize paid liberating dividends.[19] In these works James rescued a phantom theater from his dramatic fiascos, creating "events" whose failure to take place makes them rich sites for imagining relational possibilities beyond the constraints of the given.

The analysis that follows explores the formal and stylistic techniques James employs in *The Other House* and *The Awkward Age* to create the sense of alluringly inaccessible theatrical performances. In our analysis of the 1896 novel version of *The Other House*, its 1909 dramatic adaptation, and 1899's *The Awkward Age*, we will see that the most intriguing effects of all three become intelligible only when they are considered as *read* texts—but also that in these works James understands reading as a constitutively inadequate activity. Thus while James's discouragement in the theater had largely resigned him to the fact of nonperformance, he was unwilling to abandon the theater as an imaginary referent. Instead, James created a bizarre fictional medium to convey the sense that these texts are sketches for a more robust but deferred theatrical enactment. The result is to enjoin an effortful imaginative practice on the reader that both estranges her from the readerly and theatrical conventions of the period and renders visible the ideologies with which those conventions are complicit. Most radically, James prompts his readership to reconstitute itself as a ghostly theatrical public, a collective body made over in the image of the permissive coterie he depicts in *The Awkward Age*. By reason of their referential thinness, the "performances" conjured by these texts are made to feel as desirable as the social possibilities they sketch.

Thus did James's failure to conform coherently to either the protocols of the novel or the drama become a productive strategy. The unachieved theatrical events depicted in these books are a means for James to imagine what he called in *A Small Boy* "other publics" (132)—appealing but currently invisible social groupings and forms of relation. The poignancy of this project is increased by James's apparent inability to sustain it for more than a few novels. F. W. Dupee, one of the critics most sympathetic to James's aims in *The Awkward Age*, concedes that the book "would seem to lead nowhere so far as the art of narrative is concerned"; Tzvetan Todorov says the novel's formal oddity makes it "thoroughly peculiar" in "the enormous family of novels."[20] But this failure to take a legitimate place in fiction's family line is also a challenge to create the worlds and audiences that could sustain such offspring. Moreover, if these books seem to dangle without issue at the end of a novelistic lineage, this may simply be because we have not been able to identify the forms their progeny have taken.[21] After charting the frustration of sexual knowingness in

The Other House and the elaboration of a perverse group subjectivity in *The Awkward Age*, I track the migration of this collective impulse to the level of late Jamesian style, analyzing the stylistic extremity of *The Wings of the Dove* as the carrier of an insistent utopian promise. In the process, we will see how an externalizing, centrifugal social will makes itself felt even in the most apparently inward of narrative forms.

The Performance Imaginary: *The Other House,* 1896

I was with precocious passion "at home" among the theatres.
—*A Small Boy and Others*

In December 1893 James recorded in his notebooks the idea for what would become *The Other House*: "Is there something for a tale, is there something for a play, in something that might be a little like the following?" (*N*, 138–139). The generic uncertainty is notable, as is the sense that the distinction between "tale" and "play" might be of obscure importance. As he sketches his idea of a man bound by a promise to his dying wife never to remarry, James remains unsure about the generic destination of the idea. "In the first chapter of my story this young man is present—the 1ˢᵗ chapter of my story—by which I mean the 1ˢᵗ act of my play!" (*N*, 139) he hesitates at one point. The plot summary ends on a note of tentative decision—"As I so barbarously and roughly jot the story down, I seem to feel in it the stuff of a play" (*N*, 141)—but uncertainty clearly lingers. That this is theatrical material seems less a matter of conviction than aspiration: "It is the *play* that I am looking for, but it is worth noting, all the same, for the *other* possibility" (*N*, 139).

What, we will naturally ask, is the "*other* possibility"? It seems clear that James refers to the possibility of the novel—that *The Other House* is to find its home in that structure he would later term "the house of fiction" (*AN*, 46). The permutations of his initial idea, though, indicate that the story never felt fully housed to James, in any genre. A month after the initial entry, James changes his mind and says the material could be "quite the subject of a story, as well as of a play . . . Oh yes, there is a story in that . . . which would greatly resemble a play" (*N*, 146–147). When he did return to his play outline two years later, it was to develop it into a novel; *The Other House* began its serial run in *The Illustrated London News* in 1895 and was published in book form in 1896. James later described the novel to Edmund Gosse as having "its base [i.e., dramatic] origin smeared all over it," a description suggesting that the novelistic refunctioning of the story remained unsatisfactory to James.[22] That base origin would reassert itself: in June 1909 he began reworking the material back into dramatic form, and a month later the London producer Herbert Trench was considering it for production at the Haymarket Theatre.

By December the project was rejected, and a month later, working on the plan for *The Ivory Tower* (a novel he would leave unfinished at his death), James invoked the protean project in the words I have quoted above: "Oh blest *Other House*, which gives me thus at every step a precedent, a support, a divine little light to walk by" (*N*, 348). James does not specify here whether he refers to the story's dramatic or novelistic avatar, so we cannot know which version receives this encomium. But given the story's permutations, it seems likeliest that by this point the words "The Other House" had come to attach themselves less to any particular textual instantiation than to the very idea of generic indeterminacy. A work held in reserve for some emphatically "*other* possibility" had become an emblem of the possibility of generic otherness itself.

The history of *The Other House* indicates that for James this work permanently straddled a line of generic alterity. "House," after all, is more than James's well-known figure for the novel; it also names the crowd that assembles to see a play. The title *The Other House* thus involves a conceptual pun, in which the theater and the novel keep referring unstably back to each other: we are always on one side of the generic line, but the possibility of crossing is always present as a temptation or an irritant. Finally, the "house" James chooses here as the figure for the novel, the drama, and the undecidability between them also names a real (however heavily mythicized) structure. This linkage of generic indeterminacy with the space of the home threatens then not only to superimpose theatricality on domesticity—to smuggle the theatrical house into the house that encloses the family—but, more abstractly, to invest the home with some of this energy of pure potentiality. We might, rearranging slightly the terms in James's fetish title, hypothesize that this superimposition intimates another *kind* of house, a home that protects radically other forms of relation.[23]

But if the plot of *The Other House* offers a glimpse of sexual and social possibility, it also considers how transformative desires are haunted by the threat of abjection. The novel's opening establishes the spatial ground for a melodrama of spectatorship and sexual deviance:

> Mrs. Beever of Eastmead, and of "Beever and Bream," was a close, though not a cruel observer of what went on, as she always said, at the other house. A great deal more went on there, naturally, than in the great, clean, square solitude in which she had practically lived since the death of Mr. Beever, who had predeceased by three years his friend and partner, the late Paul Bream of Bounds, leaving to his only son, the little godson of that trusted associate, the substantial share of the business in which his wonderful widow—she knew and rejoiced that she was wonderful—now had a distinct voice. Paul Beever, in the bloom of eighteen, had just achieved a scramble from Winchester to Oxford:

it was his mother's design that he should go into as many things as possible before coming into the Bank. The Bank, the pride of Wilverley, the high clear arch of which the two houses were the solid piers, was worth an expensive education.[24]

We are accustomed to say that a novel's first sentences "lay the scene," but the opening lines of *The Other House* imbue the figure with an odd literalism. The passage is one of the few in the text to depart from the scenic method by making use of narrative summary. But this eminently novelistic piece of backstory constructs a highly theatrical topography, in which one house (Bounds) is the spectacularized space of "what goes on" and the other (Eastmead) is the silent, darkened space of attention—of "close, though not cruel" observation. The narrative space is thus bifurcated between two houses whose specular relations strikingly evoke the sightlines of the traditional theater. Details that James goes on to provide underline the staginess of this topography. If Mrs. Beever, Eastmead's mistress, is the bearer of a self-effacing gaze, Tony Bream "expose[s] himself" in the "showy," "bright, large and high, richly decorated" Bounds—a house that "played equally the part of a place of reunion and of a place of transit" (12). Later we learn that a stream separates the houses, and that a footbridge frames Bounds like a proscenium arch, making a picture for the residents of Eastmead. (James's notebooks were explicit about the theatrical logic underpinning this novelistic space, identifying Mrs. Beever and her friend Dr. Ramage as the "two persons to figure as the *public*, the judging, wondering, horrified world" [*N*, 140]). That Mrs. Beever's spectatorial attention is turned steadfastly toward what she insists on calling "the other house" indicates that James has mapped the generic confusion attending the inspiration for *The Other House* onto his story's setting. In ensuring that the same opening passage identifying *The Other House* as a novel also marks "the other house" of Bounds as a kind of stage, James provides a spatial allegory of his text's equivocal evolution.

As the name of the other house indicates, it is a place of large and stagey gestures (the notebook entry in which James hit on the name reads "Bounce—Bounds (house, place)" [*N*, 194]). And as that name also suggests, the exuberant theatrical forces housed there demand a firm retaining wall: Bounds must be kept safely within bounds. Fittingly, the residents of the respective houses differ as drastically as do actors from the average playgoer. Tony Bream, for example, is a handsome man with a histrionic flair: "He was a collection of gifts, which presented themselves as such precisely by having in each case slightly overflowed the measure"; he is, in short, "exaggerated" (32). A widow, Tony shares the house with his dead wife's best friend, Rose Armiger, who is right at home in the thespian atmosphere of Bounds. Her gestures are characterized as "the overflow of a cup" (39–40), and at one moment James places her "before a mirror, still dealing, like an actress in the wing, with her appearance, her make-up" (86). Rose and Tony resemble nothing so much as stage actors who have learned to make their most intimate gestures visible from the cheap seats. This scenery-chewing extravagance sharply differentiates them from the characters at Eastmead: Mrs. Beever's son Paul is a "featureless person" (181), and their shy friend Jean Martle is a "light sketch for something larger, a cluster of happy hints" (14). This contrast between the intensely embodied actors and the gauzy spectators is also, it emerges, a distinction between the deviant and the normal. Bounds is a place not only of showiness but of showy perversity: at the novel's climax, Rose, overcome with desire for Tony, will drown his infant daughter in the stream separating the two houses. Meanwhile, across the river at Eastmead, a more mild romance plays out, as Mrs. Beever tries to get her hapless son Paul to propose to Jean. If Eastmead is a house of Austenesque comedy, Bounds is a theater for an Ibsenesque tragedy.

This sense of internalized generic distinction is key to the novel's sexual politics. In its separation of the theatrical and domestic, viewed and viewing, deviant and normal, *The Other House* seems a typical document of what Priscilla Walton has characterized in an essay on the novel as "the backlash climate of the *fin de siècle*."[25] But James's take on late-Victorian sexual anxieties should be interpreted through the text's generic ambivalence. Theater, and the perverse spectacle to which it corresponds, exert an irresistible gravitational pull in *The Other House*. This is evident first on the thematic level. The outsized personalities at Bounds prove so enticing to their beholders at Eastmead that they distract the players in Mrs. Beever's marriage plot, who show no interest in marrying one another: Jean Martle falls in love with Tony and Paul Beever with Rose. The specular logic of the novel's topography is so pronounced that these infatuations of the denizens of Eastmead with those of Bounds have the flavor of theatrical crushes, as if Jean and Paul were teenagers in thrall to matinee idols. If the novel's houses respectively occupy Austen and Ibsen territory, James assures that Ibsen is where the action is: the marriage-comedy characters are so drawn to their theatrical counterparts that their love plot simply stalls out.

This plot twist already complicates the distinction of theatrical from spectatorial space that opens the novel. But that distinction is even more interestingly undermined—I want to say upstaged—by the larger question of whether *The Other House* itself "really" is, or should be, a play. A summary of the novel cannot convey what makes it so formally distinctive. The narrative passages from which I have so far quoted are deeply unrepresentative of the texture of *The Other House*: the novel mostly consists of dialogue, interrupted with stage-direction-like accounts of characters' gestures. Late James is notoriously difficult, but *The Other House* is "hard" for reasons that at first seem intellectually trivial: its difficulty has little to do with the psychological subtleties, grammatical subordinations, or metaphorical abstractions of *The Wings of the Dove* or *The Sacred Fount*. The difficulty of *The Other House* stems from its intense dialogism and descriptive parsimoniousness, and consists in simply attaining a concrete sense of where its characters are, in disentangling their elusive spatial relations to one another. The characters spend an inordinate amount of time on exactly this problem—a fact most bizarrely apparent in the climactic chapters, in which the child Effie is murdered. In the following passage Tony, Paul, and Mrs. Beever have noticed Effie's absence, and are trying with rising panic to figure out where she is. But the suspense threatens to dissolve in a ludicrous game of who's-on-first:

> "They're in the house?"
> "Not in mine—in yours."
> Tony looked surprised. "Rose and Vidal?"
> Paul spoke at last. "Jean also went over—went after them."
> Tony thought a moment. "'After them'—Jean? How long ago?"
> "About a quarter of an hour," said Paul.
> Tony continued to wonder. "Aren't you mistaken? They're not there now."
> "How do you know," asked Mrs. Beever, "if you've not been home."
> "I *have* been home—I was there five minutes ago."
> "Then how did you get here—?"
> "By the long way. I took a fly. I went back to get a paper I had stupidly forgotten and that I needed for a fellow with whom I had to talk. Our talk was a bore for the want of it, so I drove over there and got it, and, as he had his train to catch, I then overtook him at the station. I ran it close, but I saw him off; and here I am." Tony shook his head. "There's no one at Bounds."
> Mrs. Beever looked at Paul. "Then where's Effie?"
> "Effie's not here?" Tony asked.
> "Miss Armiger took her home," said Paul.
> "You saw them go?
> "No, but Jean told me."
> "Then where's Miss Armiger?" Tony continued. "And where's Jean herself?"
> "Where's Effie herself—that's the question," said Mrs. Beever.
> "No," Tony laughed, "the question's Where's Vidal?" (246–247)

The frustrations offered by the passage are, to understate the case, multiple. In addition to the manifest problem of figuring out who is where in the "offstage" area (the question with which the characters are occupied), the reader is confronted by the more basic challenge of keeping track of who is speaking here, even of remembering who is present. The laughter with which Tony Bream punctuates the dizzying round of dialogue registers the exasperation likely to greet any reader confronting the novel without pen and paper and a series of diagrams. But if it seems tempting simply to label such a passage unreadable, it is crucial to see that this unreadability is quite distinct from "modernist" difficulty. The sense of elusive spatial relations arises instead from the fact that *The Other House* appears to exist in the wrong form: most, if not all, of the passage's difficulty would be rendered moot if this text had a concrete visual presence—if instead of counting back over the lines of dialogue to see who speaks individual lines we could simply watch the characters utter them; if pronouns like "mine" and "yours" attached to visible speakers and addressees instead of floating confusingly on the page; if shifters like "here" and "there" referred to a perceptible surround instead of requiring the reader to pause and recall on which side of the river she finds herself at the moment. In other words, the passage—and the novel as a whole—reads as if it should be staged.[26]

Not that these are particularly stageable passages either: in the theater the cognitive blockage and sensory deprivation—the particular difficulty the text creates for its reader—would be lost. After its preoccupation with dialogue, the most notable feature of *The Other House* is James's frequent invocation of what a hypothetical observer *would have seen*, had there been any such spectator present to observe these events: "He might at this instant have struck a spectator as a figure actually younger and slighter than the ample, accomplished girl" (45); "It would have been equally evident to a spectator that he was a man of cool courage" (63); "Tony's face, for an initiated observer, would have shown that he was by this time watching for a trap" (159). The accumulation of such moments results in a novelistic world haunted by an unprecedented temporal condition: in place of the historical, imperfect, or present tenses in which the vast majority of novels are written, *The Other House* aspires to the past conditional.[27] Rather than mitigate the reader's sense that this world is draped in obscurity, these passages aggravate that frustration by underscoring the sensually thin medium in which the novel exists by virtue of its status as a read form. Grammatical convention dictates that a clause in the past conditional demands a counterpart in the subjunctive; James's constant conditional utterances ("Tony's face would have shown"; "It would have been evident") implicitly require a subjunctive completion: "... *if* you had seen this"; "... *had* these things passed." If the temporal protocols of the realist novel tell readers that this is how it was ("It was a dark and stormy night") or that this is how it is ("It is a truth universally acknowledged"), the temporal environment of *The Other House* delivers the more peculiar message: "You had to be there."

This subjunctive mood, not normally accessible to the novel as a form, is also, of course, unconveyable in performance. It is a textual effect, one available only by means of what James, in a preface to an 1894 collection of his unproduced plays, called "the performance imaginary."[28] The singular features of *The Other House*—its definitively unperformed status, its flirtation with unreadability—thus transfer to the reader the theatrical desire and the formal undecidability evident in the germ of the story as recorded in James's notebooks. Confronted with a novel swathed in an air of incompletion, the reader finds himself structurally obliged to hunger for the other possibility—that of performance. In the preface from which I have just quoted, James calls the publication of his rejected plays a form of "faint make-believe." In published form, he elaborates, "the covers of the book may, in a seat that costs nothing, figure the friendly curtain, and the legible 'lines' the various voices of the stage; so that if these things manage at all to disclose a picture or to drop a tone into the reader's ear the ghostly ordeal will in a manner have been passed and the dim foot-lights faced" (255). *The Other House* (written a year after these lines) is devoted to just this shadow play, subjecting its reader to the "ghostly ordeal" of imagining a performance that remains an object of hazy make-believe. *The Other House* is oriented toward the theater in the sense that performance is its desired but unachieved referent, its forever deferred outcome. It "wants" the theater and makes its reader want it; we could say that the novel intends the theater, as a cognitive act intends an object with which it never coincides.

This phenomenological peculiarity scrambles the sexual and generic politics embedded in the book's topography, giving a new torque to the opposition of Eastmead and Bounds, auditorium and stage, normals and perverts. For these antagonisms become less pressing once we recognize the extent to which the text is oriented toward performance. In a world divided between two houses that both insist on calling the other *the* other, actor and spectator prove weirdly reversible roles. We have been taught to understand Eastmead as the place of spectatorship, and so it is disconcerting to learn that the designation of alterity, and the sightlines that follow from it, run both ways: Eastmead likes to watch the dramas unfolding on the lawns of Bounds, but Bounds likes to gaze at what goes on in Eastmead's garden. As James's narrator confusingly explains, "The other side was the side of the other house, the side for the view—the view as to which [Mrs. Beever] entertained the merely qualified respect excited in us, after the first creative flush, by mysteries of our own making. Mrs. Beever herself formed the view and the other house was welcome to it" (106). The syntactic contortions of the first sentence issue in the startling news of the second: Mrs. Beever is also on display. Soon, James has turned her, metaphorically, into a circus performer:

> She had thanked God, through life, that she was cold-blooded, but now it seemed to face her as a Nemesis that she was a volcano compared with her son. This transferred to him the advantage she had so long monopolized, that of always seeing, in any relation or discussion, the other party become the spectacle, while, sitting back in her stall, she remained the spectator and even the critic. She hated to perform to

Paul as she had made others perform to herself . . . She felt, before her
son's mild gape, like a trapezist in pink tights. (137)

The passage makes clear that the novel's theatrical tropism works in particular to undermine Mrs. Beever's nondramatic status. If James's notebooks record his early intention to make her the representative of the horrified public
looking on at the unfolding drama, the novelistic world he in fact created
is continually dragging her onstage. The result is that Mrs. Beever's spectacularization threatens to overtake the murderously perverse drama at the
spotlit house across the river. Early in the novel we see Mrs. Beever react to
the unfolding events "with a certain visible rigor" (35)—and, as this erectile
description indicates, Mrs. Beever's visibility is firmly connected to hints of
her sexual abnormality. We learn, for example, that while she fails to respond
to handsome men because "for herself, somehow, Mrs. Beever was not of her
own sex" (10), she finds the murderous Rose strangely attractive: "She has . . .
a charm that I recognize" (125). Moreover, Mrs. Beever employs a "formi-
dable phalanx" of athletic parlormaids; James unsubtly names the hypermas-
culine six-foot-tall corporal of this squad Manning (116). These passages
suggest a wide range of perverse possibilities for Mrs. Beever: Is her attraction
to Rose that of the female "invert" to a "normal" woman? If Mrs. Beever isn't
a woman, is she a man? (Her surname, which lexicographers suggest already
served as slang for female genitalia, also designated in the late nineteenth
century a beard or a bearded man—thus implying that Mrs. Beever could do
double-duty in the circus as trapezist and bearded lady.)[29] If she is a "man,"
does her preference for mannish parlormaids make her a male homosexual?
Scopophilia and hysteria seem equally reasonable diagnoses. Or they would,
if the diversity of possible interpretations didn't so thoroughly frustrate the
diagnostic impulse. Rather than specify her identity, the text submits her to
a general perversification; she is the bearer of a protean but highly legible
sexual oddity.[30]

The two most crucial things to note about this spectacularization of Mrs.
Beever are, first, that it does not mark her out as the text's "real" pervert so
much as fold her into a community of deviance and, second, that this perversification has implications for the presumptive sanctity of the Jamesian
doctrine of the center of consciousness. Mrs. Beever's theatricalization results
from her attempt to occupy the position of observer, an attempt that ends
with her mirroring the perversity supposedly inhering in the object of her
gaze. James may seem to demonize the patently perverse Rose when he writes
that her "mask was the mask of Medusa" (259)—until we recall that he has already described Mrs. Beever's steely glance as "the gaze of the Gorgon" (99).
A spectacular spectator, Mrs. Beever turns out to be just as apt a representative of what Foucault called the "frozen countenance of the perversions" as
her counterpart Rose Armiger.[31] If Medusa's legendary power is to fix that

which she looks upon, the hall of mirrors set up by James's novel ensures that this petrifying energy rebounds between the normal and perverse, refusing any standpoint from which to distinguish them.

The implications of this mirroring go beyond Foucault's now familiar sense that the disciplinary technology of modern power presupposes an intimacy with its objects. Mrs. Beever's perversion is also a perversion of generic protocol, a violation of the rules supposedly governing the Jamesian novel. Mrs. Beever aspires to the psychological prestige that comes from being a Jamesian reflector, the interiorized observer who is the characterological beneficiary of the scenic principle. But Mrs. Beever's enfolding into this cast of characters allegorizes the theater's modal indifference to interior distinctions; in *The Other House*, there is no assigned seat from which to safely assist at the dramas of sexual meaning. As if in anticipation of the Artaudian theater of cruelty, the lights come up on that other house that is the auditorium, and the spectator who had hoped to enjoy the show under cover of darkness becomes the main attraction. *The Other House's* would-be center of consciousness is evacuated, and the bearer of that gaze herself hardens, under the reader's gaze, into an icon of spectacular perversity. The novel records not the differentiation of the perverse from the normal but their convergence on the terrain of the imagined performance. In order to gauge the full scope of this theatricalization, it is necessary to follow *The Other House* through another turn of the generic screw.

The Performance Imaginary II: *The Other House*, 1909

In its novelistic avatar, *The Other House* refers insistently to the play it might have been. It would be reasonable to predict that James's later decision to turn the novel back into a play would bring the story home, so to speak, to its correct form. But while there seems no reason to doubt that James wanted to see the play he wrote in 1909 performed, we can be sure that after decades of writing plays that failed to find stages on which to materialize, he was aware that publication might be the sole destination for this one as well. The play version in fact radiates effects available only through the "performance imaginary"; its most uncanny implications are intelligible only to a reader. Most strangely, when considered specifically as a read text, the play widens its perverse ambit to embrace not only each of the "other" houses but the reader who might at least have imagined herself—whatever transpired at Bounds or Eastmead—safe in hers.

James opens the first act of his play with the following stage direction: "*The geography and topography, so elaborate, so difficult, yet so possible here, all to be lucidly worked out and presented.*"[32] If the 1896 novel occupied a cognitively obscure topography, the move from the novel to the drama has not mitigated this difficulty. The "completion" of *The Other House* seems no closer at hand: James's contradictory claim that his story's setting is both "*so elaborate, so difficult*" and "*so possible here*" prompts the obvious question: Where is *here*? He could be anticipating the impending performance, relishing the idea that soon an audience will have the logic of the senses to assist in comprehending the comings and goings of his characters: "here" in this reading would refer to the stage of the play's imminent enactment. Or is it rather that that topography is so elaborate, so difficult, that it will only be fully realizable *here*, in the space of the text? The remainder of the play hardly clarifies this confusion between the logics of print and performance. After Paul Beever, at his mother's insistence, half-heartedly proposes to Jean Martle, James indicates in a stage direction that Paul

> *seems to follow* [Jean] *with his eyes as she takes her course, out of all other sight, down to the stream, through a shrubbery which marks the path to the bridge and then across the rest of the bridge to the opposite bank. He appears to wait for a renewed final sight of her, but turns away, with a drop of attention, as if it has a little puzzlingly failed him. After which, looking at his watch and coming vaguely down and across, he is aware of his mother at the opposite end of the stage: Enter* MRS. BEEVER *from the house.* (731)

The bulk of this stage direction, concerning Jean's out-of-sight perambulations, is in performative terms irrelevant. To that extent the stage direction indulges in the logic of the novelistic, in which the possibility of narrative movement affords an escape from the unity of time and place mandated by the realistic drama.[33] But James's beguilement by novelistic mobility is interrupted when we read that Paul's mother appears at the "*opposite end of the stage.*" While the opening sentences float free of the theater, here, abruptly, the stage reasserts itself as a concrete space. If the first part of the stage direction suggests that *The Other House* is "really" (or should be) a novel, the conclusion makes it seem essentially a play. There exists a third option, however—that the text is precisely neither, and that the creation of an uncannily in-between imaginary referent is the aim of the 1909 *Other House.*

One effect of such a conclusion would be to minimize the importance of the difference between the novelistic and theatrical incarnations of *The Other House.* But while both texts mutually contaminate the codes of narration and drama, these poles are not equally valued by James: if the two versions of *The Other House* only produce their effects when considered as read texts, the meaning of those effects is only clear when we recall that these texts' generic orientation—the "glamour" toward which they point—is theatrical. They share an insistent sense that the textual existence to which they are confined is incomplete even if the world they depict is "only possible here" in the space of the text. The final sentence of the stage direction quoted above suggests the defining characteristic of the impossible performances sketched by these texts. "*He is aware of his mother at the opposite end of the stage: Enter* MRS. BEEVER *from the house.*" We may by this point have become so accustomed to James's confusion of the language of the stage with the language of what that stage represents that we fail to notice the startling fact that the line literally reports the appearance of a "mother" and a "house" on a "stage." More than a lapse on the part of an inexpert playwright, this confusion of registers is a crucial aspect of the no-man's-land the text conjures. *The Other House* calls on its reader to imagine a world where a house and a mother find themselves translated to the performative environment of the stage: a domestic world operating under the sign of a pervasive theatricality.

This effect is amplified by another distinctive aspect of James's stage directions. As many critics have noted, stage directions are the component of the dramatic text that function analogously to narration in the novel. Raymond Williams observes that the drama's late-nineteenth-century bid for literary respectability involved a new emphasis on stage directions as a showcase for writerly skill, and notes that Shaw's extensive stage directions (frequently containing theatrically unrepresentable information on characters' psychology or history) are the paradigmatic example of the dramatic text's orientation toward a readership and its colonization by the logic of the novelistic.[34] More recently Elin Diamond has argued that the prestige of stage directions in the late century was linked to the will-to-interpretation central to psychoanalytic inquiry. Stage directions served to anchor the meaning of the performer's gestures, to render the performative body a legible container of interior truth.[35]

But James's unstageable stage directions function differently. Rather than foray into the possibilities afforded by the novel, they create a world existing between the poles of theater and narration—one that thereby scrambles the logic of legible personality. James's stage directions imagine a universe conditioned by the subjunctive mood. This is a world in which the tiniest gestures are pervaded by a theatrical self-consciousness, the most intimate emotions qualified by a philosophy of "as if." The following exchange between Tony and Rose is typical:

> ROSE. (*Prompt; and as with the air, for herself, of being again in possession of him.*) Do you ask that partly because you're apprehensive that it's what I propose to you?
> TONY. (*Easy; as not, to his perturbation, apprehensive on that.*) By no means, my dear Rose, after your just giving me so marked a sign of the pacific as your coming round—
> Rose. (*Taking him straight up.*) On the question of one's relation to that little image and echo of her adored Mother? (*Then after an instant; as full of a purpose of her own.*) That isn't peace, my dear Tony. (721)

The introductory "as" is so persistent in the stage directions to *The Other House* that it may escape attention how wholly odd a construction it is. It is impossible to tell whether these stage directions provide diegetic or directorial information—that is, whether they describe characters who only ever represent their emotions or whether they are not descriptions of characters at all but instructions for actors. When James says that Rose speaks "*as full of a purpose of her own*," is he telling us something about Rose (for instance, that she lacks this purpose but must feign it in order to achieve her goals in this exchange)—or informing the hypothetical actress portraying Rose of the impression she must convey to her spectators? If the latter, James's consistent use of "as" betrays a strangely naïve desire to remind the actors at every turn that they are merely impersonating fictional characters; if these stage directions have a purely directorial intention, the usual form—"*prompt; with an air of being in possession of him*"; "*full of a purpose of her own*"—would function with more clarity.

The question of how to take these stage directions is inherently undecidable; we cannot know whether to understand them according to the logic of narration (information about Rose) or that of the theater (information for the actress). They refer neither to a coherently conceived alternate reality, as would a realist novel, nor to a coherently imagined performance, as would a dramatic text, but to a reality conscious of its status as performatively constituted, a space in which the boundary between actress and character recedes into indistinction. James thereby inserts the subjunctive mood into a text that by virtue of its status as a play script already calls attention to itself as a blueprint for a hypothetical future performance; we could describe this emphatically subjunctive effect as the creation of a second-order performativity. Whether one conceives of the text's referent as a play that has expanded to encompass the entire world or as some version of the real world in which everyone behaves as if he were onstage, this impossible space has two salient features: it can only be cognitively represented via the text, and it is a place where identity is a definitionally incoherent quantity. Introducing a performative dimension into the texture of the stage directions, James refuses an interiorizing psychology any conceptual ground at all. This is a reversal of the usual critical story: far from functioning as the site at which the novel invades the theater, James's stage directions defeat the logic of the novelistic. The generic undecidability embedded in the conception of the two *Other Houses* disintegrates the concept of interiority with which James-the-novelist is so closely associated.

The implications of this corrosion of identity for any attempt to name and make perversion legible are serious. Once the functions of spectator and performer are no longer localizable in distinct individuals—once that demarcation line has taken up residence in the interiority of every person in *The Other House*—the anxious project of differentiating seer from seen can gain no traction.[36] In a crucial scene in the 1909 text, for example, Rose appears on stage and talks with Tony. She is flushed and anxious, and we shortly learn that she has just drowned the child Effie; Mrs. Beever, her suspicions aroused, moves to the back of the stage as if to depart. Importantly, James specifies that Mrs. Beever carries *"a book in her hand . . . which volume . . . she now, while she leans against the parapet, or whatever, that marks the picture here, vaguely opens as if to keep herself quiet"* (735). As Mrs. Beever surreptitiously looks on from behind the cover of her book, Tony and Rose begin to speak:

> ROSE: [. . .] (*She stands a moment, again, looking down; and then still not meeting his eyes, brings out abruptly and in different* [sic], *a lower, tone.*) Don't stand so *near* me. The Queen-Mother's waiting there (*as if he hasn't known she has stayed*)—and she's not reading; she's *watching* us.
> TONY. (*Holding his ground and not turning about to see; as if in fact amused at her fine circumspection, while he yet accepts her hint of the lowered tone.*) How in the world, with your back turned, can you *see* that?
> ROSE. (*With quiet irony and as if enjoying even the momentary passage with him.*) It's with my back turned that I see most. (*Looking straight before her; facing the spectators.*) She's looking at us hard. (736)

The interplay of sightlines is dizzying: Rose, poised at the edge of the stage, explains that a character stationed behind her is looking at "us," a pronoun in the first place designating herself and Tony and in the second taking in the hypothetical audience of *The Other House*. James's habit of scrambling the referential code of the stage directions makes this second meaning startlingly explicit. Here, for the only time in the text, the theatrical audience is not merely implied but named: there just are *"spectators"* to this scene, and Rose, along with Mrs. Beever, is openly gazing at them. If this moment would be striking enough on the stage, its most uncanny implications arise in the reading situation. If, as James claims, in the printed drama the covers of the book figure the curtain in a "performance imaginary," these lines position Rose not only at the edge of the stage but at the very border of the text we hold in our hands, returning the reader's voyeuristic gaze. The neurotic infanticide is at the height of her perverse legibility in this scene, and she is here literally surrounded by those—Mrs. Beever, ourselves—who would read her under cover of absorption in a book. But in one of the more striking of the dethematizing spatializations we have encountered, Rose acknowledges the theatrical house and in the process deflects that perversifying gaze. Her disconcerting assertion that she, in effect, has eyes in the back of her head refers, on the one hand, to the ease with which she sees through Mrs. Beever's pose of readerly disinterest. But she also seems to see through ours: she violates what D. A.

Miller describes as the "very ontology" of fictional characters, whose normal condition is to exist as a "subject of readerly perusal unable to *look back*."[37] James threatens to revoke the privileges structuring the reading situation.[38] Fantasmatically intruding on the reader's privacy, Rose rejects the presumed innocence of reading itself, outing its evident pleasure in the spectacle of deviance and combating the localization of perversity in her person.

If in *The Other House* these effects are intelligible mostly as threats (to the reader's privacy, and to her presumed normality), it is worth considering them also as the vehicle of a utopian impulse. The naming of the reader can be seen as an invasion of her privacy, or it can be seen as the end of her isolation. This scene could be described as subjecting its reader to a regime of punitive specularity; but these multiplying gazes also make for a paradise of what James in *A Small Boy and Others* labels "taking in"—an activity that he describes as offering "the very greatest pleasure perhaps I was ever to know" (145). If *The Other House* perversifies the reader by taking her in—that is, by looking at her—it also takes her in in a more welcoming sense, enfolding her in a world where that fact loses its identitarian implications: a world bathed in a boomeranging specularity defeats the ability of any particular gaze to fix its object. In the first scene of the 1909 play, Rose describes Eastmead and Bounds, despite their differences of temperament and position, as "bridged so charmingly for so easy an intercourse" (681). This is precisely the fantasy toward which *The Other House* gestures in its various incarnations: a dream of promiscuous intercourse between theater and book, actor and spectator, reader and read, normal and perverse. Crucially, *The Other House* articulates this dream not by claiming that the novel can adequately absorb and displace the theater but by persistently, even exasperatingly, emphasizing the novel's failure to be theater, its distance from embodiment and the social event of performance. In its necessary incompletion, its failure to coincide with any particular aesthetic embodiment, James's "other house" names a project yet to be achieved, a public yet to be convened. James gave this ambition its most sustained expression in the impossible performance of *The Awkward Age*.

In the Sociable Dusk of *The Awkward Age*

> Better to focus the image he closed his eyes awhile.
> —Henry James, *The Awkward Age*

The plot of *The Other House* turns on the attempt of certain of its characters to imagine themselves safely on one side of what James elsewhere termed "the queer chasm" separating stage from auditorium—a plot given point by James's indecision about which side of a generic divide his story should inhabit.[39] By the time he published *The Awkward Age* in 1899, however, James appeared to have definitively settled into the house of fiction. His generic ambivalence, if not vanquished, may at least seem to have been confined to that group of texts marked by the name "the other house"; although it resembles *The Other House* in its dialogism, James never imagined *The Awkward Age* as anything other than a work of narrative fiction. But in fact *The Awkward Age* does not so much resolve the generic impossibility of *The Other House* as wholeheartedly surrender to it. The later novel abandons the avowed desire for performance, but it aggravates the representational strangeness—and the feeling of generic wrongness—salient in the earlier book; in the process it heightens the desire for the performance it has renounced. As we have seen, James quite early associated the theater with a collective consciousness and with a permeable, almost mystically *other* domesticity. *The Awkward Age*, whose characters are described as "a collection of natural affinities" and whose chief setting is an "impossible house," is best understood (despite its self-announcement as a novel) as a blueprint for an impossible performance, and a scheme for a new form of community.[40] *The Awkward Age* not only relocates the theater's "queer chasm" inside each of its characters but makes that self-difference definitive of a social universe otherwise arranged.

For the novel's unsympathetic critics, the extremism of the novel's form has rightly been seen as related to the oddity of its content. In a novelistic world defined thematically by ramifying perversion and formally by endless conversation, sex and talk come to stand in for each other. An anonymous contemporary reviewer for the *Spectator* impugned both the moral fiber of the characters in *The Awkward Age* and the novel's dialogic mode by calling the book "a whispering-gallery of ignoble souls"; the *New York Times* critic noted that "depravity seems to be [the characters'] common bond," and complained that "perhaps James in picturing so well the minds of his creatures fails to give them permanent corporeal form."[41] Such reactions set the terms for the novel's harshest later critics. In his attack on James, Maxwell Geismar discerned a world of "evil sexuality" through the "continuous chatter" of *The Awkward Age*; Edmund Wilson claimed that the novel is filled with "a whole host of creepy creatures . . . a gibbering, disembowelled crew who hover about one another with sordid, shadowy designs."[42] For all these writers, the novel's perversity is yoked to its dialogism and the insubstantial universe that dialogism creates: the book's sexuality is one with its spectrality. Moreover, these critics note that any moral distinctions James draws *among* characters are less salient than the universal representational medium in which they are given: victim and victimizer, ingénue and rake—they comprise a "collection of natural affinities" not by virtue of their actions but in the substance of their beings.

In this emphasis on the book's ghostliness, James's detractors in fact offer a more accurate account of his achievement than do his partisans. Among the latter the keynote is struck by Percy Lubbock, who elevated the "show, don't tell" dictum supposedly embedded in the Jamesian scenic principle

into a novelistic prescription. For Lubbock, scenic construction intensifies
the concreteness of the fictional world, and *The Craft of Fiction* accordingly
commends James's work for having "solidity, weight, a third dimension." In
Lubbock's account, James's scenic novels do not just aspire to but actually
achieve the vividness of an "embodied" and "palpable" event.[43] If the first set
of critics faults James for creating novels of distressing intangibility, Lubbock and those who follow him find the same novels thrillingly concrete. For
James's defenders, the scenic principle effectively circumvents what Elaine
Scarry has called the "enfeeblement" of imagined objects.[44] In Scarry's account, verbal art begins from a disadvantage in imparting "vivacity" to its
consumers: where theater and film are "brimming with auditory and visual
commitments" (5), novels rely on the impoverished sensory data provided by
words on a page. Scarry argues that in order to make an unreal world imagi-
natively available to a reader, verbal art prompts an effort of "perceptual mimesis" (6), spurring readers to employ the same faculties of perception on
the fictional world that they would on a concretely present object of perception. The success of this operation depends on its being kept hidden from the
reader; this difficult imaginative process must happen behind the scenes, as it
were, of our readerly attention. "Reading entails an immense labor of imaginative construction" (37), Scarry writes, but this process of world-imagining
must feel all but effortless to function successfully.

It will be clear from my description of James's most strictly scenic novels
that they refuse the solidity, and the air of ease, that Scarry describes. As in
The Other House, the spatial relations of *The Awkward Age*—its "staging"—
can be baffling, often comically so. And even more incessantly than in the
earlier novel, James makes reference to what a hypothetical observer "might
even have detected" (88) had such an observer been present; what "might
have been seen" (93) had someone been there to see it; what "another pair of
eyes might moreover have detected" (121) had such eyes existed. The effect
of this amplified subjunctive spectatorship is complex. On the one hand, the
increased frequency of these evocations makes the imaginary audience for
The Awkward Age feel "bigger": the multiplication of these moments implies
that a crowd of observers watches the most private scenes from just beyond
a transparent fourth wall. On the other, the relentlessly subjunctive nature
of these invocations makes us feel even more forcefully that we are not that
audience. To an even greater extent than in *The Other House*, this device, far
from concretizing the action, causes it to recede behind a cloud of speculation; while the novel seems to take place in an imagined performative space,
and before an audience, the reader is constantly reminded of having missed
the show. The result is to make this novel of contemporary London seem to
transpire in some parallel dimension, or as if its narrated action constituted
a legendary performance whose precise look and tone was available only to
some fortunate first-night public.

Perhaps the most striking technique the book employs to complicate the process of world-imagining is its underdescription of its inhabitants. Mr. Longdon, the elderly provincial visitor to the fast London set around which the novel turns, is introduced as lacking in "mass, substance, presence—what is vulgarly called importance. He had indeed no presence, but he had somehow an effect" (20). In this gauziness he is typical of the inhabitants of *The Awkward Age*. Even when James discusses his characters' bodies, he stops short of physical description; the attribution of some definite physical effect is often a means to evade positing any actual corporeal trait. Harold Brookenham is notable—or not?—for "the acuteness, difficult to trace to a source, of his smooth fair face" (39); his father has "a pale, cold face, marked . . . by a hardness of line in which, oddly, there was no significance, no accent" (53). Mr. Mitchett boasts "little intrinsic appearance" (59), while Carrie Donner is an "apparition" (73). And Nanda, whom we first encounter via the "faded image" (27) of a photograph, is described by Vanderbank as having "no features." He elaborates: "She's at the age when the whole thing—speaking of her appearance, her possible share of good looks—is still, in a manner, in a fog" (31–32). The fogginess of these descriptions ensures that, even more drastically than *The Other House*, *The Awkward Age* conveys the impression that it exists in some incomplete, preliminary, or second-best version of itself. Or, to put this somewhat differently: the experience James creates for his reader is not (as Lubbock claims) that of witnessing a performance but of reading a play—one that has not yet been cast with the actors who will give these names bodily density.

An analysis of the referential status of play texts by theater historian Erika Fischer-Lichte clarifies the cognitive effort James thereby enjoins on his reader. She argues that the orientation of dramatic texts to a future performance makes them heavy with corporeal reference: "we cannot conceive of the dramatic character without a body, even if the character is conceived while reading a playscript."[45] James's text is similarly difficult to read without invoking some imagined "staging" that would give flesh to its ghostly frames. But where play texts can rely on an at least hypothetical enactment to lend density to their descriptive thinness, *The Awkward Age* reads like a play marked with the caveat *never to be performed*. In severing even the imagined connection between dramatic text and intended enactment, James frustrates our habitual referential expectations and creates for his reader a mild but persistent experience of cognitive impossibility. "We cannot conceive of the dramatic character without a body"—but, the novel insists, we must. This awkward injunction—and not the more familiar difficulty presented by Jamesian supersubtlety—is surely what has led critics to complain of the unique readerly effort demanded by *The Awkward Age*.[46]

It would be a mistake to conclude that James's creation of an impossible performance is "antitheatrical." Performing the awkward mental gymnastics necessary to imagine this stage, the reader has not been liberated from theatrical enactment so much as made to feel her exile from it more acutely. In this way, James's effort to spark the reader's desire to see *The Awkward Age* "put on" is intimately connected to the text's social desire, its ambition to imagine a world that would protect the radical social values described in the novel. The challenge of sustaining an image of the novel's action functions as a correlative to the challenge of sustaining a world that would harbor that action; the imaginative difficulty the novel demands of its readers is, to paraphrase Scarry, a mimesis of social effort. In enjoining on his reader an effort of mental dramaturgy, James increases both the ingenuity and the poignancy of the novel's social imagination. The phenomenological thinness of the book and the cognitive labor it demands of the reader are a constant reminder of the fragility of the social world it sketches. But if the extremity of James's formal experimentation accentuates the sense of social constraint, it can also sharpen the desire to overcome it. The sense of cognitive and social difficulty courted by the novel, far from resigning readers to "a platitude of acceptance of the poor actual," may incite us to imagine a more capacious social world.

Gauging the provocation of *The Awkward Age*, in other words, requires asking what the impossibility of *The Awkward Age* makes possible. The simplest answer to this question—one that quickly becomes fairly complex—is that the novel imagines and protects a world of sexual permission. *The Awkward Age* is distinctive not only for its formal oddity but for its attack on the power of the marriage plot to assign narrative significance to certain parts of a life story, for its refusal to identify sexual perversions with discrete individuals, for its demurral from identitarian coherence in favor of group consciousness, and for its mapping of a less punishing scene of sexual publicity than those current in the late nineteenth century.[47] The novel's obsession with the drama—in particular, its interest in the possibilities of dialogue or "talk"—is the rallying point for these interrelated efforts. And the sexual and relational permission granted to the characters in *The Awkward Age* is ample. The deviant relationships flourishing in the novel's shadows have been well documented, and excoriated, by critics such as Geismar and Wilson: the elderly Mr. Longdon's infatuation with Vanderbank at the novel's opening and his incestuously toned "adoption" of the teenager Nanda at its close; Mitchett's cash-for-sex arrangement with Lord Petherton; the latter's use of a dirty French novel as an erotic prosthesis in his wrestling match with the newlywed Agnesina; Mrs. Brookenham's pimping of her son Harold to wealthy family friends, and her apparent rivalry with her daughter for the affections of Vanderbank; the Duchess's adulterous liaison with Harold; Carrie Donner's contemplated affair with Mr. Cashmore; Tishy Grendon's predilection for skimpy dresses that present "a choice, as to consciousness, between the effect of her being and the effect of her not being dressed" (227); the universal adoption of nicknames that seem virilizing in the case of women (Mrs. Brookenham becomes Mrs. Brook) and feminizing or castratory in the case of men (Mitchett becomes Mitchy), and so on. As Vanderbank (aka Van) sighs at one point, "It's a queer life" (127): making room for homosexuality, fetishism, masochism, pedophilia, nymphomania, gender inversion, exhibitionism, scopophilia, and prostitution, *The Awkward Age* constitutes a veritable roll call of fin-de-siècle deviance.[48]

If the similarity to *The Other House* is striking, so, too, is at least one important difference. Where the earlier novel achieves a pervasive perversity by turning the houselights up to enfold its characters in a play of mutual gazes, *The Awkward Age* arrives at the same end by turning down the lights, by stressing not universal visibility but universal shadiness. The darkness that enfolds the novel's social field provides protective cover for its perversity: *The Awkward Age* never forces its inhabitants to cough up the list I have just crudely provided. It is crucial to the proliferation of these erotic possibilities that they remain conjectural, never confirmed or denied by the represented action of the novel, which is occupied not with depictions of sexual impropriety but with talk about its possibility. "The less tempered darkness favoured talk" (214), James writes at one point, in words describing the phenomenological law undergirding the medium of *The Awkward Age* itself. The novel transpires in what James calls "the sociable dusk" (217), an obscure place where visual deprivation permits—even provokes—a stream of suggestive discussion. Talk, then, is as important as sex in this novel; or, more precisely, talk is important *to* the sex in this novel. "What is *The Awkward Age* about?" Tzvetan Todorov asks in the closing lines of an essay that points to the starring role of conversation in the novel. "It is about what it is to talk, and to talk about something."[49] But in its circularity this formulation stops exactly too soon, ignoring the connection between the novel's investment in talk and its exploration of erotic possibility. The "something" that the characters are continually occupied with talking about is sex, and their talk creates the medium in which sex flourishes in various forms and with relative impunity.

The novel and the social world it narrates are both organized according to a belief in the limited but real power of talk to performatively rearrange the contours of the permissible, and to deflect attention from sexual difference as a socially or narratively significant fact. When, early in the novel, the Duchess hears that Lord Petherton "lives on" the wealthy Mitchy, she exclaims that this relationship constitutes a "social scandal." Mrs. Brookenham replies: "Oh, we don't call *that* a social scandal!" (51–52). Declaring an active disinterest in the constative question of whether Mitchy's arrangement with Petherton *is* or is *not* a scandal, Mrs. Brookenham calls attention instead to her coterie's power of designation—and, as if miraculously, the novel heeds her decree. For the remainder of the book this would-be outrage fails to achieve any narrative importance whatsoever. However briefly, her words enact the fantasy of a discursive practice that performatively cancels the pressures of sexual propriety and sexual identitarianism, "talk" that engages sex without naming it as the truth of the subject. The exchange demonstrates in miniature the labor of Mrs. Brookenham's group to protect a space of what the novel elsewhere calls "queer condonations" (149). Against what Foucault termed the "perverse implantation" of the late-century, this dethematizing labor deserves recognition as truly heroic—the more so because of its ultimate futility.[50]

In disrupting the assignment of narrative importance to sexual facts that outside of this coterie and outside of the pages of *The Awkward Age* were commonly understood as catastrophic (the recent Oscar Wilde trials provide one conspicuous example), "talk" is a key strategy.[51] An equally important effect of the novel's commitment to dialogue is its departure from the supposed Jamesian law of a central consciousness and its corresponding notion of psychological depth. If James developed this strategy in *The Other House* by means of an unstable specularity, *The Awkward Age* undermines the notion of a central consciousness even further, first by removing any topographical or characterological location through which to focalize the action such as those James begins by offering in Eastmead and Mrs. Beever in the earlier novel. This novel remains constitutively unclear about precisely whose story it might be understood to be telling. While Nanda's failed marriage plot provides the novel with its temporal horizon, the lack of all interiorizing narrative prevents her consciousness from becoming the object of preeminent interest. Trained on the doctrine of "establishing one's successive centres" of consciousness (*AN*, 296) that James's prefaces expound, we might attempt to preserve a characterological orientation for *The Awkward Age*; taking our cue from James's labeling of each of the novel's ten "books" with a proper name, we might decide that the novel is centered not on one or two central characters but on ten in succession. But if we note that the first book is named for the long-dead Lady Julia, and others for relatively unimportant players—the climactic Book VIII, for example, is named for the peripheral Tishy Grendon, seemingly because it takes place at her house—it becomes clear that the correlation of textual unit to human personality is incoherent. The books are not in any clear sense about the characters for whom they are named, and *The Awkward Age* is not about anyone in particular.[52]

By preventing us from choosing any particular character with whom to identify, through whom to perceive, or even on whom to concentrate, James leaves his reader with the sole option of cathecting the entire social scene.[53] While a perverse collectivity was an incipient possibility of the imaginary dramatic space invoked by *The Other House*, *The Awkward Age*'s abandonment of any orienting topography makes for a less anxiously policed representational universe. Along with a fixed position of spectatorship, the possibility of read-ing psychological truth off of surfaces evaporates in this novel. James posits this nonpathologizing relation between psychology and specularity in a pas-sage describing Mrs. Brook's drawing room; it is, we read,

> a place in which, at all times, before interesting objects, the unanimous occupants, almost more concerned for each other's vibrations than for anything else, were apt rather more to exchange sharp and silent searchings than to fix their eyes on the object itself. (75–76)

In its exchange of gazes, the passage may seem to belie my earlier observa-tion that *The Awkward Age* folds its characters in a saving obscurity. But the specularity described here has little in common with the Gorgon gazes of *The Other House*; indeed, in its disinterest in psychological depth, the activity described here seems hardly to participate in what we typically recognize as specularity. The "object" to which the passage refers is the unhappily married Lady Fanny, whose possible elopement is much on the minds of the coterie. But this interest does not issue in any attempt to "read" Lady Fanny, whose sexual escapades instead inspire a play of lateral glances among the salon members. And although James figures these gazes as "sharp and silent search-ings," it would be a mistake to conclude that they represent attempts at psy-chological penetration. Rather than trying to plumb one another's depths, the members of the salon tune their attention to the "vibrations" the scene produces among them; they seem to be exchanging tactile sensations as much as visual or cognitive data. The scene is strikingly close to the one in *A Small Boy and Others* in which James explains that his pleasure in the theater has less to do with the onstage spectacle than with "becom[ing] thus aware of our collective attitude . . . I am not sure I wasn't thus more interested in the pulse of our small party, under my tiny recording thumb, than in the beat of the drama" (85). In neither scene does the thrill of spectatorship derive from achieving epistemological leverage over a spectacle. (Indeed, it seems hardly necessary to *see* the spectacle.) Rather, what fuels these theaters is the appre-hension among the audience members of a depsychologized and pleasurably embodied collectivity.

James's description of Mrs. Brook's parlor serves as an account of *The Awk-ward Age* itself, and its refusal to make a scene over the sexual transgressions in which it is awash. Instead, what flourishes in this permissive atmosphere is precisely the type of collective consciousness for which James reaches in his desubjectified autobiography. "Here we are together," Mitchy declares at one point, "one beautiful intelligence" (177). The project of *The Awkward Age* is to sustain the narrative conditions under which such a corporate conscious-ness can remain a lived social reality. The importance of this project to these apparently superficial characters is palpable: one of the novel's oddest features is its characters' seeming awareness of the fragility of the medium in which their coterie flourishes. As Mrs. Brook puts it when justifying one of her recent franknesses, "If the principal beauty of our effort to live together is ... in our sincerity, I simply obeyed the impulse to do the sincere thing. If we're not sincere, we're nothing" (180). Unlike many another Jamesian character, there is nothing "deep" about Mrs. Brookenham at this moment: with nothing to hide, she has nothing to lose by publicizing her investment in the struggle to maintain the group's vitality. Her words are a precise summary of the novel's depsychologizing agenda, the resistance it offers to psychic privacy in the name of group subjectivity. The conversation in which Mrs. Brookenham utters these words concerns Mr. Longdon's decision to supply Nanda with a dowry in an effort to persuade Vanderbank to marry her—an outcome that, in detaching one of the coterie's key players, would put its collective effort out of commission. Her comment thus makes clear that the ethical project the novel outlines is menaced most frontally by the marital imperative. The marriage plot organizes all the values against which the formal and thematic peculiarities of *The Awkward Age* are ranged: in place of a studied disinterest in particular affective configurations, it privileges one relation over others; instead of dispersing interest over a collective subject, it draws attention to two psychological centers; in place of the externalizing force of talk, it seeks out and ratifies characters' internal truth; and in place of an interest in the tributaries and eddies of potentially endless conversation, the marriage plot has an overriding interest in arriving at the end of narrative.

In a discussion of the truth games entailed by aesthetic forms, Paul Morrison contrasts the "culture of spectacle" with "the dispensation of the Word," arguing that at stake in this opposition are "the modes of human subjectivity and somatic organization—perverse or otherwise—that any given aesthetic form presupposes and promotes."[54] Morrison aligns the former with the externality of the theater and the latter with the novel's "theatrically inaccessible interiority" (23) and the "heterosexualizing 'machinery'" (31) of the marriage plot. The generic impossibility of *The Awkward Age* dramatizes precisely the standoff between two generic orders and two models of psychosexual meaning; the suspense of the novel lies not in the question of whether Nanda will marry but in whether novelistic meaning will triumph over theatrical externality. The characters' most effective strategy against novelistic logic is tactical delay. Interest in the marriage plot is continually sidetracked by the pleasures of dilatory, non-utilitarian conversation, as the characters make clear in their remarkably drawn-out discussions of Nanda's romantic prospects. Concluding one such conversation on the likelihood of Van marrying Nanda, Mrs. Brook seems to be warily eyeing the narrative arc of *The Awkward Age* itself:

"Dear Van will think conscientiously a lot about it, but he won't do it . . . We shall be very kind to him, we shall help him, hope and pray for him, but we shall be at the end," said Mrs Brook, "just where we are now. Dear Van will have done his best, and we shall have done ours. Mr Longdon will have done his—poor Nanda even will have done hers. But it will all have been in vain. . . . It lacks, as I say, the element of real suspense." (178)

Synopsizing the plot of the novel in which she figures—and thereby mitigating the urgency of its progress—Mrs. Brook highlights her own utterance ("as I say") as an alternative site of interest. With a string of future perfect clauses that draw attention to themselves through the sheer oddity of their temporal orientation, Mrs. Brook talks about the marriage plot as a way to forestall moving through it.[55] If the marriage ceremony functions as the paradigmatic example in J. L. Austin's theory of performatives, Mrs. Brook's weird meandering around the possibility of such a ceremony (a meandering that renders that possibility ever more remote) is a signal instance of what Eve Sedgwick calls the periperformative. A class of utterances "around" the performative, periperformatives comment on speech acts (expressing bemusement over a dare, say, or exulting over a proposal, or voicing regret about a promise) —and in so doing can work both to render visible the compulsory nature of any specific performative scene and to "disinterpellate" speakers from it.[56]

The detachment Mrs. Brook displays over Nanda's marital prospects is commonly read either as a monstrous neglect of her daughter's interests or as an equally monstrous ploy to keep (or obtain) Vanderbank as her own lover. But it should be recognized as a disinterpellative strategy, an effort to stave off the culturally enforced marital telos. Strikingly, Nanda's speech—the only means, in this novel, to gauge what she wants—evinces the same detachment, and by using the same proleptic verbal structure. Urged by Mr. Longdon to desert her mother's sociable salon ("I wish immensely you'd get married!"), Nanda replies, several chapters before her mother's prediction, "I shall be one of the people who don't. I shall be at the end . . . one of those who haven't" (142). By her own report, Nanda falls on her mother's side of the novel's talk-story divide: "I want to hear all the talk" (97), she frankly informs Mitchy. To read through these utterances to decide that Nanda and her mother are locked in agonistic combat is not only to miss the congruence of their stated desires. It is to ignore the challenge they both mount to the power of the marriage plot to define an intelligible life. In this struggle, mother and daughter, far from being opposed, should be seen as allies. If there is pathos in *The Awkward Age*, it lies in the fact that its generic identity seems ultimately to close down these efforts to resist the logic of the novelistic.

James and His Kind

Although James appears to narrate the defeat of Nanda and Mrs. Brooken-ham's performative battle against the generic constraints of the novel as a form, a different outcome becomes visible when we attend to the fact that *The Awkward Age* also constructs for itself an imaginary theatrical public that seems oddly indifferent to the spectacle of psychic legibility. The novel's di-egetic action reaches its climax in the party recorded in Book VIII. But this party is most interesting as a scene of generic anagnorisis, the moment when the novel acknowledges the impossibility of sustaining its play-like texture and the performative project that texture expresses. The episode turns on a risqué novel—described earlier as an "impossible book" (197)—and ends with a social cataclysm that James compares to the collapse of a theater. Suit-ably the episode aggravates the confusion between novelistic and dramatic modes to the point of near incomprehensibility. The scene is confusingly set thus:

> "Mitchy's silent, Mitchy's altered, Mitchy's queer!" Mrs Brook pro-claimed, while the new recruits to the circle, Tishy and Nanda and Mr Cashmore, Lady Fanny and Harold too after a minute and on perceiv-ing the movement of the others, ended by enlarging it, with mutual accommodation and aid, to a pleasant talkative ring in which the sub-ject of their companion's ejaculation, on a low ottoman and glaring in his odd way in almost all directions at once, formed the conspicu-ous, attractive centre. Tishy was nearest Mr Longdon, and Nanda, still flanked by Mr Cashmore, between that gentleman and his wife, who had Harold on her other side. Edward Brookenham was neighboured by his son and by Vanderbank, who might easily have felt himself, in spite of their separation and given, as it happened, their places in the group, rather publicly confronted with Mr Longdon. "Is his wife in the other room?" Mrs Brook now put to Tishy. (245–246)

As with the breathlessly farcical business of the 1896 *Other House*, the dif-ficulty in picturing the action threatens to upstage the interest we might take in its content. The careful laying of the scene, far from conveying a vivid vi-sual image, makes the bewildered reader all the more aware of his exclusion from the enactment that would render the arrangement of these characters immediately comprehensible. This imaginative strain in turn lends urgency to the gathering thematic crisis: in inquiring after the whereabouts of little Aggie, Mrs. Brookenham triggers the collapse of the book's marriage plot and the dissolution of her coterie. The newlywed Aggie, we soon learn, is in an adjoining room "playing" with Petherton and an obscene French novel that Nanda, under her mother's interrogation, confesses to having read. With

Nanda's innocence revealed as compromised, Vanderbank decides he cannot marry her. He abandons her mother's circle, which now seems certain to descend into a final silence.

There is a plausible characterological motivation for Mrs. Brookenham's self-destructive initiation of this chain of events: she seems simply exhausted by the hypocritical effort of keeping up what she has earlier termed "the preposterous fiction, as it after all is, of Nanda's blankness of mind" (170). But Mrs. Brookenham's fatigue can also be described as a formal one—as if she, and *The Awkward Age* itself, were collapsing under the effort of maintaining the "pleasant talkative ring" in a generic medium that demands less dalliance and more progress, less perverse obscurity and more moral clarity, less talk and more meaning. Mrs. Brookenham's exhaustion here is doubled by the cognitive awkwardness the reader experiences in this scene, which delivers clumsily in narration a picture that cries out for a stage.

In discussing the event in the following chapter, the characters fittingly compare it to the destruction of a theater, and they do so by invoking a canonical closet drama. "It was a wonderful performance," Vanderbank tells Mrs. Brookenham.

> "You pulled us down—just closing with each of the great columns in its turn—as Samson pulled down the temple. I was at the time more or less bruised and buried, and I didn't in the agitation and confusion fully understand what had happened. But I understand now." (253)

Milton's *Samson Agonistes* makes the case against the theater in dramatic form; the poem records a theatrical disaster in the form of an unperformed play. In its hero's anguished cries to be sheltered from the gawking crowds of Gaza, the poem anticipates the inward gaze of the psychological novel—the inverse of the polarity structuring James's book, which tries to sustain the value of performance against the claims of interiority in a form that appears hostile to the endeavor. The generic contrarianism of *Samson Agonistes*, its dawdling approach to a violent climax, and its preoccupation with blindness make it a crucial intertext for James's most thoroughly scenic novel.[57] But where Milton, propagandist for the regime that closed the theaters, wrote against a restored culture of display, James writes against the novelization of everything. Milton's Samson pulls down the temple in a heroic gesture of antitheatricalism, whereas the collapse in James's novel registers as a genuine loss. In the preface to *The Awkward Age*, James makes the dramatic conception of his novel explicit by comparing his work on the book to the effort of writing a play—an activity he in turn describes as constructing a sturdy edifice: "The dramatist has verily to *build*, is committed to architecture, to construction at any cost" (*AN*, 109). James's conception of dramatic writing as architecture suggests that the social demolition at the novel's climax also describes the disintegration of the book's structural principles. "We've fallen to pieces" (253), Mrs. Brookenham insists, in words that might refer both to her circle's ill-fated shared consciousness and to the very performative conception of *The Awkward Age*.

Sheila Teahan notes that "Van's 'impossible book,' the French novel whose circulation stages Nanda's definitive and fatal exposure . . . figures *The Awkward Age* itself."[58] We might add that this moral impossibility is tied to a generic one. What is revealed in these scenes is not that *The Awkward Age* is just as sexually loose as the novel that precipitates its crisis; this does not count as a revelation at all, given the novel's unanxious harboring of deviant sexual possibility. What comes to pieces at the novel's climax is *The Awkward Age*'s attempt to shelter performance in the heart of the novel. This capitulation is signaled by the novel's now hasty march toward its close, and it is most forcefully articulated in the novel's final scene, where the play of meanings around the notion of impossibility is reduced to the question of identity which the book has been dodging with such ingenuity. Before this scene, the epithet "impossible" has been applied to a variety of objects and spaces: to the Brookenham house (50) and the "class" of people it welcomes (46), to Mitchy's conversation (64), to Tishy Grendon's parlor (71), to Van's book (197), and, finally, as Teahan notes, to *The Awkward Age* itself—the figure and container for all these. But impossibility now abruptly attaches itself to one lonely character. Not coincidentally, it does so during a conversation in which Nanda appears to avow, in the irrefutable language of the body, her passion for Vanderbank. Longdon is comforting Nanda for losing Van:

> "It would be easier for me," he went on heedless, "if you didn't, my poor child, so wonderfully love him."
>
> "Ah, but I don't—please believe me when I assure you I *don't*!" she broke out. It burst from her, flaring up, in a queer quaver that ended in something queerer still—in her abrupt collapse, on the spot, into the nearest chair, where she choked with a torrent of tears . . . "Ah, Nanda, Nanda!" [Longdon] deeply murmured; and the depth of the pity was, vainly and blindly, as the depth of a reproach.
>
> "It's I—it's I, therefore," she said as if she must then so look at it with him, "it's I who am the horrible impossible and who have covered everything else with my own impossibility. For some different person you *could* have done what you speak of, and for some different person you can do it still."
>
> He stared at her with his barren sorrow. "A person different from him?"
>
> "A person different from *me*." (308–309)

Nanda's admission of her unsuitability for marriage no longer concerns what she knows or with whom she talks, but, more insidiously, what she is: her avowal is not epistemological or social but ontological in nature. No longer the beneficiary of a circulating traffic of pleasurably impossible products, Nanda appears to rewrite herself as their impure source: "It's I . . . who have covered everything else with my own impossibility."

But might Nanda's thrice-repeated first-person pronoun imply not insistence but hesitation, a hint of resistance to the logic of identity she articulates? The most inviting of the interpretive options opened by James's refusal to delve into his characters' consciousness is the possibility that we *do* have all the relevant information, that what the characters speak is all we need know of them. Nanda's passionate disavowal of love for Van would in that case constitute flimsy evidence of its existence. Her tearful outburst would express not a long-suppressed truth but her exhaustion with the demand that she embody such a truth. From this perspective it becomes clear that Nanda has been subjected to a kind of gaslighting from all quarters—here, for example, from a friend who remains "heedless" of her protestations and whose concern takes the form of "reproach," but more importantly from the narrative conventions governing her fictive existence. Far from disclosing her real feelings, Nanda's body has been tortured into expressive significance. Her stammering self-description is less the voice of her truth than a cry for help as the walls of the novel—and the novelistic—close around her.

It is important to recognize that the contemporary theater may have made precisely the same identitarian demand on Nanda. As we have seen, the late-nineteenth-century theater was dominated by a preoccupation, borrowed from the novel, with legible psychological meaning. David Wiles has noted that the naturalist emphasis on psychic truth demanded a corresponding spectatorial disposition: "The new focus on the interiority of the actor assumes that a passive audience will lose itself in the emotions of the fictional character." This "new aesthetic code," he writes, sought to "reduc[e] a convivial audience to silence."[59] Nanda's breakdown thus implies the existence of a certain kind of audience—in Longdon, certainly, but also in that imaginary audience formed by the corporate body of the novel's readership. *The Awkward Age* has continually invoked the hypothetical observers of its action, and in this final scene James appears to be indicating what sort of observers these are: Wiles's still, expectant, silent audience is conjured here as the witness to Nanda's dramatic outburst. Indeed, we might say that our spectatorial attention—our keenness to be present at the moment of revelation—has helped to provoke this spectacular confession. Our quiet expectancy has been complicit in hounding this final identitarian truth from our victim. On this reading, James's bleak ending indicates that, in a culture pervaded by an investment in psychological meaning, any turn toward the performative will prove gestural at best. If Nanda's anguish expresses a desire for a theater that would rescue her from novelistic significance, it is a nonexistent or impossible theater she demands—one that would play to a new kind of audience.

But *The Awkward Age* does not abandon us, or Nanda, at these generic crossroads. In a striking moment of performative spatialization, the novel imagines a counternarrative to the dispiriting triumph of psychological intelligibility by organizing its readership into a different kind of imaginary public: "We," it turns out, may not be as quiescent, or as eager to extract Nanda's interior truth, as her outburst suggests. In the final scene, Nanda relays an apology from Van to Longdon for not having visited the older man. Longdon, characteristically concerned with Nanda's supposed obsession with Vanderbank, appears nonplussed: "Nanda's visitor looked so far about as to take the neighbourhood in general into the confidence of his surprise" (305). Longdon's broad histrionic gesture is strictly speaking nonsensical, since he is alone with Nanda. If James's evocation of a hypothetical spectatorship has built up for his readership a sense of itself as a ghostly theatrical audience placed just beyond the framed stage of the novel's action, this is the first time James imparts an awareness of *The Awkward Age*'s performative contours to one of its characters, and the effect is to concretize that audience and thus "our" presence at the scene. Longdon, the least showy of the book's actors, here suddenly gestures out beyond the fourth wall, as if to enlist his audience's support. But his uncharacteristic hamming betrays a panicked awareness of the unmanageable meanings being brought to this drama by its audience.[60]

Longdon's stagey surprise registers the pressure of this virtual spectatorship, and suggests that that pressure does not necessarily work to the advantage of his psychologizing agenda. James opens the novel's final book with a description of Nanda's newly furnished drawing room, and in the process introduces a subtle modification to the book's imaginary theater. "Nanda Brookenham, for a fortnight after Mr Longdon's return, had found much to think of; but the bustle of business became, visibly for us, particularly great with her a certain Friday afternoon in June" (281). While the invocation of a viewing public has been constant in the novel, until now that observing public has been designated one viewer at a time—"our" status as a corporate body only thinkable as the multiplication of so many individually designated hypothetical observers. Moreover, the conditional form of that invocation has made "our" attendance at the drama of *The Awkward Age* propositional at best. But here, suddenly, we are: James designates the viewing audience as plural ("visibly for us") and shakes off the subjunctive mood to push us into the preterite plane of the narrated action ("became"). In coalescing a group of individual spectators into the first-person plural, James repeats exactly that movement toward sociality that he attributes to theatrical attendance in his autobiography. And this appearance of the collective works to undo at the level of the readerly fantasmatic precisely the individuating catastrophe

James has just described at the level of narration. "We shall never grow together again" (253), Mrs. Brookenham has lamented after the "smash" that
dissolves her group. But James's invocation of his audience indicates that the
disbanded collectivity of *The Awkward Age* has reconstituted itself on the
other side of the novel's imaginary footlights.

A few lines later James adds a further dimension to our collective portrait.
James's ostensible object in the following sentences is Vanderbank's nervous
fluttering around the room as he prepares to bid a final good-bye to Nanda:

> Vanderbank had not been in the room ten seconds before he showed
> that he had arrived to be kind. Kindness therefore becomes for us, by
> a quick turn of the glass that reflects the whole scene, the high pitch
> of the concert—a kindness that almost immediately filled the place,
> to the exclusion of everything else, with a familiar, friendly voice, a
> brightness of good looks and good intentions, a constant though per-
> haps sometimes misapplied laugh, a super-abundance almost of inter-
> est, inattention and movement. (281–282)

On the level of narration—on the level of novelistic meaning—nothing
good is happening here: a cowardly suitor is fumbling his way through an
awkward scene with a woman he has jilted. But the obscurity of the passage,
along with its invocation of a new and thoroughly disorienting theatrical
topography, mean that what it narrates is not necessarily what it "becomes
for us." The final sentence apparently applies to Vanderbank's nervousness
as he decamps from the marriage plot. But James's separation of Van's name
from its predicates makes it difficult to connect what seems an impersonal
and overflowing "kindness" to his person, and the attributes of this kindness—superabundance, mobility, omnipresence—bespeak a quality that can
scarcely belong to one character. This kindness is more properly described as
the "pitch of the concert," the keynote of "the whole scene," than the property
of any single person.

But what is this concert? Where is this scene? James writes that this impression of kindness becomes available "for us" by "a quick turn of the glass
that reflects the whole scene." While a conception of art as a mirror held up
to nature is a commonplace of aesthetic theory, in the context of the theater
the metaphor takes on a curiously literal topographical meaning, one that
James exploits here for maximum strangeness of effect.[61] Especially in a theatrical environment where the stage has retreated behind a framing proscenium
arch, the flat plane separating actors from performers can be understood as
the surface of a mirror.[62] In staring at the stage picture the audience might
thus be described (in a way meaningless for the nonvisual media of text or
music, for example) as gazing at an image of itself. James's language opens
the possibility that the scene under description pertains not to the narrated

action at all but to the collective image of the gathered spectators who sit just outside it. The optical relations implicit in the passage indicate as much: "a quick turn of the glass," if it is to reveal anything to "us," can only be facing us. This spinning mirror offers us a glimpse of ourselves as the public comprising the imaginary audience of *The Awkward Age*.

The "whole scene" that James depicts here is then a picture of the novel's readership remade in an ideal image of a theatrical crowd—glimpsed not in motionless attentive silence but in a labile moment of "interest, inattention and movement." While James has previously described *The Awkward Age* as an off-limits performance, his language now invokes not the gauziness of absence but the plenitude of plural and embodied presence. We have not only suddenly gathered into a plural first person but have done so in the present tense ("becomes for us") of actual spectatorship. In this strange mirror scene the effort of imaginative spectatorship the book has continually demanded is suddenly released in a moment of pleasure. The glass has spun around momentarily to reflect the audience hazily constructed by all those subjunctive clauses, and we discover not only that we now are that audience but that we are engaged in conversation, laughter, movement—and a curious form of "interest" devoid of any particular object of "attention." The words echo those James employed to describe *The Awkward Age*'s coterie as engaged in an exchange of tactile gazes, intent not on extracting information but on vibrating pleasurably at the scene of sexual permission. The disposition of the audience we now constitute indicates that James has transferred the mantle of permissive collectivity from his characters to his readers.

In an important sense, then, the drama of Nanda's abjection is one to which we are not particularly attending. Just as the book moves narratively toward its conclusion, its theatrical contours widen, gesturing out beyond that plot to a collective present where a performative sociability is preserved. This may not seem to mitigate the tragedy of Nanda's—and everyone's—submission to the novel's demand for truth. But we should not underestimate the pressure exerted on the torsion of the story by our performative presence across the footlights. We have already seen how Longdon must reckon with the "neighbourhood" in making his push toward novelistic closure, and an awareness of our collective presence should alert us to how many of the dilatory energies generated by *The Awkward Age*'s "talk" survive its climax. (Even in Milton, the messenger who reports on Samson's having brought down the house is obliged to admit that "Gaza yet stands" [506].) Nanda will depart with Longdon, but there are hints that this may only be a temporary retreat before she joins her mother at the center of a reconstituted circle of social permissiveness. On his visit to Nanda, Van suggests that there is life after the novel when he tells her that she "[seems] to me to hold the strings of such a lot of queer little dramas" (287).[63] And Mitchy indicates that his marriage to Aggie will not prevent him from cultivating an ongoing conversation with

Nanda; on the contrary, his wife's promiscuity will ensure "a practical multiplication of our points of contact" (298). He assures Nanda that she will be
"saddled for all time to come with the affairs of a gentleman whom she can
never get rid of on the specious plea that he's only her husband or her lover or
her father or her son or her brother or her uncle or her cousin. There, as none
of these characters, he just stands." To which Nanda "kindly" replies, "Yes . . .
he's simply her Mitchy" (295).

"Kindness" here, as in Van's visit to Nanda, might seem like cold comfort.
But in *The Awkward Age* the word pulses with performative amplitude. It figures prominently throughout the novel and particularly at its end; we might
recall by way of explanation that "kind" is also a word for a distinguishing
generic class. James alludes to this meaning in the preface to *The Awkward
Age*, in a discussion of the extremity of the book's formal experimentation.
"Everything," he writes, "becomes interesting from the moment it has closely
to consider, for full effect positively to bestride, the law of its kind. 'Kinds'
are the very life of literature." James goes on to rail against the "confusion of
kinds" in literature (*AN*, 111), yet his words have curiously indicated that the
most interesting thing to do with the law of genre is to *straddle* it. If *The Awkward Age* is saturated with "kindness," it is kindness of precisely this variety:
a hyperawareness of generic limitations that provokes an effort at bending
their contours.

The Awkward Age, we might say, kills genre with kindness. It resists the
psychologizing thrust of the late-century drama and novel, aggravating a generic impasse in order to invoke a phantom theater. In its determined failure to function coherently either as fiction or as theater, *The Awkward Age*
issues a challenge to imagine life beyond the constraints of both forms as
given, as well as beyond the psychosexual and relational logics they support.
The awkwardness and effort the novel enjoins on the reader are a measure of
how conscious James remains of the difficulty of maintaining spaces of "queer
condonations," but in its imagination of a group that tries to do just that the
book instructs its readers in the social effort it would take to do so. A "kind"
is also a name for a human collectivity brought together by a common trait
or interest, and in bathing its imaginary landscape in kindness *The Awkward
Age* seeks to give its audience the courage of whatever collective peculiarity they might attempt to embody. If Mr. Longdon's distress at the alliances
proliferating at the novel's end represents one common reaction to any such
challenge to imagine collective change, Mitchy's encouraging response might
also be seen as the novel's:

> Mr Longdon, on his side, turned a trifle pale: he looked rather hard at
> the floor. "I see—I see." Then he raised his eyes. "But—to an old fellow
> like me—it's all so strange."
> "It *is* strange." Mitchy spoke very kindly. "But it's all right." (280)

What Does Jamesian Style Want?

Even a "star" is but a function of the total cast.
—Kenneth Burke, *The Philosophy of Literary Form*

Readers of James's last novels will respond dubiously to Mitchy's reassurances (as, to be sure, does Mr. Longdon). From the perspective elaborated in this chapter, the works of the major phase look like retreats from *The Awkward Age*'s picture of collective psychosexual agnosticism. At the level of narrative form, the communal and depsychologized vision of *The Other House* and *The Awkward Age* cedes in the late fiction to an obsession with point of view: unlike the texts we have been examining, the later novels are rigorously focalized, and their plots turn on the epistemological conundrums this narrative perspectivalism fosters. Thematically, the situation is similar. Compared to the multiplication of sexual transgressions in *The Awkward Age* and James's refusal to make anything of them, the later novels' fascinated equation of sex with narrative interest stands out all the more vehemently: James's final novels all turn on extramarital liaisons, the discovery of which is treated as eventful enough to organize even these dauntingly complex plots.

Yet far from disappearing, the performative universalism and the sense of perlocutionary petition we have traced in James's awkward stage migrate into the most recognizable feature of his late work: its style. James's interest even into his late novels in collective forms of being has been difficult to perceive because our dominant critical paradigms have seen James primarily as a writer of individuals. For example, both components of Peter Brooks's justly influential characterization of James's work as exploring the "melodrama of consciousness" tend to obscure the collectivism of James's stylistic imagination.[64] Understood as a melodramatist, James appears as a painter of starkly moralized characterological oppositions; understood as a novelist of consciousness, James appears concerned to trace incommensurate perspectives. Both James's moralism and his perspectivalism imply a poetics of division and differentiation.

In unsettling this critical emphasis, the best place to start may be with the text that looks least promising—that is, the least morally ambiguous: *The Wings of the Dove*. Of James's late novels, *The Wings of the Dove* most luridly juxtaposes the "children of light" with the "creatures of prey" (to use the terms memorably proposed by James's secretary Theodora Bosanquet).[65] Where the other fictions of the major phase offer extenuating circumstances for the moral and sexual transgressions they narrate, it is hard to make excuses for Kate Croy and Merton Densher.[66] Kate's sister is vulgar, her prospects bad, and her father exquisitely seedy, but none of this mitigates the callousness of her scheme to manipulate her dying friend into believing herself loved and giving away her fortune. It is to this severity of moral outline that Alan Hollinghurst most obviously alludes when he has one of the characters in his 2004 novel *The Line of Beauty* ask, "What would Henry James have made of us, I wonder?"—to be answered by the novel's protagonist Nick Guest, "He'd have been very kind to us, he'd have said how wonderful we were and how beautiful we were, he'd have given us incredibly subtle things to say, and we wouldn't have realized until just before the end that he'd seen right through us."[67] The remark is perfectly keyed to the chiaroscuro of *The Wings of the Dove*, which juxtaposes the much remarked "beauty" of Kate's plan with the ugliness of its motivation.

But the very moral obviousness of this plot challenges us to read it otherwise. Nick's reading of James's work as invested in a moralized teleology is apparent. Slightly less so is the way Nick claims residence in a character population defined by a shared condition: the susceptibility to being "seen right through" is, he insists, universally distributed, and so the morality tale he sketches is played out by a collectivity in which moral distinctions are strangely irrelevant. *The Line of Beauty* ends in firmly melodramatic mode, with Nick cast among the victimized children of light—homophobically ejected from the Tory household where he has ambiguously sheltered, convinced of his HIV-positive status (although, like Milly Theale before him, with no clear diagnosis of his condition) and, in a scene that cites Milly's walk through Regent's Park, savoring how his mortality lends point to the beauty of the world. Given the clarity of the moral distinctions structuring his plot, it is notable that Nick insists on speaking of himself as just another member of a community defined by a common trait. His words signal an alternative ethical economy in James's late work—one that does not render irrelevant the manicheanism so palpable to Bosanquet but that operates alongside it and in crucial respects upstages it. Perceiving this economy requires stepping to the side of James's plots, as it were, and looking at his style.[68]

Alongside the plot of moral difference is a deeply Jamesian interest in what I have called performative universalism. To begin with the second half of the term: the universalism inherent in Jamesian style is most evident in the consistency of his lines' texture. Here, chosen almost at random from *The Wings of the Dove*, are some of the sentences Nick Guest probably has in mind:

> "Oh she's grand," the young man allowed; "she's on the scale altogether of the car of the Juggernaut." (113)

> "We agreed just now that you're beautiful. You strike me, you know, as—in your own way—much more firm on your feet than I." (63)

"Well, he likes to please," the girl explained—"personally. I've seen it make him wonderful." (100)

"She understands," Milly said; "she's better than any of you. She's beautiful." (160)

"I had much rather see you myself—since you're, in your way, my dear young man, delightful—and arrange with you, count with you, as I easily, as I perfectly should." (109)

"To be seen, you must recognize, *is*, for you, to be jumped at . . . Look round the table, and you'll make out, I think, that you're being, from top to bottom, jumped at." (153)

He but "looks in," poor beautiful dazzling, damning apparition that he was to have been. (43)

Assembling these passages highlights certain obvious features of James's late style: the use of appositives and inversions, the almost Germanic deferral of grammatical closure. But it also reveals the verbal similarities that hold across the cast of Jamesian characters: in the passages above, Densher speaks to Kate about Aunt Maud; Kate speaks to Lionel Croy about himself and then to Densher about Lionel; Milly speaks to Lord Mark about Susan Stringham; Aunt Maud speaks to Densher about himself; and Lord Mark speaks to Milly about herself. The speakers, addressees, and subjects are distributed over the social landscape of the book.[69] But these characters address one another in almost indistinguishable patterns, and they laud one another with adjectives that seem interchangeable ("grand," "beautiful," "wonderful," "delightful," etc.). This uniformity will hardly be news to any reader of late James. But it has largely escaped critical commentary, perhaps because it sits athwart the supposedly paramount Jamesian dictum of the central consciousness, with its emphasis on perspectival distinctions. The above examples make clear that James's style interrupts the operation of this formal principle, inundating the drama of moral and perspectival difference in a bath of stylistic indistinction. One thing Jamesian style wants is to replace the differentiating energies of the drama of consciousness with an equally compelling vision of collectivity and universalism.

This vision of collectivity proceeds from a stylistic sharing among characters, but it also blurs the boundary between author and character in late James. The final example above bears a clear resemblance to those that come before, but it is taken from the section of *The Wings of the Dove*'s preface in which James regrets that Lionel Croy makes such a brief appearance in the novel. The sentence evinces one of the fundamental markers of Jamesian style, the self-interruption with phrases of apposition, specification, or qualification ("poor beautiful, dazzling, damning apparition that he was to have been"). Intricate as these effects of complication and syncopation can become in James, they frequently proceed from the homeliest of narrative interjections. Often it is only the choice of where to place speech tags that creates the Jamesian note. "Well, he likes to please personally"—what Kate "actually" says about her father in the example above—is ordinary enough; it is the eccentric placement of the also ordinary "the girl explained" that gives the sentence its Jamesian point and suggests a wealth of meanings in that final adverb. But far from implying that these are banal speakers lent subtlety by the way James sets them in his narration, the sentences above prompt something like the opposite conclusion. Even the stupidest characters (i.e., Lord Mark) know what an utterance gains in ambiguity through rearrangement of its particles; every Jamesian character seems to sense how idioms ("from top to bottom," "jumped at") are poeticized—ironized, given resonance, made strange—by being subjected to predication, hesitation, or inversion. It is as if these characters were conscious of a shared duty to hold up the general tone.

One of the strangest effects of this uniformity of style is thus to intimate a shared purposiveness on the part of these characters. The stylistic consistency of James's characters lends them a sense of affective and intentional surplus—as if, whatever role they occupy in the story (innocent, villain, *ficelle*), Jamesian characters retain an extradiegetic consciousness of themselves as engaged in precisely those roles and thus in a larger fictional project. Earlier I termed this distinctive ontology of Jamesian characters "performative"—not to denote an ironized distance from a role or social identity (though this is one potential feature of performance) but to convey that a secondary purposiveness akin to that of a good actor haunts the specific narrative fates of each character in late James. In an effective theatrical production, we may notice not only that Malvolio is foolish and pompous but also that the actor playing Malvolio radiates intelligence in conveying that foolishness and a sense of humor in conveying that pomposity. Such actorly purposiveness—the ability to communicate to the beholder a consciousness that has no narrative function and is often opposed to diegetic meaning—is a central feature of the phenomenology of theater (it is, in fact, this *suspension* of the suspension of disbelief that is definitive of theatrical experience as such: without it we would only be pained or exasperated at Malvolio's gullibility). It is precisely such a surplus that Charles Lamb labels, in a passage discussed in the introduction, the "perpetual subinsinuation" of stage illusion: the actor's style addresses us to the side of the plot in performance, and it is this suggestion of supplemental awareness that is one powerful effect of James's late style.[70] Equally important—and equally characteristic of successful performance—is the fact that this purposiveness is distributed universally along with the style that conveys it, crossing the most severe or moralized characterological divides. The subinsinuation of Jamesian style infuses a collaborative energy into the divisive structures of Jamesian plotting.

Even the most abject, marginal, and despicable characters are thus enfolded. Take Lionel Croy, who for some powerfully unspecified reason serves as the novel's polestar of depravity.[71] James's prefatory remarks about him continue in this way:

> He but "looks in," poor beautiful dazzling, damning apparition that he was to have been; he sees his place so taken, his company so little missed, that, cocking again that fine form of hat which has yielded him for so long his one effective cover, he turns away with a whistle of indifference that nobly misrepresents the deepest disappointment of his life. One's poor word of honour has *had* to pass muster for the show. Every one, in short, was to have enjoyed so much better a chance that, like stars of the theatre condescending to oblige, they have had to take small parts, to content themselves with minor identities, in order to come on at all. (43)

Both features of performative universalism (its connection to a sense of surplus intention, and its collective nature) are in evidence here. First, James attributes to Lionel Croy a supplementary consciousness, an awareness not only of his position in Kate's life but of his place in the architecture of *The Wings of the Dove*. (And just as Malvolio's idiocy optimally comes accompanied with a sense of actorly intelligence, the awareness James imputes to Lionel Croy lends his situation an affective dimension wholly tangential to his diegetic situation: in the opening chapters of the novel, Croy is, of course, not casually shown the door—"so little missed"—but entreated by Kate to stay.) Second, in taking on this secondary awareness, Croy ceases being utterly distinctive in the text's character-system and becomes utterly typical. The novel's plot encourages us to see Lionel Croy as the cause of Kate's misery and the source of her ambition, but in the passage above James dissolves this singularity by casting Lionel as just another member of the cast, and a representative one at that: note how quickly the passage moves from Croy's particularity to a discussion of "everyone" in the novel, and how Lionel's role as a performer is the hinge on which the move to generality turns.

In exceeding the normal ontological contours of fictional characterization, Lionel Croy is representative not only of the characters of *The Wings of the Dove* but of character more generally as discussed in James's prefaces: thus Christopher Newman is not only a gullible American in Paris but the featured performer on "a high and lighted stage"; the characters of *The Portrait of a Lady* importune James "like the group of attendants and entertainers who come down by train when people in the country give a party; they represented the contract for carrying the party on"; and Christina Light, not content with being consigned after *Roderick Hudson* to "the pasteboard tomb, the doll's box, to which we usually relegate the spent puppet," demands that James "cloth[e] . . . her chilled and patient nakedness" with her own eponymous novel, *The Princess Casamassima* (*AN*, 23, 53, 73–74). In these examples—all of them referring to an imagined theater—James's characters seem instinct not only with their "biographical" coordinates but with a shared awareness of their position in the larger fictive enterprise.

This extradiegetic consciousness thereby also intimates an alternative realm where narrative importance is more evenly allocated. If in the novels as they exist there are bit parts and major players, James's constant invocation of the theater conveys a sense of the contingency of that apportioning; the theatrical metaphor registers a democratizing pressure—holding open, if only imaginarily, the possibility of a radically flattened distribution of narrative sympathy and attention. James invokes this leveling aspect to theatricality in the preface to *The Tragic Muse*, where he writes that "no character in a play . . . has . . . a *usurping* consciousness; the consciousness of others is exhibited exactly in the same way as that of the 'hero'; the prodigious consciousness of Hamlet . . . the moral presence the most asserted, in the whole range of fiction, only takes its turn with that of the other agents of the story, no matter how occasional these may be" (*AN*, 90). While these prefatory remarks are external to the novels themselves, the stylistic extravagance of Jamesian characters insinuates an effect of performative universality into the heart of the fiction; especially in the late novels, it is the uniformity of the verbal style (we might, invoking the theatrical metaphor, call it James's "company style") that conveys this sense of a corporate consciousness and of a cooperative endeavor as the ground of the story's presentation.

This performative leveling has a special significance for *The Wings of the Dove*, whose characters radiate a sense of collective purpose from their sharply differentiated situations in the plot. Perhaps the central example of the novel's universalism is the titular image. Uniquely among James's late fictions, this novel's title is suggested by a character in the story. While the idea of embassy hovers in the conceptual background of *The Ambassadors* and *The Golden Bowl*'s title refers to an actual object in the story, only in *The Wings of the Dove* is the text's governing metaphor supplied by a character within it: Kate nominates the dove as a figure for Milly near the end of the first volume (236). The dove is thus a product of one character's linguistic inventiveness, an element of personal style.[72] Once introduced, however, the figure rapidly circulates among the characters and throughout the text, taking on shades of meaning as it does so: Milly immediately seizes on the image, pondering "straightway the measure of the success she could have as a dove" (237); and before long Densher, too, is thinking under the figure's auspices, so that when he rents new rooms in Venice he wonders to himself if any suspicion of his motive in doing so has "brushed [Kate] with its wings" (365). Even the clamor of pigeons in Saint Mark's undergoes figurative transubstantiation to become for Kate and Densher "the flutter of the doves" (373).

Surveying these proliferating meanings, it is tempting to label the image of the dove a sign of psychic distinction, an object lesson in perspective's ability to transform any object. But more important than these particular differences is the fact of the figure's circulatory success. The dove is an emblem of stylistic infectiousness—as if the provenance and destination of the metaphor were less important than the felt need on the part of the characters to spread it around. The first thing the image does is jump the novel's moralized character gulf: originated by Kate, the term immediately fascinates Milly. The second thing it does is widen its indexical reach to enfold someone originally unconnected with it, as Milly hears Mrs. Lowder's questions to her as having a "tone of the fondest indulgence—almost, really, that of dove cooing to dove" (236). Later Densher adopts the metaphor precisely to note its ramifying power, reflecting that Milly's "wings" have "lately taken an inordinate reach, and weren't Kate and Mrs Lowder, weren't Susan Shepherd and he, wasn't *he* in particular, nestling under them to a great increase of immediate ease?" (389); and by the novel's end, Kate and Densher agree that Milly's "wings" have reached out to "cover" them both (508).

This closing image of the all-encompassing wings can, of course, be interpreted as a mystification of the plot's economic engine: Milly's wings on this reading would simply be her money, and Kate's wonder at their span merely her delight at Milly's bequest and the imminent success of her plan. But in its mobility, the image resists the reduction of this equation. Or, to put this somewhat differently: the restlessness of the figure of the dove can be understood as James's attempt to hold in view the utopian promise—we could call it the promise of the redistribution of stylistic wealth—lodged in the mystification. The largesse with which Milly allows her fantastic riches to circulate signals the prodigality of style in the Jamesian universe. The dove is an emblem of the text's refusal of the economy of stylistic scarcity, its attempt to imagine a community united by a language whose sameness is an emblem of radical egalitarianism. In its refusal to observe the limits of any particular consciousness, the dove encapsulates what Stanley Cavell offers as one definition of art: a "site of the transmutation of public and private into and out of each other."[73]

James puts just such a vision of transmutation in play in the novel's final Venetian soirée, when Milly's dovelike mildness strikes Densher as a kind of tide pool sustaining the novel's characters with sublime indifference: "He moved about in it and it made no plash; he floated, he noiselessly swam in it, and they were all together, for that matter, like fishes in a crystal pool . . . She hadn't yet had occasion—circulating with a clearness intensified—to strike him as so happily pervasive" (386). As a character in the plot, Milly is of course committed to her personal lot, her desire for Densher and her anguish over her looming death. But as an emblem of style—as the dove that the text won't let us forget she also is—she must be seen as committed to making pervasive the riches concentrated on her person. And in this redistributive project, she should be understood as, strangely but palpably, a collaborator even with her chief antagonist: much like the starring actresses in "some dim scene in a Maeterlinck play" (339) to which James compares them, Kate and Milly radiate a sense of cooperating on some plane that, though not quite narratable, nonetheless happily pervades this unhappy novel. While this other scene never rises to the level of diegetic action, it makes itself felt in the texture of the characters' language and in their emotional stance toward one another. Some such imagined scene of collaboration, for example, seems necessary to explain James's insistence on what would otherwise appear only a refinement of Kate's depravity: her repeated insistence that she likes and respects Milly, indeed is a good friend to her and in some sense a supporter of her interests.[74] If we want to rescue this claim from the most banal cynicism, we should see this avowal as a local, and imperfectly instantiated, manifestation of a deeper collective project.[75]

Of course, if the transmission of Milly's money is a sign of a collaborative attempt at redistributive justice, this impulse does not play out at all smoothly in the book's narrated action. While its style bespeaks an already achieved communalism, at the level of the story the novel's redistributive energies become entangled in deception, disappointment, and death, as if James wants to stress that difference ultimately vanquishes the text's palpable stylistic universalism; indeed the word "difference" recurs insistently in the novel's final stretches as if semantically to underline the point.[76] This brings us up against what I will no doubt seem to have willfully avoided: the intransigence of the novel's plot. If the story narrated in *The Wings of the Dove* is less central to the ethical imagination of the novel than we might expect, it is not quite as marginal as I have found it necessary to claim in order to hold style in view. But the meaning of that plot is altered once set in relation to style understood with its proper degree of importance—once we recognize that in its vehemence style becomes a kind of secondary protagonist in the novel. If we understand *The Wings of the Dove* to be narrating not only the fate of a victimized heiress but the destiny of a stylistic project, the novel's plot becomes legible as the story of style's ultimate social ineffectuality, its inability to render palpable on the plane of the real its democratizing imagination. "They could think whatever they liked about whatever they would—in other words, they could say it," James writes early on about Kate and Densher's situation (97), and his words might refer not only to the prodigally stylish speakers who populate his fiction but to the prodigality of Jamesian style and, beyond that, the aesthetic itself: all of them combine a fantasmatic richness with a poignant powerlessness to see their projects materialize on the field of the social. *The Wings of the Dove* is at once a repository for the imagination of collectivity and a ruthless analysis of the damages of individuation. If its utopian image of communitarian possibility issues a perlocutionary demand on its readers, its negativity is a reminder of the conjectural nature of that performance: Jamesian style wants its vision of collectivity and it wants to record that collectivity's status as still only visionary.

FOUR

Joyce Unperformed

My brother did not go on stage except as an amateur actor in a one-act comedy by Maggie Sheehy . . . Jim, who often found relief for his feelings in stark English, said that even the virgin cheeks of his arse blushed for his part in it. It certainly did not seem so. He appeared to be quite unconcerned as if he were acting in a more elaborate kind of charade. —Stanislaus Joyce, *My Brother's Keeper*

Joycean Exposures

In *Stephen Hero* James Joyce famously claims Aquinas as a source for his theory of epiphany.[1] But Joyce's Dublin acquaintances recalled epiphany less as an effort to apprehend *quidditas* than as a cruel game of social exposure. While Stanislaus Joyce concurred with his brother's description of epiphanies as "manifestations or revelations," his account of Joyce's unnerving habit of jotting down ephiphanic material gives these words a resonance more petty than scholastic: "Jim always had a contempt for secrecy, and these notes were in the beginning ironical observations of slips, and little errors and gestures—mere straws in the wind—by which people betrayed the very things they were most careful to conceal."[2] This account is augmented by Oliver Gogarty, the medical student whose "little errors and gestures" Joyce would ironize in *Ulysses* under the name Buck Mulligan. Writing in 1937, Gogarty recalls that the young Joyce "recorded under 'Epiphany' any showing forth of the mind by which he considered one gave oneself away," and tells of a drinking party with Joyce and a medical student named Elwood during which Joyce excuses himself from the table, apparently to note some vulgarity in the progressing conversation:

"Whist! [says Elwood] He's gone to put it all down!"
"Put what down?"
"Put *us* down. A chiel's among us takin' notes. And, faith, he'll print it."
[. . .] I was trying to recall what spark had been struck or what "folk phrase" Joyce had culled from Elwood or me that sent him out to make his secret record . . . I don't mind being reported, but to be

> an unwilling contributor to one of his "Epiphanies" is irritating...
> Which of us had endowed him with an "Epiphany" and sent him
> off to the lavatory to take it down?

As Joyce scribbles away in the bathroom, Elwood and Gogarty trace their friend's new project to his sense of isolation from the Irish literary scene—particularly as represented by Lady Gregory's Irish Literary Theatre, which has failed to show interest in Joyce's promise as a playwright. "We're all on the stage," a drunken Elwood concludes, "Jayshus, we're all on the stage since the Old Lady threw him out."[3]

Its questionable authenticity notwithstanding, the anecdote offers an object lesson in the social life of an aesthetic program: Joyce's epiphanic method, commonly understood as an attempt to raise the quotidian to the level of art, emerges here as a *ressentiment*-fueled technique of public shaming. For an artist as obsessed with betrayal as Joyce, these possibilities are, of course, far from mutually exclusive. Joyce's biographer Richard Ellmann traces the genesis of Joycean aesthetics in social revenge but argues that for the mature artist the vindictive impulse gave way to a celebratory one: in the course of conceiving of *Ulysses*, Ellmann writes, Joyce's "literary aim shifted imperceptibly from exposure to revelation of his countrymen."[4] Although I will be tracing the persistence of the shaming impulse into the celebratory aesthetic of the "mature" Joyce, my goal is not to claim that Joycean aesthetics are inevitably tied to a practice of social exposure but to illuminate Joyce's career as a meditation on the ethical implications of aesthetic practice. The transformation in the function of the epiphanic agenda is ascribable less to an inevitable process of maturation than to Joyce's recognition of the ideological investments of his artistic program.

Joyce's most famous novelistic achievement—the representation of inner psychic experience—is one about which his texts evince a palpable ambivalence. Joyce wrote in a cultural context in which interiority had become firmly grounded in sexual identity, and his work can seem self-parodically illustrative of the links between aesthetically capturing a personality and sexually exposing it. While the sexual irregularities covered in Joyce's work are many, his work shows a persistent concern with male homosexuality and the gender inversion model by which his period largely understood it.[5] Gogarty's memoirs hint at the complicity in Joyce's work between psychological skewering and erotic shaming; if his account of Joyce skulking off to pen "secret" notes in the water closet enacts its own public exposure of a former friend, this may be explained by Gogarty's resentment over Joyce's exposure of *him* in the pages of *Ulysses* as someone whose sexual vulgarity threatens to spill over into sexual abnormality: in the first chapter of the novel Buck Mulligan addresses Stephen Dedalus as "my love," "sigh[s] tragically," "flutter[s] his winglike hands," "caper[s]," shows off his nude "plump body," proposes a program to "Hellenise" Ireland, and introduces the name of Oscar Wilde into a text that will worry at length about Irish martyrs to sexual puritanism.[6] Given this introduction, Mulligan's association with "the love that dare not speak its name" (9.659) is no more surprising than are Gogarty's suspicions about the punitive aspects of the epiphanic mode. From Gogarty's point of view, there is good reason to believe that Joycean "revelation" and "manifestation" are synonyms for exposure, and epiphany little more than a fancy name for a game of find-the-pervert.

From the epiphanies he wrote as a teenager to the phantasmagoria of "Circe," Joyce's interest in the sexual as the site of identitarian truth is closely linked to the idea of the theater. Elwood's response to Joyce's epiphanic practice ("We're all on the stage!") indicates one powerful sense in which the theater is connected to the impulse to expose legible personality; and Joyce in fact wrote roughly half his epiphanies in dramatic form, as if to emphasize their function of putting his contemporaries on uncomfortable display. The epiphanies embody Joyce's sense of theater as a form particularly conducive to the making visible of the fixed rules of human personality. As he put it in a 1900 school essay titled "Drama and Life," "drama has to do with the underlying laws first, in all their nakedness and divine severity."[7] These words were written by a seventeen-year-old Joyce heavily under the influence of Ibsen, and they express the coherence of Joyce's program with the new naturalist drama, itself intent on the exposure of buried psychological truth. Insofar as it aims to make a spectacle of the truth by putting it "onstage," Joyce's entire body of work can be understood as theatrical in nature.

But if, on the one hand, the young Joyce understood the drama as the form best suited to the revelation of psychological truth, he was capable of celebrating the stage in quite distinct terms. "Drama and Life" also contains a passage that shifts the essay's focus from the austere legibility of the drama to the embodied sociability of the theater. "Drama is essentially a communal art and of widespread domain . . . [Drama] almost presupposes an audience, drawn from all classes. In an art-loving and art-producing society the drama would naturally take up its position at the head of all artistic institutions" (26). The theatrical is thus allied both with a potent discourse of characterological truth and with the notion of an ideal and embodied public. While there need be no inherent contradiction between the drama's truth-telling function and the theater's social orientation, in practice these lead Joyce to an artistic and intellectual crux that produces some of his most compelling work. The doubled impulse of the theatrical toward the psychological and the social—its investment in making a spectacle of the legible individual and in reaching out to an embodied collective space—on the one hand helps Joyce perfect the interior monologue that is perhaps his definitive contribution to the modern novel; on the other, it allows him to interrogate the notion of psychosexual truth to which that technique is so closely wedded.

Joyce's epiphanies are compact expressions of this dual torsion; their formal and thematic preoccupation with the drama encapsulates Joyce's diagnostic aesthetic and its potential undoing by a crisis of gender and sexual indeterminacy. The ephiphanic experiments were in turn crucial to Joyce's play *Exiles*. Usually understood as a pale tribute to Ibsenesque naturalism, the play is also a reflection on the scenographic conventions of naturalist theater and their ethical implications. Only fitfully performed in Joyce's lifetime, the play's confinement to an almost exclusively textual existence allowed Joyce to explore naturalism's intense ambivalence about performance and its orientation toward the textual; in the course of writing and annotating his play, Joyce came to interrogate the notions of characterological truth governing naturalist dramaturgy. He would exploit naturalism's logic of psychic revelation in the opening chapters of *Ulysses* and bring it to its highest expression in the "Scylla and Charybdis" chapter that marks the end of the novel's "initial style";[8] I claim that the unparalleled character effects of the first half of *Ulysses* are directly derived from Joyce's experiments with the form of the drama. In "Circe," the novel's longest and arguably most important chapter, sexuality and theater come explosively together: with its combination of lurid eroticism and dramatic form, "Circe" begs to be read—and has been—as Joyce's most extended piece of theater-as-exposure. I understand it on the contrary as a repudiation of the logic of sexual identity and of the aesthetic codes that underwrite it, a burlesque that exposes the banality of the logic of exposure. "Circe" is less Joyce's attempt to exorcise his characters' sexual and psychic demons than his effort to defeat the will to knowledge that has shaped his career and his reader's expectations.

Central to this analysis is the fact that Joyce's investment in performance was haunted by his distance from successfully achieved performance. Because the theatrical marked the limits of Joyce's protean talent, it was among other things a potent emblem of the ideological limitations of his artistic practice. Gogarty's mention of Joyce's frustrations at the hands of Lady Gregory and the Irish Literary Theatre makes spiteful reference to the fact that drama has long been understood as the exception to Joyce's versatility. Unperformed Joyce, precisely by marking a space of failure at the heart of Joyce's encyclopedic project, thus has important implications for a reconsideration of Joycean cultural politics. Those politics have been most trenchantly critiqued by Leo Bersani in his essay "Against *Ulysses*." For Bersani, Joyce's high critical standing is a function of his shoring up of the most cherished (that is, received) Western ideas about personality, sexuality, and culture. The massive interpretive effort Joyce's novel seems to demand is, in Bersani's reading, a parody of interpretation; *Ulysses* merely prompts its exegetes to link the text's obscurities to items in a valorized inventory of Western culture: "The intertextual criticism invited by *Ulysses* is the domestication of literature, a technique for *making familiar* the potentially traumatic seductions of reading.

Even more: *Ulysses* eliminates reading as the ground of interpretation, or, to put this in other terms, it invites intertextual elucidations as a strategy to prohibit textual interpretations . . . *Ulysses* is a text to be deciphered but not read."[9] (Bersani's critique, which sees Joycean difficulty as a screen for Joycean banality, might be read as an elaboration of Gertrude Stein's remark that "people like [Joyce] because he is incomprehensible and anybody can understand him."[10]) The self-satisfaction of *Ulysses* is most apparent for Bersani in its "sublimating bookishness" (17), its dedication to the notion that "its own performance can redemptively replace all culture which it seeks to incorporate" (14).

This powerful account understands Joyce's book as embodying its own successful enactment—its own "performance," to use Bersani's term. It thus seems particularly important that Joyce's theatrical failure had made him well aware that *Ulysses* was not in fact performance; in casting its longest chapter in dramatic form, we will see, he pointed up the limits of his own redemptive project. As a text that refers to a performance that by definition it cannot achieve, "Circe" calls attention to the worldlessness of the text, its distance from an embodied social surround it can only indicate. If a distance from the social is perhaps the enabling condition for any notion of the literary, this alienation was exacerbated by a high modernism for which Joyce's work remains paradigmatic. But Joyce's interest in the theatrical makes hypervisible the social melancholy underlying modernism's self-sequestration from the body of the popular. Bersani claims that *Ulysses* marks "the successful positing of the Book—or, more accurately, of books, that is, of a certain type of professional activity—as the ontological ground of history and of desire" (16–17). Excoriating Joycean intertextuality for creating a difficulty that is ultimately trivial in nature, Bersani claims that the dense allusiveness of the Joycean text makes every reader over in the image of the professional "Joycean." The difficulty this chapter focuses on is of a different sort: not that of tallying references to the *Odyssey* or Aquinas or the Dublin newspapers of June 1904 but of envisioning an escape from the Book from within its most elaborated exemplar.

This is the project of "Circe": if dramatic form represented for Joyce the pathos of the literary's distance from the social, "Circe" is the site of *Ulysses*'s most explicit desire for the social and of the book's (and the Book's) most explicit failure. The unperformed performance of "Circe" marks it as an expression of Joyce's doubts about the redemptive force of art, the place where his discourse recognizes its inadequate relation to the real. It is correspondingly the site where Joyce most radically questions his psychologizing project and most forcefully delineates a new one. In *Ulysses* Joyce translates the sexual dialectic of occlusion and exposure into a second-order distinction between the textual and the embodied, the performed and the merely read. In flattening out the distinction between off- and onstage, revealed and hidden, Joyce shunts the energy of this tension onto a social longing, replacing a hermeneutics of sexual suspicion with an erotics of the social.

Epiphany and the Obscene Body

"By an epiphany he meant a sudden spiritual manifestation, whether in the vulgarity of speech or of gesture or in a memorable phase of the mind itself. He believed that it was for the man of letters to record these epiphanies with extreme care."[11] Joyce's first written definition of epiphany suggests that there are two kinds of "sudden spiritual manifestation": those that reveal others (through the "vulgarity of speech or gesture") and those that permit insight into the self ("a memorable phase of the mind"). In apparent accordance with this division, the surviving epiphanies divide into two formal categories: roughly half are written in narrative form, and half are presented as dramatic sketches, with designated speakers and briefly noted "stage business" enclosed in parentheses; these latter epiphanies resemble, as Raymond Williams notes, "a fragment of text of a modern play."[12] It is tempting to follow Vicky Mahaffey in mapping this "generic"—or, more exactly, modal—distinction onto the divide between self and other in Stephen Dedalus's definition of the form: "The narrative epiphanies," Mahaffey writes, "celebrate the power of the author's mind; the dramatic epiphanies reduce the stature of those around him. The epiphanies, like the manuscript novel that succeeded and partly incorporated them, present the nascent artist as an inevitable Hero."[13]

This account downplays, however, the radical instability of the objectifying energies in the epiphanies. For in fact it is *Joyce* who most often appears foolish, flustered, called out, exposed in these texts. Epiphanies 4 and 5 read in their entirety:

4

[Dublin: on Mountjoy Square]Joyce—(*concludes*) . . . That'll be
forty thousand pounds.
Aunt Lillie—(*titters*)—O, laus! . . . . I was like that too. . . . .
   When I was a girl I was *sure* I'd marry a lord . . . or something . . .
Joyce—(*thinks*)—Is it possible she's comparing herself with me?

5

High up in the old, dark-windowed house: firelight in the
narrow room: dusk outside. An old woman bustles about,
making tea; she tells of the changes, her odd ways, and what the
priest and the doctor said . . . . . I hear her words in the distance.
I wander among the coals, among the ways of adventure . . . .

Christ! What is in the doorway? . . . . . A skull—a monkey; a
creature drawn hither to the fire, to the voices: a silly creature.
—Is that Mary Ellen?—
—No, Eliza, it's Jim—
—O . . . . . O, goodnight, Jim—
—D'ye want anything, Eliza? —
—I thought it was Mary Ellen . . . . . I thought you were Mary
Ellen, Jim—[14]

In their obscurity, the epiphanies seem to justify Williams's dry comment, "I
think we have to say that they must have meant more to [Joyce] than they
now can to us."[15] This is a large part of their interest: in a writer as dedicated
to *significance* as Joyce—who once boasted that he could "justify every line"
of even his most obscure work[16]—the tendency of these epiphanies to defeat
interpretation makes them a valuable guide to the contours of Joyce's writing.
Equally important, they concentrate several formal issues that will be crucial
to Joyce's career, and these in turn mitigate the opacity of their content.

Most obviously, these two short texts indicate that the line between
"dramatic" and "narrative" forms is a blurry one; while epiphany 5 does not
include parenthetical stage directions or designate its speakers by name, its
force stems from the clash between an internalized first-person narration ("I
hear her words in the distance") and the externalizing pressure of dialogue.
The epiphany achieves its point in precisely the moment of misapprehension
of the "I" by an observer: "I thought you were Mary Ellen, Jim—." That such
misapprehension is crucial to the epiphanies—and that Joyce connected it
with dramatic form—emerges with more emphasis in the previous epiphany,
which ends on a similar note: Joyce's availability as an object to be read (or
misread) by his aunt is rendered with particular clarity by the epiphany's dialogic form. The bizarre "stage direction" introducing the final line, "(*thinks*),"
of course points forward to the technique of the interior monologue. At the
same time it illuminates the harshly externalizing force of dialogue; we are
made more aware of the potentially abusive misprisions of dramatic form
by the sudden move into Joyce's consciousness. Thus if the two epiphanies
respectively embody the "dramatic" and "narrative" modes, they do so only
to betray those modes: the first highlights the externality of dialogue by
bringing us into the mind of one of the interlocutors, while the second exposes the solipsism of the internal monologist by emerging onto a scene of
conversation. The result in each case underlines the dramatic as the mode
of potentially wounding misunderstanding between the individual and his
environment.

The distance between consciousness and the social, and the abuses to
which that distance can be put, are most legible in the thematic the epiphanies
share: in both texts Joyce is taken (or, he insists, mistaken) for a woman. The

generic boundary the epiphanies illustrate by transgressing is also a boundary
between genders; the discrepancy between the inside and outside view is emphasized by the fact that it involves Joyce's unmanning. If we take Joyce's definition of epiphany at face value, we will see Aunt Lillie's and Eliza's mistakes
about Joyce's gender as evidence only of their "vulgarity" and of Joyce's superiority. But it is equally possible that the self-evidence of Joyce's masculine
identity is being adduced precisely because it has been challenged. What the
epiphanies expose, to put this bluntly, may be less the stupidity of Joyce's rela-
tives than a *womanliness* in Joyce himself. The blurring of the line between
narrative and drama accentuates just this possibility by putting interiority
on display—by making consciousness the object of our readerly perusal. In
epiphany 4, Joyce's sense of the absurdity of being conscripted into the role
of female ingénue is easy to read as his paranoid response to a random comment: precisely by revealing the interiority which should secure a sense of
Joyce's masculinity, the epiphany reveals that masculinity as a defended, and
therefore suspect, quantity. If Joyce's mastery over his gendered self is threatened by the intrusions of the social context, that pressure is signaled most
clearly by the externalization of dramatic form. In underscoring—by moving
across—the bright line demarcating interior and exterior, the epiphanies indicate the power of the social to read, and to "fix," the content of the inner.[17]

The relation between sexuality and dramatic form is clearest in epiphany
19, a densely revealing short text (although, as we will see, *what* a literary
text can reveal is precisely the question to which it emphatically points). The
epiphany reads in its entirety:

19

[Dublin: in the house in Glengariff Parade: evening]

Mrs Joyce—(crimson, trembling, appears at the parlour door) . . .
   Jim!
Joyce—(at the piano) . . . Yes?
Mrs Joyce—Do you know anything about the body? . . . What
   ought I do? . . . . There's some matter coming away from the hole
   in Georgie's stomach . . . . Did you ever hear of that happening?
Joyce—(surprised) . . . I don't know . . . .
Mrs Joyce—Ought I to send for the doctor, do you think?
Joyce—I don't know . . . . . . What hole?
Mrs Joyce—(impatient) . . . The hole we all have . . . . . here
   (points)
Joyce—(stands up) (*PSW*, 179)

Like the other epiphanies, this one can seem maddeningly obscure: is its
point to critique Joyce's abstraction from the material facts of the typhoid

fever that killed his brother Georgie, or perhaps to ridicule his mother's prudish inability to name the anus or specify its location—if we can even be sure that it is the diarrhea symptomatic of typhoid that is being discussed here? What is clear is that the emotional power of the piece derives from its formal presentation. The thematic content of the episode—the urgent need to apprehend the body, to render it linguistically graspable—is doubled by its dramatic form. The exchange between Joyce and his mother lurches and halts when confronted by the exigent facts of the corporeal, but the "stage directions" render *their* bodies emphatically present, from the eloquent redness and trembling of Mrs. Joyce's first appearance to Joyce's final "line," which consists of a wordless display of his own body: "Joyce—(*stands up*)." These manifestations of the body underscore by contrast the physically absent body of Georgie, the alarming decomposition of which is legible in the failure of language adequately to denote it. The disturbing force of the epiphany's image of Georgie lies in its indeterminacy, not least its gendered indeterminacy. Mrs. Dedalus's language anticipates Molly Bloom's exasperated query, "whats the idea making us like that with a big hole in the middle of us" (*U* 18.151–152). But where Mrs. Bloom speaks of and from a female body in terms that make it approach a condition of universality, Mrs. Joyce means to speak universally but occasions in her son a moment of gendered panic; over the course of the short conversation, Joyce's bafflement opens confusion about whether the "hole" under discussion is the navel or is instead anal, or even vaginal in nature. However much we may want to close down these proliferating possibilities by an appeal to the obvious (Georgie of course is—isn't he?—a boy; the navel of course is—isn't it?—the only "hole" in the stomach), the epiphany's primary function is to trouble that corporeal common sense.

I have called the epiphany's description of Georgie an image, but in fact the language brought to the problem of his ailing body evades visualization. Indeed, the everyday and the etymological meanings of "obscene" converge here: Georgie's body is at once abjectly, "obscenely" punctured in a way that suggests an erosion of bodily contours or a doubling of genders *and* ob-scenely "offstage" and so beyond the reach of the language that would tame its traumatic otherness. But if there is a clear sense in which Georgie's body represents the obscene of this text, its constitutive and unrepresentable boundary, it is also true that the bodies I have discussed as emphatically present are themselves no more than designated in the textual space of the epiphany. This is most apparent in the confusing final moments of the exchange: Mrs. Joyce's deictic utterance, "The hole we all have . . . . here," is on its own unable to clarify her meaning, and the pointing gesture with which she accompanies it is the necessary supplement to her speech act. But, of course, the word "*points*" points to nothing beyond our inability to see what is being designated. Mrs. Joyce's gesture shares its decorporealized status with the epiphany's final words: Joyce employs a typographic convention ("Joyce— ") that leads us to expect a verbal utterance, but delivers instead the gesture of a body displaying itself. It is as if the Joyce of the epiphany is attempting to offer his mother his own, whole, body as a substitute for the dematerializing body of his brother, or as if his only way of assisting at this scene of linguistic failure is by proffering his mute body as witness. But this is a literally empty gesture. This body can display itself only in its absence: the "line" indicates the corporeal but never achieves its density. The dash that uncannily floats at the epiphany's end does not so much stand in for Joyce's body as point help-lessly to its invisibility.

Thus the epiphany's dramatic form means that even those "present" bod-ies suffer from the obscenity supposedly confined to the offstage Georgie; even the text's "normals" are threatened by figurative contamination with that body's lurid difference. Part of what is cognitively traumatizing about the text's wandering "hole" is its ability to function as a particularizing and universalizing sign of corporeal lack. Clearly, Georgie is in some important sense different from Joyce and his mother: the horror of impending death, and of the malfunctioning body that announces that imminence, belong to him. But Mrs. Joyce brings Georgie's body into the realm of the thinkable by rendering it comparable to everyone else's ("The hole we all have"), thereby introducing an ambiguity into the epiphanic mode's diagnostic orientation. The dramatic might have seemed to Joyce peculiarly suited to the exposure of sexual and psychic irregularity, but in its unperformed mode this perver-sity has an alarming mobility. In the absence of visibly perverse bodies, the diagnostic impulse constantly threatens to coil back on its origin. Impor-tantly, this failure of the diagnostic program stands in for a general failure of language to coincide with the world. The epiphanic text, in describing (*only* describing) an embodied real, is always an instance of failed deixis; it is its own offstage, its own obscene other. Invoking through epiphany the show-ing forth of Christ's body, the young Joyce imputed to his aesthetics a quasi-theological power to render the word flesh. But this short text suggests that epiphany might alternatively be described as making manifest only its own failure to make anything manifest. By exacerbating readerly consciousness of the absent body, the epiphany's dramatic form accentuates a malaise we have become accustomed to see as endemic to all language. But this generalized trauma takes a specific form here: the textual obscenity of the epiphany as a form finds a corollary both in the elsewhere-ness of Georgie's body and in its disturbing violation of bodily—especially gendered—coherence.

Several moments in Joyce's early writing connect what Luke Thurston terms the "problematic of literary apparition"[18] to the specific questions of male homosexuality and gender inversion; queer thematic material repeat-edly intensifies the awareness of textual impalpability. "An Encounter," the second story from 1914's *Dubliners*, reaches at least two kinds of climax when its young male narrator and the friend with whom he has ditched school are accosted by an elderly man in a field outside the city. After a "monotonous" and repetitive peroration on the attractions of young female bodies, the man walks into a field and—apparently—begins to masturbate: crucially, the reader's only clue that this perverse spectacle is under way is the narration's studied refusal to document it. The man wanders away from the children, and the unnamed narrator's companion Mahoney suddenly blurts out, "I say! Look what he's doing!" The narrator informs us that "I neither answered nor raised my eyes," and in response to this nonresponse Mahoney continues, "I say . . . He's a queer old josser!"[19]

As in epiphany 19, here the offstage quality of the event not only underlines but properly constitutes its enormity: we know the event is disturbing, and most likely sexual, precisely because the text—and Mahoney with it—can only point us toward it. And as in the epiphany, the localization of that perversity is challenged by the thematic and formal qualities of the text. Thurston notes that the story as a whole shares this traumatic moment's descriptive thinness,[20] and we might thus be led to wonder what other qualities this bodiless deviant shares with the boys whose textual existence keeps them similarly offstage. Two striking details stand out in the story's descriptive reticence. Early in the day the narrator has strained to get a glimpse of Norwegian sailors as they unload a ship docked in Dublin's harbor: "I went to the stern and tried to decipher the legend upon it but, failing to do so, I came back and examined the foreign sailors to see had any of them green eyes for I had some confused notion" (15). What this notion is we never learn, but the reader is likely to feel that some question *about the narrator* has been answered when we discover that the "queer old josser" (in the process now of describing the pleasure of whipping little boys) looks at the narrator with "a pair of bottle-green eyes" (19). Certainly the narrator's panicked refusal to look—what Margot Norris labels his "rigid ocular control"—is legible as a symptom of repressed excitement.[21] However much we may want to quarantine the story's perversity on the body of the older man, these details suggest that precisely this encounter was what our narrator has been looking for— that his openness to perverse solicitation is the legend the text deciphers.

Similarly, the reader of *A Portrait of the Artist as a Young Man* might wonder who and what precisely is put on stage when Stephen stumbles on the rehearsals for a student play in the Clongowes school chapel. From the shadows Stephen observes the scene:

> In a dark corner of the chapel at the gospel side of the altar a stout old lady knelt amid her copious black skirts. When she stood up a pinkdressed figure, wearing a curly golden wig and an oldfashioned straw sunbonnet, with black pencilled eyebrows and cheeks delicately rouged and powdered, was discovered. A low murmur of curiosity ran

round the chapel at the discovery of this girlish figure. One of the pre-
fects, smiling and nodding his head, approached the dark corner and,
having bowed to the stout old lady, said pleasantly:

—Is this a beautiful young lady or a doll that you have here, Mrs
Tallon?

Then, bending down to peer at the smiling painted face under the
leaf of the bonnet, he exclaimed:

—No, upon my word I believe it's little Bertie Tallon after all!

Stephen at his post by the window heard the old lady and the priest
laugh together and heard the boys' murmur of admiration behind him
as they passed forward to see the little boy who had to dance the sunbonnet dance by himself. A movement of impatience escaped him.[22]

As Joyce's repetition of the word makes clear, this is a "discovery" scene, an
epiphanic revelation. But is the embodied vulgarity of theatrical transvestism
any more dramatically legible than Stephen's weirdly impalpable reaction to
it? Joyce's meticulous laying of the scene—the gradual, even prurient, unveil-
ing of the feminized little boy, the lightly off-color raillery between the prefect and the boy's grandmother—contrasts oddly with the underdescription
of the scene's culminating moment. What is the "movement of impatience"
with which Stephen punctuates his spectatorship? The answer is that the gesture itself hardly matters; it is clearly a symptomatic expression of Stephen's
agitation at the cross-gender display. We don't need to see the gesture because
we can so easily read through it to its psychic meaning: Stephen has a problem—easy enough to read as a repressed identification—with the spectacle
of gender inversion.[23]

The relationship between the gesture's diagnostic efficacy and the flim-
siness of its representation is underscored a few pages later when Joyce
spells out that Stephen's irritation stems from the vulgarity of his surroundings, in particular their inadequacy to the intensity of his desire for the girl
"E— C—": "All day he had imagined a new meeting with her . . . until the
pleasantry of the prefect and the painted little boy had drawn from him a
movement of impatience" (81). The text's nervous return to this vacant gesture—and the use of the identical phrasing to describe it—betrays an anxiety
about the meanings it may convey, with the result that the heterosexualizing
explanation feels more like a rationalization. The showy impalpability of Stephen's physical response upstages the evident perversity of the painted boy's
performance, encouraging us to turn the diagnostic gaze instead on Stephen
himself. These examples suggest that the only mobility the theatrical offers
within the dynamic of exposure obeys a logic of reversibility: epiphany can
make a spectacle of others' perversity or it can cause that perversity to rebound on the subject.

But this is not the only function of the theatrical in Joyce. If the dramatic mise-en-scène can encourage a punitive gaze at an objectified spectacle, it also—by virtue of its orientation toward an embodied collective space—suggests an alternative economy of perversity. This is clearest in epiphany 23, which records one of the teenaged Joyce's dreams and in the process points beyond epiphany's collusion with sexual stigmatization.

23

That is no dancing. Go down before the people, young boy, and dance for them. . . . He runs out darkly-clad, lithe and serious to dance before the multitude. There is no music for him. He begins to dance far below in the amphitheatre with a slow and supple movement of the limbs, passing from movement to movement, in all the grace of youth and distance, until he seems to be a whirling body, a spider wheeling amid space, a star. I desire to shout to him words of praise, to shout arrogantly over the heads of the multitude 'See! See!' . . . . . His dancing is not the dancing of harlots, the dance of the daughters of Herodias. It goes up from the midst of the people, sudden and young and male, and falls again to earth in tremulous sobbing to die upon its triumph. (*PSW*, 183)

Joyce's annotators record that the boy in this dream epiphany is the recently deceased Georgie (*PSW*, 275). The text enacts a posthumous repair of his decomposing body; Joyce's words replace the unimaginably ruptured body of epiphany 19 with a vision of corporeal coherence, of a "slow and supple movement of the limbs, passing from movement to movement." Not at all coincidentally, Georgie's body—"sudden and young and male"—has now also been cleared of all suspicion of unmanning. Equally important is the biblical—and Wildean—intertext that dances into view here. What might distinguish Georgie's "lithe" and orgasmic ballet from Salomé's striptease is unclear enough to motivate Joyce's denial: "His dancing is not the dancing of harlots, the dance of the daughters of Herodias."[24] But this disavowal of gender inversion may be less important than what it licenses: an unanxious immersion in a public scene of male erotic display. Where Stephen Dedalus lets slip a symptomatic "movement of impatience" when confronted by "the little boy who had to dance the sunbonnet dance by himself," the speaker here—faced with a virtually identical scene—instead becomes a praise singer; that his enthusiasm for this scene might implicate him in sexual abnormality does not bother him enough to silence his laudatory cries. The hermeneutic of sexual suspicion to which the earlier examples submit is oddly beside the point here; the point is simply to *be here* to have this ecstatic dance ecstatically pointed out to us.

In other words, the drive to read symptomatically has been defeated, not reinforced, by theatrical display. In the movement from Mrs. Joyce's anxiously pointing finger ("here") to Joyce's ecstatic directive ("See! See!"), a celebratory deixis replaces a pathologizing one. In the process the meaning of the obscene body at the center of each of these texts has been transformed: we have exchanged the scene of psychosexual exposure for an amphitheater of erotic embodiment. This transvaluation is intimately related to the performative space this text conjures. Although it ranks with the "narrative" epiphanies, epiphany 23 offers a startlingly explicit account of the affective energies compressed in dramatic form as Joyce uses it. As we have seen, the dramatic epiphanies highlight the worldlessness of the literary artifact precisely through their orientation toward a scene of performance. The indicative "stage directions" express the fantasy that the discursive might coincide with, even call into being, a concretely embodied world. This doubled valence of the dramatic—describing something imaginary, expressing desire that it exist—is captured and given an erotic coloration in the exclamation of epiphany 23: "I desire to shout to him words of praise, to shout arrogantly over the heads of the multitude 'See! See!'" The applause offered to the beloved object is here congruent with a plea to perceive him, a demand that his presence be validated by the gathered multitude. This injunction to see is, clearly, directed equally at the reader who encounters this spectacle only via the text. The words spell out the imaginative prompt to the reader implicit in the typography of dramatic texts, where stage directions first posit a world ("Joyce—"; "Dublin: Mountjoy Square") and then animate it ("*stands*"; "*evening*"). The epiphany reveals that the world-making desire of Joycean theatricality is also an erotics—precisely a desire to conjure a new and embodied world.

It would be easy to demystify this demand for readerly witness as part of a post-Romantic ideology of genius: on this reading Joyce needs "us" to ratify the power of his creative imagination. But the appeal to his readers' corporate body does not merely verify his creative authority. It is "we," after all, who disrupt the isolating spectacle of sexual legibility through our ecstatic witness. Even as the speaker decries the multitude, that plural presence is entirely necessary to his rapturous vision. In going public, the scene of sexual deviance loses its ability to impart stigma—loses not its perversity but the spotlit isolation that renders that perversity the object of punitive specularity. The urgency with which the speaker enjoins our witness belies the fact that this transformative theater takes place only virtually: as a textual fantasm it remains unrealized. But the offstageness of obscenity shades here into a different kind of placelessness, that designated by the concept of utopia. (Indeed, one of the functions of these epiphanies is to point out that obscenity and utopia are etymological puns for each other: "offstage" and "nowhere" designate similarly tantalizing extraterritorial zones.) The dramatic mode in Joyce can serve the function of identitarian sexual scapegoating or of permissive publicity, and, as these epiphanies demonstrate, the line between the two is a delicate one. Joyce's negotiations along that line informed the most influential innovations of his later career.

Ibsen, *Exiles,* and the Scene of Sex

In the closing lines of "Drama and Life," Joyce compares the search for artistic truth to a mountain trek. Spurning the use of "dainty silks to shield us against the eager, upland wind," Joyce recommends braving the elements with the help of accurate navigational tools: "The sooner we understand our true position, the better; and the sooner then we will be up and doing on our way." The naturalist drama will play a key role in this effort, as Joyce indicates by ending his essay with a nod to his idol Ibsen: "In the meantime, art, and chiefly drama, may help us to make our resting places with a greater insight and a greater foresight, that the stones of them may be bravely builded, and the windows goodly and fair. '. . . what will you do in our Society, Miss Hessel?' asked Rörlund—'I will let in the fresh air, Pastor.'—answered Lona" (*OCP*, 29). The lines Joyce chooses from *Pillars of Society* conform precisely to the rhetoric of truth he has employed throughout the essay. Just a page earlier he has castigated the popular drama for its falsity, a falsity he equates with the stuffy and darkened theatrical space itself: "people want the drama to befool them, Purveyor supplies plutocrat with a parody of life which the latter digests medicinally in a darkened theatre, the stage literally battening on the mental offal of its patrons" (*OCP*, 28).

The confusion Joyce evinces here about "literalness" (the popular stage can hardly be "literally" feeding on an offal that, being mental, is itself already a figure) is indicative of a deeper uneasiness in naturalism over the ability of the theater to put what Joyce calls "real life" on the stage (*OCP*, 28). If naturalist theater vilified "a parody of life" in the name of the real thing, its performative medium committed it by definition to artifice. In response to this potential collision between its truth claims and its necessary theatricalism, naturalist theater developed its own rhetoric of antitheatricalism. To a startling degree, this rhetoric involved a denial of the importance of the theatrical mise-en-scène, and an appeal to the reader understood as the proper addressee of naturalist drama. This antitheatrical rhetoric was most pronounced among theater practitioners themselves. William Archer, naturalism's principle champion in England, answered charges that Pinero's *The Second Mrs. Tanqueray* would have been better as a novel by claiming that this was precisely its strength: "It is the highest praise, then, that I can find for *Mrs Tanqueray* to say that its four scenes are like the crucial, the culminating, chapters of a singularly powerful and original novel."[25] Ibsen

himself—notwithstanding his long experience as director of Norway's national theater and his powerful manipulation of stagecraft in his own plays
—often spoke as if the proper destination of naturalist theater were not the
stage but the book. Writing about his early play *Cataline* to his translator
Edmund Gosse in 1874, Ibsen explained: "I wished to produce the impression on the reader that what he was reading was something that had really
happened."[26] This address to the reader occurs over the heads, as it were, of
any actual theatrical audience. Rhetorically bypassing the scene of dramatic
enactment, Ibsen makes clear the extent of theatrical naturalism's theoretical
discomfort with the actually existing theater.[27]

His words also indicate that the naturalist dramatic text aspires to the
referential protocols of fiction: between the experience of reading and the
imagination of the "events" to which the text refers, no imagined moment of
enactment is necessary. Indeed, such an imagination would explicitly hinder
Ibsen's purpose here: the "something that had really happened" to which he
refers is patently *not* the first-night premiere of *Cataline* but the "real" (i.e.,
imaginary) events the play represents and which Ibsen's text will render palpable. The text's bid for verisimilitude, that is, depends on its not referring
to a theatrical space. Joyce demonstrates that he has taken Ibsen's lesson to
heart when, in the closing lines of "Drama and Life," he claims theater as the
handmaiden of truth by detheatricalizing—that is, novelizing—it: "'What
will you do in our Society, Miss Hessel?' asked Rörlund—'I will let in the
fresh air, Pastor.'—answered Lona." Translating Ibsen's theatrical dialogue
into the past tense and supplementing it with the inquit phrases that lend it
novelistic texture, Joyce briefly becomes not so much Ibsen's mouthpiece as
his characters' narrator.

In building his case for realism on *Pillars of Society*, Joyce invoked the
1877 play that perfected the dramaturgical conventions of naturalist theater
and marked the beginning of Ibsen's great cycle of bourgeois prose dramas.
The story of a prominent small-town man who is humbled before his community when he is forced to reveal a long-ago sexual liaison with an actress,
the play functions as a parable of the naturalist drama's uneasy truce with
its necessary theatricalism. Karsten Bernick's bland affirmation—before his
unmasking—that "the family is the core of society . . . a good home, some
true and honored friends, a little close-knit circle," is meant to be taken as
hypocrisy.[28] But the play in fact ratifies Bernick's vision of fortified privacy.
At a ceremony where he is to be honored for his accomplishments, Bernick
tells the assembled townspeople that "we have to confront the truth" (112)
before coming clean about his dalliance with the actress Marie Dorf. His sins
publicly confessed, all is forgiven; a grateful Bernick sighs, "It's as if I were
coming back to my senses now after being poisoned" (117). As these words
indicate, *Pillars of Society* proposes a homeopathic solution to the noxious
presence of theatricality: Bernick's concealment of his sexual past and his

ostentatious performance of moral rectitude are put right at a stroke by a public ritual of confession-and-expiation which the Bernick family manages with Clintonian panache.

Ibsen gives these reversals dramatic force by staging, paradoxically enough, a fear of theater. As Toril Moi puts it, *Pillars* "uses the stage and its resources (particularly the set) to expose the concealments of theatricality."[29] The opening stage direction describes the Bernicks' "*spacious garden room*"—a room whose

> rear wall is glass almost entirely . . . A portion of the garden below the steps
> can be seen, bounded by a fence with a small entry gate. Just beyond and
> parallel to the fence is a street, lined on the far side with small, colorfully
> painted wooden houses. It is summer; the sunlight is warm. From time to
> time people pass by on the street; some stop and converse, others patronize
> a little corner shop, etc. (15)

The Bernicks literally live in a glass house. The shattering of their domestic complacency is prefigured by the mise-en-scène that opens their private space to the view of the street. This condition of intense visibility is, of course, also that of the theatrical situation itself: the exposure of the Bernick house to the gaze of the village is an architectural peculiarity, but its exposure to the gaze of the theatrical crowd is part of its generic being. In brilliantly concise form, Ibsen's headnote delineates the interior space of the domestic drama and the publicity that is its limit and condition. "Maybe we ought to draw the curtains?" Mrs. Bernick wonders aloud when scandal starts to heat up—shortly after the stage directions have indicated that "*a crowd of* TOWNSPEOPLE *can be seen coming up the street*" (35–36). But the curtain cannot be brought down until the public has seen the Bernicks' secrets exposed. The play's climax is announced by a stage direction that is unusually expressive for Ibsen: "*The door to the garden is thrown open . . .* [*Enter*] TOWNSPEOPLE *of all classes, as many as the room can hold. An enormous crowd, with flags and banners, can be glimpsed out in the garden and on the street*" (109). This deeply unsettling vision of theatrical publicity threatens the stability of Bernick's newfound self-consistency even as it provides the necessary audience for its confirmation. "I ask each one of you to go home—collect yourself—look deep down into your own heart" (114), Bernick implores the townspeople, and his will to disperse the crowd is offered as proof of his commitment to sincerity and psychic consistency. The play's mirroring between the street and the theater means, of course, that Bernick is also speaking to the theatrical crowd that watches him from the auditorium. At the play's close "*the onlookers melt away through the garden*" (115) in rehearsal of the audience members' imminent departure for those domestic spaces in which they too are invited to "look deep down" and contemplate the truth of their souls.

Ibsen will never again offer such an explicit, or moralized, vision of the theatrical public that is the necessary condition for the confessional momentum of his work. The protagonists of Ibsen's later plays utter their innermost secrets to at most a few other onstage listeners. But as *Pillars* indicates, those famous conversation pieces depend for their revelatory effect on the audience's presence across the footlights. In this sense the play performs a symbolic exorcism of naturalism's necessary but rhetorically disavowed public. The obvious theatrical resonance of the Bernick's curtain-framed garden room may make us want to label *Pillars* a piece of metatheater, a kind of play-within-a-play. But its thematic insistence on psychic self-consistency, its phobic management of its own stage's openness to public view, its proposal that the ideal audience is the privately ensconced and self-absorbed individual—all these factors suggest that *Pillars* would be more accurately described as staging a *novel*-within-a-play. Certainly the play's generic contrarianism supports Peter Szondi's assessment that Ibsen's material is always that "of a novel . . . The thematic ultimately remains alien to the stage."[30] Much of Ibsen's undeniable power derives from precisely the struggle of his novelistic material with its theatrical environment. The relative bluntness with which *Pillars* stages this conflict makes it a useful guide to those later, more sophisticated explorations of interiority that Joyce was reading with such avidity when he began his writing career. In its distance from the nuances of *The Master Builder* and *Hedda Gabler*, *Pillars of Society* helpfully illustrates the conventions underlying late Ibsen's psychological precision. For this early play reveals the extent to which sexuality is the privileged domain of interiority in theatrical naturalism, the core of its concept of psychology.

As many commentators have argued, even in those Ibsen plays where characters' buried secrets are not explicitly sexual in nature, they are accessible to explanation by a sexual etiology. Szondi refers to Ibsen's technique as "analytical," and connects it to the revelations of *Oedipus*, in which the tragedy is tied to the revelation of a secret past (16). Michael Goldman picks up on the psychoanalytic hint in Szondi's work to argue that Ibsen's plays demanded a new style of performance, one that "charge[s] the actor with manifesting buried, often contradictory drives." For Goldman, this acting technique, with its focus on bringing to light "desires suppressed, repressed, censored, or denied," connects "the program of Freud and method acting."[31] Naturalist theater's psychologism and its attendant revolution in acting style coincided with the amplification of the privacy effect created by the box set that had been introduced in England in 1830 and by the end of the century largely replaced the apron stage: in naturalist theater, the closural logic of the box set is taken a step further by a stage that narrows as it recedes, frequently ending in a secluded bedroom or closet. If the box set made the interior hearth the favored locale of nineteenth-century drama, the diminishing naturalist stage—with its suggestion of retreat into ever more secluded zones of privacy—was the objective correlative to a drama obsessed with *psychic* interiority. Naturalism's orientation toward a truth associated with the sexual core of the psyche was mirrored in a stage that gave this core a physical location, the recessed bedroom that suggested the "backstage" of the mind itself.[32] All these developments—thematic, dramaturgical, performative, scenographic—worked to bolster an ideology of characterological truth best exemplified by Ibsen's comment that "before I write a single word, I have to have each character in mind through and through. I must penetrate into the last wrinkle of his soul."[33] Character, understood as something that can and must be grasped, becomes the central concern of the naturalist drama and its stagecraft.

While Joyce is profoundly influenced by naturalism, his work registers ambivalence about its epistemological avidity. Joyce's exploration of techniques to put the psyche on stage, begun in the epiphanies, is continued in *Exiles*; that exploration is pushed in the direction of a critique by that play's notorious difficulty in reaching realization on the stage. It is a commonplace of Joyce criticism that the failure of *Exiles* stems from Joyce's narrative orientation.[34] But John MacNicholas's reconstruction of the play's production history suggests that there is good reason to be wary of this critical endorsement of what may be an accident of theatrical history; MacNicholas shows that there is nothing inherently unstageworthy about the play (Harold Pinter's 1970 production, for example, was widely praised.)[35] At any rate, the play's almost total confinement to its textual ghost had serious implications for Joyce's thinking about psychic explicitation in naturalist dramaturgy. Because *Exiles* languished in a state of textual nonperformance, the ancillary textual material—particularly the notes Joyce wrote during its composition—clearly came to occupy an ever more prominent role in his conception of the play. We will see that the consequent flattening between the text and its explanation, onstage performance and textual obscene, led Joyce to interrogate the logic of truth informing naturalism itself.

Joyce's notes for *Exiles* on the one hand suggest a meditation on character wholly consonant with Ibsen's self-described "penetration" of his characters: Joyce appears to understand his people not as performatively constituted beings but as rounded characters whose plausibility is verified by the fact that more of them exists than can be demonstrated on the stage. "Perhaps it would be well to make a separate sketch of the doings of each of the four chief persons during the night, including those whose actions are not revealed to the public in the dialogue," Joyce writes to himself after composing the first act.[36] "It would be interesting," he also notes, "to make some sketches of Bertha if she had united her life for nine years to Robert—not necessarily in the way of drama but rather impressionistic sketches" (*PE*, 345). In terms of the plot of *Exiles*, these are strictly counterfactual imaginings: they will be neither represented nor referred to in the play's action. They gravitate toward specifying the truth of the play, the insinuated but never quite disclosed psychic core animating the frequently obscure action and dialogue onstage. Unsurprisingly, this truth is sexual in nature.

Joyce's play takes place on a single night in the Dublin suburbs, and follows a romantic and sexual struggle among two men and two women; *Exiles* resonates with Joyce's other fictional portraits of marriage (in *Ulysses,* especially), and it is quite clearly based on his own early life. Richard Rowan is a writer who has returned to Dublin after nine years of voluntary exile in Europe; he brings with him Bertha, the uneducated woman who has abandoned respectability to follow him, and their son Archie. Robert Hand is the friend who idolizes Richard and attempts to seduce Bertha; Beatrice is the stiff but intellectually ambitious woman to whom Robert is engaged and with whom Richard has been carrying on a high-toned literary correspondence. Although the plot's focus is on heterosexual jealousy, the lines of desire in the play are tangled; the intensity of the men's mutual attraction, in particular, approaches articulation at several points. Robert's attempt to take Bertha from Richard, which occupies the center of the play, prolongs and heightens the bond between the men, which dates from the "wild nights" the two used to share in a cottage in the suburb of Ranelagh reserved for the purpose: "We had the two keys for [the cottage], he and I," Richard tells Bertha. If the carousing involved women, he does not mention them: "Where we used to hold our wild nights, talking, drinking, planning—at that time. Wild nights; yes. He and I together" (171). Robert explicitly designates himself Richard's disciple, and his attempt to disrupt the master's marriage figures also as a consummation of his apprenticeship. As he puts it, "She is yours, your work. (*suddenly*) And that is why I too was drawn to her. You are so strong that you attract me even through her" (189). The taut chain of identification and desire between the two men is accentuated by the similarities in their first names, and by the suggestion of mutual fit and phallic manipulation in their surnames. In the weirdly interlocking, strenuous exercise in which the men are engaged, it can be difficult to know the rower from the hand.

The play, in other words, offers itself readily to psychologizing readings— and these were not slow to be produced. The contributors to a 1919 symposium in the *Little Review* a year after the play's publication agreed that homosexuality was the daring—if covert—theme of *Exiles*. Israel Solon explained that the play concerns "the fate of two men who are in love with each other," while Jane Heap confirmed that "Robert is in love with Richard, has always been." In his more circuitous formulation, Samuel Tannenbaum wrote that *Exiles* treats "one of the most tabooed and falsified motives of human conduct,—we mean homosexuality. It is true that the reader unlearned in such matters, and perhaps the author too, may not be aware that this is the theme of the play and may look for it in vain . . . [The theme can be] derived from the author's repressed but most urgent impulses . . .

Richard Rowan's, the protagonist's, homopsychism, is never once referred to in the story but is clearly to be deduced from his character and conduct."[37]

We may want to dismiss the vulgar psychologism of these readings, but they derive from an interpretive agenda exactly congruent with Joyce's own. "A faint glimmer of lesbianism irradiates this mind," Joyce writes in his notes a propos Bertha's solicitous third-act conversation with Beatrice (*PE*, 350). It is the first of a string of comments indicating Joyce's sense of the sexual determination of character. "The play: a rough and tumble between the Marquis de Sade and Freiherr v. Sacher Masoch," Joyce notes to himself. "Had not Robert better give Bertha a little bite when they kiss? Richard's Masochism needs no example" (*PE*, 351). A few lines from this comment he explains that "the bodily possession of Bertha by Robert, repeated often, would certainly bring into almost carnal contact the two men. Do they desire this? To be united, that is carnally through the person and body of Bertha as they cannot, without dissatisfaction and degradation—be united carnally man to man as man to woman?" (*PE*, 351). In secreting the truth of his characters' sexual motivation in the obscene zone of the ancillary notes, Joyce models the hermeneutics of sexual suspicion that his audience is meant to take up. Although the *Little Review* commentators had not, of course, read Joyce's notes, the equivalence of their interpretive stance seems retroactively to qualify those notes as the answer to the play's riddle.

"Do they desire this?" is also a version of the play's central thematic issue: the question of whether Bertha and Robert have consummated their extramarital flirtation is the focus of Richard's—and the audience's—obsessed attention. The hiatus between the second and third acts, during which Bertha and Robert either do or do not retire to the bedroom located at the back of the men's pied-à-terre, makes this question fundamentally unanswerable. The results of this undecidability are complex. Certainly it augments the epistemological prestige of the question itself, sponsoring a theatrical environment structured by the imperative to disclose the hidden sexual act ("We all confess to one another here," as Robert puts it at one point [220]). No less than for Ibsen, characterological truth in *Exiles* is understood to lie offstage, in a sexual scene that must be discursively represented onstage in order to be ratified by the gathered public. And Joyce's notes have ensured that the sexual meanings so apparent to the *Little Review*'s contributors have been readily available to subsequent critics eager to appear in the role of that prurient public. As Bernard Benstock observes, the willingness of the play's critics to treat Joyce's notes as having diagnostic truth value has been increased by the fact that *Exiles* is so infrequently performed: "the Joycean commentator quite casually tends to accept *Exiles* as a closet drama with additional stage directions affixed by its creator, an entity which now becomes a nontheatrical *Exiles* readily acceptable within the logic of the Joyce canon."[38] Far from contesting this critical situation, Benstock finds it wholly appropriate in dealing with a writer whose real talent was for narrative.

Critics have thus tended to treat nonperformance as *Exiles*'s ideal modality, understanding the text as addressed to them *as readers*. This presumption in turn validates the naturalist investment in characterological truth by giving an evenness of texture to the events of the play and the sexual etiologies appended in the notes. Moving seamlessly between the text of the play and Joyce's notes for it, Joyce's critics have largely ignored the differentiation of text destined for performance from text meant to remain "offstage."[39] This approach seems consonant with Joyce's own attitude to the play; but in hewing so closely to Joyce's commentary, these critics reproduce his reading rather than interpret the relation of that reading to the play itself. Considered as a designedly unperformed piece, *Exiles* arrives before readers already interpreted according to an inescapable logic of sexual truth: any difference in status between the events of the play and the sexual motivations for those events fades away. In *Exiles*-the-closet-drama, the play's various illicit sexual combinations and identifications are no less "real" for being imaginary: these fantasy events have the same ontological status as the events that performatively occur.

But *Exiles* is also the drama *of* that indistinction, a meditation on the consequences of the paratext's elevation to the status of diagnostic truth. To treat *Exiles* as if it already were a novel is to miss that the play dramatizes precisely the novelization of character. It is only once we have registered *Exiles*'s self-consciousness about the relation of text to performance that we can perceive the play's struggle with the stage logic exemplified by *Pillars of Society*. In important respects Joyce's relation to that logic verges on parody. This is first evident in a certain assertiveness—even a showiness—in the stage directions; at several moments they seem to achieve a performative life that exceeds their narrative or descriptive function. When Beatrice utters a line "*softly*" and Richard answers her "*slowly*" (122), Joyce's stage directions create a discursive and visual rhyme in the space of the text that has no relation to performative meaning. Acted, the manner in which these two lines are to be read would make them appear to an audience as quite different; read, they appear as echoes of one another. The address to the reader inherent in naturalist dramaturgy creates here a meaningless static "between" that reader and the action.

Elsewhere a distracting seepage occurs between the dialogue and the stage directions: a few lines after those I have just quoted, Richard tells Beatrice that her relationship with Robert has always "made me so reserved with you"; half a page later, when the stage directions indicate that she answers him "*with some reserve*," the echo makes it appear as if both kinds of verbal material, performative and extra-performative, were directed at some single reading consciousness (123). An almost comical textual effect occurs during a tender moment when Robert tells Richard that their reunion gave birth in him to a physical impulse: "At that moment I felt our whole life together in the past and I longed to put my arm around your neck"—an announcement which, though it does not issue in the physical contact in question, nonetheless leaves Robert "*deeply and suddenly touched*" (199). In a play in which a disavowed homoeroticism has such motivational force, the lines ensure that insofar as they are textual beings these characters will be revealed even in what they fail to do: we quite literally read the denied caress the performance only hints at. In themselves relatively insignificant, these moments cumulatively herald a theatrical environment menaced with textual meaning; this menace is so pronounced that eventually even the characters themselves seem conscious of the power of the discursive and the extra-theatrical to fix identitarian meaning.

In this context, and in light of the insistence with which Joyce's notes give voice to the diagnostic impulse, the play's refusal to disclose or represent its sexual transgressions gains a sense of ethical urgency.[40] More important, his characters use their performative position to resist the potentially terroristic condition of total psychic legibility. When we see Bertha "*suddenly withdrawing from her post*" at the window in act 3, and telling her servant Brigid, "I don't want to be seen" (235), she might seem only to be reiterating Bernick's distaste for publicity, and his corresponding desire to ratify his self-sameness on the stage of the home. But in fact the two characters function quite differently. Bernick embodies a fully theatricalized antitheatricalism, a fear of publicity that does not hesitate to make a spectacle first of his own happy family and then of his own psychological consistency. Bertha's unease is less amenable to accommodation on the naturalist stage because she contests its fundamental premise of psychological coherence. Her fear of the outside is exceeded by her fear of those heavily significant interior spaces of the stage on which she finds herself—precisely those private spaces which Bernick concludes *Pillars* by recommending to his audience.

One of the play's most mysterious passages occurs in act 2, when Bertha is alone with Robert in the "wild nights" cottage in Ranelagh. The space is described in the headnote as containing "*in the wall at back folding doors, draped with dark curtains, leading to a bedroom*" (182). The dramatically framed scene of sex will be literally spotlit later when Robert enters the bedroom and puts a pink glass shade on the lamp there, asking Bertha with leering suggestiveness, "Do you like the effect of the light?" (214); when the wind blows in from the porch, the flickering lamp becomes a taunting strobe on which Joyce's stage directions dwell with redundant emphasis: "*The room is half dark. The light comes in more strongly through the door of the bedroom*"; "*The flame of the lamp leaps*"; "*The light from the doorway of the bedroom crosses the place where they sit*" (222, 228, 229). Bertha reacts to the gothic meaningfulness of all this with anxiety, even dread: "Robert! . . . Come here quickly!

Quickly, I say!" she exclaims when Robert first disappears into the recessed bedroom, explaining later, "(*trembling*) I was afraid . . . I feared something. I am not sure what" (214–216). It is perhaps inevitable to read Bertha's wariness of these suggestive spatial semiotics in psychological terms. She may not want to betray her husband. She may be afraid of her desire to do so. She may be put off by her inept Lothario (and we could continue in this vein by inferring that the clownishness of Robert's seduction indicates that his real attraction is to Richard...).

But Bertha exhibits a similar agitation about her husband's study, which occupies an equivalent recessed space of epistemological privilege (through "*a small door*" in the rear wall [115]) in her own house. "All those things you sit up at night to write about," she reproaches Richard in act 1, "(*pointing to the study*). In there" (176); she repeats the gesture in act 3 in a discussion with her maid: "Did you not know? (*she points towards the study*) He passes the greater part of the night in there writing. Night after night . . . Study or bedroom. You may call it what you please" (241). Again, it would be easy to read these lines psychologically (as expressing Bertha's sexual frustration, or her jealousy of Richard's letter writing to Beatrice, or her feelings of intellectual inferiority, and so on). But it is less important to deduce the psychic meaning of these moments of anxiety than to note their structural congruity: in every case a performatively constituted character—"I do things," Bertha proclaims at one point (208)—protests against those sites where truth is fixed on the naturalist stage. Bertha's recriminatory conflation of bedroom and library registers a resistance not to whatever traits will be assigned to her in these spaces ("frigidity," sensuality, lesbianism, etc.) but rather to these spaces' power of designation over the meaning of her actions. As the relentlessly psychologizing reception of *Exiles* indicates, she is quite right to note that the bedroom and the library are the same space on this stage; sex in an important sense is always already written—performance is always legible—in this world. Bertha's resistance is to a theater saturated with significance.

Bertha is the characterological location of this protest, but she articulates a strategy in which all the characters participate. The universal resistance to textual pinning down is most evident in the extraordinary proliferation of unplayable—and quite literally meaningless—stage directions. The text is shot through with moments in which the text designates, bafflingly, "*a gesture*" (163, 167), "*a sudden gesture*" (178, 203), "*a sudden fervent gesture*" (188), "*a vague gesture*" (193), "*an involuntary gesture*" (199), and so on—precisely the form with which, in *Portrait*, Joyce designates the gesture that needs no specification because its sexual meanings are all too legible. The vague gesture in Joyce's first novel goes undescribed because it is a symptom, a sign of something beyond it; as such it poses no interpretive difficulty for the reader. In *Exiles* the profusion of similar gestures serves a precisely opposite function. Because the text is explicitly designed as a blueprint for enactment, the reader confronted with these oddly empty gestures (not to speak of the actors charged with embodying them) is faced with what Roland Barthes would call an inoperability in the text.[41] The stage directions I have quoted are clustered with particular density in the climactic act 2, which transpires in the harsh light emanating from the backstage bedroom in which so many of the play's sexual secrets are located. With their flatly unimaginable gestures, the characters appear to react to the obviousness of the spotlit bedroom by jamming the mechanism of psychosexual legibility. Far from capitulating to the psychologism of the naturalist stage, these movements seek to restore action to a condition of performative opacity. "I do things," these gestures say, inscrutably.

In their performative failure to mean, these gestures could not be further from naturalist convention.[42] Moreover, once we perceive the ambivalence of *Exiles*'s investment in naturalism, Joyce's diagnostic notes emerge not as statements of analytic revelation but as almost comically clueless musings on an elusive spectacle. At one point Joyce wonders just how far Bertha would let Robert go:

> It is certain that [Bertha's] instinct can distinguish between concessions and for her the supreme concession is what the fathers of the church call *emissio seminis inter vas naturale*. As for the accomplishment of the act otherwise externally, by friction, or in the mouth the question needs to be scrutinised still more. Would she allow her lust to carry her so far as to receive his emission of seed in any other opening of the body where it could not be acted upon, when once emitted, by the forces of her secret flesh? (*PE*, 351–352)

Joyce pushes the naturalist will-to-knowledge here to Jesuitical extremes. In its smutty investigative enthusiasm, the passage seems a burlesque of Szondi's Oedipal analyst. "You know the kind he is," Bertha cries exasperatedly at one point in reference to Richard. "He asks about everything. The ins and outs" (217). She might be describing her creator, whose investment here in the "ins and outs" of the scene of sex undoes its rationale in the process of articulation (does the issue of where Bertha would permit Robert to ejaculate *really* "need to be scrutinised still more?"). Far from ratifying naturalism's attachment to characterological depth, Joyce has in fact staged a confrontation between a meaning-obsessed sexual investigator ("himself") and characters who continually evade his scrutiny. It is striking that in the above quotation the final sentence is phrased as a question, as if Joyce's characters had achieved a kind of autonomy by entering a zone of privacy he cannot penetrate. In another note Joyce writes, "Bertha wishes for a spiritual union of Richard and Robert and *believes* (?) that union will be effected only through her body and perpetuated thereby" (350). The sentence both insists on Joyce's grasp of Bertha's interiority (with the italicized emphasis on "*believes*") and immediately puts that grasp in doubt (with the interjected question mark), as Joyce momentarily casts himself in the role of the wondering spectator to the psychologies he has created.

The contradictory intensity of the moment marks it as a crux in Joyce's thinking about the knowability of character. It is clear that these persistent questions—all versions of "Do they desire this?"—serve, on the one hand, to bolster the seriousness of the sexual inquiry. But read in the light of these characters' efforts not to disclose, the questions concede to them a certain opacity—even make an ethical point of not knowing. Performative beings exiled in a theatrical form that would read their desire like an open book, Joyce's characters manage to insist on their allegiance to a theatrical illegibility. In the process they allow Joyce to interrogate naturalism's interrogative impulse.

Backstage at the Library: "Scylla and Charybdis"

Joyce wrote *Exiles* as he drafted the opening chapters of *Ulysses*,[43] a book with a plausible claim to being the preeminent psychological novel in English. As Karen Lawrence's study most incisively argues, Joyce's focus on interiority and the "primacy of character" is especially pronounced in *Ulysses*'s first half: "In the early chapters of *Ulysses*, the narrative largely devotes itself to exposing the quality of the characters' minds."[44] As the foregoing analysis of his only surviving play indicates, dramatic form was crucial to Joyce's thinking about the representation of character. The naturalist drama offered a set of propositions about the central role of sexual secrecy in constituting subjectivity; from his earliest work, those propositions suggested that the psychological novel achieves its character effects by putting those sexual secrets "onstage"— a practice Lawrence aptly describes with her language of exposure. If Joyce's experiences with *Exiles* were key to *Ulysses*'s unprecedented creation of the illusion of characterological depth, this is even truer of *Exiles* regarded as a theatrical failure.

As we have seen, Joyce's play is routinely treated as a kind of closet drama, one that comes handily appended with authorial notes specifying the psychic truths motivating the onstage action. Disregarding the division between the action and its obscene discursive supplement, critics freely mingle diegesis and exegesis, regarding *Exiles* as an undifferentiated mix of textual material into which the idea of performance introduces no distinctions of importance. If Joyce's critics bear partial responsibility for this flattening, we have seen that Joyce himself puts in play a complicated interaction between the characters and the author's discourse of truth about them. Joyce, in other words, was already beginning to explore the possibilities of nonperformance: *Exiles* suggested the distinctive access to characterological truth offered by a text that would encompass symptom and diagnosis, action and truth. As he began work on *Ulysses*, *Exiles* seemed more and more likely to be confined to a textual existence,[45] and it is thus significant in this context that his major novel might (like the text of *Exiles*) be described as including its own off-stage. As Dorrit Cohn has argued, the innovation in the opening chapters of *Ulysses* consists not in incorporating transcriptions of thought into scenes composed of narration and dialogue but in the "altered appearance" of the Joycean text.[46] Dispensing with the inquit phrases that usually mark interior speech ("he thought," "Molly said to herself"), and removing the quotation marks from both spoken and unspoken dialogue, Joyce presents a dauntingly undifferentiated textual artifact. We can better perceive the impact of *Exiles*'s nonperformance on this innovation if we recall the hierarchy of truth instantiated by the orthodox naturalist stage, which opposes symptomatic dialogue and action to a diagnostic discourse of narrativized stage directions and authorial explication. The naturalist stage allots these separate orders of discourse to separate physical locations: the former onstage and visible, the latter hidden in a recessed room or an inaccessible play text. But this topographic segregation breaks down in the event of nonperformance, the absence of an embodied stage event opening the possibility of a de-differentiation between action and explanation.

In *Ulysses*, Joyce renders legible the content of interiority by lining dialogue and narration with the properly "offstage" information of the mind's content. The novel creates precisely the textualized "closet drama" that *Exiles* was in the process of becoming via the more mundane process of theatrical failure: a fully discursivized space in which the contents of those recessed closets have been pushed into view. Intermixing the material of the mind with the novel's action, *Ulysses* is a kind of backstager, a naturalist drama where the characters readily disclose the desires naturalism expends such energy extracting. The consequences for the reader are significant: in order to comprehend the action at all, we are forced to re-create those characterological boundaries the text so continually violates. Faced with an undifferentiated textual block, *we* must decide what "belongs" where, distinguishing mental from narrative material and re-secreting the former in its proper psychological containers.[47] This demand functions complexly: on the one hand, by making the reader complicit in delineating character, Joyce's text massively increases the explanatory prestige of interiority. The curious flatness of *Ulysses*, far from refusing the naturalist hierarchy of characterological truth, heightens the importance of that hierarchy by transferring the responsibility for its erection to the reader. On the other, in rendering the material of consciousness so readily available, Joyce vitiates the drama of interiority's exposure: when the scandalously obscene is everywhere present, the ability of that obscene to signify "truth" is seriously undermined.

Ulysses in fact pursues each of these strategies in succession, and it seems clear that *Exiles*'s nonperformance suggested to Joyce the strategies for both perfecting and later undoing his character effects. The first strategy, in which the drama of interiority's exposure consorts seamlessly with naturalist notions of psychic truth, reaches its apotheosis in "Scylla and Charybdis." This is the final chapter of *Ulysses* to feature the regular alternation of narration, dialogue, and interior monologue before the novel embarks on the strenuous experimentation of "Wandering Rocks" and the subsequent episodes. Not coincidentally, it is in "Scylla and Charybdis" that the dramatic genealogy of the interior monologue, and its role in anchoring identity in sexual truth, come into sharpest focus. The issue of psychic coherence in fact occupies the thematic foreground: the chapter relates Stephen's effort to convince a group of Dublin acquaintances gathered at the National Library of his off-the-wall theory that Shakespeare identified with the ghost of Hamlet's father. The conversation traverses familiar Dedalan (and Joycean) terrain: the mystery of paternity, the nature of artistic inspiration, the arcana of literary biography. But the debate is less interesting for its content (Ezra Pound termed it "a university vanity"[48]) than for its foregrounding of the hermeneutics of sexual suspicion. Stephen thinks Hamlet Sr.'s sexual betrayal is directly traceable to Ann Hathaway's adultery, and rests on this imaginary incident not only a reading of *Hamlet* but, crazier still, an interpretation of the entire arc of Shakespeare's career. In his zeal to detect Shakespeare's location in his plays, Stephen models in extreme fashion the psychological boundary marking that *Ulysses* demands of its reader.

Stephen's determination to hunt out the person behind the text is all the more notable because he is dealing with the drama, a form he elsewhere commends for its impersonality.[49] Mr. Best fatuously encourages Stephen's argument—"*Hamlet* is so personal, isn't it . . . a kind of private paper, don't you know, of his private life" (9.362–363)—but "Scylla and Charybdis" itself seems more skeptical of Stephen's psychologizing agenda. The chapter yearns instead toward the externalizing genres of theater and the philosophical dialogue: at one point the conversation is actually rendered in play script form (9.893–934), and Buck Mulligan concludes the chapter by writing a quick "play for the mummers" on the subject of masturbation (titled *Every Man His Own Wife, or a Honeymoon in the Hand*) the dramatis personae of which is reproduced in the text (9.1171–1189). Indeed, the chapter's dramatic tropism registers as a kind of allergic formal response to Stephen's preoccupation with psychological truth. Far more interesting than the debate on *Hamlet* is the competition "Scylla and Charybdis" stages between the modes of dramatic and narrative presentation. In this debate, the very skill with which Joyce explores novelistic interiority ends up a liability: "Scylla and Charybdis" in fact argues for the ethical and strategic superiority of drama. Joyce stages the move into and out of consciousness as a move between generic options, with the perversely performative squaring off against a cruelly diagnostic (and self-diagnostic) interiority. As in the epiphanies, Stephen's consciousness is adduced to "prove" his superiority or normality but ends up subjecting him to the logic of exposure he has set in motion. The interiority Stephen represents and implicitly espouses will be revealed in "Scylla and Charybdis" as hopelessly entangled with a logic of sexual shaming.[50]

As in the earlier epiphanies, Stephen's attempt to make a display of Shakespeare's sexual life ends up making a spectacle of him. This occurs, first, through the homoerotic inflection of the argumentative form in which he finds himself involved, the Socratic dialogue. "Are you going to write it?" Mr. Best asks Stephen at one point. "You ought to make it a dialogue, don't you know, like the Platonic dialogues Wilde wrote" (9.1068–1069). Best's invocation of Wilde draws attention to the queerness of the cultural tradition in which this type of intellectual debate is steeped. Stephen's preference for Aristotle over Plato hardly straightens out this tradition: if, as Best points out, Wilde is in some sense behind any fin-de-siècle invocation of Plato, Aristotle is under Plato—as Stephen acknowledges when he admits that "Aristotle was once Plato's schoolboy" (9.57). With its homosocial bonding through cultural name-dropping, the chapter toys with acknowledging what Eve Kosofsky Sedgwick has called pederasty's foundational role in the Western philosophical tradition.[51] And if the reader misses this chain of cultural signifiers, the chapter's overt thematic material is sufficiently given over to gender inversion, transvestism, and homosexuality to arouse suspicion. Stephen's theory centers on a scene of heterosexual seduction—but he finds space to declare that Shakespeare's "boywomen are the women of a boy. Their life, thought, speech are lent them by males" (9.254–255), and to wonder "what name Achilles bore when he lived among women" (9.350–351). Lyster refers to Shakespeare's infatuation with the Earl of Pembroke (9.443–445), Magee wonders if Hamlet was a woman (9.518–519), several references are made to male pregnancy (9.836–837, 9.875–877), and Stephen concludes his discourse with the suggestion that heaven is a place of perfect androgyny (9.1052).

Such preoccupations cluster, unsurprisingly, around Buck Mulligan. Mulligan shows an interest in the fate of Jewish foreskins (9.609) and the erections of hanged men (9.559–560); he claims that Bloom is "Greeker than the Greeks" (9.614–615) and that he "lust[s] after" Stephen (9.1210); he delights in rehearsing the "charge of pederasty brought against the bard" (9.732). As in the novel's opening chapter, Mulligan's good-natured performance of hypersexed masculinity threatens to overstep a line into homosexuality. Still, it is Stephen's references to homosexuality that come off as more

damningly characterizing—precisely because they are internal. Stephen's silent accusation that Mulligan is a "catamite" (9.734), his mental comparison
of Mr. Lyster to Elizabethan cross-dressed actors (9.329–330), his interior
labeling of Mr. Best a "blond ephebe," a "minion of pleasure" who puts him
in mind of "Phedo's toyable fair hair" (9.531, 9.1139)—all these references
suggest that novelistic interiority is an even more definitive stage for exposure than Mulligan's campy conversation. When Mulligan loudly proclaims
his interest in Shakespeare's male paramour, Stephen responds—or, rather,
doesn't—by silently citing Lord Alfred Douglas's "love that dare not speak its
name" (9.659). The words are meant to draw attention to Mulligan's perversity. But it is Stephen who, in keeping quiet, conforms more exactly to Douglas's iconic definition of gayness.[52] At one point Stephen seems to register the
revelatory nature of his own discourse: "What the hell are you driving at?"
(9.846), he asks himself silently just before he wonders—out loud—at the
rarity of father-son incest. Stephen's success in masking his alarm from his listeners hardly matters to the reader, who is witness to his internal queer bash-
ing and his panicked sense of its significance. Like the characters of *Exiles*
fearful of the legibility of their every move, Stephen inhabits narration as a
space of total visibility. Contrasting Stephen's mental (self-)accusations with
Mulligan's volubility, "Scylla and Charybdis" also plays out a generic struggle.
Against Mulligan's display of polymorphous perversity, Stephen stands for
psychological knowability—a principle he both advocates thematically (with
his Shakespearean inventions) and represents formally (through his status as
the narrative's focalizing agent).

In this context Stephen's ambivalent attraction to Mulligan takes on new
implications. The eroticism of their relationship renders palpable what we
might think of as the melancholy of interiority, its desire to escape its painful self-consistency. While composing the chapter, Joyce wrote a letter to his
friend Frank Budgen which excitedly reported on a possible (in the event
abortive) production of *Exiles*: apparently inspired by this immanent performance, he added the following postscript: "P.S. Last night I thought of an
Entr'acte for Ulysses in middle of book after 9th episode *Scylla and Charybdis*. Short with absolutely no relation to what precedes or follows like a pause
in the action of a play."[53] Like the unstageable stage directions of *Exiles*, the
note is tantalizingly empty: Joyce makes no mention of the content of this
theatrical interlude except to specify that it will have "absolutely nothing to
do" with the novel it punctuates. For a writer otherwise eager to submit to
a program of total aesthetic accountability, this is a remarkable ambition—
and it is important that Joyce associated this escape from significance with
the form of the theater. Joyce did not write his *entr'acte*, but in Buck Mulligan's perverse externality—perhaps even in the stupidly profane comedy
he hastily pens at the chapter's close—we can perceive an image of just such
a theatrical escape from psychic meaning. "Scylla and Charybdis" may be

characterologically centered in Stephen, but its insistent invocation of performance expresses a yearning to take interiority out of the novel, to let its characters exist in a medium of pure display.

In the library symposium at the heart of the chapter, George Russell disparages Stephen's psychobiography of Shakespeare as "greenroom gossip" (9.187). The phrase could serve for all the editorializing verbiage that surrounds and reads the performances of being: the inquisitive notes to *Exiles*, naturalism's telling stage directions, the diagnoses offered by the *Little Review*—and the putting into discourse of mental states known as interior monologue which Joyce brings to paranoid precision in "Scylla and Charybdis." At one point in the chapter, Stephen's interior discourse appears to record a dissatisfaction with the terms of its own narrative existence. Stephen's silent words report an emotion we could describe as the bibliographic sublime: "Coffined thoughts around me, in mummycases, embalmed in spice of words" (9.352–353). Stephen's horror is directed at the library's mountains of books, but his words associate the stillness of texts and the deadness of the letter with the crypt of interiority itself. In its insistent invocation of the drama, "Scylla and Charybdis" wants to substitute mummery for mummification, to replace the greenroom gossip of interiority with a community of perverse action.

The Ineluctable Modality of the Legible: "Circe"

Joyce scholarship has confirmed the integrative role "Circe" played in the conception of *Ulysses*. Joyce wrote the two famous schemata—detailing a color, technique, organ, Homeric correspondence, and so on, for each chapter—while he was at work on this longest and wildest section; it was also as "Circe" came into being that Joyce began the extensive revisions of the earlier episodes that tightened the novel's intramural coherence.[54] Both the schemata and the revisions were central to the claims to artistic seriousness Joyce would use to defend his book from charges of pornography. Pointing to the fact that the novel had been so clearly organized, so meticulously cross-referenced with itself, Joyce deflected claims that his book was a lewd and formless mess.[55] That "Circe" should be central to *Ulysses*'s bid for respectability seems counterintuitive, to say the least. Bloom and Stephen's adventures in Nighttown comprise the most grossly physical and linguistically vulgar of *Ulysses*'s chapters. But the contradiction is only apparent: the sexualization of "Circe" is entirely consistent with its role as the anchor and justification of the novel as a whole. As Joyce revised the earlier chapters his most consistent concern was to amplify the passages of interior monologue.[56] It is the solidification of the character effect, that is, that unifies *Ulysses*. If the retroactive insertion of interior monologue was one means to this end, the sexual explicitation of "Circe" was another; the vivid sexuality of *Ulysses*'s central chapter appears to confirm Joyce's understanding of sexuality as the characterizing agent par excellence. Joyce excuses the eroticism that is so central to "Circe" by enlisting it in the project of elaborating psychological meaning. If sex serves as the anchor of character, character provides an alibi for sex.

This durable chain between sex and character makes psychologizing readings of "Circe" inviting, perhaps to some extent inevitable. The sense that "Circe" is where Joyce's characters—especially Bloom—are most *known* has proven difficult to escape. The language of revelation and exposure, of psychic depth, of suppressed fantasies and repressed memories, dogs even those critical accounts eager to take their distance from vulgarly psychological readings. Hélène Cixous celebrates the episode as a post-structuralist carnival of indeterminacy (Nighttown "decomposes each and everyone into his several selves . . . without distinction of object, of subject, of interiority or of exteriority"), but is happy to read Bloom's penetration by the whoremistress Bella/o precisely as a revelation of a psychic interior: the chapter "brings to light [Bloom's] shameful desire. The most deeply buried manages to expose itself."[57] Maud Ellmann similarly insists that the theater of "Circe" must be expressing something: "When [Bloom] becomes a woman . . . we know that he has longed for subjugation; when he creates Bloomusalem, we know that he has also lusted after power; and when he is accused of a dizzying spectrum of perversions, we know that his desires speak in his accusers' tongues, together with the added frisson of chastisement."[58] But in what sense do these count as revelations? By the time we reach the fifteenth episode of *Ulysses*, we have seen Bloom fix his wife breakfast in bed and take care to stay away from the house during the hour appointed for her liaison with Blazes Boylan; we have overheard his mental plans for any number of municipal improvements; his correspondence with Martha Clifford has long since apprised us of his penchant for domineering dirty talk. We might adapt Joyce's comments on Richard Rowan to note that by the time we get to "Circe" Bloom's uxoriousness, his civic-mindedness, and his masochism need no example.

It is not an accident that these readings, otherwise so aware of the episode's complications, produce redundant interpretations of character when they deal with the sexual core of "Circe." The near inescapability of the psychological lexicon is directly traceable to the episode's use of dramatic form. But "Circe" is a reductio ad absurdum of the logic of theatrical naturalism that ends by questioning why theatrical form should authorize us in thinking something is being revealed.[59] The process initiated in "Scylla and Charybdis," in which Joyce begins to rotate into the text what in *Exiles* had remained extradiegetic diagnostic material, reaches a climax in "Circe": "Dr Bloom is bisexually abnormal," Mulligan (who should know) declares at one point: "There are marked symptoms of chronic exhibitionism. Ambidexterity is also latent . . . I have made a pervaginal examination and, after application of the acid test to 5427 anal, axillary, pectoral and pubic hairs, I declare him to be *virgo intacta*" (15.1775–1786). The categorizing appetite of sexology is being satirized here, of course, but the passage equally recalls Joyce's fervid imaginings in his notes to *Exiles*. Far from being simply another discourse to be parodied, the language of sexual diagnosis lies at the heart of Joyce's construction of characterological depth. And while it has been evident to critics that "Circe" has a pivotal place in the integrative project of *Ulysses*, the chapter is better understood as the place where the text yearns for that project's undoing.

As we have seen, naturalism naturalizes its reliance on sexual exposure by appealing to the authority of the novel and correspondingly disavowing its own theatricality. While the presence of the theatrical crowd is necessary to ratify the truth of character, naturalism is concerned to make it appear as if this truth emerged of its own accord—the result not of social coercion but of looking deep into the soul. In the exemplary case of *Pillars of Society*, scenography is central to this denial of the public element of theatrical privacy: fortified against the intrusions of the "street," the domestic stage space pretends it does not stand exposed to the eyes of the gathered spectators. But if Ibsen fantasmatically banishes the public, in "Circe" Joyce reintroduces naturalism's theatrical crowd with a vengeance: the theatrical remains the text's stubborn, if impossible, ground. The sense of the theater—an embodied space of performers and spectators—remains flickeringly but consistently available in the episode as an imaginative backdrop to the action, so that "Circe" becomes the most extreme of the theatrical spatializations we have thus far encountered. During Bloom's trial for sexual crimes, we read that he *"turns to the gallery"* to deliver his defense (15.785); the word designates a space for seated spectators both in court and in the theater, and so raises the possibility that the red-light district constituting the "real" context for the episode is itself contained in the space of a theater. Mary Driscoll's later accusations against Bloom of sexual assault are met with *"general laughter"* (15.894); as the text has not designated the presence of any spectators in the courtroom (nor, in fact, the existence of the courtroom itself), we are forced to posit the "play's" audience as the source of this merriment. Similarly, when he is threatened with violence by the Honorable Mrs. Mervyn Talboys ("I'll flay him alive") and Mrs. Bellingham ("Tan his breech well, the upstart!"), Bloom's excitement, and his shame, are connected to the sense of spectatorship: "Here? (*he squirms.*) Again! (*he pants cringing.*) I love the danger … All these people" (15.1083–1094). "All these people" could be the assemblage of characters who have been moving through the chapter, but it could also be the fantasized presence of a theater audience. Indeed, this confusion effectively conflates the population of "Circe" with the imaginary theatrical "house" watching the action.

It is the consistent availability of this *"audience"* (15.2223), this *"crowd of sluts and ragamuffins"* (15.1038), this *"bevy of barefoot newsboys"*

(15.1122–1123), these policemen designated as the *"raincaped watch . . . silent, vigilant"* (15.674–675)—it is the presence of these spectators that justifies Bloom's comment to Bello: "We are observed" (15.2800–2801). One of the most striking aspects of the chapter is its almost total failure to designate the *exits* of the scores of characters it piles onto its "stage" (Virag Bloom's comic departure, with his head under his arm, is a notable exception [15.2639]). The effect is to suggest that a burgeoning if imprecisely defined public populates the area. Although this public only some of the time seems aware of or responds to the outlandish events taking place in the foreground, it is always imaginarily available as the threat of publicity: it is the gallery to be played to, the audience to be winked at, the court of public opinion which laughs derisively or gasps in shock. This public's main role, that is, is in regulating the distribution of sexual shame, and its presence is most strongly felt during Bloom's "fall" from power through a barrage of sexual accusations. Although it is possible to locate Bloom's sexual exposure in a series of specific events in "Circe," the peculiarly fraught publicity of the episode keeps that shaming a live possibility even when the plot moves beyond it. Where naturalist theater strains away from its public status toward an imaginative destination in the book, "Circe" instead crowds a raucous theater into the intimate space of the reader's imagination.[60] In the hybrid imaginative space thus created, sexuality emerges precisely as the supposed essence of the private which is nonetheless mediated and maintained by the presence of the public. "Circe" exposes sexual exposure as the threat underlying naturalist conceptions of psychological truth.

And yet, as Bello indicates, "this isn't a musical peepshow" (15.3528). If "Circe" reveals the underpinnings of naturalist dramaturgy, it also curiously suggests that the revelations extracted by this dramaturgy are devoid of interest. There is a striking emptiness to the confessions that punctuate the chapter. Defending himself from accusations of sexual impropriety, Bloom *"begins a long unintelligible speech . . . Reporters complain that they cannot hear"* (15. 899–924). A few lines later he responds to the *"uproar and catcalls"* of the courtroom by talking *"inaudibly"* (15.935–937). Joyce most explicitly parodies the meaningfulness of naturalist confession in Bloom's titillating dialogue with Mrs. Breen: the stage directions indicate that Bloom *"meaningfully drop[s] his voice"*—only to deliver himself of a wholly meaningless avowal: "I confess I'm teapot with curiosity to find out whether some person's something is a little teapot at present" (15.457–458). Amplifying a technique first developed in *Exiles*, these lines throw up an interpretive screen, lodging linguistic and gestural unintelligibility in the space of confession. The unwillingness of these passages to satisfy the inquisitive urge emerges even more forcefully when we contrast them with the "Joyce— (*thinks*)" formulation of the dramatic epiphanies. Where the earlier text makes nonperformative drama a mechanism for unmediated access to interior truth, "Circe"'s confinement to the textual facilitates psychic inscrutability. This reticence justifies Joyce's otherwise bewildering comment to Frank Budgen that the problems that most occupied him in composing this thoroughly sex-saturated episode were those "of good taste, tact, technique, etc."[61]

This tact is paradoxically most evident in what might seem the chapter's most obscene and psychically meaningful event, Bloom's transformation into and penetration as a woman by the masculinized Bella/o Cohen. To conceive of this as a scene of transvestism is to obscure the extent of its incoherence. There is no textual justification for considering this as a moment of costume change. The frankly denotative nature of stage directions[62] insist that this is a matter of corporeal transformation: on one page we read of Bello "*squeezing his mount's* [i.e. Bloom's] *testicles*," and a few moments later he "*bares his arm and plunges it elbowdeep in Bloom's vulva*" (15.2945, 15.3089). There is no safe extra-fictional ground here, no stable vantage point from which to decide that these emphatically indicated body parts are mere illusions. And while we must imagine these transformations as corporeal in nature, the text's unstable use of gendered pronouns makes it difficult to decide finally who inhabits which gender at any particular moment. At one point Bloom is abruptly designated with "*her*" (15.2847), but a few pages later Bello (masculine for now) instructs his employees to "hold him down, girls, till I squat on him" (15.2916) and accuses Bloom of preparing himself for sex by clipping his "backgate hairs" (15.3000). Bello seems "male" here, and so for several pages we may feel confident in designating their sex play as "homosexual" in nature. But Bloom quickly becomes "*her*" again only to confuse things further by claiming to have been a "female impersonator" from an early age (15.3009–3010). And moments after Bloom's penetration by Bello, Joyce reverts to male pronouns in referring to his central character (15.3124). The passage presents the reader with an experience of cognitive impossibility: on the one hand there is no neutral textual site from which to claim that Bloom and Bella are engaged in mere masquerade, but on the other there is no clear way to picture the bodies we have been instructed to imagine as definitely "here."

The episode, in other words, is manifestly perverse, but precisely what its perversity might signify becomes ever more unanswerable. In this unthinkability, the moment occupies the epicenter of the chapter, at once the culmination and hollowing out of Joyce's conception of character. Or, more precisely: a hollowing out of character at the site of its supposed fastening—precisely at the sexual locus where naturalism would suggest we will find character guaranteed. As the clearest exemplar of the impossibility of "Circe," Bloom's vulva functions as a synecdoche for the interpretive difficulties that plague the reader of the episode as a whole. Does this orifice "mean" Bloom's fantasy of inhabiting an embodied femininity? Is it "really" Bloom's anus disguised in the language of female anatomy? (And might it then indicate that Bloom must straighten his desire to be anally penetrated by imagining himself as a woman?)[63] Is Bloom's penetration a hallucination that terrifies him or a fantasy that dazzles him? If Bloom's vulva can even be said to exist, where is it—in his idle thoughts? In his unconscious? His memory? His desire? The ease with which one might multiply interpretations runs up against the impossibility of deciding among them. The event is altogether too simple and quite literally impossible to "read": while "Circe" seems designed to prompt precisely these—and other—questions, it ultimately insists that the answer doesn't matter. With no recourse to a stabilizing hermeneutic through which to read this passage (as event, vision, repressed or conscious fantasy, symptom, joke), we can make no more of Bloom's fistfucking than of the fact that "*he performs jugglers tricks, draws red, orange, yellow, green, blue, indigo and violet silk handkerchiefs from his mouth*" (15.1603–1605). In reducing the sexual symptom to the same ontological status as a magic trick, Joyce revokes sex's explanatory privilege. Like Joyce himself as described by Stanislaus in the epigraph to this chapter, Bloom undergoes a sexual abjection with no psychic meaning. Joyce may register his theatrical humiliation on the blushing "virgin cheeks of his arse," but to the onlooker he appears "quite unconcerned as if he were acting in a more elaborate kind of charade." Bloom too suffers an exposure without being exposed, a queering with no consequences.[64]

This may seem an altogether too easy dismissal of an interpretive dynamic that Joyce's career—not to mention its critical reception—demonstrates to have considerable cultural tenacity. But in fact "Circe" conveys an acute awareness of the difficulty of its project. Despite the apparent lightness of the episode, its formal peculiarity makes "Circe" the site of *Ulysses*'s most explicit pathos—what we might call the pathos of textuality. Bloom's is the latest in a long Joycean line of textually designated obscene bodies: the uncannily pierced body of Georgie, the hauntingly indicated body of Mrs. Joyce, the obscurely sexualized body of the "queer old josser," Stephen Dedalus's spastically symptomatic body, the fantasmatically penetrated body of Bertha, the imaginarily conjoined bodies of Richard and Robert in the offstage bedroom of their suburban love nest. In a sense Bloom's body is the most explicit of these, but it is also the one that most clearly registers as materially and cognitively inaccessible. His unimaginable moment of corporealization is thus symptomatic not of Bloom's psychology but of the text's distance from the scene of theatrical embodiment. What is brought into view here is not Bloom's female identification or transvestism or masochism or homosexuality but the catachrestic nature of all linguistic utterance—and this catachresis acquires ethical force precisely by upstaging this string of possible diagnoses. An impossible scene whose image only becomes available via the medium of print, Bloom's womanly penetration is a moment of failed deixis, a pointing without a referent. It illustrates the textual's frustration and longing in the face of the real and the embodied. We might, paraphrasing Stephen Dedalus, say that "Circe" foregrounds the fact that the literary exists in the ineluctable modality of the legible.[65] Or, against Bersani's "Against *Ulysses*," we might say the episode registers not the triumph of textuality but its limit.

If the elements of frustration in Joyce have been difficult to see, this is because of the near unanimous sense that *Ulysses*, whatever else it may be, is a consummately "achieved" novel. In the case of "Circe," this most frequently takes the form of eliding the distinction between play text and performance—between, that is, a blueprint for enactment and enactment itself. Almost as inescapable as the sense that "Circe" is the site of psychic truth is the notion that it *materializes* abstractions, *literalizes* figures of speech, *visualizes* the repressed, *puts on show* the previously occluded, *renders audible* what has been silent.[66] These are of course metaphors, and as such they are reasonable descriptions of the extremity of "Circe." But it is striking how infrequently their figurative status is acknowledged, as if "Circe" were the material, visible, audible performance it only calls for. But "Circe" is a script, a text whose form demands the imagination of a successful embodiment even as it marks its distance from such an embodiment.[67] It would be more accurate to describe "Circe" not as performing anything but as underscoring the difficulty of performance; it does not deliver performance so much as it shows the will to performance in a state of suspended frustration. Even as "Circe" declares a certain blithe freedom from the normal constrictions of the corporeal, the episode multiplies images of, precisely, difficult embodiment. From the *"deafmute idiot with goggle eyes"* (15.14) who opens the chapter to our first glimpse of Bloom *"flushed [and] panting"* (15.142–143) to Ben Dollard with his *"loins and genitals tightened into a pair of black bathing bagslops"* (15.2606–2607), "Circe" presents us with warped, maimed, exhausted, embarrassed, or otherwise imperfect bodies. If the episode demands the most strenuous mental tasks of its reader, it enacts the violence of those imaginative contortions on the bodies of its inhabitants.

Markers of the effort of imagining the stage of "Circe" itself, these bodies also offer an image of the exactions of the text's obscenely utopian imagination. The demand on the reader is a constant feature of Joyce's work; but there is more than one kind of effort. If in the earlier sections of *Ulysses* difficulty arises from the demand to adjudicate the boundaries of interiority, "Circe" upends this difficulty and replaces it with another: where before we were set to work discerning and so shoring up characterological frontiers, "Circe" issues the more strenuous task of imagining a social world where these projects are rendered impossible and irrelevant. The episode heralds a new referential vector: no longer focused on the psychic interior, we are instead directed outward to a psychically flattened social world. If there is a relation between "Circe" and psychology, it is not one of explicitation or exposure but of displacement: the episode both sketches a world freed from Joyce's obsession with psychic meaning and acknowledges the difficulty of the act of social imagination it has prompted.

Stephen in the library has articulated the dream to which "Circe" gives free rein, the fantasy of consciousness uncontained in the tomb of interiority. Near the end of "Circe," Bloom and Stephen *"gaze in the mirror"* at Bella Cohen's brothel. *"The face of William Shakespeare, beardless, appears there, rigid in facial paralysis, crowned by the reflection of the reindeer antlered hatrack in the hall"* (15.3821–3824). The moment merges Joyce's two male protagonists in the image of the playwright who, "Scylla and Charybdis" demonstrates, presents a virtually inexhaustible screen for psychological speculation. But the "bisexually abnormal" bard's availability to any number of projective identitarian fantasies also makes him useless for embodying any identity in particular. A kind of universal pervert, Shakespeare also serves here as a comically random "cultural catch-all," as Christy Burns aptly puts it.[68] The bard thus functions as the sign of a release from psychic meaning into perverse display. Far from expressing anything about Bloom or Stephen, Shakespeare's apparition here is interesting precisely in its insignificance, its paralytic inexpressiveness, its banal impersonality. If this is an emotionally powerful image, it is not because it represents a psychological rapprochement between these two men but because it permits them respite from the text's surveillance. In refraining from telling us anything more about these men about whom we already know so much, the moment represents a supreme gesture of authorial tact. The perverse but unknowable playwright is an image of a shared performative immunity to psychic penetration.

"Circe" culminates with what is often considered the most psychologically affecting event in *Ulysses*, the apparition of Bloom's son Rudy as he would have appeared had he survived infancy. He is, we read, *"holding a book in his hand. He reads from right to left inaudibly, smiling, kissing the page"* (15.4958–4960). The typography of the chapter's final words invites, and then disappoints, the expectation that "Circe" will end with a word from this visitant:

RUDY

(gazes, unseeing, into Bloom's eyes and goes on reading, kissing, smiling. He has a delicate mauve face. On his suit he has diamond and ruby buttons. In his free left hand he holds a slim ivory cane with a violet bowknot. A white lambkin peeps out of his waistcoat pocket.) (15. 4963–4967).

In a pattern to which "Circe" has accustomed us, the detail of the image proliferates in excess of any possible psychic meaning. If the apparition is undeniably moving, this is then only partly because it addresses Bloom's disappointed procreative ambitions. It is, instead, as an emblem of textual fetishism and its limits that these words most forcefully register. Joyce presents his chapter's final moments in the parentheses of withheld presence: like the epiphanic "Joyce—(*stands*)" this passage gives us a line that is not one, a speech act that puts the body in place of speech and then uncannily indicates that the body itself can only ever be designated in the space of the text. On the stage on which "Circe" does not take place, these bracketed words would disappear into the fact of corporeal presence. Here they linger troublingly, challenging us to imagine the stage that could contain its inexpressive figure by giving social density to a world not policed by the threat of psychic exposure. With this final dangling parenthesis "Circe" insists on the pathos, not the transcendence, of its textuality. It suggests the formal inadequacy of the novel in which it occurs—as if this most bookish of books aspired to status as a play text to be marked up and discarded after rehearsals. Rudy's loving caress of his book offers an image of the analytic work with which we may feel tempted to answer and appease this ghostliness. But "Circe"'s utopian provocation to imagine a world not ordered by psychosexual significance will not be consoled with interpretation or research.[69] It demands performance.

Epilogue

In the Kingdom of Whomever: Baldwin's Method

"What happened to all that intuition, all that—*specialized*—point of view?"
"Beyond a certain point," she said with a sullen smile, "it doesn't seem to work
so well." —James Baldwin, *Another Country*

The claim that ends the previous chapter risks absurdity, or sentimentality: What justifies labeling utopian a demand not for the transformation of the social order but for a depathologizing of specifically sexual difference? This epilogue will not so much answer this question as demonstrate its structuring importance in the work of an author who stands in several important senses at the end of the tradition traced in *Empty Houses*. James Baldwin is not only one of the more notable Anglophone twentieth-century novelists to attempt continually and with minimal success to enter the theater. He is also one of the major inheritors of the aesthetic and political problematic we have repeatedly encountered in the course of this book. Baldwin is perhaps the most important twentieth-century novelist to seriously explore what it means to make interiority the bearer of collective desire.

The self-conscious resonances of Baldwin's career with that of the other writers treated in *Empty Houses* are notable. Most famously, Baldwin's debt to Henry James (a writer he called "my master") is evident in the shape of his sentences, in the plots of his major novels, and in the title of his most famous essay, "Notes of a Native Son"—which references both Richard Wright's *Native Son* and James's *Notes of a Son and Brother*.[1] Implicitly, Baldwin analogized his equivocal success in the theater to James's when, in the preface to the published text of his 1955 play *The Amen Corner*, he wrote of the "age-old, iron rule . . . that very few novelists are able to write plays."[2] Explicitly, Baldwin understood his European exile as modeled both on that of James and that of James Joyce—comparing, for example, his departure from Harlem for France with Joyce's exile from Dublin: a few months before sailing for Paris in 1948, Baldwin quoted Stephen Dedalus's ambition "to forge in the smithy of my soul the uncreated conscience of my race."[3] This private comparison was made public when Baldwin adopted the form of Joyce's dateline conclusions to *A Portrait of the Artist* and *Ulysses* ("Dublin 1904, Trieste 1914"; "Trieste-Zurich-Paris 1914–1921") for his own books: *Another Country* (1963) was finished, its last page tells us, in "Istanbul, Dec. 10, 1961," and *Tell Me How Long the Train's Been Gone* (1968) concludes with the words "New York, Istanbul, San Francisco, 1965–1967."[4]

Baldwin's connections to the other novelists we have examined are equally marked. Like his Victorian predecessors, Baldwin's reputation suffered from his propensity to interrupt his fictional world with sermonizing; his working name for *Another Country*—a portrait of what the narrator calls "an aimless, defeated, and defensive bohemia"—was *So Long at the Fair*, a title recalling that of Thackeray's best-known novel along with its disabused tone.[5] And although Baldwin appears never to have mentioned George Eliot in print, his work and life seem uncannily to quote hers. Like Eliot, Baldwin passed through a youthful evangelical phase to arrive at a secular gospel of sympathy profoundly influenced by the language of Christian love (in abandoning his faith while cleaving to a religious vocabulary, Baldwin can seem like the most important Victorian novelist of the twentieth century). Eliot's *Middlemarch* narrator chides us for our inattention to a mundane suffering figured as "that roar which lies on the other side of silence," while in *Just Above My Head* (1979), Baldwin castigates us for "the cool, brutal, high-pitched siren of our indifference."[6] Eliot brings her novel to an ethical climax by having Dorothea Brooke gaze out her window to perceive her estate workers as aestheticized emblems of "the largeness of the world and the manifold wakings of men to labour and endurance" (788). Nearly a century later, in *Another Country*, Ida Scott scolds her white friend Cass during a cab ride through Central Park in words that seem descended from Eliot's: "I bet you think we're in a goddam park. You don't know we're in one of the world's great jungles. You don't know that behind all them damn dainty trees and shit, people are screwing and sucking and fixing and dying . . . You've got to *know*, you've got to know what's happening" (347–348). The lexicon is recognizably twentieth-century in its profanity and its substitution of lumpen suffering for productive labor—and Baldwin's tone is accordingly more harrowed. But the sermon is classically liberal in its assumption that salvation consists in perception, preferably through glass.[7]

From a certain perspective, in other words, Baldwin's work might be said to constitute an anthology of the narrative and thematic tropes central to the novel of interiority. As we have seen, that novel becomes over the course of its development in one way ever more interior—finally locating the criteria of human truth in the sexual depths. But it has been the central claim of this book that the novel of interiority not only rehearses this reduction but also points to and protests the exacerbated distance from the public attendant on such a reduction. Baldwin's work can be understood as swallowing this tradition whole: so insistently does he force his vision of social redemption

through the strait gate of sexual truth that his work arrives at an agoniz-
ingly high degree of self-awareness about that tradition's structuring ambiguities. And in the most intriguing segment of Baldwin's career in the 1950s
and 1960s, he struggled with the issue of the novel's relation to interiority
through a turn to and then away from the drama. 1956 saw the publication
of the novel *Giovanni's Room*, which Baldwin almost immediately began to
adapt into theatrical form; his difficulties in the latter project directly inform
the innovations in the novels he worked on at the same time, 1963's *Another
Country* and 1968's *Tell Me How Long the Train's Been Gone*. These novels—
particularly *Another Country*—constitute an experiment in the possibility of
narrative fiction to apprehend collective experience. Moreover, that experiment is conducted through Baldwin's ambivalent meditation on the dominant American acting theory, known as the Method, which by mid-century
had codified the "novelization" (that is, the interiorization) of the theater
that had been gathering force over the previous century.

.   If a relentless linking of the sociohistorical and the sexual was a persistent
feature of Baldwin's nonfiction writing,[8] the prominence of the sexual as the
ultimate site of truth at first appears even more marked in his novels. Here,
for example, is Leo Proudhammer, the narrator of *Tell Me How Long the
Train's Been Gone*, remembering the clientele at the West Indian restaurant
in Greenwich Village where he worked before achieving fame as an actor:

> Here they came: two girls who worked in advertising and who lived
> together in fear and trembling, who told me all about their lives one
> drunken night. One of them found a psychiatrist, married a very fat
> boy in advertising, and moved to California and they are now very
> successful and vocal Fascists. I don't know what happened to the other
> girl. Here they came: the black man from Kentucky, who called him-
> self an African prince and had some ridiculous name, like Omar, and
> his trembling Bryn Mawr girl-friend, whose virginity he wore like a
> flag . . . here they came, the fagot [*sic*] painter and his Lesbian wife, who
> had an understanding with each other which made them brutally cruel
> to all their playmates and which welded them, hatefully, to each other.
> Here they came, the lost lonely man who worked in the shipyards and
> lived with his mother, who loved young boys and feared them and
> who jumped off a roof, here they came, the nice, middle-aged couple
> everyone was always glad to see, the husband of which couple, weep-
> ing and sweating, once threw me down among the garbage cans and
> tried to blow me—"Don't tell Marcia. Please don't tell my wife!"—
> here they came, the beautiful girl who ended up in Bellevue, here they
> came, the beautiful girl who was going to be a dancer and who ended
> up in prison, here they came, the brilliant Boston scion who liked to

get fucked in the ass, and who threw himself before a subway train—
which chopped off his head.[9]

The hypertrophy of the interiorizing imagination here is equally as extreme
as in James's *The Sacred Fount*, in which virtually every social fact has a sexual
etiology and every sexual fact tends toward the illicit. Also as in James's novel,
the attribution of deviance rebounds on the narrator—Leo Proudhammer is
himself bisexual—and ultimately on the author: as with James before him,
it has been all too easy for Baldwin's critics to see the reduction of the social
to the sexual as not only his theme but as an ideological project fueled by
personal demons.[10] But it is too simple to see Baldwin as the proponent of
the logic his narrator articulates here. Indeed, in their quasi-parodic intensity,
Leo Proudhammer's boomeranging sexual divinations demand to be read as
a skeptical meditation on the narrative convention whose logic they embody.
Proudhammer's diagnoses in fact have a habit of running aground on shoals
of illegibility—and to do so particularly in proximity to the topos of the theater. Late in the novel, Proudhammer finds himself at an excruciating cocktail
party:

> Two drama students, both male, were loudly disputing some point
> about the Stanislavski method, concerning which, as far as I could tell,
> neither of them knew anything. They hoped that I would overhear
> genially and genially interrupt and even, perhaps, find one of them
> attractive. Not that either of them was "gay"—to use the incompre-
> hensible vernacular; anybody mad enough to make such a suggestion
> would have been beaten within an inch of his life. But they were on the
> make, and what else, after all, did they have to give? Also, they were
> lonely. (451)

Once again the passage strains verisimilitude in the sheer precision of its
knowingness: one wonders how Proudhammer guesses from his restricted
narrative position that the men are interested in him, that their interest is
sexual, and how, finally, he knows that neither would allow any identitarian implication to follow from this desire. Indeed, the passage approaches
self-contradiction in its disavowal of the language of its own insights: the
claim about the "incomprehensibility" of the label "gay" collides with the
hypercomprehensibility of the sexual subjectivities of the characters, as if
Baldwin wants to insist on sexual legibility even as he disqualifies the terms
with which we might describe it. If *Tell Me How Long the Train's Been Gone*
appears on the one hand irreducibly invested in a notion of legible psychosexual meaning, it seems equally and oppositely invested in the sexual as
untellable.

It is crucial that this paradoxical insistence occurs in the context of a discussion of theatrical performance. After its extreme devotion to interiority's legibility, perhaps the most notable feature of Proudhammer's narration is its loudly voiced contempt for the theory of acting—associated with Constantin Stanislavksi and with his American interpreter Lee Strasberg—that would seem most congruent with Proudhammer's penchant for sexualized analysis. Early in the novel we encounter a gratuitous sneer at the Stanislavskian system of actor training when Proudhammer remarks, "Preparing myself for a role—I was to live with this inane concept for many years" (84); the compound reference here is to the first and third books (1936's *An Actor Prepares* and 1961's *Creating a Role*) of the influential trilogy of acting theory Stanislavski wrote out of his experience as director of the Moscow Art Theater. Much crueler is the novel's extended attack on Lee Strasberg, who had developed Stanislavski's system into the Method in the 1930s and played a key role in establishing its dominance in American theater and film as the artistic director of the Actors Studio from 1951 to his death in 1982. Strasberg appears in the novel thinly disguised as Saul San Marquand, the pretentious and simpering director of the fictional Actors Means Workshop. Perhaps unexpectedly for a writer apparently so insistent on interior truth, Baldwin's distaste for these theoreticians focuses on what Joseph Roach has called Stanislavski's "intense, even obsessive interest in the inner psychological content of an action."[11] Roach's tracing of Stanislavski and Strasberg's intellectual inheritance from Diderot's *Paradox of the Actor* (which notoriously claimed that actors need not feel the emotions they replicate convincingly on stage) makes clear that both men were well aware of the mechanical elements of the actor's craft. But the complexities of Stanislavski and Strasberg's practice notwithstanding, their published texts led to the widespread sense of the Method as a kind of wild psychoanalysis: in popular conception, Method actors were less skilled technicians than exhibitionists intent on publicly unearthing deeply buried traumas.[12]

"We begin by thinking about the inner side of a role," Stanislavski insists in the first few pages of *An Actor Prepares*, and concludes by demanding that the actor identify with his role so completely that "his eyes . . . reflect the deep inner content of his soul."[13] Stanislavski's rhetoric is overtly contemptuous of the "external" side of actor training: this landmark text of theatrical theory uses the word "theatrical" as a synonym for "dead," "conventional" (129), and "artificial" (17), and understands "theatricality" in an actor as indicative of "perverted taste" (33), "exhibitionism" (29), and "flirt[ing] with the audience" (32). Strasberg's adaptation of Stanislavski placed less emphasis on the corrupted nature of theatricality but made more overt the sexual implications of Stanislavski's focus on interior truth. In Strasberg's *A Dream of Passion: The Development of the Method* (published posthumously in 1987), actor training emerges as amateur therapy. Portions of Strasberg's book seem explicitly modeled on Freud's case studies, so that we get accounts of one actress under his tutelage who realizes that her puritanical father's hatred of acting has inhibited her physical and emotional expressiveness, of another reliving traumatic memories of Catholic confession, even of one who describes Strasberg's relaxation techniques as "directly responsible for her pregnancy."[14] This roster of women cured of long-repressed traumas obliges Strasberg to half-admit the charge that "this work really amounts to amateur analysis or 'cheap' psychiatry" (103).[15]

Baldwin's intimacy with the Method was thorough, and thoroughly equivocal. In a 1966 conversation with Charlie Chaplin, for example, Baldwin vehemently contrasted the Method to what he called "real" acting, and argued that the Method's emphasis on the actor's interiority denied the fact that "an actor had to act, had to accept the discipline of 'pretending.'"[16] Baldwin's theoretical distaste was augmented by personal experience: in 1958–59 he had worked as an assistant to Elia Kazan, one of the cofounders of the Actors Studio, on productions of Archibald Macleish's *JB* and Tennessee Williams's *Sweet Bird of Youth*; Baldwin judged the results "a *crock*."[17] But Baldwin's hostility was far from consistent. It was during the same period that Kazan suggested that Baldwin write a play "based on his evident concern with the 'private lives' of blacks and whites in the context of the civil rights struggle"— a suggestion that came to fruition with *Blues for Mister Charlie*, which was produced by the Actors Studio with Strasberg as director in 1963.[18] A fictionalization of the lynching of Emmett Till, the drama is essentially a revelation of motive, which is to say psyche: the murder occurs in the first scene, and the play's suspense depends on a series of monologues in which the characters reveal in faultlessly naturalist fashion the sexual motivations that have driven them to their acts of violence and complicity with violence. With its implicit claim that every social performance has a psychosexual backstory, *Blues* is a virtual emplotment of the Method. (Fittingly, rehearsals focused on the personal journey of Baldwin's friend Rip Torn, a southerner whose performance as the white lead necessitated what Baldwin's biographer David Leeming characterizes as a "painful descent into cultural memory"; moreover, Torn's erotically saturated acting—one historian of Method acting calls him "the character actor you always remember . . . because he's got sex in his eyes and a permanent erection"—made him the perfect embodiment of Baldwin's sexually motivated lyncher.[19]) The *Blues* production, which was critically panned, soured Baldwin's relations with Strasberg and Kazan. But when a few years later in Istanbul Baldwin was given the opportunity to direct a play himself— a 1969–70 production of John Herbert's gay-themed prison drama *Fortune and Men's Eyes*—Baldwin's disdain for his former associates did not prevent him from precisely imitating their Method. Baldwin forced his cast into two weeks of collective soul-searching before they began rehearsals, telling them his goal was a "full confession" among director, actor and audience; one of his players recalled that "Baldwin 'directed from inside,' from the perspective of individual motivation and personal pain." According to Leeming, "some said it was more like psychoanalysis than directing."[20]

How to make sense of Baldwin's impatience with the Method alongside his apparently total absorption of its procedures? One answer is perhaps already implicit in Leo Proudhammer's placing of the Method in proximity to the interrelated issues of psychic transparency, narrative point of view, and the fixing of homosexual identity. Baldwin's ambivalent closeness to the Method was also a meditation on the complex history of the theater's relation to the novel of interiority. The Method's exaltation of interiority was a direct descendant of the negotiations between theater and the novel that had produced both forms' apparent ideological convergence on the issue of psychic consistency—as well as the resistances to that convergence. The Method represents the apotheosis of the naturalist theater's absorption of the "novelistic" imperative to ratify interior truth. For a gay novelist at once fascinated by sexual subjectivity and wary of the policing functions such fascination could serve, the Method clearly constituted an irresistible event in the theory of character. Baldwin's interest in the Method should be understood not as an endorsement but as evidence of his recognition of its usefulness in exploring interiority's ideological force.

As often with the writers examined in this book, while the dramatic results of Baldwin's theatrical fascination were often conventional or misguided, the narrative consequences would be radically innovative. In the most interesting stretch of Baldwin's career, the pressure of theatrical longing pushed him not only to insist upon and then step back from the legibility of interiority but also to develop a collective fictional subject. Moreover, this collectivizing project would be leveraged by a hollowing out of the exacerbated psychic meaningfulness of homosexual subjectivity. Baldwin's second novel, 1956's *Giovanni's Room*, is narrated in the first person by the tormented homosexual David, and recounts his erotic waffling between his fiancée and the alluringly self-accepting Giovanni: its plot essentially consists of the narrator's slow and painful admission that even his denials (precisely his denials) constitute proof of his perversion. Confronted by the coterie at a Paris gay bar, David introduces his reader to the inescapable transparency of his personhood: "It was as though they were the elders of some strange and austere holy order and were watching me in order to discover, by means of signs I made but which only they could read, whether or not I had a true vocation . . . I was in a box for I could see that, no matter how I turned, the hour of confession was upon me and could scarcely be averted."[21] Giovanni's eponymous rented room is itself a figure for the "box" of gay identity—at once a space of erotic license and hideous entrapment.

The book's deliciously melodramatic sense of gay subjectivity as a zone of terrorized hypervisibility earned it, of course, an instant place in the queer canon. But perhaps the most surprising fact about the history of *Giovanni's Room* is that its creator so quickly turned to adapting it into a play. The Actors Studio staged Baldwin's first attempt at a theatrical version of the novel in a workshop production in 1958. Baldwin was optimistic about the chances for a Broadway run, and his short list for candidates to play David was a roll call of Actors Studio aristocracy: Montgomery Clift, Paul Newman, and his friend Marlon Brando. All of them were perfectly suited by their training in the Method to embody Baldwin's intensely psychologized and self-betraying protagonist. But by precisely the same token, these actors' Method training made the possibility of their accepting the role less likely. As inheritors of an acting theory that held (in Stanislavski's words) that *"you can never get away from yourself... Always and forever, when you are on the stage, you must play yourself"* (192), these actors were reluctant to provoke the inevitable biographical speculation.[22] Baldwin biographer James Campbell records that Brando excused himself by claiming to be too busy and that "no other actor whom they approached would take the part for fear of being tainted by the subject." Baldwin was undeterred, and over the remainder of his life wrote at least two more theatrical versions of the novel; according to Campbell he worked on a performance text of *Giovanni's Room* "until, literally, his final days."[23]

None of the theatrical versions of *Giovanni's Room* has been published, and none exists in a publicly accessible archive. But there is evidence of the deep oddity of the adaptation—and perhaps also some insight into why the text's difficulties occupied Baldwin for nearly thirty years. *Giovanni's Room* produces narration as the space of exposure: the novel's intensity derives from the simultaneous self-deception and self-revelation of its first-person narrator. In necessarily abandoning this narration to rework it for the non-focalized medium of drama, Baldwin's adaptation appears to have muddied the story itself, as well as creating confusion—improbably enough—around the inescapably obvious fact of David's homosexuality. In a 1958 letter to a friend, Baldwin reports on the baffling response he received from Joshua Logan, the director of the Broadway hits *Annie Get Your Gun* and *South Pacific* to whom he had hopefully sent the play text: "[Logan] feels 'let down' by the play, does not find the 'electricity of the novel' in it, does not 'care at all' about the boy and girl." Baldwin goes on to quote directly from Logan's response—"Also I found the ending very inconclusive and somehow the tragedy of the boy's [i.e., Giovanni's] death invaded the possible happiness of the girl and boy"—before offering his dry comment: "It sounds as though he has rather misread the play."[24] We cannot know whether Logan's unknowing response to *Giovanni's Room* was the result of haste, hostility, or some combination thereof. But the possibility exists that, in the absence of narration, the novel's overwhelmingly unmissable core—its protagonist's secreted and exposed homosexuality—became oddly opaque. Confronted with the technical challenge of removing narrative perspective from a text whose whole raison d'être was the sexual coloration of narrative perspective, Baldwin appears to have created a text where sexuality is rendered illegible.

This possibility is supported by the striking originality of the novel that Baldwin wrote during the years in which he first began working on a theatrical version of *Giovanni's Room*. At first glance, *Another Country* seems to bear only the most attenuated relation to its predecessor. Where *Giovanni's Room* features a small and all-white cast of characters, *Another Country* is a sprawling group portrait in which seven or eight characters, black and white, compete for narrative centrality. *Giovanni's Room* is narrated in a claustrophobia-inducing first person, *Another Country* in a disorientingly mobile third person. And where the drama of *Giovanni's Room* is resolutely psychological, *Another Country* is shot through with a sense of the limits history and politics impose on interpersonal and communal action. But these novels, so widely different, are also clearly linked by the central role played in each by the idea of sexual secrecy. Indeed, while the all-importance of sexuality remains tacit if everywhere implied in *Giovanni's Room*, in *Another Country* it becomes the explicitly avowed ground of identity: early in the novel Rufus Scott, the blues musician who at first appears to be the novel's protagonist, looks at his white lover Leona and sees her eyes "filled with some immense sexual secret which tormented her" (53). Later, another character reflects that "perhaps such secrets, the secrets of everyone, were only expressed when the person laboriously dragged them into the light of the world, imposed them on the world, and made them a part of the world's experience. Without this effort, the secret place was merely a dungeon in which the person perished" (112). Perhaps most striking about these endlessly adduced sexual secrets, as Kevin Ohi notes in his reading of the novel, is that they are without substance. "Revelation appears only in the guise of its failure," Ohi writes; the novel is filled with "secrets that maintain the characters' and the novel's consistency not through self-revelation but through their exorbitant, recalcitrant, and inscrutable weight."[25]

The idea of sexual interiority, that is, has rhetorical and dramatic force in *Another Country* out of all proportion to its specifiable content. This is all the more striking in light of the extreme specifiability of the sexual secret that anchors *Giovanni's Room*. But in fact the link between the novels—and the gulf between them—is even stranger than this: *Another Country* has less abandoned the legibility of sexual subjectivity than incorporated and transmuted it. One of the novel's central characters, the white, southern-born Eric Jones, is identified as a gay man in a few lines of what seems almost parodic clarity. The pages introducing Eric read like a condensed version of *Giovanni's Room*'s drama of occlusion, repression, and exposure:

How could Eric have known that his fantasies, however unreadable they were for him, were inscribed in every one of his gestures, were betrayed in every inflection of his voice, and lived in his eyes with all the brilliance and beauty and terror of desire? He had always been a heavy, healthy boy, had played like other children, and fought as they did, made friends and enemies and secret pacts and grandiose plans. And yet none of his playmates, after all, had ever sat with Henry in the furnace room, or ever kissed Henry on his salty face. They did not, weighed down with discarded hats, gowns, bags, sashes, earrings, capes and necklaces, turn themselves into make-believe characters after everyone in their house was asleep. Nor could they possibly, at their most extended, have conceived of the people he, in the privacy of the night, became: his mother's friends, or his mother—his mother as he conceived her to have been when she was young, his mother's friends as his mother was now; the heroines and heroes of the novels he read, and the movies he saw; or people he simply put together out of his fantasies and the available rags. (199–200)

The first sentences of the passage read like a precise anticipation of Foucault's much quoted description of the homosexual as "a personage, a case history, and a childhood . . . with an indiscreet anatomy and possibly a mysterious physiology."[26] And yet the isolating meaningfulness of Eric's sexuality has by the end of the passage become a hinge to the imagination of collectivity—a will to embody not only the women with whom Eric presumably identifies and the men whom he presumably desires but all the unspecified "people he simply put together out of his fantasies and the available rags." Are we to understand Eric's putting people together as the assembly of individual characters from gestures and phrases—or as a kind of social engineering, a putting together of individuals into new erotic and relational combinations? Baldwin's language leaves both options open, and in the process suggests that the extremity of this character's particularity opens on the intimation of collective possibility.

This sense is borne out by the novel's plot. Eric is one of the text's ensemble players, but Baldwin positions him squarely at the intersection of the novel's ramifying erotic networks. *Another Country* conveys such a strong sense of proliferative sexual recombination that we may be startled to realize how much this derives from this one character's erotic mobility. We learn that Eric has been sexually involved with Rufus, and we first meet him alongside his current lover Yves; he later embarks on a sustained affair with Cass and a briefer encounter (narrated at considerably greater length) with Vivaldo. Eric's links to the single major character with whom he has no

sexual contact—Rufus's sister Ida—are just as emphatic: in the novel's prehis-
tory, Eric has given Rufus a pair of cufflinks as "a confession of his love"—
cufflinks Rufus in turn gives to Ida, who is wearing them as a pair of "heavy
and archaic" earrings when Eric first meets her (249). Thus, although Baldwin makes it repeatedly clear that Ida dislikes Eric and his homosexuality, the
novel takes pains to underscore their symbolic marriage. Baldwin's point here
is neither to laud Eric for his erotic versatility or to claim a messianic function
for gay identity—although Eric's role has been interpreted this way by the
novel's least sympathetic readers.[27] Rather, Eric's sexuality demands to be read
as a commentary on the psychosexual reductionism of which Baldwin's work
(and the tradition explored throughout *Empty Houses*) is often accused. This
character's extreme psychic transparency—his exacerbated interiority—
becomes in Baldwin's audacious experiment the narrative site of a correspondingly intense outward pressure toward collective experimentation.

This fact in turn is directly related to the novel's engagement with the
theater. Eric is not only a homosexual whose specified identity has strangely
little to do with his actual erotic practice. He is also, and relatedly, an actor—
specifically, a disciple of the Method, a fact confirmed by the presence of *An
Actor Prepares* among the books in his rented house in the South of France
(195) and by his annotation of a role he is preparing with details from his
own emotional history: "*On this, maybe remember what you know of Yves*"
(286), he jots down at one point next to a line in the script of *Happy Hunting Ground*, the fictional play in which he will make his Broadway debut.
The item of emotional memory Eric records here highlights, of course, the
specially fraught status of sexual identity in a theory that understands performance as premised on the actor's mining of his psychic depths. As Baldwin's difficulty in finding an actor to play the lead in *Giovanni's Room* had
underlined, the Method made the stage into a potentially punitive space of
involuntary homosexual self-disclosure.[28] As far as the novel informs us, Eric
is not playing gay in *Happy Hunting Ground*, and so his choice, if that's what
it is, to use his mostly homosexual life history in preparing the role seems a
portent of his inability to succeed in the part (or, worse, to expose his queerness in the attempt). But Baldwin no sooner raises the specter of this potentially abject figure—the homosexual Method actor—than he dissolves the
psychic consistency that would render him legible. Later in the novel Eric
consults his annotations and finds that these "urgently scrawled notes . . . had
hardened into irrelevance" (392). Faced with the sheer social and erotic contingency *Another Country* records at such length, the Method has come to
seem unmethodical, a random commentary on a performance whose truth
it cannot pin down.

In drawing attention to Eric's opacity to himself, Baldwin strongly suggests that the derangement of the Method is a model for his novelistic practice. Where the Method ratifies the actor's truth *qua* psychological subject,

Baldwin repeatedly rehearses and then undoes this ratification. More than this: these scenes hint at the way the theater in *Another Country* stands for the incipient collectivization of what might otherwise appear irredeemably individual. In Eric's library, Stanislavski's text of acting theory appears alongside *The Wings of the Dove* and *Native Son*—thus suggesting the theater's mediating role between the supposed quintessentially "psychological" ground of the former and the clearly "political" scope of the latter. It is, again, not necessary to claim special political virtue for homosexuality to note that the figure of the queer highlights this incipient politicization—and the obstacles to it—in the starkest terms. Baldwin thematizes the destabilization of psychic fixity most clearly through his presentation of Eric. But in an important sense Eric's homosexuality, precisely because of its ambiguous status as psychic truth, makes him exemplary of the cast of characters in general. All of them, after all, are defined by secrets empty of content—secrets that instead of differentiating them serve to establish their potential interchangeability. Baldwin's achievement in *Another Country* is to have represented sexual individuality as the space of a yearning for the possibility of collective existence. The novel makes repeatedly clear that one of the things signified by "another country" is simply the space of other subjectivities.[29] Read in the context of the text's breathless shuttling among intensely isolated characters, that title becomes legible as a directive to move beyond the individual. *Another Country* does not *have* a collective protagonist so much as it strains toward one.

To put this in slightly different terms: in the vehemence with which *Another Country* represents privacy as pushing toward its own defeat, the novel as a whole emerges as an injunction toward the collective. It achieves this effect with strategies at once narrative and stylistic. Narratively, the shift in focalization among characters is perhaps the novel's most striking feature. *Another Country* begins firmly in the consciousness of Rufus, but after his suicide Baldwin begins to rotate the novel's focalization with disorienting frequency among the black and white survivors who attempt to mourn Rufus or to forget him. The narrative architecture that results has overtly political implications: because Baldwin paints Rufus's suicide as the result of racist oppression, the novel's "decentered and carefully balanced character system" (as Alex Woloch describes it) also makes a claim that Rufus's death, and the accusation it contains, need to be publicly claimed.[30] Equally striking is that this egalitarian injunction insinuates itself into the novel's stylistic texture. Baldwin follows Henry James in his tendency to make his characters sound indistinguishable from one another and from their narrator—with similarly collectivizing results. Like *The Wings of the Dove*, *Another Country* overlays a narrative of extreme characterological difference with a style that fantasizes the cancellation of that difference.[31]

As a condensed exhibit of these processes one stunningly strange passage will serve. The scene is one of many in which a character finds himself haunted by Rufus's accusatory ghost. The focalizing character in the following sentences is Vivaldo—but it is in keeping with Baldwin's derangement of psychic focus that such a designation hardly seems to make sense. The passage so violently unites the extremes of psychic isolation and psychic sameness that it is difficult to know whether to read it as an account of one character's sexual misery or as evidence of his interchangeability with . . . almost anyone.

> And now—now it seemed they were all equal in misery, confusion, and despair. He looked at his face in the mirror behind the bar. He still had all his hair, there was no gray in it yet; his face had not yet begun to fall at the bottom and shrivel at the top; and he wasn't yet all ass and belly. But, still—and soon; and he stole a look at the blonde again. He wondered about her odor, juices, sounds; for a night, only for a night; then, abruptly, with no warning, he found himself wondering how Rufus would have looked at this girl, and an odd thing happened: all desire left him, he turned absolutely cold, and then desire came roaring back, with legions. *Aha*, he heard Rufus snicker, *you don't be careful, motherfucker, you going to get a* black *hard on*. He heard again the laughter which had followed him down the block. And something in him was breaking; he was, briefly and horribly, in a region where there were no definitions of any kind, neither of color, nor of male and female. There was only the leap and the rending and the terror and the surrender. And the terror: which all seemed to begin and end and begin again—forever—in a cavern behind the eye. And whatever stalked there *saw*, and spread the news of what it saw throughout the entire kingdom of whomever, though the eye itself might perish. What order could prevail against so grim a privacy? And yet, without order, of what value was the mystery? Order. Order. *Set thine house in order*. He sipped his whiskey, light-years removed now from the blonde and the bar and yet, more than ever and most unpleasantly present. When people no longer knew that a mystery could only be approached through form, people became—what the people of this time and place had become, what he had become. They perished within their despised clay tenements, in isolation, passively, or actively together, in mobs, thirsting and seeking for, and eventually reeking of blood. Of rending and tearing there can never be any end, and God save the people for whom passion becomes impersonal!
>
> He went into the phone booth again. (301–302)

Opening firmly in Vivaldo's consciousness, the passage floats ever freer of this localization the "deeper" it goes. Moreover, it is precisely where Vivaldo should be most psychologically anchored—in his sexual thoughts—that he finds himself occupied by a foreign consciousness, that of the long-dead

Rufus. The vehemence of Baldwin's racializing rhetoric here tempts us to any number of plausible conclusions about Vivaldo's psychology: for example, that his imagination of sexual potency is routed through fantasies of black masculinity, or that his clinically described desire for this woman masks, or expresses, a desire for his dead friend. But the temptation to embark on these interpretations, however compelling they are individually, emerges over the course of the passage as a tease; they are not so much inaccurate as finally irrelevant to the passage's point, which is the evacuation of all such interpretive frameworks. Vivaldo's inhabitation by Rufus is not the truth of Vivaldo's desire but the preamble to a more mysterious and total voiding of psychic specificity. This voiding is expressed narratively by the bewildering swerve into hieratic peroration ("There was only the leap and the rending and the terror and the surrender") whose idiom and perspective it is difficult to ascribe strictly to Vivaldo. The passage leaves its initial psychic location so far behind that when Baldwin returns to the business-as-usual of character-centered narration ("He went into the phone booth again") we experience it as a traumatically implausible, even bathetic, reduction in scale.

In following a stunning transcendence of individuation with its violent re-assertion, the passage might be understood as encoding the movement from the interiorized sexual subject to the theatrical cast that Baldwin was simul-taneously undertaking in adapting the deeply subjectivized *Giovanni's Room* into the medium of drama. Prompting his reader to make psychosexual sense of its nuances and then rendering this project futile, this passage also makes a case for sexual interiority as exerting a pressure toward collectivity. We could, following Henry James, say that sexuality in *Another Country* is lived as the injunction to other almost anyhow; or, following Baldwin's extraordinary phrasing of a similar imperative, say that sexuality in the novel is a passport to the kingdom of whomever. Baldwin's other name for this kingdom here is the "cavern behind the eye." The image is designedly hard to grasp: what could it mean to say that whatever it is that stalks through this cavern "*saw*," or to insist that such seeing proceeds "though the eye itself might perish"? Rather than attempt to picture it, the image appears to want us, more basi-cally, to register its injunction to think beyond the limitations of point of view and its "grim . . . privacy."[32] The cavern behind the eye emerges in its impossibility as the last and the most extreme—the most painfully reduced and most ambitiously expansive—of the novelistic spatializations examined in *Empty Houses*, a figuration of interiority as a hollow space that cries out for compensation by the vision of a collective that would be, in principle, endless in scope.

The vision is certainly utopian. And, to provide the obvious answer to this epilogue's opening question, abstracting a utopian vision from the space of sexual interiority is by its nature an impossible project. Far from papering over that impossibility, Baldwin's prose becomes in its extremity a record of the painful gulf that looms between the interior and the collective, between the psychological and the political. As Baldwin has Vivaldo put it in a sentence that serves as an emblem of the novel as a whole, "I'm just a fucked-up group of people" (281): the logical and affective distress radiating from the words make clear that Baldwin's project is not to exalt the individual but to render his isolation from the collective unavoidably obvious—and obvious as the result of a process of historical damage. *Another Country*'s wrenching distortions of style and point of view, of narrative and even grammatical coherence, are precise measurements of the sociopolitical obstacles confronting Baldwin's vision of a cast of characters who are in some ineffable sense "all equal." That vision, this book has argued, is incubated by the novel of interiority and expressed most visibly in its persistent wrestling with theatrical modes of storytelling: the novel's resistance to the closure of interiority has been quite literally "a mystery approached through form." Baldwin's vision of collective existence, and that of the novel of interiority more generally, may seem sentimental, doomed to failure by virtue of its abstraction from the details of social and political struggle. But that failure, and that provocation, are those of the literary itself.

1. On modernity's intensification of the analogy between domestic and psychic space, see Diana Fuss, *The Sense of an Interior: Four Writers and the Rooms That Shaped Them* (New York: Routledge, 2004).

2. Ian Watt, *The Rise of the Novel* (Berkeley: University of California Press, 1957), 206; Sylvie Thorel-Cailleteau, "The Poetry of Mediocrity," in Franco Moretti, ed., *The Novel*, vol. 2 (Princeton, NJ: Princeton University Press, 2006), 77.

3. Georg Lukács, *The Historical Novel*, trans. Hannah and Stanley Mitchell (1962; reprint, Lincoln: Nebraska University Press, 1983), 201–206; Raymond Williams, *Culture and Society: 1780–1950* (1958; reprint, New York: Columbia University Press, 1983), 102–109.

4. Fredric Jameson, *The Political Unconscious: Narrative as a Socially Symbolic Act* (Ithaca, NY: Cornell University Press, 1981), 221.

5. Franco Moretti, *Modern Epic: The World System from Goethe to García Márquez*, trans. Quintin Hoare (London: Verso, 1996), 143.

6. Nancy Armstrong, *How Novels Think: The Limits of Individualism from 1719–1900* (New York: Columbia University Press, 2005), 25; Pierre Bourdieu, *The Field of Cultural Production: Essays on Art and Literature* (New York: Columbia University Press, 1993), 55. Armstrong's statement extends her argument in *Desire and Domestic Fiction: A Political History of the Novel* (New York: Oxford University Press, 1987) that the novel rewrites political conflicts as romantic entanglement.

7. The literature on "the public" and its relation to domesticity and psychological interiority is voluminous. Michael McKeon's *The Secret History of Domesticity: Public, Private, and the Division of Knowledge* (Baltimore: Johns Hopkins University Press, 2005) traces the emergence of modernity's public/private dichotomy, focusing on what he terms the "devolution of absolutism" in the seventeenth and eighteenth centuries: "a progressive detachment of the normatively absolute from its presumed locale in royal absolutism and its experimental relocation in 'the people,' the family, women, the individual, personal identity, and the absolute subject" (xxii). Sexuality represents a final link in this devolutionary chain (see 269–319, 323). With its emphasis on the ways sexuality comes to contain the fantasy of access to an increasingly remote public, *Empty Houses* might be understood as following the literary historical line of McKeon's argument into a period beyond the scope of his study.

Influential accounts of the nineteenth-century fading of a robust public sphere include Richard Sennett, *The Fall of Public*

Man (New York: Norton, 1974); Jürgen Habermas, *The Structural Transformation of the Public Sphere: An Inquiry into a Category of Bourgeois Society,* trans. Thomas Burger, with Frederick Lawrence (Cambridge, MA: MIT Press, 1989); and Hannah Arendt, *The Human Condition* (1958; reprint, Chicago: University of Chicago Press, 1998). Arendt's terminology is idiosyncratic: her category of "the social" designates the contamination of the properly public realm with properly private energies, and thus describes what Lauren Berlant has termed the "intimate public sphere" (see Berlant, *The Queen of America Goes to Washington City: Essays on Sex and Citizenship* [Durham, NC: Duke University Press, 1997], 1–24). But Arendt's account of the "modern discovery of intimacy" (69) coincides in its outlines with those of Sennett and Habermas. For an account supplementing Habermas's emphasis on institutions of publicness with a Foucauldian attention to discourses of sexual privatization, see Lauren Berlant and Michael Warner, "Sex in Public," *Critical Inquiry* 24.2 (1998): 547–566. For a codification of the distinct but overlapping ways in which the public/private distinction signifies, see Jeff Weintraub, "The Theory and Politics of the Public/Private Distinction," in idem and Krishan Kumar, eds., *Public and Private in Thought and Practice: Perspectives on a Grand Dichotomy* (Chicago: University of Chicago Press, 1997). I focus on the third of Weintraub's senses of "public," that of "a fluid and polymorphous sociability"—a sense which Weintraub specifies "might almost be called dramaturgic, if that term were not so ambiguous" (7).

8. Susan Gal, "A Semiotics of the Public/Private Distinction," *differences* 13.1 (2002): 77–95.

9. McKeon, *The Secret History of Domesticity*, 269. Gal's "recursive nesting" resembles McKeon's "dialectical recapitulation" (323), the process whereby the "internal" or "private" half of a given historical split between public and private is itself subject to division. *Empty Houses* hypothesizes that one function of the literary object is to retain the memory of those processes of subdivision as a formal and affective trace.

10. In an argument instructively sensitive to the ambiguities of the novel's supposed containment of politicized collectives in private subjects, John Plotz writes that "a potentially explosive singularity [thereby] comes to abide inside the deep subjects of the novel." John Plotz, *The Crowd: British Literature and Public Politics* (Berkeley: University of California Press, 2000), 190.

11. Arendt, *The Human Condition*, 58.

12. Nancy Armstrong, "The Fiction of Bourgeois Morality and the Paradox of Individualism," in Moretti, *The Novel*, 2:373.

13. Jameson, *The Political Unconscious*, 70.

14. Important critical accounts of the nineteenth-century novel's obsession with theatricality include Emily Allen, *Theater Figures: The Production of the Nineteenth-Century British Novel* (Columbus: Ohio State University Press, 2003); J. Jeffrey Franklin, *Serious Play: The Cultural Form of the Nineteenth-Century Realist Novel* (Philadelphia: University of Pennsylvania Press, 1999); and Joseph Litvak, *Caught in the Act: Theatricality in the Nineteenth-Century English Novel* (Berkeley: University of California Press, 1992). These books consider many of the authors treated here, and have been central to my thinking throughout, but none treats novelists' theatrical works; I seek to complicate these studies' consequent emphasis on the novel's an-

titheatricality. Alan L. Ackerman, Jr., *The Portable Theater: American Literature and the Nineteenth-Century Stage* (Baltimore: Johns Hopkins University Press, 1999), which discusses James's plays as well as his fiction, is an exception to this trend.

15. M. M. Bakhtin, *The Dialogic Imagination: Four Essays*, trans. Caryl Emerson and Michael Holquist (Austin: University of Texas Press, 1981), 4. Crucial recent departures from the tendency to understand the novel as antitheatrical include Lynn M. Voskuil's *Acting Naturally: Victorian Theatricality and Authenticity* (Charlottesville: University of Virginia Press, 2004) and Deborah Vlock's *Dickens, Novel Reading, and the Victorian Popular Theatre* (Cambridge: Cambridge University Press, 1998).

16. See Michael R. Booth, "Introduction," in idem, ed., *English Plays of the Nineteenth Century*, vol. 1, *Dramas 1800–1850* (Oxford: Oxford University Press, 1969); and Nina Auerbach, "Before the Curtain," in Kerry Powell, ed., *The Cambridge Companion to Victorian and Edwardian Theatre* (Cambridge: Cambridge University Press, 2004): 3–14.

17. Influential accounts of this "novelization" include Raymond Williams, *Drama from Ibsen to Brecht* (1952; reprint, New York: Oxford University Press, 1969), 244–246; and Peter Szondi, *Theory of the Modern Drama*, trans. Michael Hays (Minneapolis: University of Minnesota Press, 1987).

18. Darko Suvin, *To Brecht and Beyond: Soundings in Modern Dramaturgy* (Brighton, England: Harvester, 1984), 58.

19. On nineteenth-century stage design, theater architecture, and audience behavior, see Simon Trussler, *The Cambridge Illustrated History of British Theatre* (Cambridge: Cambridge University Press, 1994), 191–266; and David Wiles, *A Short History of Western Performance Space* (Cambridge: Cambridge University Press, 2003). For a detailed account of mid-century changes in London's West End theater district, see Jim Davis and Victor Emeljanow, *Reflecting the Audience: London Theatregoing, 1840–1880* (Iowa City: University of Iowa Press, 2001). An invaluable source on naturalist stagecraft is Christopher Innes, *A Sourcebook on Naturalist Theatre* (London: Routledge, 2000). On Constantin Stanislavski's System and its American descendant, the Method—and their close relation to late-nineteenth-century theatrical naturalism—see Joseph R. Roach, *The Player's Passion: Studies in the Science of Acting* (Ann Arbor: University of Michigan Press, 1993), 197–217; and Steve Vineberg, *Method Actors: Three Generations of an American Acting Style* (New York: Schirmer, 1994).

English director Declan Donnellan has dissented from the Method's dominance in terms resonating with the historical connections between stage design, acting style, and the domestic interior. His book *The Actor and the Target* casually conflates domestic and psychic space (the target of Donnellan's animus in the following passage, from which the epigraph to *Empty Houses* is taken, is the Method shibboleth of "concentration"): "It is important never to concentrate," Donnellan tells his actor-reader. "Concentrating is like escaping the horror house of *Uncle Silas*: we always end up mysteriously back home. Imagine you are hungry and have no food in your flat. It doesn't matter how often you search the fridge: it will remain empty. The only place to get food is outside. If you stay in, you'll starve, no matter how often you rummage around the wire racks . . . It seems so safe at home, it seems so frightening on the streets, but this is a delusion. It is not safe at home; it is only safe on the streets. Don't go home." Declan Donnellan, *The Actor and the Target* (St. Paul, MN: Theatre Communications Group, 2002), 28-29.

20. J. Jeffrey Franklin describes the Victorian supersession of "the subject of performance" by "the subject of reading," while Elaine Hadley traces a replacement of "melodramatic" by "romantic" or novelistic subjectivity in the nineteenth century. See Franklin, *Serious Play*, 126; and Elaine Hadley, *Melodramatic Tactics: Theatricalized Dissent in the English Marketplace, 1800–1885* (Stanford: Stanford University Press, 1995), 71. Friedrich Nietzsche's *Birth of Tragedy* (1872), which presents itself as an investigation into the origins of Greek drama, might more accurately be read as a report on this nineteenth-century process: Nietzsche tracks the transformation of Aeschylan tragedy (a ritual allowing "no opposition between public and chorus") into Euripidian drama (in which this massed public is dissolved into individuated "spectators" scrutinizing "*character representation* and psychological refinement"). Nietzsche associates this new order with both "*the novel*" and the "death-leap into the bourgeois drama." However fanciful as classical history, his essay constitutes a powerful allegory of the nineteenth-century theater, with the portrait of Euripides functioning as an anticipation of Ibsen's late-century psychologized dramas. Friedrich Nietzsche, *The Birth of Tragedy and the Case of Wagner*, trans. Walter Kaufmann (New York: Vintage, 1967), 62, 108, 91.

21. G. H. Lewes, *On Actors and the Art of Acting* (London: Smith, Elder, 1875), xi; Charles Dickens, *The Life and Adventures of Nicholas Nickleby* (1839; reprint, London: Penguin, 1982), 385.

22. See Carolyn Williams's reconstruction of these effects, and her excavation of their cognitive components, in "Moving Pictures: George Eliot and Melodrama," in Lauren Berlant, ed., *Compassion: The Culture and Politics of an Emotion* (New York: Routledge, 2004), 105–144.

23. Sharon Marcus, "The Theater of Comparative Literature," in Ali Behdad and Dominic Thomas, eds., *A Companion to Comparative Literature* (Malden, MA: Blackwell, 2011).

24. "Contest": Franklin, *Serious Play*, 87; "competition": Allen, *Theater Figures*, 17. Franco Moretti makes the case for a Darwinian generic history in "On Literary Evolution," in Franco Moretti, *Signs Taken for Wonders: Essays in the Sociology of Literary Forms*, trans. David Forgacs, Susan Fischer, and David Miller, rev. ed. (New York: Verso, 1988). Vlock's *Dickens, Novel Reading, and the Victorian Popular Theatre* challenges the idea of the novel's inwardness in a way that resonates with my goals here. Vlock's focus on Dickens leads to the conclusion that "the 'drama' was not supplanted by the novel in the nineteenth century but merged with it" (3). (A similar emphasis on the relatively unanxious Victorian exchange among genres informs Martin Meisel's *Realizations: Narrative, Pictorial, and Theatrical Arts in Nineteenth-Century England* [Princeton, NJ: Princeton University Press, 1983].) But in the easy dialogue his work maintained with the theater, Dickens was remarkably un-predictive of the novel's development over the years covered in *Empty Houses*. For the writers I treat, the line between the theater and the novel was frequently moralized and always the subject of intense affective investment; because for them the theater constituted not a source of easy borrowing but of ambivalent longing, these writers emblematize literary culture's increasing investment in distin-

guishing between the logics of page and stage. For earlier considerations of Dickensian theatricality, see Robert Garis, *The Dickens Theatre: A Reassessment of the Novels* (Oxford: Clarendon, 1965); and Edwin M. Eigner, *The Dickens Pantomime* (Berkeley: University of California Press, 1989). On the theatrical dimension of Dickens's public readings, see Malcolm Andrews, *Charles Dickens and His Performing Selves: Dickens and the Public Readings* (Oxford: Oxford University Press, 2006). Andrews, in demonstrating both the ease with which Dickens adapted his novels into one-man shows and his comfort before the public, shows as well how unrepresentative he was of the main current of novelistic practice.

25. Sigmund Freud, "Mourning and Melancholia" (1917), in idem, *General Psychological Theory* (1963; reprint, New York: Simon and Schuster, 1997): 164–179. On melancholia as a productively retentive phenomenon, see Judith Butler, *Gender Trouble: Feminism and the Subversion of Identity* (New York: Routledge, 1990), 73–81.

26. See Robert Stang, *The Theory of the Novel in England, 1850–1870* (New York: Columbia University Press, 1959), 120–127. Gérard Genette notes that although Aristotle is frequently cited as the source of the tripartite generic distinction among tragedy, epic, and poetry, *The Poetics* "is not yet a system of genres" but an account of modes—that is, of the difference between narrative and dramatic presentation. Genette shows that the affinities between certain modes and certain qualities are contingent (the association of drama with "impersonality," for example, dates from Renaissance theorists, who backdated it to Aristotle) *and* that these contingencies have a crucial shaping force on what writers think they are doing when they employ different modes. This insight into the contingency and felt necessity of the ideological entailments of modal differences has been crucial to my thinking. See Gérard Genette, *The Architext: An Introduction*, trans. Jane E. Lewin (Berkeley: University of California Press, 1992), 12.

27. Philip Auslander relatedly argues both against the tendency of performance theory to invest "liveness" with "cultural and ideological resistance," and indicates that the idea of liveness nonetheless acquires special status as an emblem of communitarian desire in a mediatized culture. See Philip Auslander, *Liveness: Performance in a Mediatized Culture*, 2nd ed. (New York: Routledge, 2008), 7.

28. For all its attention to historical detail, Jonas Barish's landmark work on the antitheatrical prejudice affords little purchase on theater's variable historical meanings. Antitheatricality, Barish claims, is so pervasive (his account runs from Platonism to Nazism) that it points to an "ontological malaise, a condition inseparable from our beings": hatred of the theater is so endemic to Western civilization as to virtually define it. See Jonas Barish, *The Antitheatrical Prejudice* (Berkeley: University of California Press, 1981), 2.

29. Significantly, Bakhtin's mention of Thackeray occurs in a discussion of the way "literature's sundered tie with the public square is re-established" in the novel. See Bakhtin, *The Dialogic Imagination*, 166.

30. These theatrical spaces are presided over almost exclusively by women, who thus figure as nondomestic and often overtly "bad" heroines: Thackeray's Becky Sharp and Julia Prior; Eliot's Fedalma and Gwendolen Harleth; James's Rose Armiger, Mrs. Brookenham, and Kate Croy; and Joyce's Bella Cohen. The prominence of women in this chronotopic tradition becomes even more notable in light of Nancy

Armstrong's influential argument that the paradigmatic subject imagined by the novel is a domesticated woman. This roster suggests that the history of the novel could equally be written as centered on these distinctly nondomestic figures. See Armstrong, *Desire and Domestic Fiction*, 3–27.

31. See, in particular, Nina Auerbach, *Private Theatricals: The Lives of the Victorians* (Cambridge, MA: Harvard University Press, 1990).

32. See Gordon S. Haight, *George Eliot: A Biography* (1968; reprint, New York: Penguin, 1985), 471–472.

33. Henry James, *The Other House*, in idem, *The Complete Plays of Henry James*, ed. Leon Edel (London: Hart-Davis), 1949), 736.

34. Bruce Wilshire, *Role Playing and Identity: The Limits of Theatre as Metaphor* (Bloomington: Indiana University Press, 1982), 262.

35. Bert O. States, "The Phenomenological Attitude," in Janelle G. Reinelt and Joseph R. Roach, eds., *Critical Theory and Performance* (Ann Arbor: University of Michigan Press, 2007), 29.

36. "Parabasis," in Alex Preminger and T.V.F. Brogan, eds., *The New Princeton Encyclopedia of Poetry and Poetics* (Princeton, NJ: Princeton University Press, 1993), 876.

37. Paul de Man, *Aesthetic Ideology* (Minneapolis: University of Minnesota Press, 1996), 178.

38. Joseph Kestner notes the inextricability of the spatial imagination from the temporal one (pointing out, for example, that the idea of a novelistic "scene" refers us not only to a memorable event but to the place of its occurrence). But he is uninterested in how specific situations of consumption are suggested by certain forms—and so, for example, does not mention that a scene implies not only a diegetic *setting* but an extradiegetic *theater* in which that scene is embedded. See Joseph A. Kestner, *The Spatiality of the Novel* (Detroit: Wayne State University Press, 1978), esp. 69–71.

39. Charles Lamb, "Stage Illusion," in idem, *The Essays of Elia* (1823; reprint, London: Walter Scott, n.d.), 289–290.

40. Barish offers a history of this moralization in *The Antitheatrical Prejudice*. Michael Fried's account of the reception of eighteenth-century French painting demonstrates that the moralization of performance travels far beyond the confines of the theater. See Michael Fried, *Absorption and Theatricality: Painting and Beholder in the Age of Diderot* (Berkeley: University of California Press, 1980).

41. Lamb's essay argues that such effects are suitable for comedy but not for tragedy, which he claims requires the spectator's seamless belief in character. But Lamb elsewhere acknowledged that the potentially estranging effect of the actor's intention is ineradicable from theatrical presentation *tout court*: his notorious argument that Shakespearean tragedy is unsuitable for performance is based on the signifying static produced by the "subinsinuation" of the actor's bodily presence. See Charles Lamb, "On the Tragedies of Shakespeare, considered with reference to their fitness for stage representation," in idem, *Lamb as Critic*, ed. Roy Park (London: Routledge and Kegan Paul, 1980), 85–101.

42. Olive Schreiner, *The Story of an African Farm* (1883; reprint, London: Penguin, 1995), 29.

43. Schreiner's complaint about the theater confuses actor and character: it is not the *characters* who assemble at the play's close but the bodies that have made

those characters visible. Rather than fault Schreiner for this imprecision, we might note that the confusion is an unavoidable feature of performance; no mere canvas for characterological representation, the actor's body produces meanings in excess of that character. While this has been construed as an obstacle to artistic purity—most extremely by the stage designer E. Gordon Craig, who advocated the replacement of living actors with giant puppets—the inevitability of such doubling is what properly constitutes the theatrical. See Edward Gordon Craig, "The Actor and the Über-Marionette," in idem, *On the Art of the Theatre* (Chicago: Browne's Bookstore, 1911). On Craig's theories as an expression of modernist antitheatricality, see Martin Puchner, *Stage Fright: Modernism, Anti-Theatricalism, and Drama* (Baltimore: Johns Hopkins University Press, 2002), 6, 10.

44. Suvin, *To Brecht and Beyond*, 83; Fredric Jameson, *Brecht and Method* (Verso: London, 1998), 11.

45. Jacques Rancière, *Dissensus: On Politics and Aesthetics*, trans. Steve Corcoran (London: Continuum, 2010), 79. Kenneth Burke's "dramatistic" conception of politics is apposite here: "Even a materially dispossessed individual may 'own' privilege vicariously by adopting the 'style' (or 'insignia') of some privileged class . . . Politics above all is a drama . . . One's identification as a member of a group is a role, yet it is the only active mode of identification possible, as you will note by observing how all *individualistic* concepts of identity dissolve into the nothingness of mysticism and the absolute . . . If you would avoid the antitheses of supernaturalism and naturalism, you must develop the coordinates of socialism, which gets us to cooperation, participation, man in society, man in drama." Kenneth Burke, *The Philosophy of Literary Form: Studies in Symbolic Action*, 3rd ed. (Berkeley: University of California Press, 1973), 309–311.

46. The central theoretical text is Jacques Rancière, *The Philosopher and His Poor*, trans. John Drury, Corinne Oster, and Andrew Parker (Durham, NC: Duke University Press, 2003); see, esp., 3–53. Rancière's research on French theater was published in *Révoltes Logiques* between 1975 and 1985; the essays have been collected in Rancière, *Les Scènes du peuple* (Lyon: Horlieu, 2003). For an excellent discussion of this work's relation to Rancière's later theoretical articulations, see Peter Hallward, "Staging Equality: On Rancière's Theatrocracy," *New Left Review* 37 (2006): 109–129.

47. Rancière, *Les Scènes du peuple*, 213.

48. Ibid, 214.

49. See Elaine Hadley, *Melodramatic Tactics: Theatricalized Dissent in the English Marketplace, 1800–1885* (Stanford: Stanford University Press, 1995); and Marc Baer, *Theatre and Disorder in Late Georgian London* (Oxford: Oxford University Press, 1992).

50. Rancière, *Les Scènes du peuple*, 213.

51. Vlock, *Dickens, Novel Reading, and the Victorian Popular Theatre*, 35; Rancière, *Dissensus*, 136. Bakhtin employs a similar emphasis on theater's dethematizing qualities in contrasting the characters inhabiting the "poetic" genres of tragedy and epic to those in farce: "Outside his destiny, the epic and tragic hero is nothing . . . On the contrary, popular masks—Maccus, Pulcinello, Harlequin—are able to assume any destiny and can figure into any situation (they often do so within the limits of a single play), but they cannot exhaust their possibilities by those situations alone; they always retain, in any situation and any destiny, a happy surplus of their own."

Bakhtin, of course, goes on to associate the theatrical's "happy surplus" with the novel and, ironically, to classify the drama as tending toward monologism; in doing so he embodies the most influential theoretical arm of the effort to metaphorize the theater in the name of novelistic art. As Martin Puchner notes, Bakhtin "never acknowledged that his dialogism was in fact a dramatic model." See Bakhtin, *The Dialogic Imagination*, 36, 405; Puchner, *Stage Fright*, 194.

52. On the Greek concept of *moira,* or "share," as signifying both individual fate and collective redistribution, see Bruce Robbins, *The Servant's Hand: English Fiction from Below*, 2ⁿᵈ ed. (Durham, NC: Duke University Press, 1993), 28. On the theatrical cast as a collective whose division into parts (its "casting") ambiguously suggests a conceptual unity, see Samuel Weber, *Theatricality as Medium* (New York: Fordham University Press, 2004), 41.

53. Relevant here is the psychoanalytic concept of "phantasy," which Laplanche and Pontalis define as expressing a desire not for an object but for the ongoingness of "organized scenes which are capable of dramatization." J. Laplanche and J.-B. Pontalis, *The Language of Psychoanalysis*, trans. Donald Nicholson-Smith (New York: Norton, 1973), 318.

54. Discussing the *omnium gatherum* dream episode in Goethe's *Wilhelm Meister*, Jameson refers to "a form of closure utterly distinct from plot" and connects this Goethean passage to the Nighttown chapter of *Ulysses*. Although he does not refer to theatrical space, his comments are suggestive of the spatial closure of the theater. Fredric Jameson, "The Experiments of Time: Providence and Realism," in Moretti, *The Novel*, 2:105–106.

55. Michel Foucault, *The History of Sexuality*, trans. Robert Hurley, vol. 1 (1978; reprint, New York: Vintage, 1990).

56. Michael Warner, "Introduction," in idem, ed., *Fear of a Queer Planet: Queer Politics and Social Theory* (Minneapolis: Minnesota University Press, 1993), xxvi.

57. Sedgwick, *Epistemology of the Closet*, 1.

58. On homonormativity, see Lisa Duggan, *The Twilight of Equality? Neoliberalism, Cultural Politics, and the Attack on Democracy* (Boston: Beacon, 2004).

59. Eli Zaretsky, *Secrets of the Soul: A Social and Cultural History of Psychoanalysis* (New York: Knopf, 2004), 39.

60. Fredric Jameson, "Pleasure: A Political Issue," in idem, *The Ideologies of Theory: Essays, 1971–1986*, vol. 2 (Minneapolis: Minnesota University Press, 1988), 73.

61. Armstrong, *How Novels Think*, 10.

62. On the relation between James's literary authority and his increasingly rarefied public, see Mark McGurl, *The Novel Art: Elevations of American Fiction after Henry James* (Princeton, NJ: Princeton University Press, 2001), 21. For Joyce's comment that *Ulysses* was designed to "keep the professors busy for centuries," see Richard Ellmann, *James Joyce*, 2ⁿᵈ ed. (New York: Oxford University Press, 1982), 521.

63. Isobel Armstrong, *Victorian Poetry: Poetry, Poetics, and Politics* (London: Routledge, 1993), 4.

64. Roland Barthes, "Baudelaire's Theater," in idem, *Critical Essays*, trans. Richard Howard (Evanston, IL: Northwestern University Press, 1972), 25.

65. It seems clear that even the most notorious theatrical failures might have gone otherwise: in his reconstruction of *Guy Domville's* first night, Leon Edel shows how difficult it is to know whether the play was jeered because of its quality, the presence

in the audience of a faction with a grudge against one of the actors, or a wobbly hat on one of the players. Given the accidents that affect theatrical productions, it has seemed less intellectually fruitful to attempt to solve the question of why plays failed than to trace the effects of their failure on these writers' novelistic practice. See Leon Edel, editor's foreword to *Guy Domville*, in Henry James, *The Complete Plays of Henry James*, ed. Leon Edel (London: Hart-Davis, 1949), 465–483.

66. On the limited agency of the aesthetic in modernity, see Sianne Ngai, *Ugly Feelings* (Cambridge, MA: Harvard University Press, 2005).

67. Hans Ulrich Gumbrecht, *Production of Presence: What Meaning Cannot Convey* (Stanford: Stanford University Press, 2004), xv. Gumbrecht's central examples of presence-rich aesthetic objects are theatrical: Kabuki, No, Artaud, Calderón. See 149–152.

68. On the historiographic challenges posed by theatrical phenomena, see Jacky Bratton, *New Readings in Theatre History* (Cambridge: Cambridge University Press, 2003), 3–16, 95–132; and R. W. Vince, "Theatre History as Academic Discipline," in Bruce McConachie and Thomas Postlewait, eds., *Interpreting the Theatrical Past: Essays on the Historiography of Performance* (Iowa City: University of Iowa Press, 1989), 1–18.

69. Bakhtin understands the novel's relation to other forms as parodically incorporative: the essential features of the novel, he claims, "constitute a criticism (from the novel's point of view) of other genres and of the relationship these genres bear to reality." Bakhtin, *The Dialogic Imagination*, 10.

70. Keir Elam, *The Semiotics of Theatre and Drama*, 2ⁿᵈ ed. (London: Routledge, 2002), 128.

71. For Roland Barthes, the world-reference of performative genres marks their participation in "the order of the operable"; he specifies that "*the novelistic real is not operable.*" One effect of the novel's incorporation of theatrical cues is to bring this non-operability to readerly consciousness. Roland Barthes, *S/Z: An Essay*, trans. Richard Miller (New York: Hill and Wang, 1974), 80.

72. These theatricalized novels thus seem designed to controvert Samuel Johnson's claim in the "Preface to Shakespeare" that "a play read affects the mind like a play acted." Indeed these novels might be read as elaborations on Johnson's admission, in an introduction to the printed edition of his *Masque of Hymen*, that the event "cannot by imagination, much less description, be recovered to a part of that *spirit* it had in the gliding by." Both comments are quoted in D. F. Mackenzie's essay on book history, "Typography and Meaning: The Case of William Congreve," in Giles Barber and Bernhard Fabian, eds., *Buch and Buchhandel in Europa im achtzehnten Jahrhundert: The Book and the Book Trade in Eighteenth-Century Europe: Proceedings of the Fifth Wolfenbutten Symposium, 1–3 November 1977* (Hamburg: Ernst Hauswedell, 1981), 101, 117. It is not accidental that Mackenzie's project of "trac[ing] a tradition of consciousness of the book" (93) is centered on an analysis of Congreve's landmark edition of his plays; the sensory thinness of print becomes unavoidably obvious in the case of play texts.

73. J. L. Austin, *How to Do Things with Words*, 2ⁿᵈ ed. (Cambridge, MA: Harvard University Press, 1975), 101. A large literature has grown up around Austin's terminology and its applicability to literary study. See, in particular, Stanley Cavell, "Counter-Philosophy and the Pawn of Voice," in idem, *A Pitch of Philosophy: Auto-*

biographical Exercises (Cambridge, MA: Harvard University Press, 1994): 53–128. I have been influenced by Cavell's sense of the performative as a register peculiarly sensitive to the ethical limitations of an epistemological focus on interiority, and by his sense of "the world-boundness of language" (118). On the Victorian novel's engagement with perlocutionary response in ethical life, see Andrew H. Miller, *The Burdens of Perfection: On Ethics and Reading in Nineteenth-Century British Literature* (Ithaca, NY: Cornell University Press, 2008), esp. 1–32. See also Eve Kosofsky Segwick, "Around the Performative: Periperformative Vicinities in Nineteenth-Century Narrative," in idem, *Touching Feeling: Affect, Pedagogy, Performativity* (Durham, NC: Duke University Press, 2003): 67–92, on the ways performative utterances invoke spatial imaginaries.

74. Andrew Miller discusses aesthetic reception as a state of being "perfectly helpless" in *The Burdens of Perfection*, 130-5. Miller's argument that Austen's novels "strain toward bodily animation, testing the limits of novelistic form" (132) by soliciting in readers a desire to intervene in the diegetic action is true in a different sense for the play text, which solicits in its form a collective project of performance and attendance.

75. Bert O. States, *Great Reckonings in Little Rooms: On the Phenomenology of Theater* (Berkeley: University of California Press, 1985), 127. States's account of play scripts resonates with the tradition of nonprescriptive utopianism Russell Jacoby discusses in *Picture Imperfect*. As Jacoby's title indicates, iconoclastic utopian thought emphasizes not vividly particularized images of an ideal world (as does what Jacoby calls "blueprint utopianism") but oblique hints of one. In language reminiscent of the phenomenological peculiarity of the play text as well as of many of the novels we will examine, Jacoby writes that in the utopian tradition he traces "one could 'hear' the future, but not see it." Russell Jacoby, *Picture Imperfect: Utopian Thought for an Anti-Utopian Age* (New York: Columbia University Press, 2005), xv.

76. Mary Poovey, *Uneven Developments: The Ideological Work of Gender in Mid-Victorian England* (Chicago: University of Chicago Press, 1988), 90.

77. See Shannon Jackson, *Professing Performance: Theatre in the Academy from Philology to Performativity* (Cambridge: Cambridge University Press, 2004), 13.

CHAPTER ONE   Acoustics in the Thackeray Theater

1. Gordon N. Ray, *Thackeray: The Uses of Adversity, 1811–1846* (1955; reprint, New York: Farrar, Straus, and Giroux, 1972), 115.

2. Quoted in ibid., 151.

3. Quoted in ibid., 115–116. See William Makepeace Thackeray, *The History of Pendennis* (1848–50; reprint, London: Penguin, 1972), 189.

4. Alison Byerly argues that Thackeray's ideal is "unpretentious realism, the antithesis of the 'theatrical heroic' . . . He tries to teach [readers] how to look beyond the charade to see what is real." Alison Byerly, *Realism, Representation, and the Arts in Nineteenth-Century Literature* (Cambridge: Cambridge University Press, 1997), 62, 84.

5. William Makepeace Thackeray, *Vanity Fair: A Novel without a Hero* (1847–8; reprint, Oxford: Oxford University Press, 1983), 1–2.

6. Lynn Voskuil's analysis of Victorian theories of "natural acting" as "passionate self-projection" provides a valuable alternative to critical stress on the nineteenth century's supposed antitheatricalism. See Lynn M. Voskuil, *Acting Naturally: Victorian Theatricality and Authenticity* (Charlottesville: University of Virginia Press, 2004), 31.

7. Leonore Davidoff and Catherine Hall's *Family Fortunes: Men and Women of the English Middle Class, 1780–1850* (Chicago: University of Chicago Press, 1987) demonstrates that domestic privacy was as much fantasy as reality for middle-class households in the period. But their work testifies to the prestige of the separate-spheres model and the respectabilization of the public sphere in the second half of the nineteenth century (see 416–454). John Tosh builds on their work in arguing that the domestic sphere was a central arena of masculine authority and self-conception in the period; he identifies the years 1830 to 1860 as "the heyday of masculine domesticity." See John Tosh, *A Man's Place: Masculinity and the Middle-Class Home in Victorian England* (New Haven, CT: Yale University Press, 1999), 6. Thackeray's distinctive narrative characteristics are a reaction to these discursive facts, and thus a powerful guide to the felt restructuring of public and private space. See also Christopher Castiglia's essay on the temporal components of any robust concept of publicness, "Sex Panics, Sex Publics, Sex Memories," *boundary 2* 27.2 (2000): 149–175.

8. "Depressive": Joseph Litvak, *Strange Gourmets: Sophistication, Theory, and the Novel* (Durham, NC: Duke University Press 1997), 68; "disenchanted" and "deflated": George Levine, *The Realistic Imagination: English Fiction from Frankenstein to Lady Chatterley* (Chicago: University of Chicago Press, 1981), 138; "dissociated": Myron Taube, "Thackeray and the Reminiscental Vision," *Nineteenth-Century Fiction* 18.3 (1963): 247.

9. See Lewis Melville, *Some Aspects of Thackeray* (Boston: Little, Brown, 1911), 256. Thackeray seemed unsurprised by the rejection—a reaction in keeping with the doubtful relationship he retained with his public even at the height of his career. As Anthony Trollope put it in his biography, "While performing much of the best of his life's work, he was not sure of his market, not certain of his readers, his publishers, or his price . . . He did not probably know how firm was the hold he had obtained of the public ear." See Anthony Trollope, *Thackeray* (1879; reprint, Detroit: Gale, 1968), 17, 34. Thackeray's position as the indisputably major Victorian writer most consistently to strike minor keys—of doubt, disappointment, anticipated refusal—was accentuated by perennial comparison with Dickens. See Melville, *Some Aspects of Thackeray,* 238.

10. Jacques Attali, *Noise: The Political Economy of Music,* trans. Brian Massumi (Minneapolis: University of Minnesota Press, 1985), 6.

11. Thackeray's investment in a culture of ambient noise suggests a counterpoint to John Picker's stress on the ways in which intellectual workers forged an identity as professionals through campaigns to control street noise. Similarly, Thackeray's dubious stance toward sanctified domesticity contrasts with Ivan Kreilkamp's account of Dickens's voice as "domesticat[ing] public response" by "characteriz[ing] his readers as members of an extended family in which Dickens occupied pride of place as father." See John Picker, *Victorian Soundscapes* (Oxford: Oxford University Press, 2003), 41–83; and Ivan Kreilkamp, *Voice and the Victorian Storyteller* (Cambridge: Cambridge University Press, 2005), 106.

12. Levine, *The Realistic Imagination,* 161.

13. John Carey, *Thackeray: Prodigal Genius* (London: Faber and Faber, 1977), 189.

14. H. M. Daleski, "Strategies in *Vanity Fair,*" in Harold Bloom, ed., *Modern Critical Interpretations: William Makepeace Thackeray's* Vanity Fair (New York: Chelsea House, 1987), 139, 140.

15. Georg Lukács attacks Thackeray's *Henry Esmond* in similar terms, deriding Thackeray's focus on everyday life as "the distortion of history, its degradation to the level of the trivial and the private." Lukács' characterization of Thackeray's novelistic practice as "trivializing" and "microscopic" is precisely accurate—but this is what makes Thackeray a historian of intensifying domesticity (a phenomenon that for Lukács falls outside the purview of "real" history). Georg Lukács, *The Historical Novel,* trans. Hannah and Stanley Mitchell (Lincoln: Nebraska University Press, 1983), 204, 202. On Thackeray as an early exemplar of "cultural history," see Avrom Fleischman, *The English Historical Novel: Walter Scott to Virginia Woolf* (Baltimore: Johns Hopkins University Press, 1971), 131.

16. Ian Duncan uses the same phrase to describe Dickens's modifications to the narrative patterns of Scott's historical romances: for Duncan, *Dombey and Son* represents the "end of history" because "the end of the fiction's didactic work is a transcendental patriarchal household luminous with lack of social content." Dickens in this account narrates the end of history as a consolation, whereas a similar evacuation in Thackeray results in a depressing sense of loss, of mere ongoingness. Ian Duncan, *Modern Romance and the Transformations of the Novel: The Gothic, Scott, Dickens* (Cambridge: Cambridge University Press, 1992), 246.

17. William Makepeace Thackeray, *The Four Georges,* in *The Works of William Makepeace Thackeray,* vol. 26 (New York: Scribner's, 1903–4), 133.

18. See John Sutherland's note on page 884 of the Oxford edition.

19. Tracing the history of the book as an expressive visual medium, D. F. Mackenzie claims that the Protestant antipathy to the image that resulted in the 1642 closing of the theaters also encouraged a dissociation of word and image in serious literature. Mackenzie notes that Thackeray's illustrations of his own work represent "a significant"—and, we might add, quite lonely—"act of reintegration." See D. F. Mackenzie, "Typography and Meaning: The Case of William Congreve," in Giles Barber and Bernhard Fabian, eds., *Buch and Buchhandel in Europa Im Achtzehnten Jahrhundert: The Book and the Book Trade in Eighteenth-Century Europe: Proceedings of The Fifth Wolfenbutten Symposium, 1–3 November 1977* (Hamburg: Ernst Hauswedell, 1981), 99. The connection Mackenzie posits between theater and book illustration provides a historical reason for the ambient theatricality of Thackeray's images.

20. Susan Stewart, *On Longing: Narratives of the Miniature, the Gigantic, the Souvenir, the Collection* (Durham, NC: Duke University Press, 1993), 95.

21. Eli Zaretsky, *Capitalism, the Family, and Personal Life* (London: Pluto, 1976), 34.

22. Geoffrey Tillotson remarks on Thackeray's fondness for the word "little" in *Thackeray the Novelist* (Cambridge: Cambridge University Press, 1954), 92.

23. The terms are, of course, adapted from those Marx uses in the opening lines of the nearly contemporaneous *The Eighteenth Brumaire of Louis Napoleon* (1852). Marx's figuration of 1848 as a repetition-in-miniature of the French Revolution has

uncanny resonances with Thackeray's novel; for both writers, trivialized repetition is the historical modality specific to the mid-nineteenth century. See Karl Marx, *The Eighteenth Brumaire of Louis Bonaparte* (1852; reprint, New York: International, 1963).

24. Philippe Ariès, *Centuries of Childhood: A Social History of Family Life*, trans. Robert Baldick (New York: Vintage Books, 1962), 98.

25. Karen Chase and Michael Levenson, *The Spectacle of Intimacy: A Public Life for the Victorian Family* (Princeton, NJ: Princeton University Press, 2000).

26. Thackeray's biography—in particular the status as bachelor and single parent he assumed after Isabella Shawe Thackeray's institutionalization for insanity—is often conscripted to support these readings. The tendency to read Thackeray biographically, and to read the biography as a glum homage to the domestic, has been strong ever since Trollope gave this theory its formulation in his 1879 biography: "Just at that period of life at which a man generally makes a happy exchange in taking his wife's drawing-room in lieu of the smoking-room of his club, and assumes those domestic ways of living which are becoming and pleasant for matured years, that drawing room and those domestic ways were closed to him." Trollope, *Thackeray*, 40.

27. Juliet McMaster, *Thackeray: The Major Novels* (Toronto: University of Toronto Press, 1971), 13.

28. George Speaight, *Juvenile Drama: The History of the English Toy Theatre* (London: Macdonald, 1946).

29. A congruent evolution occurred when the home stereoscope "domesticated" the cosmorama and panorama in the 1860s. See Richard D. Altick, *The Shows of London (*Cambridge, MA: Harvard University Press, 1978), 233.

30. Roger B. Wilkenfeld, "'Before the Curtain' and *Vanity Fair*," *Nineteenth-Century Fiction* 26.3 (1971): 308.

31. Thackeray hit on the puppetry metaphor while visiting the family of his friend Eyre Crowe. He had begun to frequent the Crowes' house in Paris at the height of his expatriate phase, taking time out from attending theater, frequenting prostitutes, and courting Isabella Shawe in order to entertain the Crowe children with drawings and to meet "a variety of English artists and writers dwelling temporarily in France" (Ray, *Thackeray: The Uses of Adversity*, 176). The amalgam of bohemianism and domesticity represented by the Crowe ménage—at precisely the moment when Thackeray was considering trading one for the other—perhaps contributed to his decision to take the puppet theater as the emblem of a broader sociohistorical transition.

32. For a critique of the "decline" thesis of nineteenth-century theater, see Voskuil, *Acting Naturally*, 1–19.

33. Michael Booth, "Early Victorian Farce: Dionysus Domesticated," in Kenneth Richards and Peter Thompson, eds., *Essays on Nineteenth Century British Theatre* (London: Methuen, 1971).

34. See Hermann von Pückler-Muskau, "In Praise of Macready's Macbeth," and Leigh Hunt, "Macbeth without Poetry," both in A. M. Nagler, ed., *A Sourcebook in Theatrical History* (New York: Dover, 1952), 475, 472.

35. Jim Davis and Victor Emeljanow, *Reflecting the Audience: London Theatregoing, 1840–1880* (Iowa City: University of Iowa Press, 2001), 184, 173. Davidoff and Hall's *Family Fortunes* discusses the return of the Birmingham middle classes to the theater district (438).

36. Simon Trussler, *The Cambridge Illustrated History of British Theatre* (Cambridge: Cambridge University Press, 1994), 221. See also David Wiles, *A Short History of Western Performance Space* (Cambridge: Cambridge University Press, 2003).

37. See J. R. Planché, "Tribute to Madame Vestris," and Charles Mathews, "Olympic Drawing Rooms," both in Nagler, *A Sourcebook in Theatrical History*, 462, 464.

38. Quoted in Jacky Bratton, *New Readings in Theatre History* (Cambridge: Cambridge University Press, 2003), 79.

39. Davis and Emeljanow, *Reflecting the Audience*, 218.

40. Giorgio Agamben, *Infancy and History: Essays on the Destruction of Experience*, trans. Liz Heron (London: Verso, 1993), 130.

41. Harold Bloom, introduction to idem, ed., *Modern Critical Interpretations: William Makepeace Thackeray's* Vanity Fair (New York: Chelsea House, 1987), 3.

42. This last detail is a mistake on Thackeray's part, since earlier in the novel the portrait has been depicted as full-size (203). Or has the picture submitted to the law of diminution governing the second half of the novel?

43. Gordon N. Ray, *Thackeray: The Age of Wisdom, 1847–1863* (1958; reprint, New York: Farrar, Straus, and Giroux, 1972), 234.

44. Planché, "Tribute to Madame Vestris," 463.

45. On the play's composition and the housewarming production, see Ray, *Thackeray: The Age of Wisdom*, 234, 391. On the increasing prominence of private middle-class entertainments in the period, see Davidoff and Hall, *Family Fortunes*, 436–437.

46. William Makepeace Thackeray, *The Wolves and the Lamb*, in *The Works of William Makepeace Thackeray*, 28:373.

47. See ibid., 374, 445.

48. See Davidoff and Hall, *Family Fortunes*, 416–454. On the discursive management of gender in urban space, see Judith R. Walkowitz, *City of Dreadful Delight: Narratives of Sexual Danger in Late-Victorian London* (Chicago: University of Chicago Press, 1992).

49. William Makepeace Thackeray, *Mrs. Perkins's Ball*, in *The Works of William Makepeace Thackeray*, 24:30.

50. Bakhtin writes that "the boundaries of each concrete utterance as a unit of speech communication are determined by a *change in speaking subjects* . . . The utterance is . . . a real unit, clearly delimited by the change of speaking subjects, which ends by relinquishing the floor to the other, as if with a silent *dixi*, perceived by the listeners (as a sign) that the speaker has finished." The narration of *Mrs. Perkins's Ball* disconcerts by suggesting the uncertainty of its own boundaries as utterance—by suggesting that the privilege of the speaking position might be usurped at any moment, whether the floor has been ceded or not. See M. M. Bakhtin, *Speech Genres and Other Late Essays*, trans. Vern W. McGee (Austin: University of Texas Press, 1986), 71–72.

51. William Makepeace Thackeray, *Lovel the Widower*, in *The Works of William Makepeace Thackeray*, 28:197.

52. See William H. Rideing, *Thackeray's London: A Description of His Haunts and the Scenes of His Novels* (London: Jarvis and Son, 1885), 5.

53. See Tillotson, *Thackeray the Novelist*, 27. *Lovel's* narration accords with Dorrit Cohn's description of interior monologue as "generally contain[ing] flurries of unanswered questions, exclamations, invocations, invectives, or curses addressed to various absent persons, human or divine." Dorrit Cohn, *Transparent Minds: Narrative Modes for Presenting Consciousness in Fiction* (Princeton, NJ: Princeton University Press, 1978), 92.

54. On Thackeray's proclivity for such in-between narrative positions, see Andrew H. Miller, *Novels behind Glass: Commodity Culture and Victorian Narrative* (Cambridge: Cambridge University Press, 1995), 28.

55. Tosh, *A Man's Place*, 108.

56. The resonance of the name, and the observing-bachelor position, with Henry James's Ralph Touchett, is suggestive for a genealogy of Jamesian spectatorship: the question that Ralph frequently provokes in readers—namely, in what context *could* he perform?—has a specific antecedent in Thackeray's text.

57. Eve Sedgwick reads *Lovel* as demonstrating the bachelor's "basic strategy" of "a preference of atomized male individualism to the nuclear family (and a corresponding demonization of women, especially mothers)." Because Batchelor's "male individualism" is informed by an exclusion from the family, it is perhaps less aptly described as a "preference" or "strategy" than as a manifestation of *amor fati*—making a virtue of necessity. See Eve Kosofsky Sedgwick, *Epistemology of the Closet* (Berkeley: University of California Press, 1990), 192.

58. J. Jeffrey Franklin, *Serious Play: The Cultural Form of the Nineteenth-Century Realist Novel* (Philadelphia: University of Pennsylvania Press, 1999), 126.

59. Tillotson, *Thackeray the Novelist*, 92.

60. On *Vanity Fair*'s economies of frustration, see Miller, *Novels behind Glass*, 14–49.

61. Lauren Berlant, *The Female Complaint: the Unfinished Business of Sentimentality in American Culture* (Durham, NC: Duke University Press, 2008), 1.

62. Sharon Marcus, *Apartment Stories: City and Home in Nineteenth-Century Paris and London* (Berkeley: University of California Press, 1999), 85.

63. We might describe Batchelor's affection for working-class boardinghouses as slumming, and conclude that it amplifies his gentlemanly prestige. But this would misread the distress everywhere evident in Batchelor's voice, and so miss how such strategies of privilege can be analyzed as articulations of social discontent. On the temporary boardinghouse stay as middle-class prerogative, see Leonore Davidoff, "The Separation of Home and Work? Landladies and Lodgers in Nineteenth- and Twentieth-Century England," in Sandra Burman, ed., *Fit Work for Women* (New York: St. Martin's, 1979), 75. For an analysis of the way "middle-class cultural power revolved around an affirmative staging of desires or behavior that had also been defined as illicit," see John Kucich, *The Power of Lies: Transgression in Victorian Fiction* (Ithaca, NY: Cornell University Press, 1994), 42.

64. The *Oxford English Dictionary*'s earliest citation of "semi-attached" is *Lovel*. But Thackeray may also be referring to two popular and almost exactly contemporaneous novels by Emily Eden, *The Semi-Detached House* (1859) and *The Semi-Attached Couple* (1860). Thanks to Sharon Marcus for drawing my attention to Eden's work.

CHAPTER TWO George Eliot's Lot

1. George Eliot, *Essays of George Eliot*, ed. Thomas Pinney (London: Routledge, 1963), 435 (hereafter *E*).

2. Eliot's interest in the problematic nature of metaphor may have derived from Max Müller's *Lectures on the Science of Language*, which she read in 1862. See George Eliot, *The Journals of George Eliot*, ed. Margaret Harris and Judith Johnston (Cambridge: Cambridge University Press, 1998), 107 (hereafter *J*); and Gillian Beer, *Darwin's Plots: Evolutionary Narrative in Darwin, George Eliot, and Nineteenth-Century Fiction* (1983; 2nd ed., Cambridge: Cambridge University Press, 2000), 114.

3. This emphasis on the drama's formalization may seem odd in the context of the vibrant nineteenth-century theatrical culture discussed in the introduction and chapter 1. Eliot, who had in recent years been rereading Aristotle and Greek tragedy, appears to be thinking of the austerity of the classical drama rather than the melodrama and burletta of her own time. On Eliot's reading of the classics, see J. W. Cross, ed., *George Eliot's Life as Related in Her Letters and Journals*, vol. 2 (Edinburgh: Blackwood, 1885), 401–404; and Gordon S. Haight, *George Eliot: A Biography* (1968; reprint, New York: Penguin, 1985), 378.

4. George Eliot, *The George Eliot Letters*, ed. Gordon S. Haight, 7 vols. (New Haven, CT: Yale University Press, 1954–55), 4:119, 132 (hereafter *L*).

5. On Eliot's friendship with Faucit, see John Stokes, "Rachel's 'Terrible Beauty': An Actress among the Novelists," *ELH* 51.4 (1984): 771–793.

6. Lewes added that he thought the text "eminently suited for an opera (and I hope will take that shape)" (*L*, 453), but refrained from saying whether Eliot shared this view.

7. Joseph Litvak, *Caught in the Act: Theatricality in the Nineteenth-Century English Novel* (Berkeley: University of California Press, 1992), 162; J. Jeffrey Franklin, *Serious Play: The Cultural Form of the Nineteenth-Century Realist Novel* (Philadelphia: University of Pennsylvania Press, 1999), 98.

8. Daniel Cottom, *Social Figures: George Eliot, Social History, and Literary Representation* (Minneapolis: University of Minnesota Press, 1987), 139, 189; Franco Moretti, *The Way of the World: The Bildungsroman in European Culture*, trans. Albert Sbragia (1987; reprint, London: Verso, 2000), 223; John Kucich, *Repression in Victorian Fiction: Charlotte Brontë, George Eliot, and Charles Dickens* (Berkeley: University of California Press, 1987), 118; Catherine Gallagher, *The Industrial Reformation of English Fiction: Social Discourse and Narrative Form, 1832–1867* (Chicago: University of Chicago Press, 1985), 252.

9. This chapter considers *The Spanish Gypsy* in the context of Eliot's novels and of narrative forms generally. But there are a number of theatrical and poetic genres from which *The Spanish Gypsy* draws inspiration. We might align Eliot's text with the Romantic closet dramas of Shelley and Bryon, and the Victorian verse plays of Arnold, Browning, and Tennyson. Eliot herself claimed kinship with the classical and Elizabethan tragedy (see "Notes on the Spanish Gypsy and Tragedy in General," in J. W. Cross, ed., *George Eliot's Life as Related in Her Letters and Journals*, 2:44–49, and L 428). But *The Spanish Gypsy*'s formal oddity renders its relation to these genres tenuous: it is less stageworthy than classical tragic texts but more insistent about its

performative ambition than closet drama and Victorian dramatic poems. Thematically *The Spanish Gypsy*'s most proximate reference points are the melodrama of race and the Orientalist spectacle, although here too Eliot's text troubles the ideological coherence of these genres. On the Romantic poets' equivocation about the performative destination of their closet dramas, see Michael Simpson, *Closet Performances: Political Exhibition and Prohibition in the Dramas of Byron and Shelley* (Stanford: Stanford University Press, 1998); on the Orientalist drama, see Edward Ziter, *The Orient on the Victorian Stage* (Cambridge: Cambridge University Press, 2003).

10. In this it is quite different from 1870's *Armgart*, a shorter dramatic poem Eliot never intended for the stage. Armgart anticipates the treatment of the Countess Alcharisi in *Daniel Deronda* with its story of a woman who forsakes marriage to pursue her singing career. Armgart's lover complains that "too much ambition has unwomaned her," a judgment the poem confirms by punishing her with the loss of her singing ability: "Song is gone, but nature's other gift, / Self-judgment, is not gone," Armgart laments, thus heralding her newfound status as an untheatrical, disciplined, interiorized—in short, "good"—Eliot heroine. George Eliot, "Armgart," in idem, *The Complete Shorter Poetry of George Eliot*, ed. Antonie Gerard van den Broek, vol. 1 (London: Pickering and Chatto, 2008), ll. 53, 872–873. On Eliot's career-long preoccupation with the performing female body, see Rosemarie Bodenheimer, *The Real Life of Mary Ann Evans: George Eliot, Her Letters and Fiction* (Ithaca, NY: Cornell University Press, 1994), 161–188.

11. Isobel Armstrong, *Victorian Poetry: Poetry, Poetics, and Politics* (London: Routledge, 1993), 361; Herbert F. Tucker, *Epic: Britain's Heroic Muse, 1790–1910* (Oxford: Oxford University Press, 2008), 425. See also Deborah Epstein Nord, *Gypsies and the British Imagination, 1807–1930* (New York: Columbia University Press, 2006), 99–124, Alicia Carroll, *Dark Smiles: Race and Desire in George Eliot* (Athens: Ohio University Press, 2003), 51–60, and Bernard Semmel, *George Eliot and the Politics of National Inheritance* (New York: Oxford University Press, 1994), 103–132.

12. Lewes wrote in July 1873 that he and Eliot had discussed "novel and play Deronda." Quoted in Haight, *George Eliot*, 471–472.

13. George Eliot, *Romola* (1862–63; reprint, London: Penguin, 1996), 86.

14. I take the notion of a "staring contest" from D. A. Miller's analysis of Hitchcock's 1937 *Young and Innocent*. As in the film, where the camera's unflinching gaze appears to provoke the blink that signals the guilt of a murderer, Eliot's steady narrative attention simply seems to wear down Tito's resistance. See D. A. Miller, "Anal Rope," in Diana Fuss, ed., *Inside/Out: Lesbian Theories, Gay Theories* (New York: Routledge, 1991), 132–133.

15. See Pam Morris, *Imagining Inclusive Society in Nineteenth-Century Novels: The Code of Sincerity in the Public Sphere* (Baltimore: Johns Hopkins University Press, 2004), 180; Alexander Welsh, *George Eliot and Blackmail* (Cambridge, MA: Harvard University Press, 1985), 342; and Philip Fisher, *Making Up Society: The Novels of George Eliot* (Pittsburgh: University of Pittsburgh Press, 1981), 131.

16. For one of Eliot's first readers, the extremity of Tito's internal self-difference increases his plausibility: Henry James wrote in 1866 that "in the career of Tito Melema there is a fuller representation of the development of character" than anywhere

else in Eliot's fiction. Henry James, "The Novels of George Eliot," in idem, *Literary Criticism: Essays on Literature, American Writers, English Writers* (New York: Library of America, 1984), 931.

17. Neil Hertz reads the juxtaposition of these deaths as a comment on the equivocal nature of "confession" under conditions of uncertain agency. Neil Hertz, *George Eliot's Pulse* (Stanford: Stanford University Press, 2003), 147–150.

18. David Carroll argues (a propos Savonarola's punishment) that "martyrdom ultimately becomes another term for the human condition in the sombre world of George Eliot's fiction." But Savonarola only stands for a general humanity insofar as we understand human existence to correspond to the novelistically observable life. The case is strong for seeing Savonarola as a martyr to the novel as a form. See David Carroll, "George Eliot, Martyrologist: The Case of Savonarola," in Caroline Levine and Mark W. Turner, eds., *From Author to Text: Re-Reading George Eliot's Romola* (Aldershot: Ashgate, 1998), 119.

19. Lewes does not say if these topics are connected—whether, that is, they discussed the representation of psychological problems in her new novel (there are many) or if their conversation touched on her creative work and his research into psychology.

20. George Eliot, *Felix Holt, the Radical* (1866; reprint, London: Penguin, 1995), 19, 23.

21. "E. S. Dallas, review, *The Times*, June 1866," in Carroll, *George Eliot: The Critical Heritage*, 269.

22. Franklin, *Serious Play*, 102.

23. "Romantic and perfunctory": Carroll, *George Eliot*, 333; "political crudeness": Sally Shuttleworth, *George Eliot and Nineteenth-Century Science: The Make-Believe of a Beginning* (Cambridge: Cambridge University Press, 1984), 142; "petty cynicism": Raymond Williams, *Culture and Society: 1780–1950* (1958; reprint, New York: Columbia University Press, 1983), 107; "no more absurd moment exists in all of Eliot's novels": Fisher, *Making Up Society*, 153.

24. George Eliot, *The Spanish Gypsy*, ed. Antonie Gerard van den Broek (London: Pickering and Chatto, 2008), Book I, ll. 1095, 1110–1111. Subsequent citations are given parenthetically with book and line number; citations to stage directions are abbreviated s.d. and cited by page number.

25. Ziter, *The Orient on the Victorian Stage*, 3.

26. Even Adam Bede's Dinah Morris—the only other of Eliot's "good" heroines to be introduced to the reader at a public gathering—is fated by the novel to give up her preacherly vocation. And the effectiveness of Dinah's antiperformative performance is felt most strongly by Bessy, the girl who, listening to Dinah's lecture on modesty, feels "very much as if the constable had come to take her up and carry her before the justice for some undefined offence." See Eliot, *Adam Bede* (1859; reprint, London: Penguin, 2008), 34 (hereafter *AB*).

27. As noted by Lou Charnon-Deutsch in *The Spanish Gypsy: The History of a European Obsession* (University Park: Pennsylvania State University Press, 2004), 115.

28. George Henry Lewes, *The Spanish Drama: Lope De Vega and Calderon* (London: Charles Knight, 1846), 106. See also Lewes's 1875 essay on "The Spanish Theater," which refers to the "invariable dance, 'bayle nacional,' which the Spaniards

seem to consider as necessary a part of the entertainment as a 'comic song' used to be (happily used to be) with us." Lewes, *On Actors and the Art of Acting*, 243.

29. On the heightened character effects achieved by free indirect style, see Michael McKeon, "Subjectivity, Character, Development," in idem, ed., *Theory of the Novel: A Historical Approach* (Baltimore: Johns Hopkins University Press, 2000), 485. On Eliot's free indirect discourse as a privatizing phenomenon, see Kucich, *Repression in Victorian Fiction*, 138. In an essay that has been crucial to my thinking about this issue in Eliot, Carolyn Williams argues that "what seems distinctive about [Eliot's] use of the melodramatic tableau is its capacity to turn both inward and outward—a visual, temporal, and rhythmic dynamic suggestively homologous with the function of free indirect discourse in novelistic narration." Williams connects Eliot's use of the tableau in her fiction to her enthusiasm for melodramas like Leopold Lewis's *The Bells* (1871), and argues that *Daniel Deronda*'s "novelistic imitation of the melodramatic tableau becomes fully significant only within an understanding that . . . these two quintessentially modern, bourgeois genres might be seen, in this respect, to be working on the same set of problems." My reading suggests that in turning her would-be theatrical tableau in *The Spanish Gypsy* into a narrated scene in free indirect discourse, Eliot had already intuited the homology between the two formal devices in her own generically ambiguous work of the 1860s. See Carolyn Williams, "Moving Pictures: George Eliot and Melodrama," in Lauren Berlant, ed., *Compassion: The Culture and Politics of an Emotion* (New York: Routledge, 2004), 106, 136.

30. To align the Brechtian Verfremdungseffekt with the theater's resistance to psychic rationalization is in a sense to hijack Brechtian theory, which understands itself as "epic" while disparaging the mystifications of the "dramatic." But Brecht's claim to have overthrown theatrical convention misrepresents the extent to which his innovations derive from nineteenth-century stage practice. The melodramatic tableau—much like the Brechtian gestus—freezes characters in socially significant arrangements and demands critical interpretation on the part of the audience. See Bertolt Brecht, "The Modern Theatre Is the Epic Theatre," in idem, *Brecht on Theatre: The Development of an Aesthetic*, trans. John Willett (New York: Hill and Wang, 1964).

31. William Dean Howells, "*The Spanish Gypsy*," in Stuart Hutchinson, ed., *George Eliot: Critical Assessments*, vol. 1 (Robertsbridge: Helm Information, 1996), 258; Sylvia Kasey Marks, "A Brief Glance at George Eliot's *The Spanish Gypsy*," Victorian Poetry 21.2 (1983): 186.

32. On the "creaturely" as "life captured at the (ever shifting and mutating) threshold of the juridicopolitical order," see Eric L. Santner, *On Creaturely Life: Rilke, Benjamin, Sebald* (Chicago: University of Chicago Press, 2006), 86.

33. "Man and citizen are political subjects and as such are not definite collectivities but surplus names that set out a question or a dispute (*litige*) about who is included in their count . . . Political predicates are open predicates: they open up a dispute about what they entail, whom they concern and in which cases": Rancière's words confirm that Eliot's theatrical typography is the formal sign of her attempt to think the scope of the political community. See Jacques Rancière, *Dissensus*, trans. Steven Corcoran (London: Continuum, 2010), 68.

34. James Buzard, *Disorienting Fiction: The Autoethnographic Work of Nineteenth-Century British Novels* (Princeton, NJ: Princeton University Press, 2005), 283.

35. The portrayal of Annibal may also have been indebted to Eliot's absorption of Darwin's theories, which as Gillian Beer has argued performed "the leveling of man with other species" without understanding this as a "punitive enterprise." Beer, *Darwin's Plots*, 61.

36. My thinking throughout this section has been influenced by Alex Woloch's analysis of the novel's "character-system" as a site of struggle between the claims of individual subjectivity and narrative structure. Theater's defining collectivity may lend it an ethical valence less structured by the economy of scarcity Woloch finds at the heart of narrative forms. See Alex Woloch, *The One vs. The Many: Minor Characters and the Space of the Protagonist in the Novel* (Princeton, NJ: Princeton University Press, 2003), esp. 1–42.

37. Bruce Robbins, *The Servant's Hand: English Fiction from Below* (1986. 2nd ed., Durham, NC: Duke University Press, 1993), 28–29.

38. See Martin Esslin, *The Field of Drama: How the Signs of Drama Create Meaning on Stage and Screen* (New York: Methuen, 1987).

39. Hutchinson, *George Eliot: Critical Assessments*, 1:244–245.

40. Jacques Rancière, *The Philosopher and His Poor*, trans. John Drury, Corinne Oster, and Andrew Parker (Durham, NC: Duke University Press, 2003), 226.

41. Armstrong, *Victorian Poetry*, 3.

42. In a November 1867 letter to Frederic Harrison, Eliot defines "the word 'culture' as a verbal equivalent for the highest mental result of past and present influences" (*L*, 395): she is practically quoting Arnold's definition of culture as "the best that has been thought and said in the world." Matthew Arnold, *Culture and Anarchy* (1869; reprint, New Haven, CT: Yale University Press, 1994), 5. On the connections between *Felix Holt* and Arnold's writings of the 1860s, see Gallagher, *The Industrial Reformation of English Fiction*, 230–236; and Morris, *Imagining Inclusive Society*, 183–184.

43. Arnold, *Culture and Anarchy*, 44, 32. That such "action" was not to involve working-class political assembly is made clear in Arnold's contention that "monster processions in the streets and forcible irruptions into the parks, even in professed support of this good design, ought to be unflinchingly forbidden and repressed" (135).

44. See Tucker, *Epic*, 425; and Nord, *Gypsies and the British Imagination*, 122.

45. J. W. Cross, *George Eliot's Life as Related in Her Letters and Journals*, 2:42–43.

46. George Eliot, *Middlemarch: A Study of Provincial Life* (1871–72; reprint, London: Penguin, 2003), 95.

47. George Levine, introduction to idem, ed., *The Cambridge Companion to George Eliot* (Cambridge: Cambridge University Press, 2001), 11.

48. See the searchable full-text version at http://www.princeton.edu/~batke/eliot/middle/. "Fate"/"fates" and "destiny"/"destinies" each occur five times.

49. Once, in one of Eliot's self-authored epigraphs, the word denotes the contingency of gambling: "Oh, sir, the loftiest hopes on earth / Draw lots with meaner hopes" (177).

50. Fredric Jameson, "The Experiments of Time: Providence and Realism," in Franco Moretti, ed., *The Novel*, vol. 2 (Princeton, NJ: Princeton University Press, 2006), 122.

51. John Plotz limns the complexities in such novelistic incorporations of the crowd in his reading of Brontë's *Shirley*, which he describes as "an open-eyed reckoning of the cost and consequences of choosing privacy over the public world." Much less explicit than Brontë's novel about the collective's relation to interiority, *Middlemarch* nonetheless performs such a reckoning imagistically and semantically. See John Plotz, *The Crowd: British Literature and Public Politics* (Berkeley: University of California Press, 2000), 184.

52. On the similarities and crucial differences between these plots, see Nord, *Gypsies and the British Imagination*, 100–101, 122.

53. See Litvak, *Caught in the Act*, 147–194. Catherine Gallagher identifies the actress and the prostitute as two figures Eliot invokes to manage her anxieties about female authorship in "George Eliot and *Daniel Deronda*: The Prostitute and the Jewish Question," in Ruth Bernard Yeazell, ed., *Sex, Politics, and Science in the Nineteenth-Century Novel: Selected Papers from the English Institute, 1983–84* (Baltimore: Johns Hopkins University Press, 1986): 39–62.

54. George Eliot, *Daniel Deronda* (1876; reprint, London: Penguin, 1995), 3.

55. On the scene's theatricality, see David Marshall, *The Figure of Theater: Shaftesbury, Defoe, Adam Smith, and George Eliot* (New York: Columbia University Press, 1986), 207; Litvak, *Caught in the Act*, 164–166; and Audrey Jaffe, *Scenes of Sympathy: Identity and Representation in Victorian Fiction* (Ithaca, NY: Cornell University Press, 2000), 146–147.

56. "Who—or what—speaks these questions?" asks Andrew Miller. He reads the lines' unlocatability as a meditation on free indirect discourse as a strategy that "intensifies the conditions of mutuality and separateness." See Andrew H. Miller, *The Burdens of Perfection: On Ethics and Reading in Nineteenth-Century British Literature* (Ithaca, NY: Cornell University Press, 2008), 90–91.

57. Amanda Anderson, *The Powers of Distance: Cosmopolitanism and the Cultivation of Detachment* (Princeton, NJ: Princeton University Press, 2001), 119.

58. See Aamir Mufti, *Enlightenment in the Colony: The Jewish Question and the Crisis of Postcolonial Culture* (Princeton, NJ: Princeton University Press, 2007), 95–96.

59. Nicholas Dames notes that Eliot deleted this detail in the Cabinet edition of the novel, apparently in response to reviews (such as Henry James's) pointing out the repetition of the coat-collar pulling. Nicholas Dames, *The Physiology of the Novel: Reading, Neural Science, and the Form of Victorian Fiction* (New York: Oxford University Press, 2007), 154.

60. On Mirah's theatrical stylizations of her antitheatricality, see Lynn M. Voskuil, *Acting Naturally: Victorian Theatricality and Authenticity* (Charlottesville: University of Virginia Press, 2004), 117–127.

61. Fredric Jameson, *Brecht and Method* (London: Verso, 1998), 11.

62. Deborah Vlock, *Dickens, Novel Reading, and the Victorian Popular Theatre* (Cambridge: Cambridge University Press, 1998), 37.

63. The obvious exceptions are Julius Klesmer and Catherine Arrowpoint, whose marriage defies the ethnic boundary marking otherwise prominent in the text. James Buzard therefore claims Catherine as the "true heroine" of the novel, and writes that "readers today may be forgiven for wishing to seize upon the minor interruption

in the workings of Eliot's narrative engine" supplied by Catherine's refusal to give up her Jewish lover. But Deronda offers more than this "minor" consolation to the multiethnic imagination—on the condition that we not try to extract a political or ethical vision from one of its characters and focus instead on the ethnically heterogeneous "show" it calls into imaginative being. See Buzard, *Disorienting Fiction*, 298.

CHAPTER THREE Henry James's Awkward Stage

1. Henry James, *A Small Boy and Others* (1913; reprint, London: Gibson Square, 2001), 1.

2. On the radicalism of James's conception of the self in *A Small Boy and Others*, see Ross Posnock, *The Trial of Curiosity: Henry James, William James, and the Challenge of Modernity* (New York: Oxford University Press), 167–192.

3. For readings of, respectively, the scene with Marie and that at the Louvre as primal episodes of queer self-understanding, see Joseph Litvak, *Caught in the Act: Theatricality in the Nineteenth-Century English Novel* (Berkeley: University of California Press, 1992), 210–219, and Michael Moon, *A Small Boy and Others: Imitation and Initiation in American Culture from Henry James to Andy Warhol* (Durham, NC: Duke University Press, 1998), 31–65. My reading questions the logic that would select any one scene as primal.

4. David Wiles, *A Short History of Western Performance Space* (Cambridge: Cambridge University Press, 2003), 11.

5. Describing a strikingly similar scene, Roland Barthes makes explicit the relation of sociality to the derangement of syntax: "One evening, half asleep on a banquette in a bar, just for fun I tried to enumerate all the languages within earshot . . . I myself was a public square, a sook; through me passed words, tiny syntagms, bits of formulae, and no sentence formed, as though that were the law of such a language . . . Then, potentially, all linguistics fell, linguistics which believes only in the sentence and has always attributed an exorbitant dignity to predicative syntax." Roland Barthes, *The Pleasure of the Text*, trans. Richard Miller (New York: Hill and Wang, 1975), 49.

6. On the shared metaphorics of drama and consciousness in the writings of the James siblings, see Frances Wilson, "The James Family Theatricals: Behind the Scenes," in Jonathan Freedman, ed., *The Cambridge Companion to Henry James* (New York: Cambridge University Press, 1998), 40–62.

7. On this point, see Anne T. Margolis, *Henry James and the Problem of Audience: An International Act* (Ann Arbor, MI: UMI, 1985), 57.

8. Dorothy Hale critiques James's conception of the social as "minimalist"—defined by the interaction between human subjects rather than encompassing the "beliefs, values, and behaviors that belong to a group of characters." She claims further that Jamesian novel theory encourages a mystified view of the social, in which reading a novel takes the place of engaging with human subjects. I understand James as less complacent about the novel's self-sufficiency, and thus about its ability to stand in for social interaction. And, as we will see, the "beliefs, values and behaviors that belong to a group of characters" are exactly James's preoccupation in *The Awkward*

Age. See Dorothy J. Hale, *Social Formalism: The Novel in Theory from Henry James to the Present* (Stanford: Stanford University Press, 1998), 8, 14.

9. Eve Kosofsky Sedgwick was among the first to recognize James's wrestling with the late-nineteenth-century moment of sexual definition, in *Epistemology of the Closet* (Berkeley: University of California Press, 1990), 182–212. Crucial work on James and sexuality includes Hugh Stevens, *Henry James and Sexuality* (Cambridge: Cambridge University Press, 1998); Eric Haralson, *Henry James and Queer Modernity* (Cambridge: Cambridge University Press, 2003); and Kevin Ohi, *Henry James and the Queerness of Style* (Minneapolis: University of Minnesota Press, 2011). See also Litvak, *Caught in the Act*; and Moon, *A Small Boy and Others.*

10. Paul Morrison, *The Explanation for Everything: Essays on Sexual Subjectivity* (New York: New York University Press, 2001), 36.

11. For accounts of the post-theatrical period that narrate James's embrace of the novel, see Sergio Perosa, *Henry James and the Experimental Novel* (Charlottesville: University Press of Virginia, 1978); Joseph Wiesenfarth, *Henry James and the Dramatic Analogy: A Study of the Major Novels of the Middle Period* (New York: Fordham University Press, 1963); and Walter Isle, *Experiments in Form: Henry James's Novels, 1896–1901* (Cambridge, MA: Harvard University Press, 1968).

12. Leon Edel, *Henry James, The Treacherous Years: 1895–1901* (1969; reprint, New York: Avon, 1978), 261.

13. Henry James, *The Art of the Novel: Critical Prefaces*, ed. R. P. Blackmur (1934; reprint, New York: Scribner, 1962), 106 (hereafter *AN*). The young Alice B. Toklas reportedly thought that *The Awkward Age* "would make a very remarkable play and I wrote to Henry James suggesting that I dramatise it." Gertrude Stein, *The Autobiography of Alice B. Toklas* (New York, Vintage, 1933), 4. James's decision to write novels that resembled plays was a more radical solution to his theatrical preoccupation than the one he had found in *The Tragic Muse* (1889–90), which ranges a series of focalizing characters around an actress who alone remains inaccessible to narrative penetration; where the novels we will consider find ways to distribute the theatrical modality's psychic agnosticism among the cast of characters, *The Tragic Muse*'s thematic approach reads as a more conventional treatment of theater as the novel's alluring other.

14. Michel Foucault, *The History of Sexuality*, trans. Robert Hurley, vol. 1 (1978; reprint, New York: Vintage, 1990), 42.

15. On de-psychologization in James, see Leo Bersani, "The Jamesian Lie," in *A Future for Astyanax: Character and Desire in Literature*, new ed. (New York: Columbia University Press, 1984); and Sharon Cameron, *Thinking in Henry James* (Chicago: University of Chicago Press, 1989). I am indebted in particular to Bersani's reading of Jamesian sociability as a "struggle against a crippling notion of truth," and to his emphasis on Jamesian "talk" as the strategy of a performative conception of the self (130). Hugh Stevens has more recently read Jamesian ambivalence about psychological legibility as a space-making strategy for non-normative sexual expression; see Stevens, *Henry James and Sexuality*, 1–19, 117–144.

16. Henry James, *The Notebooks of Henry James*, ed. F. O. Matthiessen and Kenneth B. Murdock (New York: Brazilller, 1955), 348 (hereafter *N*); Henry James, *Selected Letters of Henry James to Edmund Gosse, 1882–1915: A Literary Friendship*, ed. Rayburn S. Moore (Baton Rouge: Louisiana State University Press, 1988), 149.

17. Henry James, *The Scenic Art: Notes on Acting and the Drama: 1872–1901*, ed. Allan Wade (New Brunswick, NJ: Rutgers University Press, 1948), 3.

18. On James's late-century preoccupation with Ibsen, see Michael Egan, *Henry James: The Ibsen Years* (London: Vision, 1972).

19. Elin Diamond, *Unmaking Mimesis: Essays on Feminism and Theater* (London: Routledge, 1997), 26.

20. F. W. Dupee, *Henry James* (New York: Sloane, 1951), 196; Tzetan Todorov, "The Verbal Age," *Critical Inquiry* 4.2 (1977): 365.

21. A partial list would include the dialogue-heavy novels of Henry Green, Ivy Compton-Burnett, Ronald Firbank, and, improbably, Ernest Hemingway. On Hemingway's admiration for James (he once referred to *The Awkward Age* as "the shit") and his later disavowal of that admiration (he also called James's writing just "shit"), see Haralson, *Henry James and Queer Modernity*, 190, 173. An important extraliterary descendant of this period in James's work is Jacques Rivette's film *Céline et Julie vont en bateau* (1974). Partially based on *The Other House*, the film turns James's meditation on the novel and theater into an allegory of theater's relation to film.

22. Henry James, *Letters*, ed. Leon Edel, 4 vols. (Cambridge, MA: Harvard University Press, 1974–84), 4:82.

23. Three years after transforming *The Other House* back into the play he had always felt it (also) was, James used the titular phrase to describe just this kind of domestic alterity. *A Small Boy and Others* refers to the New York home of James's cousin Albert as "the other house, the house we most haunted after our own" (63). This house, described as "our alternative domestic field" and inhabited by the James's glamorously orphaned relative, "spoke to me of a wild freedom"; it provokes James's assertion that the unparented state entailed "an air of possibilities that were none the less vivid for being quite indefinite" (63–64).

24. Henry James, *The Other House* (1896; reprint, New York: New York Review of Books, 1999), 5–6.

25. Priscilla Walton, "'The Tie of a Common Aversion': Sexual Tensions in Henry James's *The Other House*," *The Henry James Review* 17.1 (1996): 13.

26. As a *Saturday Review* notice put it, "When [James] is not putting dialogue into the mouths of these characters, he is engaged almost wholly in providing that necessary description of their movements, their smiles and sighs and general stage-business, which in the theatre the spectator would see with his own eyes." See Kevin J. Hayes, ed., *Henry James: The Contemporary Reviews* (Cambridge: Cambridge University Press, 1996), 250.

27. The classic account of fictional temporalities is Gérard Genette's *Narrative Discourse: An Essay in Method*, trans. Jane E. Lewin (Ithaca, NY: Cornell University Press, 1980), 212–262. Although *The Other House* is largely narrated in some form of the past tense, the insistence of the "would have" construction strains the coherence of what Genette terms "subsequent narrating" (220).

28. Henry James, "Note" to *Theatricals: Two Comedies*, in idem, *The Complete Plays of Henry James*, ed. Leon Edel (London: Hart-Davis, 1949), 255.

29. "Beaver," in Jonathan Green, *The Cassell Dictionary of Slang* (London: Cassell, 1998), 72.

30. On the fin-de-siècle's "often contradictory explanations of inversion and homosexuality," see George Chauncey, "From Sexual Inversion to Homosexuality:

Medicine and the Changing Conceptualization of Female Deviance," *Salmagundi* 58–59 (1982–83): 129.

31. Foucault, *The History of Sexuality*, 48.

32. Henry James, *The Other House*, in idem, *The Complete Plays of Henry James*, ed. Leon Edel (London: Hart-Davis, 1949), 701. (Note that Act First does not open the play itself, which begins with a prologue corresponding to the first book of the novel. Act First corresponds to the novel's second book.)

33. Bert States notes that "the difference between theater's causal flow and the novel's is primarily one of the range and mobility of the narrative eye." Bert O. States, *Great Reckonings in Little Rooms: On the Phenomenology of Theater* (Berkeley: University of California Press, 1985), 135.

34. Williams, *Drama from Ibsen to Brecht* (1952; reprint, New York: Oxford University Press, 1969), 246.

35. Diamond, *Unmaking Mimesis*, 32–34. Diamond's discussion occurs in the context of an analysis of Elizabeth Robins and Florence Bell's 1893 play *Alan's Wife*. Robins, a friend of James who performed as Mme de Cintré in the 1890 adaptation of *The American*, made her name in fin-de-siècle London playing Ibsen's neurotic heroines. Given their intimacy and James's interest in Ibsen at the time he conceived of *The Other House*, it is likely that James had Robins in mind as a model for the Ibsenesque Rose Armiger. James penned his notebook entries on *The Other House* a few months after *Alan's Wife* had its short run (in May 1893); he may have been specifically influenced by Bell and Robins's play, which features an infanticidal woman and, as Diamond demonstrates, uses stage directions to disrupt the naturalist insistence on interior truth. On Robins's friendship with James, see Elizabeth Robins, *Theatre and Friendship: Some Henry James Letters* (New York: Putnam's, 1932).

36. The drama of Mrs. Beever's spectacularization, which preoccupies the 1896 novel, becomes irrelevant once *The Other House* has been translated into the dramatic medium; nor is Mrs. Beever spared the effects of the text's second-order performativity: she, too, speaks "as if" (see, in the play's prologue alone, 684, 685, and 687).

37. D. A. Miller, *The Novel and the Police* (Berkeley: University of California Press, 1988), 213.

38. Alan Ackerman notes that James's work of the 1890s is "filled with references to an imagined, extradiegetic audience." The present instance is unusual in that this extradiegetic awareness is imputed to a character within the diegesis. Alan L. Ackerman, Jr., *The Portable Theater: American Literature and the Nineteenth-Century Stage* (Baltimore: Johns Hopkins University Press, 1997), 212.

39. Henry James, *The American Scene* (1907; reprint, New York: Penguin, 1994), 148.

40. Henry James, *The Awkward Age* (1899; reprint, New York: Penguin, 1987), 84, 50.

41. Roger Gard, ed., *Henry James: The Critical Heritage* (London: Routledge and Kegan Paul, 1968), 282; Hayes, *Henry James: The Contemporary Reviews*, 328–329.

42. Maxwell Geismar, *Henry James and the Jacobites* (Boston: Houghton Mifflin, 1963), 175; Edmund Wilson, "The Ambiguity of Henry James," in F. W. Dupee, ed., *The Question of Henry James: A Collection of Critical Essays* (London: Wingate, 1947), 192.

43. Percy Lubbock, *The Craft of Fiction* (1921; reprint, New York: Viking, 1957), 178, 182.

44. Elaine Scarry, *Dreaming by the Book* (New York: Farrar, Straus, Giroux, 1999), 4.

45. Erika Fischer-Lichte, *The Show and the Gaze of Theatre: A European Perspective*, trans. Jo Riley (Iowa City: University of Iowa Press, 1997), 296.

46. See Elizabeth Stevenson, *Henry James: The Crooked Corridor* (1949; reprint, New Brunswick, NJ: Transaction, 2000), 150; and Isle, *Experiments in Form*, 168.

47. For an argument connecting *The Awkward Age*'s anti-identitarianism to "the backhanded sway of an anal erotics," see Michael Trask, "Getting into It with James: Substitution and Erotic Reversal in *The Awkward Age*," *American Literature* 69.1 (1997): 110.

48. Jonathan Freedman argues that James's late-career project is to bring "under firm control the uneasy and often uncanny play with contradictory possibilities [including sexual and identitarian ones] that marks the British aesthetic movement." In its sexual permissiveness and generic contrarianism *The Awkward Age* sits uneasily in Freedman's domesticating trajectory. Jonathan Freedman, *Professions of Taste: Henry James, British Aestheticism, and Commodity Culture* (Stanford: Stanford University Press, 1990), 132.

49. Todorov, "The Verbal Age," 371.

50. Foucault, *The History of Sexuality*, 36. In his preface to the novel, James referred to this failed group effort as a source of the novel's pathos: "The circle surrounding Mrs. Brookenham, in my pages, is of course nothing if not a particular, even a 'peculiar' one—and its rather vain effort (the vanity, the real inexpertness, being precisely part of my tale) is toward the courage of that condition" (*AN*, 105).

51. On the influence of the trials on the novel, see Paula V. Smith, "A Wilde Subtext for *The Awkward Age*," *The Henry James Review* 9.3 (1988): 199–208.

52. It is perhaps significant that *The Awkward Age* was the first novel James composed entirely via dictation; Sharon Cameron analyzes this practice as "call[ing] into question in a perfectly mundane way the site or location of consciousness" via the externalization it introduces into composition. See Cameron, *Thinking in Henry James*, 32.

53. On this point, see Dupee, *Henry James*, 197.

54. Paul Morrison, *The Explanation for Everything: Essays on Sexual Subjectivity* (New York: New York University Press, 2001), 31, 19.

55. In this she echoes the grammatical strategy of Daniel Deronda's mother, whose antinovelistic performance I discussed in chapter 2.

56. Eve Kosofsky Sedgwick, *Touching Feeling: Affect, Pedagogy, Performativity* (Durham, NC: Duke University Press, 2003), 67–91; on disinterpellation, see 70.

57. That James is invoking Milton's version of the Samson story in connection with *The Awkward Age*'s generic status is suggested also by the echo of the poem's final line (" . . . And calm of mind all passion spent") that he uses to describe Rose Armiger in the novel version of *The Other House*: "She had sunk into a seat at a distance from him, all spent with her great response to her sudden opportunity for justice" (214). See John Milton, *The Complete Poems* (Harmondsworth, Penguin, 1998), 511.

58. Sheila Teahan, *The Rhetorical Logic of Henry James* (Baton Rouge: Louisiana State University Press, 1995), 156.

59. Wiles, *A Short History of Western Performance Space*, 152. James derided the British theatrical public as "well dressed, tranquil, motionless; it suggests domestic virtue and comfortable homes; it looks as if it had come to the play in its own carriage, after a dinner of beef and pudding." James, *The Scenic Art*, 101.

60. He thus engages in an inept version of what Bruce Robbins identifies as the servant's "complicity with the house," her "reaching out for the old participatory public" from within the confines of the novel. See Bruce Robbins, *The Servant's Hand: English Fiction from Below*, 2nd ed. (Durham, NC: Duke University Press, 1993), 58.

61. James's theatrical criticism makes frequent use of the mirror as mimesis's central figure. See James, *The Scenic Art*, 22, 93.

62. On the gradual triumph of the proscenium arch, see Simon Trussler, *The Cambridge Illustrated History of British Theatre* (Cambridge: Cambridge University Press, 1994), 218–222; and Iain Mackintosh, *Architecture, Actor and Audience* (New York: Routledge, 1993), 26–40.

63. Is it coincidence that James's wording here echoes that of Thackeray's Batchelor, who boasts of his privileged access to the "queer little drama . . . unfolding itself" for his observation at the Lovel household? See *Lovel the Widower*, in *The Works of William Makepeace Thackeray*, vol. 28 (New York: Scribner, 1903–4), 271, and the discussion of the passage in chapter 1.

64. See Peter Brooks, *The Melodramatic Imagination: Balzac, Henry James, Melodrama, and the Mode of Excess* (1976; reprint, New Haven, CT: Yale University Press, 1995), 153–197.

65. Cited in Robert Pippin, *Henry James and Modern Moral Life* (Cambridge: Cambridge University Press, 2001), 17.

66. In *The Ambassadors*, Chad Newsome's caddishness does not preclude the sense that his dalliance with Mme de Vionnet may have been initiated in good faith, and, in *The Golden Bowl*, Charlotte and Amerigo's decision to marry a father-daughter duo to financially enhance their own liaison is matched in ethical dubiousness by the self-absorption of that father and daughter.

67. Alan Hollinghurst, *The Line of Beauty* (London: Picador, 2004), 140.

68. Robert Pippin reads James's work as asking what constitutes morality in a world that has lost the institutional structures that facilitate ethical decision making. Pippin opens and closes his study with analyses of *The Wings of the Dove*; it is my sense that he does so because of the moral clarity offered by its plot. Pippin reads James primarily as a teller of exemplary *stories*: he translates the text of *The Wings of the Dove* into a parable ("A remarkably intelligent woman of little means is in love with a talented man of equally few prospects . . . They meet a dying, very young American heiress . . .") because the ethical valence of the novel has, for Pippin, everything to do with what happens to its characters. His conclusion that Kate and Densher's plan fails to take Milly into account as an ethical agent seems as undeniable as it is incomplete. Faced with Pippin's plot synopsis, one wants to respond, "Well, if you put it *that* way . . ." But James never does put it that way, and that difference—the difference of Jamesian style—harbors a collectivist imagination only tangentially related to the differentiating moralism of his plots. An interest in style could add a

dimension to precisely the ethical questions Pippin illuminates in James's work; his argument that "such freedom as is possible in modernity cannot be achieved alone," for example, is supported by the shared nature of Jamesian style. See Pippin, *Henry James and Modern Moral Life*, 1, 176. On style's ethical and political significance, see Leo Bersani and Ulysse Dutoit, *Forms of Being: Cinema, Aesthetics, Subjectivity* (London: BFI, 2004); D. A. Miller, *Jane Austen, or the Secret of Style* (Princeton, NJ: Princeton University Press, 2003); and Ohi, *Henry James and the Queerness of Style*.

69. Not at first glance a terribly broad landscape in class terms, of course. "For the most part an ethical literature has come to reflect the closure of class," Fredric Jameson writes, "whether it is that of Jamesian aristocrats or Bunyan's tinkers. Ethical maxims and categories only work within a situation of homogeneous class belonging." But the situation is more complex: the cast of *The Wings of the Dove* includes an heiress but also professionals (Densher is a journalist, Susan Stringham writes fiction for magazines) and petty bourgeois (Kate's sister, the parson's widow Mrs. Condrip, and potentially Kate herself); the impression of "aristocracy" derives from the stylistic intelligence these characters uniformly display. Indeed, the story is explicitly that of a penniless character attempting to convert cultural or stylistic capital into financial security. See Fredric Jameson, "The Experiments of Time: Providence and Realism," in Franco Moretti, ed., *The Novel*, vol. 2 (Princeton, NJ: Princeton University Press, 2006), 110.

70. Charles Lamb, "Stage Illusion," in idem, *The Essays of Elia* (London: Walter Scott), 289.

71. But see Eve Sedgwick's claim that the namelessness of Croy's crime indexes male homosexuality. As we will see, James's invocation of a theatrical metaphor in describing Croy's character ontology relocates him from the margins of the text to its symbolic center; one result of the performative universalism of *The Wings* is thus the deterritorialization of the queerness narratively secreted in Croy's person. Eve Kosofsky Sedgwick, *Tendencies* (Durham, NC: Duke University Press, 1993), 73–103.

72. That James's title derives from Psalms 55:6 ("Oh that I had the wings of the dove") does not invalidate the point: since Kate initially mentions doves but not wings, the effect of James's title is to suggest not that Kate is citing scripture but, more strangely, that her author is performing a scriptural riff on *her*.

73. Stanley Cavell, *Cities of Words: Pedagogical Letters on a Register of the Moral Life* (Cambridge, MA: Harvard University Press, 2004), 41.

74. Kate and Milly's friendship was the most drastic alteration James made to the plot from his initial notebook record of the novel's germ. The notebooks insist that the two central women of his story *"must not love each other"* (*N*, 172); but Kate and Milly's mutual love becomes the central fascination of the novel. Sianne Ngai's claim that antagonism between women may be a way "to critically negotiate rather than simply disavow or repudiate" the desire for female collectivity is suggestive for *The Wings of the Dove*, where female envy seems both indistinguishable from erotic fixation and an incipient form of alliance. See Sianne Ngai, *Ugly Feelings* (Cambridge, MA: Harvard University Press, 2005), 163.

75. In his crucial essay on "The Performing Self," Richard Poirier interprets what I am calling the unifying effects of Jamesian style as an expression of authorial self-enhancement; Poirier frankly reads Jamesian extravagance as a form of "imperialism" over the real, supporting the claim with reference to James's deathbed identification

with Napoleon Bonaparte. There is obviously much to be said about the cohabitation in aesthetic practice of dreams of world domination with images of utopian
possibility. We might provisionally note that in dictating letters specifying renova-
tions to the Tuileries and the Louvre, James may be understood as disarmingly clear-
sighted—even from within his delirium—about the power fantasies fueling any
artistic career. And it is intriguing that even this overweening fantasy contains an
image of redistribution: James's Napoleon letters appear to have been addressed to
his siblings William and Alice, and to invite them to share the bounty of "our young
but so highly considered Republic at one of the most interesting of minor capitals"—
the last phrase serving as a strikingly modest description of the position James's work
occupies in what Pascale Casanova calls the World Republic of Letters. See Richard
Poirier, *The Performing Self: Compositions and Decompositions in the Languages of
Contemporary Life* (1992, reprint; New Brunswick, NJ: Rutgers University Press,
1971), 110; Pascale Casanova, *The World Republic of Letters* (Cambridge, MA:
Harvard University Press, 2007). For the text of James's deathbed letters, see Leon
Edel, *Henry James, The Master: 1901–1916* (1972, reprint; New York: Avon Books,
1978), 552–553.

76. "Nothing was stranger than such a difference in their view of it" (455); "It
made him also think, but with a difference" (456); "He was conscious enough, in
preparing again to seek her out, of a difference on that score" (474); "But she differed
with you?" "She differed with me. And when Kate differs with you—!" (479); "The
difference was that the dusk of the afternoon—dusk thick from an early hour—had
gathered" (481); "They asserted their differences without tact and without taste"
(482); "Yet all the while too the tension had its charm—such being the interest of a
creature who could bring one back to her by such different roads. It was her talent for
life again; which found in her a difference for the differing time" (501).

CHAPTER FOUR Joyce Unperformed

1. James Joyce, *Stephen Hero* (New York: New Directions, 1944), 211–213.

2. Stanislaus Joyce, *My Brother's Keeper: James Joyce's Early Years* (New York:
Viking, 1958), 124.

3. Oliver St. John Gogarty, *As I Was Going Down Sackville Street: A Phantasy in
Fact* (New York: Reynal and Hitchcock, 1937), 294–296.

4. Richard Ellmann, *James Joyce*, 2nd ed. (New York: Oxford University Press,
1982), 196.

5. See Joseph Valente, "Joyce's (Sexual) Choices: A Historical Overview," in
Joseph Valente, ed., *Quare Joyce* (Ann Arbor: University of Michigan Press, 1998),
13. If male homosexuality operates for Joyce as a synecdoche for sexual irregularity
in general, it also offers an exacerbated image of the shaming potential inherent in
any notion of sexuality as interior truth. On the constitutive relation between gay
identity and "insult," see Didier Eribon, *Insult and the Making of the Gay Self*, trans.
Michael Lucey (Durham, NC: Duke University Press, 2004).

6. James Joyce, *Ulysses* (1922; reprint, New York: Random House, 1986), 1.48,
1.502, 1.600–601, 1.729, 1.158, 1.143 (hereafter *U* where not clear from the context, with chapter and line number).

7. James Joyce, *Occasional, Critical, and Political Writing* (Oxford: Oxford University Press, 2000), 24 (hereafter *OCP* where not clear from the context).

8. See Karen Lawrence, *The Odyssey of Style in* Ulysses (Princeton, NJ: Princeton University Press, 1981).

9. Leo Bersani, "Against *Ulysses*," *Raritan* 8.2 (1988): 28.

10. Robert H. Deming, ed., *James Joyce: The Critical Heritage*, vol. 1 (New York: Barnes and Noble, 1970), 283.

11. Joyce, *Stephen Hero*, 211.

12. Raymond Williams, "*Exiles*," in Colin MacCabe, ed., *James Joyce: New Perspectives* (Sussex: Harvest, 1982), 106.

13. Vicki Mahaffey, "Joyce's Shorter Works," in Derek Attridge, ed., *The Cambridge Companion to James Joyce* (Cambridge: Cambridge University Press, 1990), 187.

14. Joyce, *Poems and Shorter Writings* (London: Faber, 1991), 164–165 (hereafter *PSW*).

15. Williams, "*Exiles*," 106.

16. Quoted in Ellmann, *James Joyce*, 702.

17. Joshua Jacobs writes that Joyce's "epiphanic mode" stages Stephen/Joyce's "alternating mastery and helplessness before his nascent sexuality and the extent to which he can define his intellectual and psychical self as discrete from his context." Epiphanies 4 and 5 suggest that these in fact constitute one and the same problem. See Joshua Jacobs, "Joyce's Epiphanic Mode: Material Language and the Representation of Sexuality in *Stephen Hero* and *Portrait*," *Twentieth Century Literature* 46.1 (2000): 21.

18. Luke Thurston, *James Joyce and the Problem of Psychoanalysis* (Cambridge: Cambridge University Press, 2004), 21.

19. James Joyce, *Dubliners* (1914; reprint, London: Penguin, 2000), 18.

20. Thurston, *James Joyce and the Problem of Psychoanalysis*, 23.

21. Margot Norris, "A Walk on the Wild(e) Side: The Doubled Reading of "An Encounter,"" in Valente, *Quare Joyce*, 31.

22. James Joyce, *A Portrait of the Artist as a Young Man* (1914–15; reprint, London: Penguin, 1992), 77–78.

23. Valente observes that *Portrait*'s "homosexual energies are indissociable from Stephen's phobic denial of them." Valente, "Thrilled By His Touch," in idem, *Quare Joyce*, 49.

24. As the opening of *Ulysses* makes clear, this is not the last time Joyce makes use of Wilde's work as a metonym for male homosexuality. Joyce's 1909 essay "The Poet of Salomé" demonstrates his ambivalent attraction to a diagnostic account of Wilde's life and work. On the one hand, he hints darkly at "certain circumstances regarding the pregnancy of Lady Wilde and the infancy of her child which, in the opinion of some, partly explain the sad mania (if it can be so called) that would later drag him to his ruin." On the other, he claims that "it is not worthwhile shadowing him as the Parisian spies did," and describes Wilde's "fantastic myth, his work" as "a polyphonic variation on the relationship of art and nature, rather than a revelation of his psyche" (*OCP*, 148, 150–151).

25. Quoted in Michael Booth, ed., *English Plays of the Nineteenth Century*, vol. 2 (Oxford: Oxford University Press, 1969), 335. Archer's antitheatrical rhetoric

would not stop him from rejecting Joyce's first dramatic effort, *A Brilliant Career*, on pragmatic theatrical grounds. Archer returned the play (which Joyce sent him in 1900) with a note indicating that "for the stage, of course—the commercial stage at any rate—it is wildly impossible . . . I do not know whether you really want to write for the stage." Quoted in Ellmann, *James Joyce*, 79.

26. Quoted in Christopher Innes, *A Sourcebook on Naturalist Theatre* (London: Routledge, 2000), 75.

27. In her reminiscences of playing Hilda Wangel in *The Master Builder*, Elizabeth Robins similarly praised the audience by dematerializing it: "It was as if one played not only, as the good old advice directed, 'to the last row in the gallery,' but farther still, to an audience invisible. And this feeling was not disturbed by the sounds from the actual audience." See Elizabeth Robins, *Ibsen and the Actress* (London: Hogarth, 1928), 47–48.

28. Henrik Ibsen, *Pillars of Society*, in idem, *The Complete Major Prose Plays*, trans. Rolf Fjelde (New York: Plume, 1978), 33.

29. Toril Moi, *Henrik Ibsen and the Birth of Modernism: Art, Theater, Philosophy* (Oxford: Oxford University Press, 2006), 221.

30. Peter Szondi, *Theory of the Modern Drama*, trans. Michael Hays (Minneapolis: University of Minnesota Press, 1987), 17.

31. Michael Goldman, *Ibsen: The Dramaturgy of Fear* (New York: Columbia University Press, 1999), 19, 26–27. Goldman defends Ibsen's dramaturgy against Szondi's charge that it is essentially novelistic in nature. But the similarities of Goldman's and Szondi's accounts suggests that their disagreement lies less in how to describe Ibsen's innovations than in whether these can make for effective theater. See ibid., 39. Moi's *Henrik Ibsen and the Birth of Modernism* amply demonstrates how Ibsen's antitheatricalism coexists conceptually and practically with powerful theater.

32. See David Wiles, *A Short History of Western Performance Space* (Cambridge: Cambridge University Press, 2003), 230–233; and Elin Diamond, *Unmaking Mimesis: Essays on Feminism and Theater* (London: Routledge, 1997), 28.

33. Quoted in Innes, *A Sourcebook on Naturalist Theater*, 13.

34. Hugh Kenner's comments (Joyce "loses control" of *Exiles*; it is "not much of a play," "capital farce," etc.) are exemplary. Hugh Kenner, *Joyce's Voices* (Berkeley: University of California Press, 1978), 24–25.

35. John MacNicholas, "The Stage History of *Exiles*," *James Joyce Quarterly* 19.1 (1981): 9–26.

36. James Joyce, *Poems and* Exiles (London: Penguin, 1992), 353 (hereafter *PE* where not clear from the context).

37. See "*Little Review* Symposium on *Exiles*," in Deming, *James Joyce: The Critical Heritage*, 1:150, 153, 150–151.

38. Bernard Benstock, "*Exiles*: 'Paradox Lust' and 'Lost Paladays,'" *ELH* 36.4 (1969): 744.

39. See ibid.; Mahaffey, "Joyce's Shorter Works"; Suzette Henke, *James Joyce and the Politics of Desire* (New York: Routledge, 1990); John MacNicholas, "Joyce's *Exiles*: The Argument for Doubt," *James Joyce Quarterly* 11 (1973): 33–40.

40. See Marian Eide's reading of this refusal in *Ethical Joyce* (Cambridge: Cambridge University Press, 2002), 48.

41. On "operability" as the characteristic feature of performative genres, see Roland Barthes, *S/Z: An Essay*, trans. Richard Miller (New York: Hill and Wang, 1974), 80.

42. As represented, for example, by Gerhard Hauptmann's *Vor Sonnenaufgang*, which Joyce translated from German in 1901 as *Before Sunrise*. Hauptmann repeatedly specifies the meaning of potentially opaque performative signifiers: "*Mrs. Krause comes in . . . Mien and attire expressing arrogance, stupidity and a ridiculous vanity*"; "*He presses still closer beside her. She lets him do so but with a look that tells how loth she is to suffer him*"; "*In her look are shown surprise, contempt disgust and hate.*" We could also contrast the opacity of Joyce's stage directions with the uncanny visual precision of Shaw's description of Morrell's library in *Candida*: "*The wall behind him is fitted with bookshelves, on which an adept eye can measure the parson's casuistry and divinity by Maurice's Theological Essays and a complete set of Browning's poems, and the reformer's politics by a yellow backed Progress and Poverty, Fabian Essays, A Dream of John Bull, Marx's Capital, and a half a dozen other literary landmarks in Socialism.*" The stage direction (so obviously directed at Shaw's reader that we should perhaps designate it a "reader direction") expresses in clearest possible form the naturalist fantasy of a stage rendered legible. Joyce's departure from these models is drastic, and I would thus differ with Martin Puchner's assessment that "Joyce's *Exiles*, printed before it was staged, fully participates in the literarization of stage directions." *Exiles*'s stage directions—unlike Hauptmann's and Shaw's—work to drain literary meaning from its characters' unimaginable actions. Jill Perkins, ed., *Joyce and Hauptmann: Before Sunrise: James Joyce's Translation* (Canoga Park, CA: Huntington Library, 1978), 62, 87; George Bernard Shaw, *Candida*, in idem, *Plays Pleasant* (1898; reprint, London: Penguin, 2003), 94; and Martin Puchner, *Stage Fright: Modernism, Anti-Theatricalism, and Drama* (Baltimore: Johns Hopkins University Press, 2002), 85.

43. See Ellmann, *James Joyce*, 394, 401.

44. Lawrence, *The Odyssey of Style*, 14, 12.

45. Between 1916 and 1918 Joyce entered numerous negotiations to stage the play, but with the exception of a Munich production engineered by Stefan Zweig, they came to nothing. See Ellmann, *James Joyce*, 412, 423, 444.

46. Dorrit Cohn, *Transparent Minds: Narrative Modes for Presenting Consciousness in Fiction* (Princeton, NJ: Princeton University Press, 1978), 62.

47. Joyce was impatient with readers who failed to see the need for this segregating operation or who performed it unsuccessfully. "That didn't take place at all," he corrected a friend about an incident in "Nausicaa," "only in Bloom's imagination." See Ellmann, *James Joyce*, 513.

48. "Pound on *Ulysses* and Flaubert," in Deming, *James Joyce: The Critical Heritage*, 1:265.

49. See Joyce, *A Portrait of the Artist as a Young Man*, 233.

50. On the game of positionings around homosexuality in "Scylla and Charybdis," see Colleen Lamos, *Deviant Modernism: Sexual and Textual Errancy in T. S. Eliot, James Joyce, and Marcel Proust* (Cambridge: Cambridge University Press, 1998).

51. Eve Kosofsky Sedgwick, *Epistemology of the Closet* (Berkeley: University of California Press, 1990), 55.

52. See Lamos, *Deviant Modernism*, 149.

53. James Joyce, *Letters of James Joyce*, ed. Stuart Gilbert, vol. 1 (New York: Viking, 1957), 149.

54. Michael Groden, *Ulysses in Progress* (Princeton, NJ: Princeton University Press, 1977), 167–178.

55. See Paul Vanderham, *James Joyce and Censorship* (New York: New York University Press, 1998).

56. Vanderham quotes the following passage from "Lotus Eaters," italicizing Joyce's late additions: "[Bloom] tore the flower gravely from its pinhold smelt its almost no smell and placed it in his heart pocket. *Language of flowers. They like it because no-one can hear. Or a poison bouquet to strike him down.* Then, walking slowly forward, he read the letter again, murmuring here and there a word. *Angry tulips with you darling manflower punish your cactus if you don't please poor forgetmenot how I long violets to dear roses when we soon anemone meet all naughty nightstalk wife Martha's perfume.* Having read it all he took it from the newspaper and put it back in his sidepocket." Vanderham's presentation reveals that Joyce's late insertions of interior discourse gave *Ulysses* its characterological density; without the italicized sentences the passage has the scrupulous flatness of *Dubliners*. See Vanderham, *James Joyce and Censorship*, 79.

57. Hélène Cixous, "At Circe's, or the Self-Opener," *boundary 2* 3.2 (1975): 387, 396.

58. Maud Ellmann, "The Ghosts of *Ulysses*," in Augustine Martin, ed., *The Artist and the Labyrinth* (London: Ryan, 1990), 199.

59. Given Joyce's engagements with naturalism (as reader and expositor of Ibsen and as translator of Hauptmann), it is striking that "Circe" has not to my knowledge been considered in this context. Cheryl Herr offers an account of the episode's references to pantomime, music hall, and melodrama, while L. H. Platt reads "Circe" in terms of the Irish Literary Theatre. See Cheryl Herr, *Joyce's Anatomy of Culture* (Urbana: University of Illinois Press, 1986); and L. H. Platt, "*Ulysses* 15 and the Irish Literary Theatre," in Andrew Gibson, ed., *Reading Joyce's "Circe"* (Amsterdam: Rodopi, 1994), 33–62.

60. In invoking a space defined by these theatrical acoustics, "Circe" is quite distinct from Flaubert's *Temptation of St. Antony*, the closet drama to which it is frequently compared. Flaubert's stage directions are inundated with the narration of consciousness; in making the stage directions the carrier of interiority, the *Temptation* represents a colonization of the theatrical by novelistic devices, precisely the inverse of Joyce's project. Similarly, the public conjured by "Circe" is the knowable crowd of the gallery, the court, the theater; compare this small public to the "hippodrome full of people" through which Antony at one point makes his way or his encounter with a parade of "idols of all nations and all ages." Where "Circe" consistently has Bloom playing to the intimate publicity of the embodied crowd, the *Temptation* is better characterized as a hallucinatory encounter with the sublime. Gustave Flaubert, *The Temptation of St. Antony*, trans. Kitty Mrosovsky (1874; reprint, London: Penguin, 1983), 80, 163. Phillip Herring's book on Joyce's revisions to *Ulysses* reveals that the initial versions of "Circe" included much Flaubertian incorporation of psychological narration into the stage directions. When he revised the chapter, Joyce did so in the direction of theatrical convention, purging the stage directions of any account

of what characters are thinking. See Phillip F. Herring, ed., *Joyce's Notes and Early Drafts for Ulysses: Selections from the Buffalo Collection* (Charlottesville: University Press of Virginia, 1977), 191–262.

61. Joyce, *Letters of James Joyce,* 1:149.

62. See Wladimir Krysinski, "Poland of Nowhere, the Breasts of Tiresias, and Other Incongruities, or: Referential Manipulation in Modern Drama," in Michael Issacharoff and Anna Whiteside, eds., *On Referring in Literature* (Bloomington: Indiana University Press, 1987), 138–157.

63. As Lamos claims in *Deviant Modernism* 151–153.

64. Compare the combination of affectlessness and humiliation in the images of both performing-Joyce and penetrated-Bloom with Leo Bersani and Ulysse Dutoit's description of a sexually inviting image of St. John the Baptist painted by Caravaggio: "He is indifferently available, ready for anything, but this massive indifference itself can be read as an inarticulate protest against representational *use*. The opacity of his deteriorating flesh is also the resistance of a contemporary body to a veritable industry of symbolization. He'll do anything, but he won't let us forget that that's all he's doing: agreeing, without interest and without rebellion, to do as he has been told. There is an enormous if only potential political explosiveness in this represented refusal, on the model's part, to be an image for anything else, to play a role that might allow his own miserable life not to be seen. To insist so uncompromisingly on his own corrupted being is almost to proclaim the dignity of his seediness." Leo Bersani and Ulysse Dutoit, *Caravaggio's Secrets* (Cambridge, MA: MIT Press, 1998), 47.

65. See *U,* 3.1: "Ineluctable modality of the visible."

66. Suzette Henke claims that in "Circe" Boylan's "penile equipment is ostentatiously on show"; Hugh Kenner argues that the episode "place[s] all figures . . . on the plane of the visible and audible"; Joseph Allen Boone refers to its "externalized embodiments"; and Maud Ellmann claims that "everything is *on show* in this chapter." Henke, *James Joyce and the Politics of Desire,* 117; Kenner, "Circe," in Clive Hart and David Hayman, eds., *James Joyce's* Ulysses: *Critical Essays* (Berkeley: University of California Press, 1974), 346; Boone, "Staging Sexuality: Repression, Representation, and 'Interior' States in Ulysses," in Susan Stanford Friedman, ed., *Joyce: The Return of the Repressed* (Ithaca, NY: Cornell University Press, 1993), 194; Ellmann, "The Ghosts of *Ulysses,*" 214.

67. Despite its wildness, the episode is extraordinarily faithful to the typographic conventions of play scripts; on this point see Kenner, "Circe," 341.

68. Christy L. Burns, *Gestural Politics: Stereotype and Parody in Joyce* (Albany: State University of New York Press, 2000), 48.

69. Cheryl Herr's research into "scripts, playbills, advertisements, newspaper reviews, theatrical memoirs, diaries and reminiscences" reconstructs the real-world theatricality on which "Circe" draws. But the thoroughness of her investigation downplays the fact that the textuality of "Circe"—its status not as play but as playless script—keeps it at a remove from the popular world to which it alludes. Herr's impressive research repairs the social isolation of "Circe," but it does not read it as one of the main concerns of the text. See Herr, *Joyce's Anatomy of Culture,* 103.

EPILOGUE In the Kingdom of Whomever: Baldwin's Method

1. See David Leeming, "An Interview with James Baldwin on Henry James," *The Henry James Review* 8.1 (fall 1986): 55; and idem, *James Baldwin: A Biography* (New York: Knopf, 1994), 55. Baldwin's citation also makes us hear the echo in James's title of the abolitionist slogan "Am I Not a Man and a Brother?"

2. James Baldwin, *The Amen Corner* (1968; reprint, New York: Vintage, 1998), xi.

3. Leeming, *James Baldwin*, 55.

4. James Joyce, *A Portrait of the Artist as a Young Man* (1914–15; reprint, London: Penguin, 1992), 276; *Ulysses* (1922; reprint, New York: Random House, 1986), 18.1610–1611; James Baldwin, *Another Country* (1962; reprint, New York: Vintage, 1993), 436; *Tell Me How Long the Train's Been Gone* (1968; reprint, New York: Vintage, 1998), 484.

5. Baldwin, *Another Country*, 317. On *Another Country*'s working title, see Leeming, *James Baldwin*, 68.

6. George Eliot, *Middlemarch: A Study of Provincial Life* (1871–72; reprint, London: Penguin, 2003), 194; James Baldwin, *Just Above My Head* (1979; reprint, New York: Dell, 2000), 96.

7. On *Another Country*'s liberalism, see William A. Cohen, "Liberalism, Libido, Liberation: Baldwin's *Another Country*," in Patricia Juliana Smith, ed., *The Queer Sixties* (New York: Routledge, 1999).

8. To take just one representative moment: in *No Name in the Street*, his 1972 account of a trip to the deep South, Baldwin casually takes the "shriveled faces" of the whites he encounters as "an exact indication of how matters were with them below the belt." See Baldwin, *The Price of the Ticket: Collected Nonfiction 1948–1985* (New York: St. Martin's, 1985), 483.

9. Baldwin, *Tell Me How Long the Train's Been Gone*, 373–374.

10. Eldridge Cleaver's *Soul on Ice* notoriously uses Baldwin's homosexuality as grounds for lurid diagnostic fantasies ("Many Negro homosexuals, acquiescing in this racial death-wish, are outraged because in their sickness they are unable to have a baby by a white man") and for a dismissal of Baldwin's political seriousness. Cleaver's attack is notable for its viciousness, but its logic is basically identical to that of the more genteel opinion published in the *New York Times* in 1998 that Baldwin's "social commentary invariably was a disguised discussion of the problems of being James Baldwin . . . This interior drama gave his essays their intense appeal of intimacy and urgency, but their insistent subjectivity sabotaged their effectiveness as social commentary." See Eldridge Cleaver, *Soul On Ice*: (1968; reprint, New York: Delta, 1991), 128; and Michael Anderson, "Trapped Inside James Baldwin," *New York Times*, March 29, 1998. On black nationalists' rejection of Baldwin's work, see Henry Louis Gates Jr., "The Welcome Table," in Susan Gubar and Jonathan Kamholtz, eds., *English Inside and Out: The Places of Literary Criticism* (New York: Routledge, 1993).

11. Joseph R. Roach, *The Player's Passion: Studies in the Science of Acting* (Ann Arbor: University of Michigan Press, 1994), 204.

12. On the Method's psychologism, see Steve Vineberg, *Method Actors: Three Generations of an American Acting Style* (New York: Schirmer, 1991); and Mel

Gordon, *Stanislavsky in America: An Actor's Workbook* (London: Routledge, 2010), 125–149.

13. Constantin Stanislavski, *An Actor Prepares*, trans. Elizabeth Reynolds Hapgood (1936; reprint, New York: Routledge, 1989), 16, 212.

14. Lee Strasberg, *A Dream of Passion: The Development of the Method* (New York: Plume, 1987), 97–104.

15. Elsewhere Strasberg distanced himself from the psychoanalytic resonances of the Method's emphasis on "emotional memory": "The emotional thing is not Freud, as people commonly think. Theoretically and actually, it is Pavlov." Quoted in Roach, *The Player's Passion*, 216.

16. The paraphrase is Leeming's, in *James Baldwin*, 261.

17. Quoted in James Campbell, *Talking at the Gates: A Life of James Baldwin* (New York: Viking, 1991), 127.

18. Leeming, *James Baldwin*, 156.

19. Ibid., 232; Vineberg, *Method Actors*, 243.

20. Leeming, *James Baldwin*, 306–307. See also Magdalena J. Zaborowska, *James Baldwin's Turkish Decade: Erotics of Exile* (Durham, NC: Duke University Press, 2009), 141–195.

21. James Baldwin, *Giovanni's Room* (1956; reprint, New York: Dell, 1988), 39, 64.

22. Stanislavski, *An Actor Prepares*, 192.

23. Campbell, *Talking at the Gates*, 126. See also Zaborowska, *James Baldwin's Turkish Decade*, 273.

24. Quoted in James Campbell, "Room in the East," *Times Literary Supplement*, June 15, 2007, 4.

25. Kevin Ohi, "'I'm Not the Boy You Want': Sexuality, 'Race,' and Thwarted Revelation in Baldwin's *Another Country*," *African American Review* 33.2 (1999): 264.

26. Michel Foucault, *The History of Sexuality*, trans. Robert Hurley, vol. 1 (New York: Pantheon, 1978), 43.

27. See Cleaver, *Soul on Ice*, 132, 136; and Claudia Roth Pierpont, "Another Country: James Baldwin's Flight from America," *New Yorker*, (February 9, 2009), 106.

28. Baldwin's description of Eric anticipates not only Foucault's analysis of the homosexual but also Hal Hinson's account of Montgomery Clift in his essay "Some Notes on Method Acting": Clift has a "way of nestling a character within himself as if it were a secret, something to be hidden away, or so delicate that it would be bruised by the light." Hal Hinson, "Some Notes on Method Acting," *Sight and Sound* (summer 1984): 202; quoted in Vineberg, *Method Actors*, 150. Vineberg makes explicit the suggestion lurking in Hinson's language when he characterizes Clift's late-career roles as "old-maidish" and marred by the inadvertent exposure of a "flabby, feminine underside" (152).

29. Baldwin writes, for example, of Vivaldo's sense that Ida is determined "to frustrate . . . any attempt on his part to strike deeper into that incredible country in which, like the princess of fairy tales, sealed in a high tower and guarded by beasts, bewitched and exiled, she paced her secret round of days" (173).

30. Alex Woloch, *The One vs. The Many: Minor Characters and the Space of the Protagonist in the Novel* (Princeton, NJ: Princeton University Press, 2003), 372.

31. For evidence that such echoic effects among characters, and between characters and narrator, are fully deliberate in Baldwin, see the extraordinary segment in his final novel *Just Above My Head* in which the narrator Hall Montana imagines in minute detail a lengthy erotic encounter between his brother Arthur and a lover named Guy. Hall's narration imagines Guy referring to the "mathematic" of history before going on to draw the reader's attention both to the unusual poetry of the phrase and the impossibility of his own access to it: "Who, then," Hall asks, "in such a fearful mathematic, to use Guy's term, is trapped?" It is perhaps needless to add that this phrase, invented by Hall and attributed to Guy before being "cited" again by Hall, sounds suspiciously like the Baldwin of the nonfiction. See Baldwin, *Just Above My Head*, 500.

In addition to the narrative and stylistic features discussed above, we might add to the list of *Another Country*'s conflations of privacy and publicity the extended description of an abstract painting that forms the backdrop to the final encounter between Eric and Cass in the Museum of Modern Art. The painting is said to take "a flying leap, as it were, from the wall, poised for the spectator's eyeballs"—even as "it seemed to stretch endlessly and adoringly in on itself" (405). This imaginary painting, which Baldwin gives nearly inexplicable prominence, seems designed precisely to defeat the distinction between theatrical and antitheatrical abstract art that Michael Fried articulated in his landmark essay "Art and Objecthood"—published four years after Baldwin's novel. See Michael Fried, *Art and Objecthood: Essays and Reviews* (Chicago: University of Chicago Press, 1998), 148–172.

32. My reading here is indebted to Ohi, "I'm Not the Boy You Want," 268.

Note: Page numbers in italic type indicate figures.